NELSON

BEATTON (North Pine) RIVER

ALASKA HIGHWAY

BLUEBERRY RIVER

WONOWON

CAMERON RIVER

HALFWAY

HORSESHOE CR.

CREEK

BUTLER RIDGE

DUNLEVY CR.

A. CARDER CR.

GOLD BAR

BRANHAM FLATS

HUDSON HOPE

CUST CR. BULLHEAD MTN.

MT. GETHING

PORTAGE MTN.

PEACE RIVER CANYON

JOHNSON CR.

MAURICE CR.

BEATTIE PEAKS

MOBERLY RIVER

CARBON RIVER

MABLE PAS

DS

SCHOOLER CR.

FARRELL CREEK

BEAR FLATS

CACHE CREEK

PEACE RIVER

MOBERLY RIVER

PINE RIVER

P.G.E.R.

WILLOW CR.

CHARLIE LAKE

MURDALE

MONTNEY

NORTH PINE

ROSE PRAIRIE

CECIL LK.

BOUNDARY LK.

UMBACH CREEK

BEATTON RIVER

DOIG RIVER

MILLIGAN CR.

FORT ST. JOHN

TAYLOR

CLAYHURST

KISKATINAW RIVER

SUNSET PRAIRIE

GROUNDBIRCH

EAST PINE

MOBERLY LAKE

PROGRESS P.G.E.R.

BEAR MTN.

DAWSON CREEK

ROLLA

KILKERRAN

POUCE COUPE

COUPE RIVER

BISSETTE CR.

TOMSLAKE

TUPPER

SWAN LAKE

TREMBLAY CR.

KISKATINAW RIVER

TO GRANDE PRAIRIE

N.A.R.

JOHN HART HIGHWAY

CHETWYND

P.G.E.R.

PINE R.

LONE PRAIRIE

HASLER CR.

PINE RIVER

MURRAY RIVER

GWILLIM LK.

SUKUNKA RIVER

MURRAY RANGE

AZOUZETTA LK.

PINE PASS

MISINCHINKA RIVER

PARSNIP

FT. McLEOD

MT. RUTT

PINE

BRITISH COL.

ALBERTA

BOUNDARY

This Was Our Valley

Earl K. Pollon

and

Shirlee Smith Matheson

Detselig Enterprises Ltd.
Calgary, Alberta

© 1989 by **Earl K. Pollon**
and **Shirlee Smith Matheson**

Canadian Cataloguing in Publication Data
Pollon, Earl K. (Earl Kitchener)
This was our valley

Includes index.
ISBN 0-920490-92-1 (bound). --ISBN 0-920490-91-3
(pbk.)

1. Hudson's Hope (B.C.) – History. 2. W.A.C.
Bennett Dam (B.C.) – History. 3. Williston Lake (B.C.)
– History. 4. Dams – Environmental aspects – British
Columbia. I. Matheson, Shirlee Smith. II. Title.
FC3849.H82P64 1989   971.1'1   C89-091210-6
F1089.5.H82P64 1989

First printing: September, 1989
Second printing: May, 1990

Detselig Enterprises Limited
P.O. Box G 399
Calgary, Alberta T3A 2G3

ISBN 0-920490-92-1 hb
Printed in Canada   SAN 115-0324   ISBN 0-920490-91-3 pb

To Bonnie and Bill,
who loved the river
and to the people of the Peace
who made this story possible

Acknowledgements

The authors give special thanks to journalist Mark Lowey. His knowledge of the issues presented in this book, his sensitivity to the North and its inhabitants, and his faith in the authors' voices provided both professional and personal encouragement.

Sincere thanks to David A.E. Spalding and William Sarjeant, who provided copies of articles pertinent to the paleontological issues presented in the chapter, "Beneath These Waters," and who contributed personal accounts and editing expertise to this section.

We thank C.W.J. (Chris) Boatman, vice-president of corporate and environmental affairs, and other B.C. Hydro supervisors and engineers whose contributions are noted in the book, for their cooperation in answering our questions, (pertinent and sometimes impertinent) in our attempt to provide B.C. Hydro's position.

We wish also to thank Yvonne Trainer, for her work in selecting and editing the poems from *Beneath These Waters* for inclusion in this book.

Finally, the authors wish to thank all those who responded to our requests for information, who agreed to taped interviews, and who provided letters, reports and personal diaries so the book could truly reflect the inside stories.

In some cases, names of contributors have been withheld at their request; however, their assistance is gratefully acknowledged.

Cover photo: Dave Kyllo (standing at back) guides river boat through Ne Parlez Pas Rapids on the Peace River. (photo credit: K. Kyllo)

Contents

Detselig Enterprises Ltd. appreciates the financial
assistance for its 1989 publishing program from
Alberta Foundation for the Literary Arts
Canada Council
Department of Communications
Alberta Culture

Part One

Learning Our Legends

Introduction
Challenging the Wild Country

The Peace River in central British Columbia is part of one of the world's most extensive and complex watersheds, the Mackenzie. The Peace begins in the north with the headwaters of the Finlay River at Thutade Lake in the Stikine Plateau; the Finlay flows north-east for 50 miles, straight north for 50 miles, then breaks into the Rocky Mountain Trench from the west. Picking up the waters of the Firesteel and Toodoggone rivers, it tumbles down the southern ranges of the Cassiar Mountains, curving in a great 30- mile arch. After picking up the Fox, it flows south-east following the Rocky Mountain Trench in a straight line. By then it has dropped almost 1,000 feet from its source. Cascading down the trench, it picks up river after river until it arrives at the Forks.

Racing from the south to meet it is the Parsnip River, which has been joined by the Crooked (becoming the Pack River at McLeod Lake) and the Nation.

Head of the Peace River Canyon
(L. Gething)

1

A sudden, last-minute twist of the Finlay prevents the two rivers from meeting head on at the Forks. But it is here they marry, the brown waters of the Parsnip uniting with the blue glacial flow of the Finlay to become the Peace.

The Peace River is the protagonist in our story – this offspring of the Finlay and the Parsnip that, like a headstrong child, crashes straight into the Rockies through the only navigable water-level gap in the 2,000-mile trench.

The largest branch of the Mackenzie system, the Peace, is 1,050 miles long including its main branch, the Finlay. It flows east for 300 miles, dropping about two and one-half feet for every mile. At Peace River Crossing in Alberta, where it is joined by the Smoky, the river turns north, cutting through steep sandstone cliffs. Its bed widens and flattens until, 815 miles from its source at Finlay Forks, it enters the Slave River to become part of an ecologically sensitive area called the Peace-Athabasca delta.

The headwaters of the Peace, where this story takes place, has produced the most volatile history of the 1,050-mile river; it is here that the Peace River canyon puts a stop to river travel. Here, its turbulent waters drop 215 feet in 20 miles.

"This magnificent theatre of nature has all the decorations which the trees and animals of the country can afford it," Alexander Mackenzie noted in his diary, enroute from Peace River Crossing upstream to the canyon.[1]

But Mackenzie's tone changed abruptly when he encountered the canyon. Having been warned against attempting to line his canoes up the rapids, and avoiding the Indian portage for fear of ambush, Mackenzie and his men chose to traverse the canyon the only way possible: on foot.

> Monday, 20 May, 1793: We now continued our toilsome and perilous progress with the line West by North, and as we proceeded the rapidity of the current increased, so that in the distance of two miles we were obliged to unload four times and carry everything but the canoe . . . At five we had proceeded to where the river was one continued rapid. . . . At length, however, the agitation of the water was so great that a wave striking on the bow of the canoe broke the line and filled us with inexpressible dismay as it appeared impossible that the vessel could escape from being dashed to pieces and those who were in her from perishing. . . . The men were in such a state from their late alarm that it would not only have been unavailing but imprudent to have proposed any further progress at present, particularly as the river above us, as far as we could see, was one white sheet of foaming water.

Echoing Mackenzie's dismay was Simon Fraser, on his journey from Rocky Mountain Portage to Finlay Forks in 1806. Leaving early in the morning, it took all day to reach the head of the portage: "It was ten o'clock at night when we got to the upper end of the Portage. The road is amazing bad and the Portage is at least 14 or 15 miles long."

At the foot of the Peace River canyon, the head of navigation to the east and entry to the untouched wilderness of the Rocky Mountain Trench to the west, was situated a trading post. It was called Rocky Mountain Portage House in 1805 when Simon Fraser established it on the south side of the river. Later, it became the property of the Hudson's Bay Company in 1821 after their amalgamation with the North West Trading Company. The post was abandoned in 1825 to punish the Indians for a massacre that had occurred at Fort St. John in 1823. For several years there is nothing written about the post, until gold was discovered in early 1861 on the Parsnip River near the Forks, followed by discoveries in 1868 on the Omineca River and 1871 in the Manson Creek area. The name of the post changed with its new prosperity and, like its history, the name's origin remains an enigma. It was called Hudson's Hope, or, sometimes, the Hope of Hudson.

The first recorded mention of Hudson's Hope, according to the Hudson's Bay Company, was in a letter sent to York Factory by a James Forsyth in 1869. Some say it could have been so named because the Hudson's Bay Company owned the post. Another version, more typical of Hudson's Hope's character, is that it was named for a prospector named Hodgson who discovered gold in the canyon, left for Edmonton to get together an outfit, and always hoped to return. The word "hope" has also been traced to mean a small, enclosed "blind valley," especially a smaller opening branching out from the main stem and running up to the mountain ranges.

From journals written by explorers and others throughout the 19th and 20th centuries, there's evidence that the Peace River canyon above Hudson's Hope retained its reputation for inspiring fear and awe in the hearts of men.

Chief Trader John McLean, employed by the Hudson's Bay Company from 1821-45, wrote:

> The Rocky Mountains came in view on the 8th of October, and we reached the portage bearing their name on the 10th, the crossing of which took us eight days, being fully 13 miles in length, and excessively bad road, leading sometimes through swamps and morasses, then ascending and descending steep hills, and for at least one-third of the distance so obstructed by fallen trees as to render it all but impassable. I consider the passage of this portage the most laborious duty the Company's servants have to perform in any part of the territory; and, as the voyageurs say, 'He that passes it with his share of

a canoe's cargo may call himself a man.'"[2]

In 1899, the original post was torn down and rebuilt on the north side of the river at the end of the portage trail. The Hudson's Bay Company sent out a surveyor to site and record seven acres of land on the plateau, running parallel to the Peace River for five miles, and back from the river an average width of two miles.

Mining engineer J.D. Galloway recorded a linear description of the challenges in travelling from Summit Lake near Prince George to Hudson's Hope by river:

> From Summit Lake the route is by the Crooked River, McLeod Lake, the Pack River and then the Parsnip River to Finlay Forks. Half a mile below Finlay Forks are the Finlay Rapids, which should not be run except by skilled canoemen familiar with them. A short portage on the south bank can easily be negotiated and the boat can be lined around the edge of the rapids. Going down the Peace River the next rapids are the Ne Parlez Pas, 45 miles above the head of the Rocky Mountain Canyon, and although it is possible at certain stages of the water to run these rapids, it is much better not to take the risk. The water flows with a deadly smoothness but great speed, and breaks almost silently over a hard sandstone bank with a drop in the centre of about four feet.

Leading a boat through the Ne Parlez Pas rapids
(Hudson's Hope Museum)

Galloway goes on to describe some future possible use for the country:

The important known mineral-deposits of the Peace River District consist of coal and placer gold. It is known that an extensive area is underlain by coal, and it is also known that the field as exposed at the Rocky Mountain canyon and on the Carbon River carries very high-grade coal. Development and mining of the coal field has of course not proceeded far owing to lack of transportation and market.[3]

Settlers didn't immediately flock to Hudson's Hope, although it's considered to be the third-oldest community in British Columbia. While it possessed all the natural elements vital to industry – water, coal, timber – it remained a hidden oasis, undiscovered by all but a few. Surveyor/civil engineer Charles Horetzky and Professor John Macoun (a noted Canadian scientist, later to become assistant director and naturalist of the Geological Survey of Canada) recorded their journey in 1872 while on a pathfinding expedition for the Canadian Pacific Railway. Inspector J.D. Moodie of the North West Mounted Police trekked through Hudson's Hope to slash out a potential highway from Edmonton to the Yukon, in the process opening access to a mountain pass later named the Laurier Pass. In 1873, General Sir William F. Butler explored the Finlay and wrote *The Great Lone Land* and *The Wild North Land*, two books still used for detailed research of the Finlay wilderness. Butler had this to say about the river's deadly force:

> Some 50 miles west of St. John, the Peace River issues from the canyon through which it passes the outer range of the Rocky Mountains. No boat, canoe, or craft of any kind has ever run the gauntlet of this huge chasm; for five-and-thirty miles it lies deep sunken through the mountains; while from its depths there ever rises the hoarse roar of the angry waters as they dash furiously against their rocky prison. A trail of 10 miles leads across this portage, and at the western end of this trail the river is reached close to where it makes its first plunge into the rock-hewn chasm.[4]

A.R.C. Selwyn, then director of the Geological Survey of Canada, made a trip down the Parsnip to the Forks in 1875. Warburton Pike, a well-educated Englishman whose goal was to live on the edge of civilization, travelled in 1890 from Calgary north to the Barren Lands. He arrived, homeward-bound, in Hudson's Hope in October of that year. To his great folly he chose to ignore advice given in Hudson's Hope and forged ahead, ill-equipped, through the Peace River Gap by canoe and up the Parsnip River. The party found itself lost and starving in the mountains, with no guns or snowshoes, and inadequate clothing. They were forced to turn back, but became lost. Thirty-two days after they had set out from Hudson's Hope, they arrived back where they started from, very near death. Anyone in Hudson's Hope could have told Pike of the Nation River, and to not confuse its unique high cliff landmarks with his sought entry to the Pack River.

After the first wave of explorers into the area, the next significant movement north came from prospectors seeking gold. But the fertile valleys and flats of the Peace were soon forsaken by prospectors who moved on to seek gold in other valleys. Glittering from the river bars of the Peace, the placer gold yielded itself only in bits and pieces. Later, during the Depression of the 1930s, home-made sluice boxes were set up by local residents on Two-Mile Bar at the head of the canyon. More boxes followed on Brenham Flats and on almost every bar scattered along the Peace, into the Finlay and up to the Omineca, Osilinka, Ospika, and down to the Parsnip and the Nation Rivers. The gold is still there, made even more elusive by the waters of Williston Lake reservoir behind the Bennett dam.

The Nation River
(L. Gething)

With the gold-seekers came freighters, trappers, surveyors, geologists, provincial police and wayfarers. It was not until 1912 to 1915 that settlers came from Alberta, over the old Edson Trail, just ahead of the railway that never managed to find its way to Hudson's Hope.

The problem of transportation was optimistically tackled as early as 1878, when plans for a rail line through the Peace River Pass to the Skeena area were proposed. In the early 1900s the proposal was made again, and a federal charter (a written document granted by the government entitling the holder to particular rights, privileges and obligations, and defining the route) was obtained to construct the rail line from the Peace River Block west through the Peace-Finlay area to

Stewart, 120 miles north of Prince Rupert. D.A. Thomas had taken out leases on the coal deposits of Carbon Creek and also had a rail charter from Edmonton to the Pacific, via either the Nass or Skeena Rivers. In 1915, the Dominion Telegraph reached Hudson's Hope from Fort St. John and a wagon road was extended from Hudson's Hope to East Pine. But World War I intervened, and put a stop to local progress.

The original voyageurs' highway, the river, again provided access to the country for the sternwheelers that broke the eternal silence of the north with their sharp whistles, finally connecting Hudson's Hope to the outside world. Beginning with Bishop Grouard's *St. Charles* in 1903, the sternwheelers operated from the rapids called Vermilion Chutes in Alberta, 525 miles upstream to Hudson's Hope. In 1905 the Hudson's Bay Company put their sternwheeler, *S.S. Peace River*, into operation; it was 110 feet long and could carry 40 tons of freight. The *S.S. Peace River* was replaced by the *Athabasca River* in 1915, which could carry 110 tons, and again by the famous *D.A. Thomas* which ran the river from 1919 to 1929. Built at the then staggering cost of $119,000, she could carry 100 passengers and more than 200 tons of freight.

The boats no longer come, although many people in Hudson's Hope recall the excitement of their visits, bringing not only transportation and freight shipments but also the reassurance that Hudson's Hope was part of the outside world. The people who stayed to make Hudson's Hope their home sometimes still need that assurance, but the whistle no longer comes from the river, or from the silent black caves of coal, or from the ever-dwindling stands of timber. The call is there, but it comes from strange new directions.

In his report to the surveyor general in Ottawa in 1922, Dominion Land Surveyor L. Brenot wrote:

> With untold mineral wealth, untold water power, large tracts of agricultural land and being the head of navigation, Hudson's Hope should be one of the foremost towns of the North.

In 1923, the first load of coal was barged down the river to Peace River Crossing, the head of the Edmonton-Dunvegan and B.C. Railway. It seemed that Hudson's Hope's resources were finally becoming important to the outside world. But the river's seasonal changes hampered transportation schedules. The boats encountered sand bars, changing water levels, ice and spring run-offs. A railway was the answer and three main routes were proposed: the Monkman Pass, the Pine Pass and the Peace Pass. The Monkman Pass (from Rio Grande near Beaverlodge south-west to Kinueso Falls, along the Red Willow River – a tributary of the Wapiti – then south and west through the Monkman Pass to the highway at Hansard), was considered too expensive and presented engineering difficulties. The Pine Pass and the Peace Pass were both investigated.

Surveys were made by the Pacific Great Eastern Railway through the Pine Pass route, with connections to Hudson's Hope, Fort St. John and Dawson Creek. Whichever of the two routes was chosen, it looked as though Hudson's Hope would be connected to rail. In an article titled "P.G.E. Extension Assured," in the November, 1945 issue of *Construction World*, then B.C. premier John Hart wrote that a joint committee appointed in October, 1945 had submitted a report to the government regarding northern extension of the railway. In the report, the Peace Pass route was established as the only one with the requisite grades and which could tap the known resources. Hudson's Hope, "the centre of known resources," was to be selected as a temporary eastern terminus, with Finlay Forks considered a strategic point for the development of Central Northern British Columbia. The committee pointed out that "a million tons a year of available freight would justify an extension north. This initial million tons should be derived from minerals (coal) and forest products. This tonnage can be obtained should the coal of Carbon River and Hudson Hope be proved in volume and quality as now indicated." The report also said there was already an awareness of the coal potentialities of that district. "In the Carbon Creek area, private companies, desirous of carrying out development work, sent in engineers who made a report that within a 50-square mile area, there was a potential 2.7 billion tons of high-grade coal with ash content ranging from 1.5 to 2 percent." Cost of the rail line's construction from Quesnel to Hudson's Hope was estimated at $20 million, with no serious difficulties being envisioned.

From the Alberta side, the Northern Alberta Railway was also anxious to connect its rail line from Hines Creek into the British Columbia portion of the Peace. This line would connect at Fort St. John (a distance of 90 miles), or if deemed advisable, continue on to Hudson's Hope (an additional 65 miles). The battle of the passes had begun, with the Peace country caught in the middle, and nothing happening.

> Once, many years ago (between 1910 and 1915) decisions were taken in connection with the planned railroad projection into the Peace River district that went far in the shaping of the country's present form and character,"

says a brief presented by the Inter-Provincial North Peace Boards of Trade on the Railroad Requirements of the Peace River, 1953.

> We see plainly today how short-sighted and ill-advised some of the decisions were; how the development of the country has been warped and retarded – not because the initiative or the money was

lacking, but because these were misspent.

The crowning perversion was the turning of the main line west from McLennan towards the B.C. Border. At this point rails from Edmonton were to meet the rails from Vancouver which, having negotiated three mountain ranges, were to carry the Peace River to Vancouver. . . . What was to be the mainline of the E.D. (Edmonton-Dunvegan) and B.C. shifted from Dunvegan to Peace River Crossing, where a dual purpose bridge was built, over went the rails to Berwyn, Fairview and finally to Hines Creek, where the truncated end has waited, in vain, for the inspiration and courage that will carry it to the vast riches of the Fort St. John, Hudson's Hope, Finlay Forks, Ingenika River and Stewart areas."

The report recommended strongly that a rail line from Prince George centred on the valleys (the Parsnip, Manson, Omineca, Finlay, Ospika, and Peace, which form the Finlay Forks area, and farther north, the Ingenika) would not only provide feeders, but would help build up the Pacific and coastal trade. There was also the fascinating possibility of a railway to Alaska, the short route which would go through the Finlay valley.

The people of Hudson's Hope and the North Peace District did everything within their powers to penetrate the morass of bureaucracy. Their efforts, requiring a determination akin to that of the Peace River forging through the one gap in the trench, came to naught.

George Murray, newspaperman and politician who represented the Cariboo in both provincial and federal ridings, wrote an article illustrating the ongoing hope of the Peace River residents. It appeared in the Vancouver *Sunday Province* (September 28, 1930) under the title of "Promised Land":

> . . . New railway lines, new towns and a rush of building in the older towns; settlers on the move; perspiring road gangs building highways through a wilderness; airplanes speeding prospectors into the hinterland; survey outfits with pack horses, putting in stakes for the new coast outlet – this is the Peace River country in 1930.
>
> Truly the Peace is the promised land . . . ."

Every report about the area contained strong words: challenge, untapped potential, progress, resource-rich. There was an equitable climate, land that could grow wheat or vegetables, yield minerals beyond the wildest dreams of prospectors. A land waiting for settlers. Beyond the land twisted a river, as wild as the land itself, a river that, with man's ingenuity, could be tamed some day to produce something useful . . .

Notes

[1]From *Voyages from Montreal on the River St. Lawrence through the Continent of North America to the Fraser and Pacific Ocean in the Years 1789 and 1793*, Sir Alexander Mackenzie, London, 1801.

[2]From *Notes of a Twenty-Five Years' Service in the Hudson's Bay Territory*, John McLean, London, 1849.

[3]*Peace River Mining Division*, Annual Report of the Minister of Mines for 1923, Province of British Columbia, J.D. Galloway, Victoria, 1924.

[4]*The wild North Land, being the story of a Winter Journey with Dogs, across Northern North America*, General Sir William Francis Butler, London, 1874.

The Mighty Peace

You wend your way forever and forever,
Your ripples splash to dampen shoring rocks;
You know no master, this, the Peace so mighty,
For you are harnessed not by dams or locks.

The foamy whitecaps on your breakers leap!
The rolling, boiling eddies lurk below.
How long you've been, how long to be, I ask you?
Hark! You answer, "Only God can know."

"I've been running now for endless eons,
I've smashed my way through mountains, plain and dale.
Oh, you foolish men along my shoreline!
Your greatest efforts are to no avail.

"I've watched you come, the red men ere Mackenzie
And ere the red, there was the primal man.
All have ever strived for peace enduring
Yet none has ever lived a life to plan.

"All have ever strived for life eternal,
But from each race and tribe I take my toll.
Upon them all, I place this ancient blessing:
'Rest in Peace, Believers in a Soul.'

(written in 1945 by E.K. Pollon)

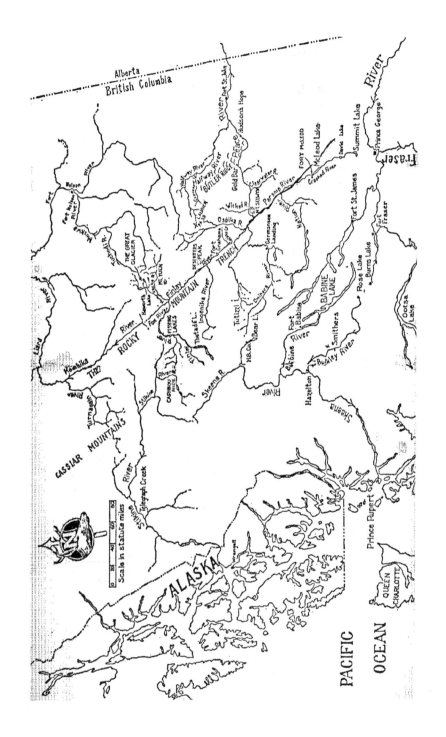

1

The Christmas Card Village

The wheels on the worn axles chattered as the old wagon bounced over roots and holes in the rutted trail. Giving a violent lurch, the wagon almost tossed my 11-year-old sister, Phyllis, off the mattress that topped the load. Suddenly the rear wheels snagged on a tree root and the wagon came to an abrupt stop.

"Doc! Roanie! Giddap there!" My father, Jack Pollon, slapped the leather driving lines. The horses lunged into their collars, lifting the wagon over the root, but the wheels hit the bottom of the deep hole on the other side with a deadening split.

"Whoa, dad! A felloe has broken," I shouted from where I was walking behind.

"Damn! That makes seven broken felloes since leaving Lone Star," Dad grumbled. "I don't think this wagon is worth the money we allowed for it on that account. Still, if we hadn't taken it, we'd have nothing."

Alfred Nelson, Nels Flatekval, Albert Savoir and my brother Art went in search of a birch tree to make another felloe, the outer circle of the wheel attached by spokes.

Alfred, Nels and Albert (a Metis, then called a half-breed) had decided to come west with us when we left Lone Star, Alberta. They had no money, so Dad had been doing all the financing on the trip.

Dad and I blocked up the back axle and removed the broken wheel. We knocked off the steel tire and placed it on the fire to heat in preparation for fitting it back onto the wooden parts after we had replaced the felloe. The men returned shortly with a piece of birch and the repairs were started.

Phyllis had wandered up to the brow of the hill where she could get a better look at the valley and the river flowing below.

"Earl! Earl! Isn't this pretty?"

13

I straightened up from drilling a hole for the spoke seat and joined her at the lookout point.

"It almost takes your breath away," I said slowly. "Makes you wonder if it's real."

We stood looking down into the deep valley. The Peace River writhed among the hills like an olive-green python. Dense forests of spruce, pine and aspen extended from its banks, broken by occasional clearings where spirals of smoke arose like fumes from Aladdin's lamp.

"Is that the Rockies, Dad?" I asked. "That blue chain of mountains with the snow on them?"

"Yes. That's them."

"They must be the highest mountains in the world. How far away are they?" asked Phyllis.

"They aren't the highest, but they are the second-longest range in the world. Thirty-five, 40 miles away."

"For gosh sakes! Will you guys stop admiring the scenery and give us a hand with this wheel?" Art yelled.

I reluctantly turned away from that breathtaking view at Cache Creek (later known as Bear Flats) and went back to work.

We made a few more miles that day taking us closer to our destination of Hudson's Hope. It was late July and saskatoon berries hung in clusters. As we walked along we carried kettles to hold the berries that we picked. When it was time to camp for the night we had far more than we needed for supper. Dad preserved the rest for winter use. We would need them as we had little money.

Dad, Phyllis and I had come from Saskatchewan to Notikewan, in the Peace River country, in the fall of 1929 when I was 13. Dad and I worked for Slim Jackson in his sawmill that winter, Dad doing the cooking and I working in the bush bucking and skidding timber. Art joined us in the spring of 1930.

When Art arrived Dad and I were busy building a grocery store and stopping place; we had applied for, and received, a post office called Lone Star. By the spring of 1931 the big Depression was well under way and our stock was all out on jawbone (I.O.U.s). Our bank account was nil. Late in 1930 the government had started issuing relief cheques to the settlers but as this paltry sum was hardly enough to live on they could pay nothing on old accounts. That's when Dad made the decision to move west.

"We'll collect what we can and get the hell out," Dad said. We ended up with three horses, the rattle-trap wagon, an old coal-oil lantern, a used scythe and innumerable promissory notes but not one dollar in cash. Dad sold for cash what he could of the little remaining stock, loaded the balance on the wagon along with the junk we had managed to accumulate, and away we went.

Now here we were – half-way between Fort St. John and Hudson's Hope – intending to travel as far as the wagon road extended into the mountains, or to a likely looking place where we hoped we could settle and make a living. What better place than one where someone else had once "hoped"?

The trail we followed must have been the original Indian pack-horse route, for it went where no self-respecting engineer would survey out a road – straight down over steep grassy hills, then up to the top again. Although we locked the hind wheels of the wagon, causing them to slide when coming down the hills, we would often have to cut a tree and drag it behind to keep the wagon from running over the horses.

We had to do this on the steep hills of the Peace at the Halfway River where Philip Tompkins ran a small trading post. When we arrived there the Halfway River was in flash flood stage. We took Phil's advice to wait until it subsided before attempting to cross it. In a few days the river went down and Eric, Phil's eldest son, drove our horses and wagon across, as he knew the ford. The river was still high enough to overflow our wagon box, wetting our supplies, including our natural-leaf tobacco. This was pretty important to us as Dad made his cigars from it, and Art and I our cigarettes. We hung the tobacco on the red willows to dry and, although it never tasted quite right after that, we smoked it anyway.

We followed the trail as it meandered through the jack-pine groves out to the edge of the river and back into the foot of the hills, making its way toward the mountains. Along this trail nestled the odd pioneer's cabin, hidden among the groves as if seeking sanctuary from the hustle and bustle of a civilized world.

"Whoa, Doc, you over-sized ancient hunk of buzzard bait!" Dad shouted.

Doc, a big bay gelding, was about twice the size of the little roan mare hitched beside him in the double-tree, and about twice her age as well. This was probably the most mismatched team to ever arrive in the Hudson's Hope territory.

We pulled up to the edge of the bench on which we'd been travel-ling, just before the trail dropped down to the flat below. Almost due west of us, at the centre of a pass in the low range of mountains, we saw a large mountain shaped like a volcano that seemed to stand alone, like a sentinel guarding against unwanted intruders. We learned this was Bullhead (later changed to Portage) Mountain. To our north was another knob, located at the southern end of the Butler Range. This was known locally as Butler Mountain (until some bright soul later changed its name to Bullhead and Bullhead's to Portage Mountain.)

Looking south and west from these guardian mountains we could see still higher mountains, two shaped like a woman's breasts.

"Say," said Art, "I'll bet those are called Tit Mountains."

He wasn't so far wrong. They are the Squaw Tit Mountains.

In the valley, we saw some log buildings scattered here and there throughout the aspen and pine flats.

"That must be Hudson's Hope," said Art.

"It doesn't look like much of a town to me. Those shacks look like they've been dropped by a prairie tornado," I said.

"It's sure pretty though, the way those cabins peek out through the trees. I'll bet in the winter it looks like those Christmas cards with the white frosting on them," said Phyllis, describing it with an 11-year-old's eyes. She gave a more apt description than we men could ever have done. I say men: Art was 14 and I was 15.

The flat on which the buildings stood was 600 to 800 feet across. The streets were winding trails just wide enough for wagons or sleighs. Some cabins had only a footpath leading up to them.

"It is kind of pretty," Art admitted.

"Well, guess we may as well drive on down the hill. You'd better put a smooth lock on those hind wheels. It looks pretty steep. I think we'll camp here for a day or two and look around," Dad said.

We had all expected to see a much larger town. As we drove in we counted the buildings: a log cabin and barn (which, we learned, had once belonged to Doctor L.G. Fredette, the region's first veterinary surgeon). A very large two-storey log structure was the old *Diamond P* that had been built in 1914 for a store and trading post, but was now vacant. Across the trail was a two-part, low-slung log building that belonged to Jim Ruxton. Then an impressive two-storey log structure that housed the Hudson's Bay Company store. South, on the banks of the river, stood the Bay manager's two-storey log house. The next building, still under construction, had a sign that said "Hudson's Hope Hotel – Bob Ferguson, Prop." A little old poplar cabin overlooking a spring that bubbled out from beneath the bench where the village sat was the home of Charlie Paquette, the oldest living pioneer of the Peace River country.

Near the log building which housed a restaurant belonging to

Ted Boynton, was a trading post owned by Henry Stege. To the south of the post was another old building which had been a Revillon Frères trading post. Stege now used it for a warehouse. It contained everything from groceries to hardware, worn clothing, Indian-made moccasins, mercury (used in gold-washing), and God knows what else.

To the west were more sod-roofed shacks and one large log building still under construction. The double-dove corner work on this building indicated craftsmanship. It belonged to Leo Rutledge.

A neat frame building, surrounded by a carrigana hedge, was painted a bright yellow, the only bit of colour in town. It provided a startling contrast to the naturally weathered logs of the other structures. This was the Government Telegraph Office.

The school house was easily identified by the large bell mounted on its roof and the flag flying from a tall, unpainted pine pole.

Another tiny old log cabin had been Hudson's Hope's first post office, established in 1912. It had been built by Colonel MacIntosh.

In the middle of a clearing was another two-storey log building: Hudson's Hope's first church. It was Roman Catholic, but no longer in use.

West of the telegraph office was a cluster of buildings belonging to Neil Gething, one of the earliest pioneers who, in 1912, had staked 60 square miles of coal in the area. About 100 feet south of Gething's we saw another small log building. It was the new post office and the Post-Master was Fred Monteith.

When we finished our ride around town someone mumbled, "So this is Hudson's Hope. It sure doesn't amount to much."

We all nodded in silent agreement.

We camped in town for a few days and rode around on our saddle horses in search of a place to settle. In our travels we came upon a wagon trail that led us up to Joe Turner's gate. We had been told that Turner was one of the early settlers who had arrived in 1914; he now had one of the largest herds of cattle in the country, something over 100 head.

From Turner's gate the wagon road narrowed into a packhorse trail, although farther up the hills on the main plateau we could see the remains of a narrow grade. We later learned this rough grade had been hand-built by Jack Thomas in 1922, to haul freight by sleigh out to two oil rigs on Lynx Creek and Red River. Although they did not hit oil, the rig on the Red River had tapped a small amount of gas, enough to produce a very low flame if ignited by a match.

Except for the fading scar left by this narrow grade and the deep groove of the original Indian pack trail, which had been reinforced by trampling hooves of horses and game over many years, nature had reclaimed this land, leaving nothing to indicate that man had ever existed here.

We rode north on this trail a few miles, past a small slough lying to the south. Beside it was an Indian grave, noticeable by its hewed covering and surrounding picket fence, which gave it the name: Graveyard Slough.

A short distance to the west we came upon a scattering of settlers. On being informed that a sawmill was located in the vicinity, I said to Art, "This looks okay to me. I might be able to get work here."

First, though, we had to pitch a temporary camp until we found a suitable place to build a cabin. We were informed in town that if we took the Portage Trail west about six miles we would find a wagon trail branching off to the north that more or less followed a survey line as far north as the old derrick on Lynx Creek. With a little axe work we were able to follow a pack trail about a mile east of the wagon road. There we pitched camp.

A few days later, Alfred Nelson shot the only double-palm-antlered moose that had ever been killed in this country. Both the front and back set of palms were identical in points and shape, although the back end measured a 51 inch spread while the front reached 54. Not realizing the antlers' value we left them there, until someone in town told us American hunters would pay a good price for a freak set such as these. Albert Savoir and I went back to get them, but a bear had beat us and carried them away.

Shortly after this, Alfred, Albert and Nels struck out on their own. This was a help because it cut down on the grub consumption, but our money was almost gone and we had to find work soon.

2
The Character of Hudson's Hope

In the early fall Dad, I, and a fellow by the name of "Racehorse Ed" Clifton, got jobs at Wes Gething's sawmill falling logs. When this work was finished, Gething asked me to take a trip with my team and his sleigh down to the Aylard Mine to get some supplies for his mill. I took with me Nels Flatekval and Willard Freer who were also working at the mill.

We could only come within three-and-a-half miles of the mine with the sleigh, because the road ended there. The mine was in the Peace River canyon at river level. We tied one horse near the sleigh at the top of the hill and took the other one with us, along with a couple of oat bundles. By the time we reached the mine building it was dark. We spent the night with Paul Porter and Charlie Anderson (the son of Sergeant Anderson of the North West Mounted Police) who were trapping out from there that winter.

The following morning we made a toboggan out of an eight-foot sheet of galvanized sheet metal, loaded it with a 100 pound keg of nails, four rolls of tar paper and a few other items. Our trouble began when we started back up the steep grade of the pack trail to reach the top of the canyon. Our supplies continually slid off the toboggan, sometimes rolling 200 feet down, forcing us to stop and repack. It was dark by the time we reached the sleigh and we were exhausted. We had very little sleep the night before as we had spent most of the night talking to Porter and Anderson, but because we were out of horse feed we had to start back that night. The weather was cold, but not extreme; however, being tired, we got chilled just sitting on the sleigh. We took turns, one driving, the others walking, to keep warm.

Our way home meant crossing an area that was thought to have been the old river channel before the last glaciers moved in and closed it, forcing the river to change its course around the south side of Bullhead Mountain. Flatekval and I were walking along when he

19

yelled, "There's a moose! Run!" Run I did, and jumped right into the sleigh. We looked around, but couldn't see an animal.

"Alright, Nels, where's the moose?" I asked.

He never answered for he had gone to sleep while walking and had dreamed of the moose.

I stayed on at the sawmill after the bucking and felling was finished to try to get work skidding the logs out with old Doc. Our harness, one of the items we had taken on an outstanding account, was in poor shape and would not stand up to the work. Wes Gething had to let me go.

Meanwhile, Dad had chosen a spot for our cabin about a mile north of Graveyard Slough beside Lynx Creek where a nice spring was located. When I returned home, I helped work on the cabin.

One day I was tacking in our windows, made from flour bags coated with candle wax, when we heard the yelping of approaching dogs. We all looked and beheld a strange apparition: a dog team followed by a tall lean man with a red bandanna tied around his ears. Frost had formed on the tufts of hair stuck up around the bandanna, giving a halo appearance to his otherwise bald head. He wore a light grey flannel shirt open to his belt, making it plain to see that he had on no underwear. When he jumped from behind the carry-all of his toboggan to speak to us, we were further amazed to see he was wearing shorts, which left his knees and legs exposed from the bottom of his shorts to the top of his Indian-made mukluks. We stood there gaping, not believing our eyes, for it was at least 10 degrees below zero.

"Hello there! Geake's the name. I must have missed the trail to the Halfway River, got on the trail to your place by mistake."

He smiled and shook our hands. His name was Edward Mayo Geake, and he had been a commander in the Royal Navy. Only later did we learn more about this strange man from stories told to us by his trapping partner, Jim Ruxton.

Ruxton and Geake were partners on the rivers of the north country for some years. Geake lived according to his own code, and led a varied and adventurous existence. He came from a well-known English family, Ruxton told us, and during World War I commanded a destroyer and was at the Dardanelles and Zeebrugge. He was in the British Diplomatic Service for a few years and spent part of that time in Harbin, Manchuria. He then immigrated to Canada and became familiar with the north country, taking up holdings near Pouce Coupe and at the forks of the Halfway River.

Geake was the originator of the Polar Bear Club in the Peace country and likely its only member. He was known to crack the ice on the Halfway River and go swimming when the weather was 30 degrees below zero. Peace country residents, constantly fighting the bitter cold, shuddered at the thought of this strange habit.

Geake was a noted "dog man" and was always accompanied by one or all of his well-trained team of Alsatian Huskies which he had named after the apostles. They were vicious dogs and once, when they turned on him, he pulled his hunting knife to defend himself. Before the fight was over, he had killed several.

In 1934, several years after our initial meeting, Geake was hired by the Bedaux Sub-Arctic (Citroen) Expedition to take charge of an advance expedition of 50 pack horses carrying gasoline and other supplies. The expedition was making a unique overland trek from Edmonton to the Alaska Panhandle and the Pacific coast. Local packers were being paid $4 per day by Bedaux, a wonderful wage during the Depression. A lavish and incredible venture, the Bedaux Expedition involved almost 50 people (including M. Bedaux' wife, her companion and her Spanish maid), more than 130 horses carrying supplies as outrageous as canned Devonshire cream, pâté de foie gras, silver cutlery and cases of champagne. One horse carried ladies' shoes, another hundreds of French novels. The purpose of the expedition was to try to take five Citroen half-tracks, already proven in tropical jungles and the Sahara Desert, from Edmonton through the Peace country via Fort St. John. After untold hardships (and nearly $250,000) the expedition was called to a halt near the Sifton Pass at the Liard-Finlay divide.

In 1935, Geake went off prospecting for an English company and made a valuable gold discovery in New Guinea. Returning to Canada in 1938, he spent several days with the Ruxtons – then living in Roberts Bay – before leaving with a Major J.C. Hartley on a trip to Durango State in Mexico. Their mission was to locate a lost treasure of Aztec gold hidden by Spanish priests who had followed Cortez on his trail of conquest and plunder. Geake and Hartley were camped a few miles from the village of Bear's Head (Village Cabeza de Oso) when they were shot by bandits. Hartley was killed instantly. Geake was badly wounded but managed to escape in the truck with Hartley's body. Geake made it to the village, but died shortly afterwards. The bandits robbed the camp and escaped into the wilds of the Sierra Madre Mountains.

We were quickly meeting our Hudson's Hope neighbours as we built our cabin. As there was no dry timber nearby, we built the walls and roof from green poplar poles; the roof was further covered with moss and cut-gut slough hay (so named because of its sharp saw-toothed edge), with a 12-inch layer of soil on top. Combined with a dirt floor, it was colder than billy-be-damned. The green timbers of the walls acted as cold conductors, inviting Jack Frost in as our fire died out. As our old stove wasn't very good, the fire went out frequently during the night. The job of relighting it fell to whoever froze out first. Many mornings we awoke to find our hair and blankets embroidered with a tatting of hoar frost.

During the winter of 1931 we ate more wild chickens and rabbits than we have in all the rest of our lives. We survived, thanks to our .22 rifle and copper snare-wire; moose and deer were not plentiful in those years. Phyllis used to drag in the rabbits she had caught in a short snare line near the cabin. They would be kicking and crying, and she could not bear to kill them. Art or I would have to do it.

One day during the winter Dad and Art went to town together, leaving Phyllis and I at home. We were both very hungry as all we had to eat was a little flour and salt mixed with water and dried out on the stove. We had been unable to kill a chicken or rabbit for several days, so I decided to go hunting farther afield. Taking the .22, I walked into the valley to hunt on the flats of Lynx Creek. After hunting all day and finding nothing, I was on my way home when I came to a thicket of spruce where I could see red squirrels scampering in the branches. They proceeded to give me a scolding in angry chatter. I had been hungry when I left home, but now I was famished. I shot seven.

But, oh, those devils were tough! The only parts with any meat on them were the hind legs, which were like spruce-flavoured golf balls and just as rubbery. However, they did enhance the flour and water gruel.

We made trips in to Hudson's Hope every 10 days for supplies. That winter of 1931 was extremely cold, and our clothing was not as warm as it should have been for a winter in the Peace River country. Whoever made the trip to town put on the warmest clothing we had.

I arrived in town one afternoon when the temperature was 50 below. I spent what little money I had for supplies at Henry Stege's store, then went over to Ted Boynton's restaurant to get good and warm in front of his big box wood heater before starting back home. I was soaking up the heat when Boynton came in from the kitchen with a cup of coffee.

"Drink this, bejeezus," he said, holding out the cup.

"I haven't any money."

"Who the hell asked for money? Just drink it. You look cold."

"I'm darn near frozen," I replied with a shudder.

During our conversation, Jack Pennington, who ran the freighting outfit and livery barn, walked in.

"I'm taking your pony down to my barn," he said to me. "You're not going out on the trail again today. It's too damned cold for man or beast."

"But I've got to go home! They will be expecting me. They'll worry if I don't turn up."

"A hell of a lot better if they worry a little and you get back alive than for them to still worry and find you frozen to death on the trail," Pennington replied, and without further ado he took my saddle horse down to his livery barn.

In the meantime, Boynton had been setting grub on the table. "Sit up and eat," he ordered. "I've got lots of blankets. You can sleep on the floor."

The next morning while I was dressing, Boynton came in with a new pair of Indian moccasins and socks. "You'd better put these on. Your footgear don't look too good and it's still 50 below."

I accepted without arguing, having found arguments useless with these men.

I was about two miles out of town, a little north-west of Joe Turner's place, when I met Art coming along the trail looking for me. He had on an old pair of leather shoes and his feet were almost frozen. We had to light a fire and thaw out his shoes before he could get them off. We stayed there about an hour until he got warmed up. I gave him the new pair of socks Ted Boynton had given me and then we continued on home. I rode and he walked, for if he had been riding his toes would have frozen in less than a mile in those cold leather shoes.

That Christmas of 1931 we received a pleasant surprise: a parcel had been left at the Post Office for us. It contained a turkey, candy, nuts and some good used clothing. Attached was a card wishing us a Merry Christmas. To this day we have never found out the identity of the kind people who brightened that day for us.

3
"Merry Christmas, You Sons a Bitches!"

After the first winter, living became a bit easier. I got on again at Wes Gething's sawmill. Instead of wages, I received lumber for my work, which I traded for other commodities we needed.

Dad, Art and Phyllis moved into town when the snow was gone. I went in after I finished working at the mill.

Dad had been doing the odd job around town to keep a little flour in the bin, and had noticed a good deposit of limestone located where the big spring gushed from under the bench where the village was built. The trail down to the boat landing ran alongside this lime deposit.

Jack Pollon (Earl's father)
(Hudson's Hope Museum)

The day I came into town, Dad said, "Earl, I think I'll try my hand at burning lime. My father and I used to burn it years ago in Manitoba."

We walked down to where he and a few others had their tents pitched. Dad showed me the lime deposit and explained what he had in mind for building the kiln. We went to work on it right away, using

25

a type of black powder the Hudson's Bay Company sold in 10-pound metal drums to blast our kiln out of the solid limestone formation. We thought this powder had once been used in Indian trade for old muzzle loaders.

The pit we blasted was eight feet in diameter at the top, tapering to five feet on the bottom. The bottom was in line with the base of a limestone cliff located a yard away from the edge of our pit. After we had finished the pit, we blasted a 30-inch-round tunnel from the foot of the cliff into the pit. The fire-box in the kiln was in line with the opening of the tunnel and consisted of lime rock.

We filled the pit, heaping it with limestone, and then started the fire in the fire-box, letting it burn at a very low heat for several hours until it had evaporated the moisture in the arch stones. Failure to do this could cause the stones to explode with steam pressure, allowing the whole structure to collapse. After the moisture was removed, we brought the fire up to maximum heat using a mixture of dry and green wood. A burn could take from 60 to 85 continuous hours, depending on fuel.

Jack Pollon's lime kiln
(Hudson's Hope Museum)

When we had finished burning that first kiln, Hudson's Hope took on a fresh white look.

Dad gradually built up a market for lime. We shipped through Maurice McGarvey and Vic Peck, who were both river-boat freighting, to Taylor Flats where the lime was picked up by the consignor. The freighters often found other sales for us, taking lime in lieu of cash for freight payment, which they in turn bartered or sold.

It became known throughout the north that we were burning lime, and our sales increased until we were also shipping with Harry Weaver on his boat, Beulah, whenever he made a trip up from Peace River Crossing with freight.

We often shipped by the Hudson's Bay boat, Weenusk, to Peace River Crossing. Other Hudson's Bay boats then carried the lime to various outposts in the Arctic Circle. We continued to ship this way as long as there was river freighting. The last tonnage shipped by river was in 1945, when Harry Weaver came up to get 100 tons of coal from the Peace River Coal Mines and bought what lime Dad had on hand.

That same spring Ted Boynton was having trouble with his well. There was plenty of water running through, as this was part of the flow that gushed from the big spring below the town. However, there were only six inches of water in the well, which rested on a conglomerate formation (rounded water-worn pebbles or gravel cemented together, forming an impenetrable mass), and Boynton could not dip a full pail.

A fellow by the name of Brown had run up quite a board bill with Boynton. Brown was a teller of tall tales; to hear him, he had been everywhere and done everything. One day Boynton asked him if he knew anything about blasting powder.

"You bet I do! I've handled powder on most of the big construction jobs in Canada!"

"Good. You can deepen my well to pay off some of your board bill."

"Sure, Ted. Nothing to it. I can fix it up in jig time. I'll need about half a keg of powder and some fuse."

The next day Boynton bought the powder and fuse, and Brown went to work. He made several trips down and up the well, then stepped into the kitchen of the cafe. "She's ready to blow!" he announced. "I've lit the fuse."

The well, which was 26 feet deep, was only about five feet from the back door of the restaurant, and only about 15 feet away from the east end of Henry Stege's store. No one thought to warn Stege that there would be a blast. In a few minutes a terrific WOORUMPH resounded. The restaurant leapt into the air. The well went to hell. To this day, none of us knows where Brown went.

Henry Stege waddled out of his store with a loaded shotgun under his arm. The blast had cleared his shelves and broken both windows. Not knowing what to do about this eruption, wanting to shoot Brown but not being able to find him, Stege started shooting cats. Henry usually kept three or four female cats. They all had kittens, the kittens had grown into cats, so Stege's original cat herd had multiplied many times over. Stege was no hell of a shot and couldn't tell his cats from anyone else's, so he shot all in sight. After running out of ammunition, or targets, he waddled back into his trading post to clean up the mess. There was a real shortage of ball-bearing mouse-traps in Hudson's Hope after that.

The summer of 1932, when we weren't burning lime, we were out on the homestead building a cabin of pine logs on the quarter-section that Dad had homesteaded near Graveyard Slough. We picked a good many hundred pounds of blueberries, for which we received 10 cents a pound.

One morning Dad and Art decided to go into town for supplies. Phyllis was staying with a new friend, Cathie Osborn. When Dad and Art saddled up the roan mare and Prince, the colt we had, they found the horses all lathered up. We wondered what had upset them, but didn't give it too much thought. The big horse, old Doc, had not been able to paw through the winter and had died.

I read for a while, then dozed off, when suddenly our dog Mickey went out of the lean-to as if ready to tear something to pieces. I grabbed our old .303 Lee-Enfield rifle. It had a safety slide which prevented any shells from entering the firing chamber as long as it was in place. As I ran out, Mickey came in, resulting in a collision which knocked over the box where we kept the water pail. For once the pail was full. It landed on my bedroll. I scrambled to my feet, still clutching the rifle, and made it out the door this time.

About 25 yards away was a large grizzly, standing up on its hind legs. I put the rifle to my shoulder, working the bolt, took aim and pulled the trigger. The gun went "click." My stomach lurched. Again I worked the bolt and pulled the trigger. Again the rifle clicked.

I ran back to the shelter, fumbling with the rifle, and only then discovered I had forgotten to pull the safety slide. Out I went once more. By this time the bear had decided to leave. I got one shot at him just as he left the clearing, but I was shaking so badly I know I missed, which was just as well. I was too scared to have gone up to the bear even if it had dropped.

Dad and Art had still not returned by dusk, so Mickey and I, being cowardly souls, moved inside the walls of the half-built cabin and barricaded the doorway. Before they returned the next day I moved my blankets back out to the wickiup.

Late in October we moved back into town and went to work for

Henry Stege. Dad and Art plastered his store and whitewashed it with our lime, and I did some carpentry work on Stege's new warehouse.

Henry Stege was about five feet seven inches tall, weighed 260 pounds, and, in place of hair, had shiny knobs sticking up all over his head. His spectacles were generally resting on his forehead, especially when he was looking for them. How he managed it I have never figured out, but he always seemed to have a three-day beard. His year-round footgear consisted of moccasin rubbers and wool socks; he would slip his feet into the rubbers, so the backs of them folded over, and waddle along shuffling his feet, no doubt to keep the rubbers on. I suppose the fact he couldn't reach his feet was the reason he allowed the backs to fold under. Unless he was angry, he wore a smile that reached from ear to ear.

Henry Stege
(Hudson's Hope Museum)

In 1933 Henry Stege put up the town's largest building, a three-storey frame structure. He moved out of his old log trading post and put in a fairly good stock. As the Depression deepened, his shelves carried less and less, and his accounts more and more.

That fall, there were four of us working on his warehouse (Bill Carter, Herb Coulson, Tom Johnson and myself). Henry, carried away with all the excitement of construction and plastering, proceeded to tie into his lemon extract and get plastered himself.

Periodically he would come out of his little store and read us the riot act: "Pound dem nails, you sons a' bitches! Pound dem nails!" Then he would turn around and waddle back into the store.

One morning late in October there was a skiff of snow on the ground and the weather was chilly. Stege was still on his binge, routinely coming out to give us the usual order to "Pound dem nails!" When Johnson asked him if he had any cotton gloves in his store because his hands were cold, Stege exploded.

"Vot in hell vill you do ven it gets *cold*?" he demanded.

"Pack a bloody heater, you silly old goon!" Johnson replied, lowering his voice at the end of the sentence.

Stege padded back into the store to think that one over. He came out again in five minutes and fired me.

The next morning I went in to get my wages. Before I had a chance to open my mouth he shouted, "Vot de hell you doin' down off dat roof?"

"You fired me yesterday. I came to get my pay."

"Did like hell fie' you. Get back up on dat roof and pound dem nails!"

I went back to "pound dem nails." We needed the money.

Art was plastering the building one day when he heard some anguished shouting coming from inside. "Help! Help! You bastids!" He went in to Stege's small lean-to bedroom-kitchen-office and found him wedged between the bed and a huge safe, unable to free himself. Art tried to pull him free while Henry continued to shout, "Pull, demmit! Pull, demmit!"

Art finally pulled him loose and received a blast for his efforts. "Vot de hell are you doing in heah?"

"I came in to give you a hand. I heard you calling for help."

"Didn't need no goddamn help," Stege snarled, following Art outside. "Get to vurk."

Christmas in Hudson's Hope was a big time of the year. Before the trappers left for their traplines in the early fall, the date was set for the school concert. To change this date after it had been set was strictly taboo, as the trappers would already have given their donations or left them with Henry Stege who, in turn, gave them to the woman who was looking after the funds. The trappers also returned from the line to attend the concert and dance, held in the old log schoolhouse.

Presents were bought for every child in the district, regardless of the length of time they had resided here, or their race, colour or creed. No childs' feelings were ever hurt by not receiving a present from old Santa Claus, although sometimes a fast shuffle was made to cover an unexpected guest.

People came from 35 or even 50 miles to attend this gala affair. Teachers would have their pupils learning their parts for weeks; if there was a shortage of students, adults would pitch in to fill a part in the two-hour program.

After the concert, Santa put in his appearance to the delight of the children even though they knew it was Henry Stege or Fred Monteith. After the concert came the dance, which could last all night or, in many cases, into the following day.

Christmas morning, after the children had opened their presents and each husband had soundly kissed his wife a Merry Christmas (often the only gift she received), someone would make a move to visit his next-door neighbour. There would be a round of hand-shakes among the men and kisses for all the girls and, of course, a small drink of cheer. It was small if you were wise! From there they would pick up the neighbour and go on to the next house in line – more kisses, more drinks. Old grudges were cast aside. This was a time when everyone could shake hands and make up without losing face.

In 1933 the usual concert and children's Christmas Tree presentations were held in the old schoolhouse. Henry Stege was appointed Santa Claus, having the right build for the job.

Jack Pennington and I were to get him dressed and take him down to the schoolhouse with Pennington's team and cutter. But when we arrived at Stege's trading post, Henry had been into his rum bottle and had taken on a bit more than he could conveniently carry. When we tried to pull on his red britches, Stege took a header under a table loaded with Indian moccasins, socks, and a collection of odds and ends. The table upset, scattering this accumulation of trade goods. It took us about five minutes to extract him from that mess. We just got him on his feet when he tipped over again. It was like trying to dress a roly-poly doll weighing 260 pounds whose balance wheel has come loose. His weight equalled the combined weight of Pennington and myself. We finally decided the best way to put on his pants was while he was in this prone position. Amid many "Mit! Mit! Mit! Vot de hell's de matteh mit yous?" we managed to get him into his costume. Then Stege insisted that he wear his beaver coat, cap and mitts over his Santa Claus suit.

On arriving at the schoolhouse, Stege ordered us to "Vhiten me up! Vhiten me up! Trow some snow on me! Vhiten me up!"

"I think a bucket of water would do more good," Pennington muttered.

With Jack on one side and me on the other, we finally weaved our way in through the schoolhouse door. The children were shouting, "Merry Christmas, Santa Claus!"

Henry completely forgot what occasion it was and started to

address a board of trade meeting: "Ladies and gentlemen. Vot! Vot! Vot de hell? Oh, Merry Christmas, you sons a bitches!"

By this time, not only the children were shouting but the adults as well. Pennington and I just turned him loose and he wobbled between the narrow aisles of the chairs, which helped keep him upright, to the stage. There he planted himself, straddle-legged, and cheerfully passed out the children's gifts as they were passed to him by the teacher, Miss Jean Cameron.

Stege always donated candy and nuts for the children's Christmas Tree and invariably wound up with about 50 pounds of the twisted Christmas mix on hand. He would pass this out to the kids whenever they entered his store, or if he saw them going by on the street.

Henry Stege had a great deal of faith in Hudson's Hope, and predicted it would some day be another Pittsburgh. His politics were strictly Conservative, but he was a civic-minded man who gave freely of his time and money toward anything that looked beneficial to the area or to the people.

Stege's time ran out in 1946. He didn't live to see the completion of his visions. With his passing, the north lost one of its most progressive and dedicated pioneers who spent a fortune and a lifetime trying to develop this country.

This is the Land

This is the land where the old die young,
The land where the young die old.
This is the land of timid men,
This is the land of the bold.
This is the land of sixty below,
Of a hundred and ten in the shade.
This is the land that will steal your heart,
A land of which you're afraid.
This is the land that is slow to condemn,
Yet mighty fast to atone.
This is the land of the towering peaks
With her fertile valleys low;
This is the land of the driving gales,
A land where your gardens grow.

This is the land, the friendly land,
The land of the gentle Peace
That wends her way through the mountains high.
Her waters never cease.

4
Lazy Stroke of the Paddle

Late in March of 1933, a party came in and asked Jack Pennington to take them to Mount Selwyn to do some work and assaying. Jack wasn't too enthusiastic about making the trip that late in the season. He pointed out that the ice would be turning rotten, and if it was too bad they would have to turn back. I was going with them to test ice ahead of the team and sleigh, Leo Rutledge was going part of the way with us, and Larry Gething was going up to work for them.

We left Hudson's Hope early in the morning, travelling with two teams above the Rocky Mountain Portage. The first night we got as far as the old portage cabin that Jim Beattie had built years before, and there we stayed overnight with three Englishmen who were using the cabin that winter (Bob Clark, Percy Stamp and Shorty Moane). The following day we travelled up-river about six miles and camped again. The snow was deep and heavy and it made rough going for the teams.

We intended to travel on ice from this point, so Rutledge left to take one team back to town. We were all in bed and the campfire had pretty well burned down when Leo walked back into camp carrying a pair of corked climbing boots; they had apparently fallen off one of our sleighs half-way back toward town. Rutledge knew that the man who owned them would be needing them before a boat went up in the spring, and therefore felt obliged to return to our camp with the boots. To save his horses he had walked back. The fellow who owned the boots muttered only a curt "thanks," damned little remuneration for 22 miles of hiking on a once-travelled sleigh trail.

Rutledge had something to eat, then walked back to the team and continued on into town that night.

From the time we started ice-travelling, it was obvious we were in for a rough trip. In places the ice was solid, clear and blue, but often we found ourselves facing rotten ice on three sides and were forced to retrace our steps and choose a new route. Sometimes it took Larry

35

Gething and I more than an hour to find a safe passage by testing the ice with axes every step of the way.

It took two days to reach the Adams' place above Twenty Mile Ranch. The weather became milder and the ice more rotten. On the south side of the Peace River from Adams' we came to a complete halt. Gething and I could not find safe passage. We tried all sections of the river with the same results: rotten ice.

"We'll have to turn back," Jack Pennington said. "I knew it was too late in the year to make this river trip."

One of the men exploded. "Oh for God's sake! I've had plenty of experience with ice-travelling. I can find some way through."

"If Earl and Larry say there's no safe ice, I don't think there is," Pennington said. "I don't doubt we can break trail around this section and even find a trail clear to Mount Selwyn, but you're forgetting one thing: we have to come back down this river with the team and sleigh. At the rate we've been going, that will be impossible."

The men argued until finally Pennington said, "Okay, go ahead."

Muttering about our incompetence, one of the men took an axe and meandered up the river. Suddenly we heard a shout and saw that he had dropped one leg through the ice and was hung up on his crotch. He now sang a different song.

"Let's get the hell out of here before we drown!" he screamed.

I crawled onto the sleigh with Pennington, both chuckling a little. Back at Twenty Mile point we unloaded the party on a sandbar that was free of snow. It was one of the windiest points on the river and Gething, who had to stay with the men, never forgave Pennington for this. They had to stay there for over a month until the river cleared of ice and the first boat made its trip in the spring. Gething said afterwards that the only compensation on that trip was that the assays taken on site were extremely high.

When a second company came in, the two companies planned a town of 3,000 people at the mouth of the Wicked River. The people of Hudson's Hope were quite excited about this prospect. Samples were taken out for assaying by the two companies, but unfortunately they proved to be far below those tested on site and the project was dropped, bursting another bubble. The country was following its usual pattern: small booms, bigger slumps.

After Jack Pennington and I returned from the aborted trip, I went to work for Leo Rutledge.

Rutledge was born in Boise, Idaho, and came to Canada in 1920; he lived with his parents in Grande Prairie, Alberta, until 1928. That year, when Rutledge was 17, he struck out on his own to go "down north" (as everyone here says, because our rivers flow downstream to the Arctic). When Rutledge arrived at Peace River Crossing he caught the first boat, which happened to be going upstream to Hudson's Hope. Deciding to stay for a few weeks, he is here still.

In 1930 Rutledge found his anchor in life when Fred Gaylor, the telegraph operator, brought in a beautiful English girl, Ethel Haines, to do housework for his wife. After a two-month courtship, Ethel and Leo were married.

I worked for Rutledge splitting his wood that spring of 1933, and in the summer I felt myself becoming restless. Work was scarce as the 1929 stock market was beginning to affect the north. Guiding was still the main source of income during the summer months, but the guiding outfits were not getting the long hunting trips of previous years. Government surveying had also pretty well been suspended. Trapping still predominated over all else in the winter months. Some seeked their fortunes by gold-washing on the Peace River and her tributaries, but most people just eked out a bare existence and many not even that.

Wicked River
(L. Gething)

Having a limited choice as to what I could do to earn my keep I decided to go on a bit of an adventure: I bought a small rowboat for a couple of dollars, invested a few more dollars in grub and kicked my boat from the landing on the 21st day of June.

The river was at peak flood stage, so once I was in midstream I had little to do. Every so often I would make a lazy stroke with my paddle to correct the bow. Riding on the crest of midstream, I had no worries about back-channels or sweepers lining the shore.

The shores of the Peace River were alive with the beginning of spring. An old she-bear cuffed an unruly cub into orderly parade with his brother and sister. A doe deer danced and pirouetted, proud of the fawn that flanked her. A cow moose farther downstream raised her head, scented the breeze, then shouldered her calf out of sight among the red willows. An eagle soared, scanning the river and slopes in search of prey to feed its young, hidden somewhere on a rocky crag or atop a towering snag. A bumble bee inspected my craft for a moment, defying aeronautics as it hovered with its over-large body and under-sized stubby wings, then buzzed away to the north shore which was ablaze with early roses.

The river. Adrift on her bosom, a sense of tranquillity enveloped me. I was filled with an inexplicable longing, a feeling I had never experienced before. I allowed my thoughts to escape, to rise and light on the fluffy clouds; to drift with them. I was free. Free. Dreaming on the murmuring waters of my river, for that is how I began to think of her.

I camped that night a few miles below Taylor, and the following morning kicked off again. I decided to camp for evening on an island in the Many Islands group. Here, the river breaks up into many channels and the water is lazy and slow. As I drifted onto the shore of one of the small islands I noticed a tree leaning out over the river which would be handy to tie up to. After I had snubbed my boat I picked up my grub box, tucked it under my arm, stepped onto the gunnel and leapt ashore, landing among scattered clumps of gooseberries.

I was suddenly overcome with the most horrible, sickening sensation I have ever experienced. Looking down, I saw I had landed on a six-inch ball of grey water snakes. With a squawk, I leapt six feet further onto a big blow-down tree, where I stood frozen with horror as I realized the island was a moving mass of snakes. Everywhere I looked were balls of snakes, and hundreds more writhed around me in a half-drugged fashion, all covered with a milky-looking slime.

I stood for what seemed like a hour on that big Balm of Gilead (black poplar) tree, wondering how to get back into my boat without wading through snakes. I walked along the tree to where the limbs began, a distance of 50 feet, looking for bare ground. There was none. The balm on which I stood was the only place that wasn't crawling.

I decided to take a running jump. The tree lay parallel to the river, about 12 feet away, so I had to make a sideways broad jump. I must have set some kind of record for I landed well out in the river, up to my armpits in water, still hanging onto my grub box. I scrambled in over the side of my boat and got to hell out of there.

The next morning I arrived at what is known today as Early's gardens. I decided to restock my grubstake there, buying vegetables, butter and eggs. I paid 10 cents each for a nice bunch of vegetables, a large loaf of homemade bread and a dozen eggs. I'd had only two dollars when I left Hudson's Hope; now I was down to a dollar and 25 cents.

I drifted down to Peace River Crossing that day, where I traded my boat for a guitar. I stayed around town for a couple of days, then caught a freight to Edmonton, where I spent another few days searching for work, sleeping wherever night happened to overtake me, eating out of my packsack.

There were hundreds of unemployed men also looking for work. I was a little better off than most, as I had grub and a little cash. It was the same all over: no work any place. I thought, What the hell? I might as well go back to Peace River.

I went down to the freight yards and immediately got grabbed by a yard bull, who asked me where I was from and where I thought I was going. I told him I was from God's country, and I was going back to God's country.

"Where is that?" he asked.

"The Peace River, where else?"

"There's a freight leaving in a few minutes and I won't be looking. Be damn sure you're gone when I do look."

"Leave that to me!" I replied.

There were quite a few more fellows aboard who were also heading back to the Peace River Country. The freight was met at Peace River Crossing by a cop who kicked us all off. I hoofed it across the bridge and hooked a freight again as far as Grimshaw. There I met an acquaintance who gave me a lift north as far as Lone Star, the place we'd started from in 1931. From there I walked to Deadwood, where I put in the summer helping my uncle and cousins until harvest time. Then we went stooking in Berwyn, but an early September frost had spoiled the crop so I got laid off. Back I went to Notikewan, 100 miles away, where I got a job on a threshing outfit. We were paid by the bushel, so everyone worked hard. I ended up with $100 when we finished the run. I was rich!

While threshing that fall I met a man named Jack Hodgson, who told me that Hudson's Hope was named after his father. The man was quite old and rather vague on all points, but he said his father had spent a season washing gold above the Peace River canyon and had done very well. He came out for supplies in the fall and talked of nothing else during the winter but returning. He said if he could divert the water in the canyon, he would find an Eldorado. Towards spring he took sick and never returned, but always hoped he would be able to go back. Hudson's Hope? Who knows. I liked this version of the origin of the town's name, and believe it is closer to the truth than it having been named after Henry Hudson in his search for the North-West Passage.

After threshing, I formed a partnership with a fellow named Dick Harding who was building a huge log barn that would hold 14 teams. The grain teams, which came from as far north as Fort Vermilion that winter, often gave us wheat in exchange for overnight stops; elevator prices then were 33 cents a bushel.

About March, my feet got the travelling itch again, so I sold out my grain equity to Harding and headed west.

One of the men riding a freight I caught invited me to spend the night at Hines Creek and I accepted. The following morning I started the long hike to Fort St. John.

The cut-off trail had not been used a great deal; one or two sleds had been over it that winter and the snowfall had been heavy. It would have been much easier to walk a two-inch beam than to tramp over that two-and-a-half inch sleigh track carrying a 50-pound pack. The depressions left by the horses' hooves were off-stride for a man, and by the end of an eight-hour day of slipping into and scrambling out of those tracks I wasn't sure whether I was walking on legs or pillars of fire. I began to go snowblind, and realized I was getting in bad shape. Then I remembered an old-timer, Charlie Paquette, telling how to make snow-glare glasses using a piece of wood charred black, with slits cut out for the eyes. I cut a notch in this chip of wood to fit my nose and tied it on with string. It really worked. I also rubbed my cheeks, nose, and above my eyebrows with charcoal.

My eyes and legs were giving me trouble enough, but then I got another problem: my rear end galled. Again I called on one of Paquette's stories for a cure. I cut a small poplar limb about an inch-and-a-half long and three-eighths of an inch in diameter, peeled the bark off and slipped it between my buttocks for a roller bearing.

I was pretty seedy looking when I reached Fort St. John. My face was covered with fuzz and charcoal, and I stared with bloodshot eyes. I was wondering what to do when I saw a middle-aged woman walking briskly down the street. She stopped.

"Hello, there. You're not from around here, are you?"

"I'm from Hudson's Hope," I said.

"Have you a place to stay for the night?"

"No. I was going down to the livery barn to see if they could put me up there."

"That's not necessary. You're welcome to come and stay at the Abbey if you like. We can fix you up with a bed."

This was my first meeting with Miss Monica Storrs, an English missionary and Good Samaritan of the Peace River country who, regardless of weather conditions would ride, walk or boat her circuit. In later years I was to meet her on the trail in 50-below weather leading her pony, icicles hanging from her eyebrows and lashes, her coat covered with frost. Despite these discomforts she always had a ready smile and a cheerful greeting.

When I got back to Hudson's Hope, Dad put me to work with a crosscut, taking out wood to burn in his lime kiln. I helped Dad burn one kiln of lime, which was all he had orders for at the time.

And that's how we got through the worst years of the Depression.

5

Hazards of the River

About the middle of May, 1934, King Gething told me that Carbon River's Charlie Jones was looking for some help and asked if I was interested in a job. He said the pay didn't amount to much, 15 dollars a month and found. King was going up in a few days on his regular mail run from Hudson's Hope to Finlay Forks and Fort Grahame, and I could travel with him.

King's boats were still beached, so when we went across the portage, King's father, Neil, and I gave him a hand with caulking, tarring and launching.

One evening after work Neil and I walked down to the head of the Rocky Mountain Canyon where the Peace River narrowed to a gorge about 175 feet wide. I picked up a rock and threw it across.

The shelf we were standing on was pitted with urn-shaped holes up to four feet in diameter, some as large as seven or eight feet deep. Neil told me these had been created by the effects of swirling water and pebbles.

"You know," Neil said, "some day there will be a huge powerplant built here, probably butting against that low hill on the south-west side and into Bullhead Mountain on this side. The canyon is three or four hundred feet deep there."

I laughed and threw another stone. In this wilderness? Impossible. These waters could never be tamed.

The following morning we started up-river. Having more freight than one boat could handle, King called on Bud Stuart to operate a second boat for him. Even then both were overloaded.

The old engines moaned in protest, pushing against the boiling current. I lay on top of the freight, with my head pillowed in the palms of my hands, to while away the hours it would take to reach Carbon River. The drone of the motor lulled my senses to all but the beauty and vastness as we slowly wound our way along the cutbanks and around the bends of the Peace River. This was the first time I had travelled up the river so early in the year.

There are a few days after the country casts off its mantle of winter, and before the Wolverine and Rocky Mountains release their winter snows, when the south slopes of the hills are touched with a faint tinge of green. The tree buds burst forth, giving a mottled effect to the brown stains left by fall, all backed by the majestic peaks still wearing winter nightcaps. The Peace River, like an opal, reflects the green of the dense spruce and pine forests that line her shores. The scene appears like the canvas of an inspired artist who has hurried to reproduce his first impressions lest he forget them.

The drone of the motor died away, bringing me out of my trance. We were coasting to shore, where the Carbon River split to enter the Peace at two different points.

Charlie Jones squaring a log for his house by the Carbon River
(Hudson's Hope Museum)

Standing on the beach to greet us were Charlie and Madge Jones. The Jones' had their home and beautiful gardens on the triangular island framed by the two branches of the Carbon, and bordered on the north by the Peace.

Charlie had come to Hudson's Hope in 1912 from the Ozark Mountains in the United States. He joined the Canadian Army in 1914 and served until 1918. While with the forces, he met and married Madge.

Marge was a tall, angular girl about 50 at that time. Charlie was a small active man, at least 20 years her senior. He was an avid reader and inclined to dramatically retell the stories, placing himself in the leading roles. In the Peace country, Charlie had trapped, prospected, held a job as fire warden, and was the originator of the Gold Bar Post Office, which opened at Carbon River and later moved to Twenty-Mile. At this time he was living on his army pension.

Jim Beattie's daughter, Girlie, was doing housework for the Jones' that summer. My job for Charlie was to milk his goats, tend the gardens, and break some land (from which a couple of starved-out prospectors had already cleared the brush) with his one horse and walking plough.

One afternoon when I was working on the land I heard some shots coming from the north side of the river. Going down to the shore to investigate, I found a pack outfit waiting on the north shore. I took a small boat that Charlie kept for fishing and rowed across. There waiting were Harry Garbitt, Dr. Brown and an Indian packer. Dr. Brown was the Indian Agent and they had just come from the Halfway Indian Reserve. Harry Garbitt was acting as outfitter and guide. They were now headed to Moberly Lake via the Carbon River watersheds to pay Treaty there.

When I had ferried their party across the river they set their wickiup camp on the west side of the upper Carbon.

That evening after I had finished milking the goats, I walked across the bridge that Jones had built over the upper branch of the Carbon to get to his billy-goat pens and new land that I was breaking, to visit Harry Garbitt and Dr. Brown. It had started to drizzle a bit in the afternoon but now it was raining quite heavily.

During the evening, Garbitt got telling of his experiences in the early days in the Peace River country, after his arrival in 1896.

"My first trip in from Edmonton was quite an experience," he said, and laughed. "I was pretty young and green. Hadn't been out from Scotland very long. A couple of fellows hired me as a horse wrangler and to help in herding horses up to the Peace country. When we left Edmonton we had seven head of horses. One morning I got up to turn the horses out of the rope corral to graze and by gawd, there were eight horses! A few days later the herd had increased by several more. Then one morning they were back down to the original seven.

"We were packing up when two North West Mounted Police rode into camp and demanded to see bills of sale for the horses. One of my bosses produced them. The police asked me a few questions, if these were the horses we had started out with from Edmonton, and I said yes.

"The next night we had the missing horses back again." Garbitt chuckled. "I guess they had been tipped off that they were going to be investigated, so they'd separated the stolen horses and driven them back into the bush during the night. They paid me 50 cents a day more than we'd agreed to in Edmonton!"

Garbitt and Dr. Brown pulled out with their pack outfit in the morning, although it was still raining hard. It was too wet for me to do any work, so I stayed indoors and read. The Jones' had a large library compiled of Vancouver Public Library discards (some of which eventually found their way into the Hudson's Hope Museum).

It rained steadily all that day and night, and was still raining the following morning. I could see the rivers were rising. In the afternoon I got cabin fever. Fed up with lying around, I put on my slicker and went outside for some fresh air. There was a rumbling to the south and I could see the odd lightning flash. I went back in and told Charlie we were getting a thunder storm at the head of the Carbon.

"We just might get a little water if it keeps up, what with having three days of rain already and the snow still in the mountains," Jones said.

The Carbon River had now risen several feet. I watched as the first forerunner of the thunderstorm's freshets came down river with about a 12-inch front of water. Behind it came another front even higher than the first. It seemed every time I blinked my eyes the river was higher. I became worried. The triangular island where we were consisted of about 10 acres of land. I suggested to Jones that it might be a good idea for us to leave the island and cross over the bridge onto the mainland.

"Oh, she won't get much higher," he replied. "It never has before."

Well, it got higher alright. The bridge went out over the little Carbon, as we called the one branch. Then we were truly marooned, with only one small rowboat that could carry two people.

The small vale across the island between the house and the Peace River filled with water. I became really worried. Charlie and Madge were old. That left Girlie and I to try to do something if it became necessary. I was hoping it wouldn't.

I again suggested to Jones that we leave the island. He again predicted the water wouldn't get any higher.

Although the little Carbon was the smaller branch, it seemed to be carrying the bulk of the flood waters. The water now was dark and muddy and had built up enough power to spew clear across the Peace River, giving the illusion of a four-foot mud dam sandwiched between the jade waters of the Peace. Still Jones refused to leave the island. And he was the boss.

The river continued to rise. It now ran between the house and the Peace River through the vale, covering Madge's flower beds. All that could be seen of them was a rose bush and a few tulips being baptized as the current ducked their heads beneath the surface.

The river rose until it was now running through the dense growth of large spruce trees on the island; the west side of the island was quickly being washed away by the surging current of the little Carbon. Large spruce fell one after the other as the banks cut away. Now the water was lapping at the doorsill of the house. The tulips gave up to a superior power, went under, and stayed there.

A small wavelet stealthily broke over the doorsill and ran into the living room. Girlie took a cloth and wiped it up. More water broke over the sill. She swiped at it aimlessly. Now a continuous trickle overlapped the doorsill. She gave up.

The peals of thunder and rain had stopped an hour ago but still the water continued to rise. Jones had long since given up prophesying and admitted he had no idea just how high it might go. He had never seen anything like this before.

As we watched, the water peaked at the doorway then started to recede almost as quickly as it had come up. The tulips reappeared, bedraggled and beaten. The rosebush came into sight, now minus its blossoms. The pansy bed was covered with silt and debris, not a pansy showing. Still standing, but with only a single shredded blossom on its stem, was a bleeding heart.

The rest of the garden was a silt-laden mass. What had been one of the beauty spots of the north, developed with all the loving care that this man and woman could put into building a home, was now a desolate waste.

As the water receded to its proper channels, it seemed to carry with it the hopes of this no-longer-young couple. Now there was nothing but the dismal sight of a ruined garden that could not possibly be replanted with any hopes of it bearing that year. A large part of the island was gone: two acres on the west side had been completely washed away.

Madge and Charlie Jones stood looking out the window, arms around each other's shoulders, and wept without tears. Girlie and I almost shed tears for them, for many times in the evenings they had told us of their dreams of making this little island in the Peace the show-place of the north.

I stayed with the Jones' for a few weeks, until things were straightened out, then I returned to Hudson's Hope.

6
Billy-Goat Wham

In the spring of 1935 the Indians came to Hudson's Hope from the North to trade their furs.

One morning I decided that Chit, as I called our little bronco, needed some exercise as he had been standing in the barn for several days. I led him out and tied him to a fence rail while I put on the saddle. When I had cinched the saddle I stepped back, and he kicked me. I hauled off and kicked him in the belly in return. I then untied him and took him out of the corral. The show was on.

Even as I started to mount the little hammerhead, he began to pitch. I managed to get into the saddle and was putting on a darn good ride until he bucked his way down into a stand of small poplars as thick as sheep's wool. My left stirrup caught on a tree, forcing it up around my ankle. I quit riding for show and started to ride for my life.

I grabbed the saddle horn with one hand. My right leg hit a tree, knocking my foot through the stirrup. Then I was really scared. I grabbed the front of the saddle with my other hand.

The Indians had seen the horse pitching and now they were all standing around the edge of the trees, whooping and hollering. This excited the cayuse still more. Having lost both the reins in my effort to hang onto the saddle, I made up my mind that if I left that horse, the saddle would go with me. I wished the cinch would break but no such luck. The horse bucked clear through the poplar stand, came out on the north side, then turned around and pitched his way back through them again. My face was cut, my hands ripped from the branches, and I was tiring. But so was the cayuse, for when we came back to the opening he just stopped, blew his nose, then turned his head as much as to say, "How did you like that?" I didn't, and told him so in no uncertain terms.

While I was cussing him, old Indian Dan came up to me. "How much horse?"

"Too much horse," I replied. "Give me $40 and he's yours."

"Me buy him. You come Hudson's Bay, me give you money."

I was so mad, as well as being broke, that I sold him. He had made me look like a fool. I didn't like that.

The next day I was standing in front of the Bay post when I saw the Indians coming on horseback, whooping and kiyiing. Ahead of them was Chit. I watched them for a while, but they were not having any luck catching him. I finally went over to where they had their wickiups. Chit was standing among a bunch of their pack horses. They still had not caught him.

I had whip-broken him to come when I called him by name. I picked up a small piece of quarter-inch rope lying among their junk, snapped it, and shouted, "Chit!" He left the other horses and came over to me. Old Dan was excited. "How you do that?"

"Just call him by name and snap the rope," I replied.

He tried it. I guess they way he slurred "Chit" didn't sound good to the horse, because he just wouldn't go to Dan when he called. Dan gave me a pair of beaded moccasins for catching the horse for him.

Two or three years later I saw Dan in Hudson's Hope again. He said, "I takum home horse, let um go. No more catchum. Horse crazy. Wolves eatum. Good!"

The summer of 1935 was a wasted summer, with the exception of meeting Bonnie Goodvin. I was only nineteen. How I would like to waste more seasons like that one!

Lloyd Gething, Bud Stuart and Pete Kyllo were going to buy out Charlie and Madge Jones, who had decided to quit the country after the flood the year before. The three men planned to start the Lobstick Fishing Lodge. I was to work for them. They had taken out logs the winter before, so a little work had been done on the new building. Then something happened and the deal fell through.

We all decided to go gold washing for the summer, so moved down to what we knew as Indian Head Flat – flat broke – and there we stayed for several weeks until our grub ran out. Our gold washing was not profitable. But then, we didn't work very hard at it. A good share of our time was spent fishing, hunting, daydreaming. Every few days we would head for the Hope for a party, which sometimes lasted three days.

That fall, Lloyd Gething went back to teaching, Bud Stuart headed for the U.S.A., Pete Kyllo went back to the farm in Alberta and I kept the gold washing outfit and moved down to Morgan Flats where the Goodvins were washing gold. The rich bar the attraction? No, no. Their niece, Bonnie, was the magnet that drew me to that gold bar.

I had first met Bonnie in Hudson's Hope when she had come up to visit her aunt, uncle and cousin. She was a little on the plump side, but she had the most beautiful hair of any woman I've ever seen, long golden blond. That trapped me right away. I immediately left her cousin, Frances, who I had been going with, and concentrated on Bonnie. But she was only 14, and I was 19. I knew I would have to wait to let her grow up.

That summer at Morgan Flats was when we started to get together. In the evenings we would walk along the river's edge, or take the boat and paddle across the Peace to a back-eddy where there was good fishing. We'd spend the whole evening out there sometimes, fishing and flirting.

October 24, 1935 was a beautiful day, warm as any day in June, with a soft warm west wind. But the following day I woke with a start to hear Joe Goodvin shouting, "Earl, get up! Our stuff is being washed away!"

I jumped off my bunk and peered out the tent flap. The wind was a driving gale from the east, and when I drew back the flap I was almost blinded by lashing snow. I looked toward the river where we had set up our mining outfit. Our boat, which had been tied to a rock on the gravel bar, was floating upstream against a five-mile-an-hour current. The tie rope, working like a drag, kept the bow downstream. Goodvin was out in swimming-water, trying to head off the boat. Luckily he managed it, because that was the only boat we had. Our mud boxes, blanket boxes and everything else on the bar were also afloat. The river had come up over eight feet during the night. We were through gold washing for that season.

That afternoon when the slush ice started to run we boated our stuff across the river to the road on the north shore. Goodvin and I took turns rowing, the other standing in the bow giving directions and breaking the way through the slush with a long-handled shovel. When the bowman saw an opening in the slush he'd shout, "Give it hell!" or "Hold it!" At times the boat was completely surrounded by floe ice. Our arms ached as we made trip after trip with that small boat, moving the Goodvin family and all their belongings to safe ground.

That night the temperature dropped still lower. It would have been impossible to force our way through the ice the next morning, because it had frozen into large solid blocks, filling the river from bank to bank. I walked 30 miles that day to get a team to come and move us down to the Hope.

That winter, my brother Art was trapping on Jim Ross' trapline on Kobes Creek when he ran short of grub. He asked me to give him a hand to pack more out. My snowshoes were in bad shape so first I had to repair them with babische made from a frozen moose hide. The large Remington folding belt knife I was using was as sharp as a razor. It folded onto my centre finger at the first joint, nearly severing it.

I had to call on Mrs. Peck to give it an overhaul. It was late at night and the lights were out. Still, I knocked on the door.

"Who's there?" she shouted.

"Earl. I damned near cut my finger off with a clasp knife."

"Too bad it wasn't your throat!" was her reply.

I turned and started back out of the yard and had just reached the gate when she shouted, "Where the hell do you think you're going? Get back here, you fool!"

That was Mrs. Peck . . . give you hell, then first aid. I have never known her to refuse help to anyone, even if she was at loggerheads with someone. She would accept no pay for her services, just say, "give someone else a hand when they need it."

In the spring of 1936 I went up-river looking for work.

Billy Mahaffy had a gold mining outfit up on Brenham Flats, for some reason referred to by the residents as Bullshit Flats. He had received a placer mining outfit in lieu of wages from the Peace River Gold Dredging Company, which he had arrived with in 1922. I was the first one to show up at the Flats looking for work that spring, so I got a job.

Bill Mahaffy's gold mining outfit on Brenham Flats
(Hudson's Hope Museum)

Billy's initials were W.A.M. and, because he always sported a small grey goatee, we called him Billy-Goat-Wham (not to his face, though!). He was a short, wiry Irishman and his goatee would quiver whenever he was angry. Mahaffy was angry most of the time.

Although he and Jim Beattie had been partners on a fur farm, Billy now had an extremely violent hatred of Jim. To get a rise out of him, all one had to do was mention Jim's name. Billy's whiskers would quiver, his chin would jut forward, and he would screech, "Jim Beattie! Fah!" His false teeth, which did not fit very well, would shoot from his mouth, making him still more angry. Then he'd jut his chin out still further and suck air into his mouth to recapture his teeth. I have yet to see anyone keep a straight face when that happened.

That summer my brother Art also got a job working for Mahaffy. One day he mentioned that he had to go down to Jim Beattie's to get some tobacco.

Mahaffy's chin shot out and his goatee quivered. "Jim Beattie!" he spat. "Fah!" That time he missed catching his teeth and they landed on the ground. "Now see what you've done! Fah!"

"You opened your own mouth, Bill," Art said, laughing.

"Fah!" he muttered as he stamped away toward his cabin, carrying his teeth in his hand.

Bill Mahaffey examines sluice box to see if it's time
to change blanket. B. Braden looks on
(Hudson's Hope Museum)

George Brandon and his wife Laura were also working for Mahaffy that summer. Laura was doing the cooking while George worked in the gravel pit. Vern Peck and I were working night shift, and sleeping in a tent a few feet away from the cache where the cookhouse supplies were stored. One forenoon we were awakened by a hell of a start. We stuck our heads out from under the edge of the tent. Laura was standing on the porch of the cache, which was built up on posts about six feet off the ground to keep out the rodents. Mahaffy was standing on the ground below.

"You goddamned scrawny-necked diseased old son-of-a-bitch!" Laura yelled. "I have a good mind to come down and make a bow tie out of that syphilitic old neck of yours! I will too, if you give me any more of your dirty old Irish tongue!"

"Fah! You are a wasteful woman! Cooking macaroni and cheese when there are potatoes! I put the lock on the cache so I can ration out the food."

"By god, you hired me to do the cooking and the men are working hard. They need a lot more than potatoes! As long as I'm doing the cooking, they're going to get it too!"

"Then from now on you're not doing the cooking! I'll do it myself."

That ended Laura as our cook. The grub took an immediate turn for the worse.

One day King Gething stopped at the Flats on his mail trip upriver. Lynch Callison was with him. Mahaffy, of course, invited them for dinner. It consisted of potatoes, pigweed greens, and rhubarb with damn little, if any, sugar in the rhubarb. After they had eaten, Callison thanked Mahaffy for the dinner, then said, "Work hell out of these men, Billy. But remember, they are like the old horse – you have to feed them to get the work out of them – so keep lots of hay in their manger."

I guess Mahaffy got the hint; the grub improved a bit after that, but not much.

We received two dollars plus board for nine blistering hours shovelling gravel in the open pit placer mine. Our work clothes consisted of a pair of pants, and low moccasin rubbers. Boots were no good, as the gravel would get into them and it was too hard to take them off to dump it out.

I finally got fed up with the grub and one morning I just "packed my turkey" and headed down to Morgan Flats where the Goodvins were working again that year. Bonnie had gone home to Demmitt, Alberta, and without her presence, half the attraction I had found there the year before was gone.

I thought about Bonnie, reliving our previous summer together here on the river, recalling the feel of that long golden hair. I called her "my river girl," and her personality was very much like the river: easy-going on the surface, but lots of depth. I felt I was just getting to know her. She was really a flirt. I could get jealous as hell when I'd catch her flirting with someone. She would flirt with her eyes and her laugh, her smile. In my books she was the most beautiful girl I'd ever met.

7

Setting Off for Manson Country

One evening the Goodvin men, Joe and Uncle Johnny, decided to go hunting on Brown's Island about two miles below Morgan Flats. They were taking the rowboat, so before they left they took me over to the north side of the river to Rainbow Rocks to fish, while Jennie stayed in the camp. We were out of meat, so if they didn't get anything we were almost sure to have fish for dinner.

It was one of those warm August evenings when the sun has lost its searing heat and settled into the mountains. About 200 yards upstream from our camp on the south side of the river the big 12-foot waterwheel, built by the Goodvins to pump water into their sluice-box for washing gravel, turned slowly, catching the reflections of the setting sun on its fresh-peeled pine spokes and the hand-hewn paddles as they rose from the river.

Goodvins' gold-washing outfit at Morgan Flats on Peace River
(Hudson's Hope Museum)

My mind again drifted on one of its fanciful trips. A flock of ducks on the river quacked to each other, no doubt discussing preparations for the migratory trip south. I had taken off my moccasins to let my feet dangle in the cool waters of the river. I resented every tug on the line that forced me out of my dreamy state long enough to remove a Rainbow, a Dolly Varden or a Grayling.

I had just mildly "damned" the last tug and started to pull in my line when my dreams suddenly came to earth with a thud. Up-river was a large bull moose swimming in the water. I jumped to my feet. "Jennie! Get the Luger! Go up to the water wheel. A moose is going to land above there."

Jennie heard me and came running from the cabin. "Joe has the Luger! He was short of shells for his rifle so he took the Luger too."

"Take old Ring, then, and go up there and keep him in the river. I'll drive him back in on this side if he tries to land here. We can drive him down to Brown's Island where Joe and Uncle Johnny are hunting."

Jennie ran along the south shore, calling for the dog as she ran. As soon as the moose saw Jennie and the dog he turned and swam back to the north shore. I had my moccasins on by now, and had picked up an armload of stones. When he tried to land on the north shore, I bombarded him. He turned and started back for the south side.

When he got close to the south shore, Ring started to bark, causing him to turn and head back toward me once again. All this time the current was carrying him farther down river towards Joe and Uncle Johnny. Jennie and I were shouting, "Joe! A moose!" as loudly as we could.

He continued to swim aimlessly back and forth between us until we reached a point about a mile downstream from where we had started. He was on Jennie's side of the river when he suddenly shook his antlers and made a bee-line for my side. I knew he was going to try and make a landing against me, fearing me less than he did the dog. As he neared the shore I started throwing rocks at him again, hitting him on the head and antlers. This time he refused to turn back, although I kept hitting him with rocks until he had his front feet on bottom. Then I turned tail and made for a black poplar close to the shore.

I had just climbed high enough when he trotted up to the base of the tree with his head down and his bristles standing on end. He stood at the foot of the tree shaking his head for about five minutes, then took off toward the second bench. I slid down the tree to the ground. He came trotting back. I shinnied up the tree again.

He started away, and again I slid down the tree, thinking the moose would come back to tree me once more. Nothing doing. This time he headed for new country. He climbed up on the second bench and ran east along its brow. As he trotted along the bench, Joe and Uncle Johnny spotted him from Brown's Island.

The moose turned and ran down the bench towards the river to where Joe and Uncle Johnny were waiting on the island. Joe ran for the boat, concealing himself below the gunnels. The moose jumped into the water without a pause, and swam across to where Joe was kneeling in the boat. Joe shot him with the Luger when he landed on the beach beside his boat.

Joe and Uncle Johnny said that was the fattest moose they had ever killed. Jennie rendered 130 pounds of tallow from him.

After the moose hunt, my fiddle-feet again got the best of me. Joe Goodvin gave me a riding saddle for my wages and I headed back to the Hope. I was restless for the rest that year, staying a few days here, a few days there, never long anywhere.

In the spring of 1937 I learned there was work down at Taylor Flats. I stayed there for a month or two, then worked on a farm, then went to work for Maurice McGarvey. While there, Mac told me of some of his experiences around the Manson Creek country. His stories intrigued me, and during the summer I did a lot of thinking about that country. Daignault was operating his Northern Ventures Project there; the Consolidated Mining and Smelting Company was also at Manson, as well as several smaller companies. Finally I made up my mind to go have a look-see.

In the latter part of August, Lloyd Gething stopped in on his way back from attending summer school. This called for a celebration. We had one, too, lasting three days at Taylor Flats and continuing two more days as we went up to the Hope with Mac on his regular mail trip. During the past few years, Gething had been teaching school at Moberly Lake. When he started there, most of the children spoke no English so he had had to learn to speak their language – Cree. When we arrived at the Hope there was a wire for Gething. He read it, then handed it to me. "Ye Gods, I've been appointed to teach at Taylor this year. Now I have to live down our past week! I asked for a transfer but I sure didn't expect the Taylor School or I never would have gone on a wing-ding there."

That brought our partying to a hard stop. I went back to Taylor and put in another month working for Mac McGarvey. I returned to the Hope and on the 12th of November, I decided to head for Manson Creek, against the oldtimers' advice. I would have done well to listen to them, for they knew what they were talking about.

When I was ready to leave, I weighed my pack. Fifty-five pounds. It contained a suit of Stanfield's wool underwear, a heavy black wool jumbo sweater, a spare pair of socks, a three-cell flashlight along with spare bulbs and batteries, cooking utensils, a three-pound lard pail, a handleless aluminum frying pan and my grub. These supplies were wrapped in a six-by-six tarpaulin and lashed to a home-made packboard. I also carried a pair of 60-inch snowshoes, a hunting knife on my belt, and a small trail axe which I carried in my hand.

The first day of the trip I stopped overnight with Jack Thomas about 17 miles out. He entertained me with a few tales about his life in this country, but said nothing about his life before he came here in 1908. (I later found out his name was neither Jack nor Thomas, that he had chosen to start a new identity when he came to the country). He told of one trip he made north with a Texan and a Mexican who had come into the Peace country by the old Edson Trail. They had gotten lost while crossing from Edson to Grande Prairie, and when they arrived in Hudson's Hope they were at loggerheads, each blaming the other for having become lost. From Hudson's Hope they wanted to go north on a prospecting trip but, not wanting to get lost again, hired Thomas to guide them.

"When we left the Hope they were both carrying revolvers," Thomas said, "one in his hand, the other in a holster at his hip. I didn't realize how bitter they were when we left the Hope or I would never have started out with them. After we were on the trail it got worse. They made as if to shoot each other a time or two, then let it drop. The first time it happened, at Red River, I tried to get them to turn back. They insisted we go on. The farther we travelled into the hills, the more their hatred built. When we reached what is now called Twemble Lake, I refused to take them any further. I tried to talk them into coming back with me, but they refused. I took what grub I needed to get back to town, then left them on their own.

"A few days later a mining party coming out from Bluebell Mountain found them both dead. They had shot each other. One was hit between the eyes, the other through the heart. The men who found them formed a miners' jury and buried them right there. The police were angry they had not been summoned to conduct an investigation, but the bodies were starting to get high, according to the men, and the evidence was plain enough for a blind man to see. Besides, it saved a lot of taxpayer's money doing it that way.

"Local residents called the lake Dead Man Lake after that, but somehow it got changed to Twemble Lake," said Thomas.

The next night I stayed at Jim Beattie's, 34 miles out. I laid over a day there at Twenty Mile Ranch and helped Beattie butcher a beef.

Before leaving the Hope I had gone to the post office and picked up all the letters for the men on the upper river. I had one for Billy Mahaffy. To deliver it meant going out of my way south a couple of miles on Brenham Flats instead of cutting across. When I arrived at Mahaffy's he was glad to see me and insisted that I stop for dinner. It was a cold blustery day with the wind blowing out of the north. He promised me something "to warm the cockles of my heart." It sure did! I had heartburn all the way to Schooler Creek, where I spent the night in Mahaffy's trap cabin.

Up to this point I had been travelling overland. When I left Schooler Creek, I started to travel along the river's shore. Although the mist from the water had glazed the shore rocks with ice, the ice had not formed enough for me to walk on it. I spent a good deal of time picking myself up after falling on the slippery rocks. Then I came to one place where the ice had formed along shore and, as far as I could see, it looked okay. I took a chance and went out on it. I travelled on the ice for about two miles, only to discover that it ended in open water on all sides. The only thing to do was to retrace my steps. By the time I arrived at the Black Rocks where Red Kinsman had literally denned up for the winter, I was played out.

Kinsman had dug a hole about four feet deep, eight feet wide and ten feet long. He had then built around the hole above the ground with logs until there was room to stand up, if you were not too tall. For a roof he had lain some logs flat on top of the walls and shovelled the dirt from the hole over them. If you bumped the walls or roof, the dirt would trickle down into your grub. For a door, he had cut a hole about two feet square in the logs. To enter his "cabin" you had to back in, letting your feet down until they reached bottom.

As I climbed up the bank to the cabin I shouted, "Halloo the house!," a standard greeting used when approaching a cabin in the wilderness. Kinsman came scrambling out on his hands and knees. The whites of his eyes were startling as they shone through his rough red beard and the dirt on his face. He had a revolver in his hand and looked like a crazy man. I suppose at that time he was getting very close to that stage.

His greeting was very abrupt, but hospitable. "Oh, it's you, Pollon. I was going to cook some steak. You're just in time. I haven't washed my dishes yet."

I think he meant he had not washed them since he had moved up there in the summer, for they were coated with grease and soot. Kinsman had not washed himself either – at least, I don't think he had. It was difficult to tell the true colour of the two-inch growth of beard on his face, for it was coated with lamp black, stove ashes, and griddle grease.

Red Kinsman was a shell-shock case from the First World War, and he would pace back and forth like a caged animal on a short runway he tramped out in the snow. When he came to the end of his runway he would make an abrupt about-face, his hands behind his back, still clasping his revolver. He would keep this up for hours at a time. When he started to pace, he forgot about anything he might have been cooking, or anything else he might have on the go. My brother Art claimed that Red Kinsman ate more burned food than anyone else in the north country. He should know: he trapped with him one winter.

After Kinsman had put the steaks on, he scrambled back out through the hole and started to pace. When the steaks were cooked, I gave him a shout. He came scrambling back in, saying, "Forgot all about them. Forgot all about them."

That was about the extent of our conversation for the evening. When it came time to roll in, I looked with dread at the accommodation he indicated. Kinsman had made his bunk out of round poles. He had not covered them with anything, or even bothered to hew off the high spots.

The last time I saw Kinsman alive was the year before he disappeared. The following summer, Kinsman left a note in a cabin on the portage on Mel Kyllo's trapline saying "GOING TO END IT ALL." He left a promissory note for $125 owed by my brother Art, who had bought Kinsman's trapline on Kobes Creek and still owed him this amount. Kinsman endorsed the note to my father, and he also left Dad his .22 rifle. When the note was found, Mel Neil and Mel Kyllo went out looking for him. Approaching the cabin, they shouted the usual, "Halloo the house!"

They were answered by a moan. Knowing Kinsman's shell-shocked condition, they wondered if they should enter. Slowly they worked their way toward the cabin, talking to Kinsman, asking if he was all right, trying to pinpoint the exact location of his voice. They finally summoned the courage to shove open the cabin door, only to discover old Billy-Goat-Wham Mahaffy curled on the floor clasping his knees to his chest. He had become ill while walking across the portage and had taken refuge in Red's hut. To this day, Red Kinsman's body has never been found.

The next day I arrived at the Ottertail (named Brewster Creek on the map). Ice had formed on the rocks in the river, which was too high and swift to try to wade across in that condition. I shouted until I attracted the attention of Fred Chapman, who occupied a cabin on the other side of the stream. Chapman shoved his canoe into the Peace and brought it down to the mouth of the Ottertail, then up the creek to where I was waiting.

When the Peace had been a lot higher, an ice-jam had formed below the Ottertail. The jam had now gone out, leaving a ledge of ice about four feet above the level of both rivers. The current from the Ottertail spewed out and went underneath the ice in the Peace River.

Chapman guided his 12-foot Peterborough canoe alongside the shelf of shell-ice on which I was standing. I dropped my snowshoes in, then reached out and down with my pack to place it in the canoe. Suddenly the ice on which I was standing gave way and down I went, landing spread-eagled on top of my pack in the canoe. The sudden weight of me and my pack landing in the bow of that short canoe caused Chapman's end to go straight up, nearly throwing him out. I was busy for a minute or two helping to keep the canoe balanced, while Chapman cursed me.

"You goldarned Cheechako! Don't you know how to get into a canoe? I've never seen such a stupid damned thing in my life. If we'd have rolled this, we wouldn't have had a snowball's chance in hell. We'd have been swept right under the ice on the Peace!"

"Well," I thought, "there goes the best hot rum toddy you can get." Fred Chapman was famous for them.

I managed to get straightened around in the canoe, but I still wasn't out of trouble. Chapman cussed me all the time we were paddling our way back to his landing, and continued to cuss while we were pulling out the canoe.

But he forgave me for scaring the hell out of him after I gave him his mail. He even came across with the hot rum toddy.

8

Mishaps and Mysteries

After I left Fred Chapman's the going was a lot easier up to Finlay Forks because I could travel on the ice in most places. Where that was impossible I could wear my snowshoes, for the main range of the Rocky Mountains is deep snow country.

When I arrived at Finlay Forks I stopped to visit the game warden, Vic Williams, who asked if I would keep track of the wolf kills I saw on my way to Manson Creek. I then delivered the mail to the store owned by Roy MacDougall and Allen McKinnon, and also dropped off a small roll of insulated wire ordered by Roy Sharp, the radio operator. They advised me that the best way to travel to Manson was over the Wolverine Range by way of Manson Creek.

This country was all new to me. Coming up the Peace I had known the location of all the cabins so could arrange to make one every night. After I left Finlay Forks, travelling by way of Manson Creek, my mileage was cut considerably as I had to start making camp in the middle of the afternoon. I carried no blankets, bedroll or gun in my pack, so the protection these cabins offered was highly desirable.

When no cabin was within range, I was forced to make a "siwash" camp outdoors. First I took off my snowshoes, using one as a shovel to remove snow from the spot I had chosen for my campfire. After I had the site cleared, piling the snow on the wind-side, I cut wood, trying to estimate how much I would need for the night. I also cut spruce boughs for my bed, laying them on the bare ground beside the pile of snow. Then I shoved two poles into the snowbank and hung up my six-by-six tarp in an attempt to retain a bit of the heat from the fire.

Supper preparations were simple: first I put my tea billy (a three-pound lard pail) over the fire so I could drink tea while waiting for supper to cook. Next I made bannock by throwing two teaspoons of baking powder and one teaspoon of salt into my flour bag, stirring it into the flour in the top part of the sack. After mixing it with enough flour to make a one to one-and-a-half pound bannock, I poured water (or, if I could spare it, milk and water) into a hollowed-out spot in the middle and mixed it, still in the bag, to form a fairly stiff cake. I then placed the dough in my frying pan, setting the pan up on its side with the dough facing the fire. When that side was browned sufficiently to stiffen the dough so it could stand on edge, I took the half-cooked bannock out of the pan and set it on a chip of wood, the uncooked side facing the fire.

I then sliced my bacon and placed it in the frying pan, letting it simmer very slowly over coals I had scraped to the side of the fire. By the time the bacon was cooked, the bannock should also be ready. Sometimes my timing was off and I had to eat the bannock half-raw.

One of the most interesting bush recipies I ever came across was "swizzled bum-gut," cooked for Paul Porter and I by Bill Brady one summer when we were on a prospecting trip in the Klawli country, up near the headwaters. One day when Brady was left at camp he shot two moose with his .22 rifle and short shells. He had a dandy supper ready for us that night.

"What do you call this?" asked Porter, surveying the meat twined around sticks by the fire.

"Swizzled Bum-Gut," Brady said. "Ever eaten it before?"

"No, but by God, you can cook it for me any time. It's good chewing!"

Brady explained how it's done: "Take the large rectum gut and wash it real well, inside and out. Then turn it inside-out, shake a little salt on both sides, tie the ends up so the juice can't run out, and wrap it around a small stick. Shove the point of the stick in the ground, or in the snow near the fire which has burnt down to a bed of coals. Keep turning slowly, sprinkling a little salt on the outside once in a while. When it starts to swell with steam, punch a small hole in it with your knife. That's it. Keep turning it until it's cooked."

I reached for another piece, but Brady speared one for me. "Try this piece, Earl. It's the root of the tongue."

I started chewing and found it as stretchy and tough as inner tube, but the flavour was good. "Do you know what you're eating?" Brady asked.

"Yeah, the root of the tongue."

"Yep. From right underneath the tail."

I jumped up, ready to drive Brady one. Porter grabbed my arm, spinning me sideways. I kicked over the tea-billy as he swung me around. Porter and Brady were both laughing.

"That's a good one on you, Earl," Porter said. "You said you were hungry enough to eat the ass-end out of something."

"What are you laughing at, Paul?" Brady said. "You ate the other one."

That ended Bill Brady as our cook.

When it came time to sack in for the night, I took off my clothes and put on my underwear, which I wore only to sleep in, and then put on my jumbo-knit sweater, pants and parka. I was then ready for a night of freezing on one side and burning on the other, curled up like a husky dog sleeping on a chip pile at 50 below, nose tucked under tail.

On my journey up to the Manson country, I had to pass through a section of the Wolverine Mountains where, a few years previously, a cyclone had blown down a strip of timber several miles wide. This windfall timber was so high and thick in places that even the moose turned back. I had to buck the windfall all one day.

After I had fought my way through, I came to a pine tree with a message inscribed on it. The tree had been blazed with an axe, and the message was printed in pencil: "IF YOU LOVE YOUR GOD OR YOUR COUNTRY, TURN BACK, OR YOU'LL CURSE THEM BOTH. MILES OF WINDFALL AHEAD."

I believe this message had been left years before by a fellow named Louis Vegan, although the name at the bottom of the blaze had been obliterated by pitch. The message itself, protected by the clear pine pitch that covered it, was as legible as if it had been painted over with shellac.

The weather had turned cold the night before I had planned to arrive at Manson Creek. I'd spent most of the night cutting wood. Dry wood was hard to find there, especially by flashlight. In the morning I had travelled only 100 yards when I came across a lovely cabin belonging to trapper Jean-Marie situated on the edge of Manson Lake. I groaned as I thought of all the needless work I had done cutting wood, and the uncomfortable night spent freezing, unable to sleep when, so close, was fuel, a bedroll and a good cook stove, all in a warm comfortable cabin.

I made Manson that day, and spent the night with Roy Cunningham, the Hudson's Bay Post manager, where I restocked my supplies.

The following day I had not travelled far when I came to a small cabin on Slate Creek. I saw smoke spiralling out of the stovepipe so I decided to stop and get directions. My knock was answered by an old wizened man named Billy Steele. He had just begun to eat dinner when I knocked, so he invited me to join him. I intended to only have dinner and continue on, but I stayed for three days. Steele had been a mining recorder for 44 years in 1937; prior to that he had been in partnership with Charlie Paquette, freighting with pack horses throughout the Cariboo Country. When he found out I was from Hudson's Hope, he wanted all the news about his old friends.

That night Steele dug out an old diary and read some entries: "Charlie Paquette and I arrived in Manson this morning. Chinks gave us a little trouble. Charlie soon settled it with a pick handle." The year? I forgot to ask.[1]

After leaving Billy Steele's, I hung around Germanson Landing for a few days awaiting word on a camp attendant job at one of Diagnault's outlying camps. When no word came, I packed up to follow the Omineca River back to Hudson's Hope.

After travelling a couple of days I came to a long stretch of clear blue ice on the river. I slid out onto it, using my snowshoes like skis, whistling like a Dipper, when I came to a small skiff of snow about three feet wide and 30 feet long in the centre of the blue ice. Without thinking I strode onto it. The air left my lungs with a gush as I fell through clear up to my armpits. My arms automatically flew out sideways; my axe went sliding across the ice.

The water beneath the ice was going like a mill race. It caught my snowshoes, shoving their tips up against the underside of the ice while the heels hung down, catching the full pressure of the water, putting a terrific strain on my legs and arms. I struggled until I freed my toes from the toe-bars of the snowshoes, instantly relieving the pressure on my legs.

With my arms spread out, I could keep myself from being pulled into the water by the current. But it was impossible to lift myself clear of the water and back onto sound ice. As I struggled, the strip which had looked like snow kept breaking up, and the current pulled me downstream to the lower end of the patch. To make matters worse, I still had my pack on and could not get free of it with my arms spread out.

Between my fighting and the pull of the current, I came to the lower end of the snow patch, where I managed to free myself of my pack, throw it onto the ice and pull myself up. From my safe position, I could see what had given the illusion of snow: at the top end of the open hole was a large boulder that had caused the current to split. What had looked like snow was nothing but frozen foam. The clatter of my snowshoes had concealed the sound of rippling water in the open hole.

The weather in the last few days had become extremely cold. I kicked off my snowshoes and looked around. I knew I had to do something, and fast. I looked along the riverbank as far as I could see, hoping for a cabin, for I was sure I would not last long enough to get a campfire going.

If there is a cabin, I thought, it has to be on that bend about a half-mile downstream. I ran to retrieve my axe, then picked up my snowshoes and pack, which I swung onto my back. The straps had already frozen. I tucked my snowshoes under my arm and lit out for the bend in the river, running stiff-legged as my pant legs, too, were frozen.

By the time I reached the bend in the river my hands were numb, but I had made a good guess. There was an old shack.

When I looked in the doorway I saw the cabin was full of packrat gatherings: twigs, leaves, mushrooms, all tinder dry. I dropped my axe, snowshoes and pack and scooped up an armful of this debris and carried it outside. I made two trips, then cut the tie rope on my pack and opened it, taking out the small waterproof can of matches. A skim of ice formed on it immediately. I knocked it off with my hunting knife and pried off the lid, shaking a few matches onto the pile of debris. By this time my hands were so numb that I could not pick up a match. I managed to get one clenched between my teeth and struck it against the bottom of the tin, which had been roughened with a knife before starting out on the trip. The matchstick broke in two. I picked up another with my teeth and struck it. It lit. I dropped it among the matches lying on the debris and they ignited, setting fire to that pile of leaves and twigs. Thank God for the packrats, despite their smell.

After I had warmed up a bit I went back inside the shack and, digging around in the litter, found what was left of an old stove made from two square, four-gallon coal-oil cans and some stovepipes. There were not enough pipes to reach the ceiling but I set up this makeshift outfit as best I could, aligning the pipes with the stovepipe hole in the roof. I hung my tarp over the door opening, my parka over the window opening, and lit a fire in this smoky set-up to dry out my clothing and grub. I did not have to cut wood . . . the rats had saved me that trouble . . . although I did have to feed the stove almost continuously. I got no real sleep, but did doze a little between restocking the stove and turning my parka to get it dry.

The next day I had good going, but did not travel too far before stopping at another abandoned cabin. This one was in far better shape than last night's hotel: it even had a door, although over the years the bottom had been partly eaten away by porcupines and other rodents. I plugged the hole by kicking snow up against the door, and hung my parka over the window opening.

This cabin contained a hand-hewn table and a bunk made from

boards about an inch and-a-quarter thick. The table and bunk were also partly chewed away. The stove was factory-made, and even had a door. After I had cut enough wood for the night and had eaten supper, I sat by the stove. The light from the open stove door cast my shadow onto the wall and the ceiling where it hovered like a monster. Whenever I moved my hands or arms, it reached out as though to grab me.

Something about the bunk struck me as strange. I stared at it for some time, then realized that the boards had only been eaten out in the centre. They had not been chewed at the sides, which is the usual way with rodents. Curiosity getting the better of me, I got up to examine it closer with my flashlight. Suddenly it hit me: if a man had been shot or knifed in the chest while lying on the bunk, his blood would have spread in just such a pattern! The rodents would have chewed out the wood where the blood soaked in.

After pondering the mystery for a while, I said "to hell with it," and prepared to make up my bed. I used my packboard rope, which I had cut in half the day before, to hang my tarp from the ceiling. This made a crude hammock that hung partly over the stove, giving me the benefit of the heat.

I stepped onto the bunk and crawled into my hammock, carrying my flashlight and my damp can of tobacco with me. Rolling up my jumbo-knit sweater for a pillow, I tried to get comfortable. My feet hung over, dangling six inches above the bunk. I had closed the stove door after filling it with wood, so the cabin was as black as the inside of a coal mine.

Suddenly I awoke with a start. I didn't know how long I had been sleeping but the fire had burned out, and I had the uncanny feeling that something had pulled on my foot. I lay still for a second. It came again, twice in quick succession. I lunged to a sitting position, bumping my head against the roof-beam. With the sudden shift of weight the rope holding my tarp let go. Down I went, my head and shoulders striking the stove. I scrambled to my feet in the dark, fumbling for my flashlight, and switched it on.

There on the bunk sat a big fat packrat. Without thinking I threw my light at it. I missed the packrat, but sure raised hell with the flashlight, breaking the glass and bulb, and putting a dent in the side of the battery tube.

The next day the weather turned extremely mild. The snow stuck to my snowshoes, making it hard travelling. Along the way I had seen plenty of wolf-kills and wolf tracks, but had not actually seen any wolves. That night a large pack howled around my siwash camp until almost daylight, making it three nights in a row with very little rest. I had tried periodically to spot them with my flashlight, but couldn't seem to catch them. The next morning I found their sign within 100 feet of my camp. After leaving the camp they had strung out, one behind the other. Every so often I could see where the one that had been breaking trail had jumped aside to let the rest pass him. The next in line would then do the trail-breaking, so none of the pack would become overtired.

The trail they made was good enough to allow me to take off my snowshoes and carry them under my arm, walking in my moccasin rubbers. I followed their trail for several miles until it left the river on the south side upon reaching some open water.

I had gone a mile or so along the river when I became thirsty. In one place the water was open right up to the rocks on shore. I kicked off my shoes and got down on my knees for a drink, shoving my mouth into the water like a horse. After I had finished drinking I raised my head and looked squarely into the yellow eyes of a big grey wolf about 30 feet away on the opposite side of the open water. As our eyes met, the wolf turned and fled. I suppose my white parka had blended with the snow behind me and the wolf, coming down to drink, had not noticed me until I moved.

I made a siwash camp that night as well. When I awoke in the morning I found the temperature had fallen during the night. I had been making such poor time the last few days that I decided to pull out without lighting a fire, so just took time to eat some frozen rice that had been left over from the night before. I had not gone very far before I was wishing I had warmed it up. My stomach was giving me hell.

As I came into a canyon on the river I spotted a beautiful little peeled-log cabin on the south shore. I quit the river and walked up to the cabin. Inside, I found the name "Nat Porter." I had heard of Nat before, and had met his brother Paul a few years ago down at the Aylard Mine in the Peace River Canyon. My stomach was giving me such a bad time I decided to lay over in Nat's cabin. I was pretty sure I was in the Black Canyon on the Omineca. If so, I was not far from the Finlay River.

The next day I had travelled only a mile or so from Nat Porter's cabin when I came to another. Seeing smoke drifting from the chimney, I decided to stop. It belonged to Carl Johnson, who invited me to spend the night because he had not seen anyone since coming out on his trapline in September. He had about 24 hours worth of questions to ask, mainly about Stalin, whom he referred to as "Stallion-the-old-sonofabitch." My stomach was still a bit sore, so I mostly answered Johnson's questions with grunts. I had drifted into a sound sleep when I came to with a start. Johnson was shaking me. I looked at the clock on the table: four o'clock in the morning. He had just wakened me to talk some more.

In the morning Johnson advised me to cut across country from his cabin in order to save six miles of walking. I had intended to follow the Omineca to where it entered the Finlay, then down the Finlay to the Forks, but I took Johnson's advice, much to my sorrow. Before I left his cabin, I unloaded my pack of all my grub except for a bacon and bannock sandwich, because I intended to restock at Finlay Forks that night. My stomach was still bothering me, so I ate little breakfast.

The trail where it left Johnson's cabin was plain to see – all new blazes. After I had been travelling for a couple of hours, I stopped to munch my sandwich. I had come to the edge of a big muskeg and could see a blazed tree about 100 yards out on it. As I neared it, I saw another one about 100 yards further on, a little to my right. As I passed each small blazed tree I could easily see the next one farther on, but suddenly when I looked for the next blaze I could see no more.

I glanced at the last blaze I had passed about 50 yards behind me. It didn't look quite right. I snowshoed back, only to discover that the "blaze" on the small swamp spruce had actually been made by a deer or moose rubbing the velvet off his antlers. I was lost, and I knew it.

I didn't have the slightest idea how far back I had lost the real blazes, but I had only an hour or so before dark. I turned on my tracks, not wanting to camp in that muskeg country, and followed them until I finally found the right blazes. They had come straight up to the edge of the swamp, then turned sharply to the left. By the time I found the right trail, it was almost dark.

I followed the trail a short distance and came out to the edge of a small lake, which I realized was Meridian Lake. Johnson had mentioned it, advising me to walk to its south end. He hadn't blazed the trail past there.

I hustled around and gathered a little dry wood before it got too dark to see. I didn't get enough to do me all night, but it was all I could find. While I was setting up camp, the wind increased until it was drifting the snow across the lake. I had no protection from the wind whatsoever, because I had camped right on the lake shore. What had been clouds earlier in the day now turned to snow.

I sat by the fire for a while, but the wind kept driving the smoke wherever I sat. I finally got fed up with the wind blowing into the camp and cut two poles, shoved them into the snowbank and hung my tarp on them. I was getting damned hungry, and now I was sitting in the poorest camp of the whole trip on undoubtedly the longest and hardest day of all.

The wind kept swirling around, first catching one edge of the tarp and then the other. It caught the smoke from the fire with every swirl and drove it back in under my shelter. I sat crying with frustration and the stinging smoke, cursing myself for my own stupidity in missing the blazes, for leaving my food at Johnson's. After several hours I felt so hungry I decided to search through my junk to see if I had anything left at all. I found two packages of Fleischmann's yeast and a little bit of tea in a canvas bag. Mrs. Peck had given me the yeast for a blood condition, saying "Now you be sure and take this!" I boiled up the tea and drank it, then mixed in the yeast with the tea-leaves, let it soak a bit, and ate it. What a horrible concoction. And how little!

After I had eaten that mess, I sat by the fire trying to keep out of the smoke. My mind chose that moment to remember the oldtimers' warning before I had started out on the trip: "Don't go! Remember what happened to Gunthier!"

Gunthier was a prospector and amateur astronomer who lived around Hudson's Hope for a few years washing gold on the Peace, the Finlay and some of their tributaries. It was in this same Muskovite Lake country where I had gotten lost that Gunthier had lost his way, never again to be seen alive. Vic Williams, the game warden, had formed a search party when Gunthier failed to show up at his appointed time. The party of men and dogs hunted for several days without success. They found his sign a place or two in the timber but lost it whenever his tracks entered muskeg or open country.

A trapper, Jean-Marie, told me the rest of the tale. The strange thing was that tracks made in the early part of winter, then covered by heavy snowfall, will show again after a warm Chinook has taken off the new snow. That is how the searchers found Gunthier's body – by tracing his old tracks. He was found on the west slopes of the Wolverine Mountains on Jean-Marie's trapline, sitting by a cold campfire, surrounded by astronomy books. He'd had no food, and either froze or starved to death.

Such were the stories that crowded my head through one of the most frustrating and self-pitying nights I have ever endured. In the morning, when grey dawn broke and the wind and snow subsided, I spotted two moose browsing on the willows within 100 yards of my camp. They were lucky I wasn't a wolf.

I followed Johnson's directions from Meridian Lake to Finlay Forks, and hadn't travelled very far when I came out to the brow of the hills, as he said I would. The weather had lifted a little, and I could make out the Wolverine Mountains to the west. When I looked down into the valley I spotted a rising spiral of smoke. What a welcome sight! My snowshoes seemed to lose half their weight as I headed for that cabin.

When I knocked on the door it was answered by Tom Batty. He and his wife and baby were living there that winter. I told them what had happened, beginning with my stomach cramps the day before reaching Porter's cabin. "You must be damned hungry!" Batty said, tossing me an orange. I gulped it down like a starving husky would gobble an inch-square of bacon. He passed me a cup of scalding hot coffee. That followed the orange, almost as fast. When I arrived, Batty had just been mixing up a batch of sourdough hotcakes for their breakfast and by this time the first griddle was cooked. He set them in front of me. I forgot all I had ever read from the columns of Emily Post. I shoved them into my mouth as fast as I could swallow. Batty kept cooking and I kept eating until the batter ran out. Tom looked at my empty plate and said, "Are you still hungry?"

"I am."

He then made me several slices of toast and fried a couple of water-glass eggs. When he asked if I was still hungry, I lied and said "No." I was ashamed for having eaten so much of the Battys' food, and tried to pay them for it. They refused to accept any money, so I thanked them for their hospitality and continued on my way.

MacDougall trading post/homestead at Finlay Forks
(Hudson's Hope Museum)

I spent that night at the trading post at Finlay Forks, restocking my grub supplies, then the next morning stopped in to report the number of wolf kills – 18 – to Vic Williams.

The trip back from this point would be easy. I stopped at a cabin on Selwyn Creek where, years earlier, Lee Parsons had left a sign on the door saying "I tore the cover off my eiderdown to make a parka. Started downriver yesterday and had to turn back. Wind blowing gale and 20 below zero. The wind in this damned Pass could blow the stars out!"

The next day I stopped in to see how Red Kinsman was making out. He was okay, just a little dirtier.

I was whistling and walking right along when I came opposite the Carbon River. I was getting close to home and was sure now I would make monkeys out of the oldtimers by coming back alive in spite of their dire predictions.

"Hello, Earl!"

I stopped, startled, and looked around for the voice.

"Over here on the island." There stood Bob Beattie. "Come on over and spend the night!"

I looked at the river and could see that the ice was not very good. "How long has that jam been in?" I called.

"Long time!"

I looked it over again, and did not like what I saw. I went up to the bench and cut a 20-foot-long safety pole and started across. I could feel the ice jam squirming beneath me. Before I was very far, I was wishing I had stayed on the north shore and gone on down to Brenham Flats as planned.

When I got to the south side I came to an open stretch of water about 50 feet wide, but it was not deep. I jumped in and waded to shore, where Beattie was waiting. "How long did you say that jam's been in?" I asked.

"Long time!" Beattie laughed. "Two or three hours." Seeing my look of horror he added quickly, "I wanted some company to travel with . . . have to go to the Hope tomorrow to get my Christmas supplies. My family is here with me. When I heard you coming downriver I said, 'Here comes the Whistler! Now I'll have some company.'"

The next morning Beattie and I headed for the Hope, intending to make the 46 miles that day. At dusk, as we started across the portage on the last lap of our journey, we met Bob's brother, Jim and his family on their way home from the concert dance. We arrived in town on the evening of December 23.

The first man I met in town was oldtimer Fred Monteith.

"Glad to see you back, Earl," he puffed. "Damn, damn, damn. Shouldn't have done it. Worried all the time you were gone. Why didn't you write? Should have, you know. Damned fool thing to do."

That was as close to a scolding as Fred Monteith ever gave anyone.

Note

[1]Note: if anyone knows the whereabouts of Billy Steele's diary, kindly forward it to the Provincial Archives in Victoria, for it contains much important data on the Cariboo country.

The Dipper

There's a little brown bird in the mountains. We call him the dipper.
You can find him along rivers where water is free of ice.

The dipper's a bird that's not pretty,
His colour's a dirty slate-brown.
But I'm sure from the gloomiest face
He can wipe the saddest frown.
His actions are dippy and jerky,
His coordinations are rough,
But he sure is a cute little fellow
And we have to admit he is tough.
He dips down underwater,
Comes up with a "cheerupa" song.
He does it at fifty below zero
And he'll do it the whole day long.
He will perch himself on a willow
And sing when a storm's in the blow
With notes that are sweeter and clearer
Than any canary I know.
I remember one time in the mountains
When I felt I hadn't a friend.
The clouds lay low in the valleys,
I was thinking my life I might end.
When I heard this marvellous singing!
I knew it! The Dipper's sweet song!
Then things seemed brighter and brighter,
He made rights from out of wrongs.
A good many years are behind me
Since the Dipper redeemed me from Hell,
Now when I feel gloomy and grumpy
I think of this bird, and I'm well.
His song, you bet I still hear it!
His music so sweet and so clear:
"Cheerupa! Cheerupa! Cheerupa!"
Things could be worse, never fear.

9

Grown Men Dreaming

When I finally decided, in 1939, to stop my wandering and settle down for a while, the woman I chose for a wife was "my river girl," Bonnie Goodvin. I left the decision to the toss of a coin. It landed "marriage" side up.

I had been writing to Bonnie steadily over the past year, but had not thought seriously about marriage until that winter. She was still down at Laidlaw, B.C. I decided to write and ask her if she would consider marrying me. I thought we had a pretty good chance of making a go of it; she'd been raised in the outdoors and liked it, and so did I. She was foolish enough to say yes. When she accepted, she signed up for a lifetime of hard work.

Bonnie and Earl Pollon

Bonnie came up to Hudson's Hope in June. We delayed our marriage until we were sure that all signals said "go." On July 7, 1939, we "went."

Plans were made for Bob Ferguson, Justice of the Peace, to perform the necessary mutterings. People tried to convince us to get married in the newly built St. Peter's church, but we were not churchgoing people.

Lloyd Gething was to be best man, and Phyllis the bridesmaid. The four of us started walking to the old log hotel, owned by Bob Ferguson, for that was to be our church. Suddenly I stopped. The ring! It was still in the post office. I had sent for it C.O.D., and now I had spent all my money on household needs and didn't have enough to get it. I took off, leaving three people staring after me. I found Art first and was in luck: he had a five-spot I could borrow. I dashed to the post office, got the ring out of hock, then ran all the way back to the hotel.

Ferguson put his reading glasses on the end of his nose and gave us the works. By the time he had finished, I was no longer sure what I was saying. Ferguson, peering over his glasses, said: "Well, that's all I can do. The rest is up to you."

We spent our honeymoon in Ted Boynton's private cabin, until Phil Tompkins sent word that I was needed for a job down at the Halfway River. The honeymoon was over.

King Gething hauled us and our household effects in his Model A Ford truck down to the Halfway River, where we set up housekeeping in Mac McGarvey's old winter-stop mail cabin. Mac never used this cabin during the summer because he hauled the mail by boat, camping along the river. It was only 10 by 12 feet, and had a pole roof covered with sandy soil.

Our first day there it started to rain, and kept on raining all night. The roof started leaking within a few hours. By morning, water was coming through in several places; by evening it was dripping all over the place. I had hung a six-by-six tarp to the roof poles in hope of directing some of the water off our bed. We were in bed about 10 minutes when the weight of the water, which had filled and bellied out the tarp, proved too much and the tarp let go in one corner. Down came the deluge.

There is nothing like a tub full of cold water to dampen the ardour, at least until you get up, wring out the blankets and turn over the mattress.

I fixed the roof, and we stayed at the Halfway until fall, then moved back to Hudson's Hope. A few days later I got another call from Phil Tompkins, saying there was a job for me with the public works department. About $5,000 had been appropriated for upgrading the road between Fort St. John and Hudson's Hope. Our job was to build some new sections and repair others using two crawler tractors, a 1929 gas Cat and an old 30 tractor. These machines had no canopies, so we were always getting clobbered by flying chunks or broken tree tops. We just accepted the risk, along with the prestige of being an operator at the rate of 35 cents an hour.

"The Hump" road 10 miles east of Hudson's Hope
(Hudson's Hope Museum)

We were to build a water-level grade seven miles east of Hudson's Hope, at what was known as "The Hump." We struggled for two days, then gave up because it was a solid shale bank. The allotted money wouldn't have gone very far working that section. If Frank Clark, the district engineer, wasn't around, we would sometimes "lose" survey stakes, especially on the Hudson's Hope side of the Halfway River where the survey went through a couple of coulees. It would have taken a lot of time and money to fill those coulees, money that could be better spent for extra miles of construction. It would appear these stakes were never found, for the sharp "S" bend we made to avoid the coulees is still there.

We worked our way to Hudson's Hope with the tractors, then started building the present grade up the hill west of town. The money lasted into December. We had not quite reached the top of the hill when they shut us down, but Phil Tompkins made some kind of deal with the department (I believe he supplied the fuel) that allowed us to finish the last 300 feet. More than 30 miles of road was completed for the lousy sum of $5,000, and the grade we built in 1939 is still used today.

In the spring of 1940, Bill Kruger hired me to help him build three boats: one 44-footer, one 32-footer, and a small 16-footer to run around in until we had the bigger boats finished. When we had the runabout built we put it in the water, but never used it until one day Bonnie and her cousin, Frances Goodvin, walked the 17 miles across the portage to visit me.

Joe and Jennie Goodvin had given Bonnie and I an old cookstove they had left at Morgan Flats when they moved to Demmit, and we decided now was the time to retrieve it, using our newly built boat. When we headed upriver to Morgan Flats, there had not been enough weight in the boat to settle it below the level of the first 10-inch board. But when we started back downstream with the cookstove, the boat began to leak. I was in the bow with the stove behind me and the two girls were in the centre. Bill Kruger was in the back with his huge work dog, Spider.

I quickly began to bail, but soon lost ground. The girls started bailing, but the boat sank lower. The green lumber used for building the hull had shrunk in the sun, and now the water was forcing the oakum caulking from the seams.

When the water began to pour in halfway back from the bow, Kruger quickly made for shore, giving the kicker full power. Just as the bow touched bottom on the gravel bar, the stern went under. We pulled the boat onto the bar and caulked the seams with pieces of an old shirt.

It took us 10 days to build the three boats. When that job was finished, I went to work for Mel Kyllo who had a contract to produce 750 tamarack telegraph poles. After the poles were cut and peeled, they had to be delivered along the telegraph lines as far downriver as Bear Flats (Cache Creek). Kyllo decided to make them into rafts at Hudson's Hope and push them down with a boat and kicker.

The first night we stopped at Farrell Creek. When it was time to go to bed, Kyllo picked up his bedroll and went into the old Farrell cabin. I took one look in there and the smell of packrat nearly knocked me down. The rest of the crew also chose to sleep out on the grass.

In the middle of the night we heard a scream, followed by Kyllo running out of the cabin, holding his ear and dragging his bedroll. The packrats had bitten a chunk out of his ear. The next morning, Kyllo went back inside for his pants and shirt. We thought he'd hollered the night before, but it was nothing compared to the cussing we heard now.

"Look what those sonsofbitches did to my belt and braces! They ate every goddamned bit of leather from my braces, and there's nothing left of my belt but the buckle!" Poor Kyllo had to tie up his pants with string until we got back to Hudson's Hope.

When we had finished delivering the poles, Lloyd Gething asked if I'd be interested in going gold washing up the river. I thought it was a hell of a good idea. As soon as Gething finished teaching school, we headed up the Peace River. I had built a small water pump using an old three-horse Evinrude motor for power. Bill Kruger took us upriver with his boat because we didn't have one of our own, and dumped us off at Ten Mile on the south side of the river, where we found some nice showings of colour.

When the pocket was cleaned out, we walked up to Brenham Flats. The year I had worked there for Billy-Goat-Wham I had noticed Mahaffy's clean-up was erratic; some days we would take out several ounces of gold, then very little. I think we were cross- working the pay streak at Brenham.

Billy-Goat-Wham was no longer at Brenham Flats; he had gone outside after becoming ill in 1938. He had turned his property over to one of his nephews, who had given some boys from Saskatchewan permission to operate a gold-washing show on the property. They were washing by hand, wheeling the gravel with a wheelbarrow. Gething and I got their okay to move in on the Old Glory Hole where Mahaffy had been operating. This called for a bigger and better pumping outfit than we had, so Lloyd Gething and I hiked back to Hudson's Hope where we bought an Old Star motor from King Gething and borrowed a three-inch pump from Vic Peck.[1] Bonnie came back to Brenham Flats with us to do the cooking, and we were in business.

I looked over all the junk left at Brenham by the Peace River Gold Dredging Company and figured we could build a hoist winch using the old pulleys and car transmissions. It was a queer-looking deal when finished. All we had for power was an old two-horse water-cooled Fairbanks Morris engine. I took the power from the engine through a car transmission, figuring on using low gear to do the lifting and reverse for letting the cars back down into the pit.

We loaded up our first car with a half-yard of gravel, then gave our hoist a try-out. The motor couldn't pull it, even with all the reduction we had made through the belts and transmissions. Gething and I stood there looking at that useless set-up that had taken so much work and cash, wondering what to do.

Then I remembered an experience Les Bazeley had when he was hauling the mail up to the Hope using a 1929 Federal Scout truck. Bazeley couldn't get up Dry Creek hill. When he tried racing the motor and dropping the clutch to get it to jump up the hill, the truck would threaten to rear over backwards. Then he turned it around to try going up the hill backwards. He raced the motor, dropped in the clutch, and the truck took off up the hill. I suggested to Gething that we reverse the cable and use the transmission in reverse for more pulling power.

We started it up. When we engaged the belt-friction, the old engine went put-chuckchuckchuck, put-chuckchuckchuck and pulled the car loaded with gravel up the steep pitch. The two boys who were working at Brenham could hardly believe their eyes. By pulling the cars in reverse we had a better and faster winch, because we could use high gear for letting them back down into the pit.

By the time we had everything working well, Gething had to return to teaching school. This left us short-handed to run the outfit, even though we had amalgamated with the two Saskatchewan boys. We also brought in Al Chapple to augment our crew.

Chapple and I would work all night repairing the junk, then work all day shovelling or running hoist. By the time we had things running fairly smoothly, freeze-up drove us out. We had not made enough to even cover our expenses. And to top it off, Bonnie was pregnant. We returned to Hudson's Hope.

While I had been upriver during the summer, George Packwood had started a coal mine. At least, he had opened up a seam of coal and intended to bring it into production. He only had the portal in about 30 feet. I got a job with the outfit, but it came to a crashing end.

The bunker had already been built when I went to work, but there was only a single track up to the mine portal from the top of the bunker, a distance of over 400 feet straight up the face of the mountain. Packwood wanted to put in a spur track that would come down past the bunker to the bottom, where he dumped the mine timbers off his old Federal Scout for loading onto the mine car. He asked me to build a frog, or switch, so we could put in this spur line.

Packwood wasn't there all the time, because he also had to look after his trucking business at Baldonnel and his truck run into Hudson's Hope, the first steady trucking service into the district. Often Howard Massey, who was doing the mining for Packwood, and I were the only ones there.

About eight o'clock one morning, Massey went up to the mine while I went to repair the bunker where a big chunk of coal had broken a plank. I finished that job and, about eleven o'clock, went into the bunkhouse to work on the frog, nailing steel strips onto the two-by-four woodwork. I was whistling away when I heard a scream: "Look out below!" I ran outside. Glancing up toward the mine, I saw the mine car hurtling down the mountain. At times it was five or six feet above the track, sailing like a swallow; then it would settle gently onto the track, only to leap again, gaining speed with every leap and foot it travelled.

Tipple at Peace River Coal Mine (present site of Bennett dam)
(Hudson's Hope Museum)

At the top of the coal bunker was the tipple (where the cars tipped and the coal drained out), which had been built on pole pilings 10 to 12 feet high. The car landed right in the middle of the tipple. Timber flew every which way. The car made another final leap, this time clearing the 70-foot-long bunker and sailing across a 30-foot-wide coulee. Crash! It hit a tree about 40 feet up in the air. Dead silence. Then, from a black mushroom cloud of coal and rock dust came a set of car wheels . . . end . . . over end . . . over end. The axle holding the wheels together was now "U" shaped. Down came the tree-top, its eight-inch trunk snapped like a matchstick. Down came the rock with which the car had been loaded. Finally, down the mountain came Massey, travelling almost as fast as the car. "Are you all right? Were you hit?"

Massey had been blasting the foot wall of the mine to give a little more clearance for the car. When he had come out with the car, he had stumbled and missed the winch cable hook.

That closed down the mine: no more coal car, no more job.

Packwood did not give up on this venture, but reopened the following spring and was to run for several years.

After the mine shut down, I got the odd job: four bits here, a dollar there. I was becoming a bit desperate for money, because Bonnie was expecting in January.

On New Year's Day, 1941, we had planned only a small dinner for Dad, Bonnie and myself out of one roasting hen. During the day, a couple of bachelors came to wish us Happy New Year. Bud Stuart also came along to say hello, and let it slip during the conversation that they had no chicken, turkey or moosemeat for dinner.

"Bud, go up town and get Elna and the kids and bring them here for dinner," Bonnie said.

When Stuart left to bring his family, I took another look at that old hen. She was still the same scrawny bird. The two bachelors were still there and, of course, when Bud and his family were invited, two more invitations had to be extended.

"For crying out loud," I whispered to Bonnie when she came into the kitchen, "I realize that according to the Bible, Christ fed the multitudes with a couple of fish and a little bread, but how do you figure on feeding this many people on this little hen?"

"I'll make chicken pot pie," Bonnie said brightly. "That way there'll be plenty for all."

"I don't feel like chicken pot pie."

"You're going to get chicken pot pie, like it or not!"

"If I'd known it had to feed this many, I wouldn't have bothered cleaning and plucking it. That way it might have given us all a mouthful, even if it was partly guts and feathers."

"Oh, stop your grumbling. There will be enough for everyone. You just wait and see. If we run short, I have a roast of moose."

"By God, I won't wait too long or the thing won't even reach me," I said.

Bonnie made the chicken pot pie and I ate it. There were seconds all round.

After New Year's, Bonnie caught a ride with the mail team to Fort St. John to have the baby. The 60-mile trip took three days.

After she had gone, Bruce Peck came along. "Get out that beer barrel," he said. "We have to put on a batch to celebrate the birth of your first child."

He supplied the malt, sugar and hops, and left them with me. I warmed up water with the malt and sugar in it, then poured it into a wooden barrel. I put the hops and yeast cake into a 10-pound sugar sack, then went outside to find a stone to sink the sack to the bottom of the solution. Snow covered the ground, so I couldn't find a stone. I had started back to the house when I noticed the head of an axe lying on a shelf in the porch. Just the thing. I shoved the axe head into the sack and sunk it into the mix.

Dad was there the night I bottled the beer. I siphoned the bottles full and capped them. Then I remembered the axe head. I took it out of the sack – at least what was left of it – for the brew had eaten away the cutting edge, leaving gouges one-half inch deep. It had also eaten away at the eye. It was ruined. What's worse, so was the beer.

"I'll have to throw it all out," I said to Dad. "It won't be any good."

"No, don't do that," Dad said. "It should be all right."

After arguing the point for a while I gave in.

"Alright, we'll keep it," I said, "but I'm going to drink two bottles right now. If it kills me, we'll know it's not safe."

I proceeded to drink two bottles as fast as I could get them down. The results were entirely unexpected. It didn't make me sick, but it sure made me drunk. When I sobered up, I found that Dad had joined me in the test and had become as inebriated as I. One bottle had a person singing and dancing. Two bottles, good-night.

"No more boozing and carousing for me," I declared when I recovered. "From now on, I'm a family man."

Just after New Year's I found a job paying two dollars a day, for 10 days. It was almost enough to pay the hospital account of a dollar a day for the mother's stay and an additional 50 cents a day for the baby. Doc Kearney charged $25 for his services. I could only give him $15. A year later when I was in Fort St. John, I paid the balance. He had never sent me a bill. When I handed him the money, he didn't even remember I owed it.

When Bonnie arrived back at Hudson's Hope with our son, Harley, I met them with a dog and sleigh to haul them home, because we lived a mile from town. I then started hauling feed from Red River for Mel Kyllo with a team and sleigh, making one round trip per day. This meant getting up at four o'clock in the morning, walking into town and taking the team from there, loading the feed on at one end of the trip and unloading it at night on our return. I never got home before ten o'clock in the evening.

Harley was not too considerate of his old man. He was fed at ten p.m. and was supposed to feed again at two a.m., but his stomach and the clock appeared set for two different time zones.

In the spring of 1941, the two brothers from Saskatchewan with whom Al Chapple and I had worked the year before came back with a third brother. Chapple and I were supposed to go back up to Brenham Flats to wash gold with them again. Now they no longer wanted Chapple, because they had the third brother to take his place. I said, "That lets me out too."

I did intend, however, to move onto the bars along the river and build a different type of gold washing outfit than any that had been used here before: a portable belt conveyor system for moving the gravel. I made the one-foot by 30-foot belt from green beef hides.

Lloyd Gething came along one day when I had the conveyor built and said, "Why don't we go and have a look at the northern part of Brenham Flats? There were some darn good samples taken out of those test pits years ago."

No sooner said than done. And thus we passed our days, grown men dreaming. For that is how the North was built.

Note

[1]The pump was made by Joe McFarland, who also invented the McFarland Wolf Snare Lock which was the most positive non-slip lock invented for snaring animals.

10

Fiddle-Feet

That spring of 1941, we at Hudson's Hope realized that the war would affect this country. An airport was built at Fort Nelson, and other projects provided much-needed work for many of us.

While Lloyd Gething and I had been washing gold at Brenham Flats, Lloyd's brother King travelled north to Fort Nelson to use his river-boating experience working for Knox McCusker. King then sent word to Bud Stuart that he could get him a job on the river. When Bud sent his wife, Elna, some money, he also sent word that there was work for all the fellows around the Hope.

Four of us made a raft, drifted down the Peace River to Taylor, and caught a ride to Fort St. John where we were all hired. When we arrived at Fort Nelson, we were put to work grubbing stumps (digging them out with shovels, or using axes to cut roots) at what we called the "prison camp" at Beacon Station. A few days later King sent word that Lloyd Gething, Al Hamilton and I could get on river-freighting if we wanted.

That spring the last Cat trains hauling supplies for construction of the Fort Nelson airport had been caught in the spring breakup, and had abandoned their load at what is called the Horse Track on the Sikanni Chief River about 180 miles upriver from Fort Nelson. These supplies would be needed before freeze-up, so they had to be brought down by scow and boat. Lloyd Gething and Al Hamilton were put to work handling scows; I was taken up-river to build them.

The Sikanni Chief is an odd river; when it's low, there's barely enough water to float a dry leaf. During spring run-off, there's more water than her channels can handle. With the spring flood comes the driftwood – lots of it – which jams the channels. So the water heads across a flat, carving a new channel, in some places through standing timber two to three feet thick. Lacking enough water to wash the trees away, the river just scours the dirt from the roots, leaving the trees standing or leaning downstream. We called one of these places the

Valley of Ghosts; it was a solid forest of drowned timber and looked like a gathering of lost souls as the current caused the trees to weave and sway.

On the way up, Mac (Knox McCusker) did most of the cooking, if you could call it that. He was a civil engineer and a good surveyor, but a terrible cook. He'd peel the spuds while the boats were on the move; when we landed for dinner, he'd drop them in a galvanized pail, slop in some water, and put this on the campfire. When the spuds were half-cooked, he started opening tins, beginning with a five-pound tin of bully beef, then adding peas, corn, diced carrots and beets – anything that struck his fancy. When it was cooked it looked like something you used to slop the hogs, hence the name "Mac's Swill Bucket." He didn't add to its appeal by calling to us, "Come and get your dog vomit, boys!"

Knox McCusker was also an outfitter and guide, and had contributed in mapping the north country before the Second World War. His maps were a big help in laying out the Alaska Highway although he received little, if any, credit. When he was on the river with us he looked like a farmer in bib overalls: a slouch hat that dropped around his ears, a red shiny face in need of a shave, and a baby-faced smile with a similar disposition.

We got up the river with the kicker boats to what the boys called "scow camp," about 15 miles below the Horse Track, and unloaded the lumber for a new scow. The two carpenters and I got off there, and set up camp that day. Next morning I got up and cooked the breakfast: I was cook as well as carpenters' helper. We started working on the scow right after breakfast.

The second night I awoke from a deep sleep, feeling that everything was not as it should be. I could hear a drizzle of rain on the tarpaulin, but was sure that was not what had awakened me. I lay there listening a minute or two, letting my eyes shift around our shelter. From the light reflected by the river, I could make out the form of a bear standing at the end of my bed. I let out a squawk and leapt to my feet, taking the blankets with me to hold as a shield. The bear, surprised as I was, scrambled up the tree where our ridgepole was attached, knocking down a shaving mirror.

"A bear! A bear!" I shouted.

One of the carpenters scrambled from his spring cot. "Where? Chase it down!"

"Chase it down yourself if you want it," I replied.

The bear slid down the tree, landing with a thump on its hind end, and ran toward the river. But it continued to haunt our camp for the rest of our stay.

We were located 165 miles north of Fort Nelson, so we couldn't afford to lose any grub. One of the carpenters remembered that a Cat-train caboose (pulled behind a string of Cats, and used for a bunk-house) had been left about five miles back on the trail. We figured if we recovered it, we'd have storage for our supplies. To make the trip, we loaded our food and bedrolls on a little stoneboat that had been used to haul supplies when the tractor had been brought in. There was no room left on the stoneboat for the tallow – used to mix with the hard tar for pitching the scow - so we put it in the oven of the tin camp stove and turned the stove over on its oven door. We arrived at the abandoned caboose that night.

Next morning we discovered why the caboose had been aban-doned. We spent more time cutting and packing logs to get the tractor out of bogs than we did in actual travelling. We made it back to camp about sundown. Our tin camp stove was ripped to pieces and the tal-low gone. The bear was still there, cocky as ever.

She continued to hang around camp like a half-wild dog, investi-gating everything as soon as we went to work. But at least she was no longer able to get into our grub, now stored safely in the caboose.

When the woodwork of the scow was completed we were unable to pitch it, because the bear had eaten our tallow and grease. We finally built a deadfall trap, baiting it with a chunk of bacon and some honey smeared on a dish towel. We wired this to a trip-stick that was supposed to spring the trap, causing a heavy log to fall upon the prey. The bear came back to camp, lumbered straight into the trap, ate the bait and backed out. We baited the trap again, thinking she had just been lucky. She sat on her rump about 20 feet away, watching us. As soon as we finished the trap, in she went. Same thing. We got a 50-foot rope, tied it to the trip-stick, and baited the trap again. This time when the bear went in we pulled the rope, tripping the trap ourselves and finally catching her. We had lots of grease then for pitching our scow.

By then we had to put ourselves on rations because our food was nearly gone. The boats were due to pick us up on the seventh day. We finished the scow on the eighth day and waited, day after day. Still they did not come.

On the nineteenth day we built a boat from a few scraps of lumber left over from the scow. It was 40 miles down-river to Kennai, where there was more grub. The boat could only carry one man, so one carpenter took it, leaving on the twentieth day. On the afternoon of the twenty-first day, we heard the kicker boats coming – a most welcome sound.

We found we were not the only ones who'd had trouble; King

Gething had suffered a heart attack coming up-river. I suppose it was partly due from frogging the boats (wading in the water and dragging them by hand). He stayed at the scow camp while the boats continued up to the Horse Track. I went with the boats, running the kicker that King had been operating.

King Gething and Leo Rutledge
(Hudson's Hope Museum)

I was in the lead with my boat when we pulled into the Horse Track landing. But as I started to land, I changed my mind in a hurry. A bear, its face covered with froth, was standing on top of the bank about 15 feet above the landing.

"Jesus Christ, that bear has rabies!" someone shouted.

I swung back into the current and idled the motor, holding the boat in the stream. Another bear looked over the bank. A ball of froth hung from its muzzle.

"That one has rabies, too!"

We idled our boats in the stream until one of the men ordered us to pull in so he could shoot them with his .22 revolver. He shot one and knocked it down. The other ran away.

I landed the boat and we walked up the bank to the supply dump. It was the worst mess I have ever seen. Wherever we looked were great balls of froth, some a good two feet high, some green, some pink. Unwound rolls of toilet paper littered the bush. A tent that had been set up to cover the food was in tatters, and case after case of canned fruit and vegetables were scattered on the ground. Most of the tins had been chewed.

Here we discovered the mystery of the rabid bears: a 50-pound tin of baking powder had been ripped open and partly eaten. Where the bears had retched after eating it, they left a ball of froth tinted to the shade of whatever they had just consumed. We dressed out the animal that was shot, intending to have fresh bear steak for breakfast, and laid out the hind quarters on a log to cool. At dusk someone said, "I think I'll pack those hinds of meat in, just in case the bears come back." He was too late. They already had.

When we arrived back at the scow camp with our loads of freight, we found King Gething had taken a turn for the worse. We were to bring the tractor down on the scow, but before we could load it we used it to make a channel in the river for the scow's passage. We then loaded up the scow and pushed it by hand through the shallow water into the deeper water below.

We hit trouble when the boats went through Sikanni Rapids. It was difficult enough taking a boat through without hitting rocks, but when the boys tried with the scow there just wasn't room and they hit a boulder, shattering a plank in the hull. Ray Smiley quickly grabbed the tractor's hydraulic jack, a short piece of 2" x 8" plank, and a gunny sack. With the water boiling up around him from the fractured plank, he crawled beneath the tractor, wrapped the sack around the plank, then set the jack on top of it, working the jack until it pushed against the bottom of the tractor. This plugged most of the leak, allowing time to pull up onto a shallow bar and make repairs.

It took us several days to get to Fort Nelson. When we arrived, King was flown out.

In August, the water ran so low that we stopped using scows and hauled the freight in boats down to Kennai. Our boats were built to carry four tons, and we freighted everything: tower steel, four-ton rolls of cable, rolls of roofing, kegs of nails and bolts, windows and doors. We were usually overloaded and the loads were awkward and hard to balance.

The side streams flowing into the lower end of the Sikanni Chief all drain muskeg country, and the water is the colour of old tea. One day Lloyd Gething, Ernie Jervis and I were a little late coming back to camp for supper. When we got back, the tea pail was hanging over the fire and Al Hamilton was cooking the grub. We each poured ourselves a cup of tea. Gething added milk and sugar, Jervis just milk, and I took only sugar.

"Ye Gods!" shouted Gething. "This tea is terrible!"

Jervis tasted his and made a face. "It tastes like muskeg water that has laid in a cow track for a week!"

I took a sip of mine. "I don't think there is any tea in this rotten water at all!"

Al Hamilton stood grinning like a coyote over a pile of guts."Al, you sonofabitch!" Jervis shouted. "You didn't put any tea in this water, did you?"

"Hell, no," Hamilton replied. "With the taste you fellows have for knick-knacks, I didn't think you'd know the difference between swamp water and tea anyway." We carried our own grub box after that.

One morning I woke up, shoved the tarp off my bed and got a face-full of snow. About eight inches had fallen during the night. This provided a cheerful start to the day. Things proceeded to go from bad to worse.

I was heading upstream on wide-open throttle when I suddenly ran out of river. I coasted to shore and docked the boat a little hard. Somewhere I had lost the channel. George McGarvey pulled up alongside with his boat, calling out, "What are you doing in this dead end channel?"

"Damned if I know! I thought it was the main channel."

"So did I," said McGarvey.

We started walking up the gravel bar. There was no water anywhere in the river. "There's our problem," someone said, pointing ahead. "That slide that has been working all summer has finally closed the river off altogether."

The slide came from a mile above, tumbling millions of tons of clay clear across the valley and the river and back into standing timber.

We returned to the boats and picked up a little freight at Kennai. But when we got back to Fort Nelson, we learned we were not in very good standing with the company. They sent out a plane to confirm our story of the landslide.

The river work ended abruptly and the company put us to work at the main camp, grubbing stumps. I had been working only a couple of days when one of the head men came over and asked if I wanted to go moose hunting.

"We haven't been able to land a plane here for several days and our meat supply is gone," he explained. "We have several hundred men to feed. We got permission from Victoria to send men out to kill wild game for the camp."

"Sure, I'll go," I said. Anything beat grubbing stumps, as far as I was concerned.

When I got to the river to take the boat, I found that George McGarvey was to be the other hunter. He would be the kicker-man on the trip, because we were taking the boat he had been running all summer. He brought our grub down in two gunny sacks and threw them into the boat. When we made camp that night, McGarvey set up the wickiup while I prepared supper. I looked in one sack: strawberry jam and bread. I looked in the other sack: more strawberry jam and bread, and a couple pounds of butter.

"Where's the rest of the grub, George?" I asked.

"It's in those two bags."

"There's nothing here but bread and jam!"

"That's all I brought," McGarvey said.

We had toast and jam for supper.

The next morning I heard rain drizzling on the tarpaulin. While I lay there, trying to talk myself into getting up, I heard the brush crack. That's funny, I thought. McGarvey must have decided to turn over a new leaf and cook breakfast.

I closed my eyes to enjoy a little extra sleep and heard the brush crack again. I grabbed my rifle and looked out the shelter to see a bull moose standing 50 feet away. I fired and it went down. I glanced back into the tent and saw McGarvey raise the side of the tarp, shove his rifle out and shoot. I ran outside. There was a cow moose scrambling to her feet within 10 feet of our shelter. McGarvey had shot her in the brisket. She was up and running, but I fired again and down she went. I turned back to where I shot the bull and McGarvey fired again as the animal had gotten up.

We walked over to the bull and cut his throat. My hands were covered with blood when I walked back to the cow, with my rifle on full-cock and my finger on the trigger. I went to kick her to see if she was dead, and my bloody hand slipped on the trigger and I nearly shot my foot.

The moose hunt rounded out my summer at Fort Nelson. I stayed on a few more days, growing more restless and homesick. One morning when the weather cleared enough for the plane to fly out, I pulled the pin.

At home, I found that Bonnie had put up a real grub stake: pickles, fruit, jams and jellies, and she had enough carrots, beets, turnips and spuds to last a couple of years. Even the tomatoes had ripened on the vine. After my summer's work I had more than enough money to last us through the winter.

But nothing was happening around Hudson's Hope, so I started getting restless. One morning I said, "Let's get out of here and go to the coast."

"What?" Bonnie said.

"Let's go to the coast and get in on some of the big wages down there."

"What about all my canning? What about Speed?"

"We can take the dog. To hell with the canning. We can buy all the grub we want out there."

This argument continued four or five days. I eventually won – or maybe I should say I lost – because she finally gave in, against her better judgment. I thought about the amount of food we left behind a good many times during some of the lean years to follow.

We decided first to stop at Demmit, Alberta, to visit Bonnie's folks. The Goodvins were running a railroad tie camp there. Before I knew what had happened, I found myself attached to a broad-axe for the next year. I had never hacked ties before in my life. I wish to hell I had never hacked them to this day.

Our second son, Pat (Robert Earl), was born February 18, 1942.

That summer I worked harder than I had ever worked in my life. Bonnie, too, as far as that goes. I felled the trees and did the broad-axe work. Bonnie did the bucking with a swede saw, and the peeling. I made 15 cents per tie the first year, then 16 cents the following summer.

In 1943, we got fed to the teeth with making ties so we decided to return to Hudson's Hope. We never did reach the coast.

On my way home through Fort St. John I saw Phil Tompkins, who was hiring men to go north to cut lumber for the bridge to be built across the Liard River. I hired on as edgerman,[1] at the unheard-of wage of $1.35 per hour, but my first job was to run the steel-wheeled tractor.

We left Fort St. John in a convoy of six trucks, some owned by Tompkins, some by the army. The Alaska Highway had just been bulldozed through the previous summer, and it was a mess. We were amazed at the number of trucks we saw smashed and scattered along the right-of-way – averaging almost a truck a mile. Some vehicles had been demolished by crashes, others had burned. The snow around some of the crash sites was red with blood.

We came to the foot of a hill with our convoy and found the highway blocked with vehicles. Headlights pointed every which way, some sweeping the skies like searchlights, others pointing down over the side into what looked like a bottomless chasm. I walked up the hill toward the shambles of trucks, where a group of black men stood hunched together like a herd of cattle with ice on their backs. They were shuddering with cold, their thin clothing unsuited to the extreme November temperatures. Some wore leather gloves, others had none. All wore leather shoes. I asked what had happened.

"Y'all see that big truck with the Cat on it? That damned thing came down the hill backwards and pushed the other trucks off the road. The ones that weren't pushed off all backed off trying to get out of the way."

"Is anyone in that truck down at the bottom?" I asked.

"I suppose there is. He sho' as hell was in there when it went over."

"What the hell was the idea of the trucks tailing each other that close? Why didn't they let the lead truck get to the top before the next one started?"

"Mister, this is the army. We had orders to keep our convoy tightened up."

I asked these men where they were from. "We's mostly from Georgia and Alabama, and by Jesus, I wishes I was back there! It's too damned cold up here for us boys."

I could never understand why the American Army didn't send men from the northern states who were more or less acclimatized. I blame the army for a good many accidents on that lonely stretch of road. They sent men and boys improperly-outfitted, and inexperienced in handling trucks in icy conditions.

When we arrived at our first campsite on the Liard River, it was a pretty dismal scene. The snow was three feet deep, with a cold northeast wind blowing off the river. Leo Rutledge, our foreman, was the first man out of the truck. Then came Ted Boynton, our cook, with a smile on his face that would have put Sam McGee to shame. "Boys," he said, "the first thing we need here is a fire so I can make a pot of coffee. Nothing ever looks so bad after you get a cup of hot java in your belly, be Jesus."

There were 10 of us in the pilot crew to set up camp for the P.F. Tompkins sawmill. The main crew was to follow later. We were all northern men and had been chosen for our experience in mill and bush work, as well as our ability to take a hard time, if need be. After we had set up the cook tent and a couple smaller ones to sleep in, we began to set up the mill. I don't know whether Tompkins had overestimated our ability to get things done or whether we were just too slow, but before we were ready for them the men started arriving by the dozen. One load got there in the middle of the night. The tents were large enough to sleep five men comfortably. We wound up with

10 in each. Leo Rutledge and I doubled up on a single bunk so I could give mine to two other men.

The new men were madder than stirred-up hornets. Tompkins had rolled the van with them in it. The van also carried several sacks of flour, sugar, salt, tea, lard and butter. Plus one air-tight wood-burning heater that had been going when the truck rolled. The men were bruised, burned, battered and had lost all their liquor. They cursed Tompkins for rolling the truck, they cursed Rutledge and I because they had no place to sleep, and they saved the biggest curse for themselves for being 500 miles north of nowhere.

"Where has our happy little family gone?" drawled Rutledge that afternoon.

"Damned if I know, but I don't like the way things are stacking up here. These men are bunching up and doing too much beefing. It will lead to trouble, sure as hell," I said.

We did not have enough tools to put them all to work. An idle logger is a bitchy bastard at the best of times, and under these conditions they were a mean bunch. Eventually, everything straightened out, but the work went slowly. Most of the men were improperly dressed, so they had to keep returning to the bonfire to get warm. Some wouldn't leave it.

My job was to haul water by tractor for the boilers at the mill, along with water and wood for the camp. The weather stayed cold, and then turned colder. I hauled the water on a stoneboat in 45-gallon drums with their tops removed. I had to fill them by hand from an opening in the river ice. When I started work in the morning, my moccasins were dry; by night, the splashed water had formed ice, which built up until my feet looked twice their normal size.

The thermometer continued to drop to between 40 and 50 below. When we ate, the angry rows would start. Men sitting near the stoves inside our large dining tent would start turning down the drafts; men on the outside near the walls of the tent would shout, "Keep your goddamned fingers off those stoves and let them snort! It's cold over here!"

The food would freeze on our plates while we were eating. Coffee or tea that slopped over into the saucer would freeze solid. Most of the men ate wearing their outside work clothes, including gloves and caps.

After we had the mill set up to cut lumber for the main camp, Rutledge took sick. We could actually feel the heat from his body when we sat close to him. A couple of days later I came down with the same thing. Our heads ached, our temperatures soared, our noses ran, and we coughed continuously. The coughing was the worst part. If one dozed off, the other would wake him up by coughing. Then we would both lay there sweating, swearing, coughing and blowing our noses. We didn't have a thing to take except Pinex Cough Syrup. Ted Boynton mixed it with honey for us.

One night when we were at our sickest, we awoke to the lonely wail of a saxophone. It played only a few bars, then stopped. In those few bars one could hear a boy crying for his mother, a man pining for his wife, for his children, the torture of a soul damned to the pits of hell – or to the frozen Arctic.

"Why didn't they let him play on? That was beautiful," Rutledge said.

"It was. That boy was a long way from here in his thoughts."

"I wish he would play more. No, I wish he hadn't played at all. He's made me homesick."

Rutledge dozed off while I lay there, wondering. I could still hear that lonely cry. What was this man – all these men – thinking of? Would this be the war to end all wars? If there was a God, why did He let this senseless war go on killing and maiming, not only the bodies but the souls and spirits of millions? Would construction of the Alaska Highway draw Canada and the United States closer, making one nation out of two? How were Bonnie and the kids making out?

North of the Liard River was an American Army camp. On Christmas morning the temperature plummeted to 55 below. One of the soldiers reached under his cot against the tent wall and pulled out a 40-ounce bottle of over-proof rum. He tossed it to his buddy. "Merry Christmas. Have a drink."

His friend caught the bottle, removed the top, tipped it up and started to drink. He gasped, and shoved the bottle back. The soldier thought his friend was chicken – he would show him how to drink rum! He tipped the bottle back and took a long drink.

The first boy to drink lived, although he was hospitalized for a long time. The second boy, the owner of the bottle, died. That liquor would have been very close to the same temperature as the weather outside: 55 below. It froze their throats and stomachs. How were they to know better? They were from the deep South and it was probably the first time they had ever seen snow, let alone weather cold enough to freeze hard steel to the brittleness of glass.

I quit my job in the latter part of January, and caught a ride down the Alaska Highway with an army four-by-four truck, the coldest thing I have ever ridden in. Even the driver wore an extra-heavy mackinaw coat. When we arrived at the Sikanni Chief River, it was 72

below. As we started down the hills we could see the Alaska Highway stretched out like a long stiff ribbon; exhaust fumes from the
trucks hovered in the valleys. The sun hung like a cold red ball above
the horizon, sun dogs guarding its frozen circle.

Note

[1]An edgerman is one who feeds the edger to trim the bark off the edge
of the lumber. A good edgerman can pay for his wages many times over by
judging the least amount that can be taken off to give a straight edge.

11

Caught in Nature's Trap

In the winter of '43, I went to work for King Gething, who had recovered from his heart attack and was operating a coal mine. It was there I got to know Jack Adams, who had come north on the Chisholm Trail. He told me tales of his life as we sat around enjoying our second cups of coffee.

In 1905, Adams had made a trip to Siberia with a Seattle mining company that the Russian government had allowed to go in and mine for two years. All the company mined in bullion it could keep, but its mining records were to be turned over to the Russian government.

When the two years were up, the company ship arrived to take the men home. On their way out, a Russian gunboat forced their ship to hove to by firing a shot across its bow. The Russians came aboard and seized the bullion, informing the captain that the company would have to deal through their government to get it back – completely ignoring papers that confirmed the original deal. After the incident, the company offered to pull in to Juneau, Alaska to land any of the men who wanted to stay.

"I decided to stay" said Jack Adams, "and landed without any clothing fit to wear. Even my shoes were completely shot. I had to whittle boards to put in the bottoms for soles."

Adams stayed for a year and staked a mining claim. He then went south to Seattle, where he bought a gasoline-driven pumping outfit and took it back to Alaska. This deal depleted the funds of Adams and his partner.

"After we had that outfit working, we were the envy of the other miners, for a time at least. One morning we started up our pumping engine and everything went haywire. The governor had stuck. My partner and I knew very little about gas-driven motors at that time. We both lit out running to get away from the crazy thing, looking back from the safety of the timber just in time to see it blow up. The

101

flywheel and piston went sailing through the air and started to roll. We were back on a bailing bucket again."

When Adams was in Juneau, he made a voyage through the North West Passage. He knew the north country as well as any man living at that time. He had diamond-drilled with Boyle Brothers in the Liard country and knew the Finlay River and its watersheds; he and his wife, Lucille, first settled there in 1913.

They came to Hudson's Hope in 1919 and built a big home they called "All's Well" in 1920 just above Jim Beattie's at Twenty Mile (Goldbar). They later built a log lodge at Summit Lake. From there they went to the Bahama Islands where they built another home.

Jack and Lucille Adams' home 36 miles up the
Peace River above Hudson's Hope, built in 1914.
Now under Williston Lake.
(Hudson's Hope Museum)

Lucille Adams was the first white woman to live in the Finlay valley. She reminded me of a beautiful hummingbird with her darting mind and sunny disposition, sipping the interesting nectars of life, never hovering long to sip of any one blossom. At 90 she still appeared to be the same sharp-minded, life-loving woman I had met over 35 years ago.

In the summer of '44, Mel Kyllo and I did some logging for George Packwood who was operating his own mine again and had brought in a small mill to cut some lumber. After the first two or three days, Kyllo and I stopped speaking to each other. If one undercut a tree, the other just shook his head indicating that it should have been undercut to fall the other way. When we had a tree down and were bucking it up, one would try to play the other out by stepping up the tempo on our cross-cut saw. We made good money. With our tempers up, we felled and bucked 120,000 feet of logs in 12 days.

This job ended when Leo Rutledge came along and asked if I would like to go trapping with him that winter. He had sold his trap-line and bought out Donald MacDonald's and Ralph Osborn's farms, intending to become a rancher, which he did in later years. But in the sale agreement for his trapline, he reserved the right to trap it one more winter with a trapping partner. I had no trapping equipment so had to buy everything, with the exception of one dog.

We left for the line on September 22, 1944. When we arrived at Ne Parlez Pas Rapids I nearly lost the boat and our grubstake. We were "lining" the boat up through the rapids, I on the bow and Rutledge on the stern with a push pole and rope which was attached to the stern. I had a bridle on the front of the boat, a rope attached to the gunnel. I let the bow swing a little farther than it should have and could not pull it back towards shore. Rutledge had to wade into the river and push like mad to shove the stern out, taking the pressure of the current off the bow. We were both in the water by the time we got it under control.

The Ne Parlez Pas Rapids had a long history of swamping travellers; Henry Stege and Jack Wiesener once lost all their trading supplies at this same spot. They were lining their boat when suddenly the bow swung crossways in the current and side-hauled on a boulder, dumping their trade goods and cash. The incident created such a disagreement they split up their partnership. Stege came down to Hudson's Hope and established a trading post; Wiesener went back up the Finlay and started his own post there.

When Rutledge and I started up the trapline, I found I still had a lot to learn about the woods. I had spent some time in the bush, but I was green to the methods of keeping alive in the mountains. Rutledge was a good teacher, with the ability to get his point across without making you feel inferior.

I was to trap the upper end of the Eau Claire River (better known as the Clearwater) and its tributaries, while Rutledge trapped the lower end and Point Creek. I had to pack in most of my supplies before trapping season opened, and before winter set in. I loaded my dogs and myself with every ounce we could carry. Some of the dogs were carrying 65 pounds. I carried about 75 or 80 pounds along with my snowshoes and rifle. It seemed foolish to carry snowshoes at this time of year; but Rutledge warned me I could be caught in a freak snowstorm and have a hard time getting out.

He helped pack in a load of grub and took me over most of the line. When it came time for us to part, I felt pretty small. I was alone, with nothing for company but my dogs and the towering peaks that surrounded me. They were both beautiful and terrifying.

When the first snow fell, I was afraid to cross under the snowslide areas of the mountains. I could see where slides had wiped out everything in their path, filling the valley with tons of snow. After passing under these areas a few times I grew more confident and ignored them, in the early part of the winter anyway. Later, when the snow became deeper, I gave them the respect they deserved.

Rutledge had a way of telling a tale with a moral to it. I came very close to getting into trouble when I failed to remember one of his tales. His story was about Louie Stranberg, who had trapped the Clearwater one year. Stranberg was hiking down the line when he came to a spot where the river had flooded his snowshoe trail. This was at the foot of a gravel bank several hundred feet high. Stranberg, without thinking, had climbed up the edge of the cutbank and snowshoed across its face. He had almost reached the opposite side when the snow let go. The slide picked him up and carried him onto the river, and buried him to his armpits. It took hours to dig himself and his snowshoes out of the heavily packed snow.

Rutledge had pointed out this dangerous cutbank when we had gone up the river on our first trip. One day, I was about a third of the way across its face when I remembered the tale. I immediately made a slow turn and pussy-footed out of there.

Another hazard on the line was a burned-over area where the tops of trees had all broken off. The snow sometimes built up on the flat-topped trees (even the ones only four or five inches thick) until it formed a ball that might be three feet deep and weigh several hundred pounds. Rutledge had warned me to always look up before I blazed a dead tree, because the slightest jar could release these huge balls of ice and snow.

I had brought four dogs with me: Speed, my lead dog, and Silver, and two others that were crosses between Irish Staghound and Husky. This is a vicious mixture and hard to control. They were sired by Bushman, a purebred Irish Staghound brought into the country by Bradford Angier (author of *At Home in the Woods* and several other books).

At any of the northern outposts where trapping was the mainstay, there were always dogs, hundreds of them. The great operatic chorus of the northern huskies, part wolf, part dog, half tame, half wild, is something to be remembered when heard for the first time.

They lament the injustice of man who, when not working them, keeps them on a tether. At night their cry is a fearful hellish pandemonium when they raise their heads, giving vent to their resentment in heart-rending, hair-raising laments.

Once I came to a trap containing a live fox. It had been caught in what we call a block set, made by cutting a block of wood about six inches thick and three to four feet long, bevelled on the end so when the block leaned against the tree the bevel end was flat. On this sat the trap, nailed to the tree. Anything caught in the trap would usually knock the block down, leaving the animal suspended in the air.

When the dogs spotted the fox, the two Irish Staghounds tried to run past me to get at it. I had my axe in one hand and my heavy rifle in the other. I knocked one of the dogs down with the axe handle and the other with the rifle barrel. Both out cold. I ran to where the fox was fighting, doing a jig on its hind legs, to escape the trap. I hit the animal with my axe handle, but it ducked and I struck its trapped leg. This knocked the fox loose. Before it could get away, I grabbed its throat. I threw the animal onto the snow and landed on top of it. The two dogs had come to and were trying to get at the fox, but ended up nipping me. Speed and Silver then wanted to do battle and they too joined the fray.

I jumped up, still choking the fox, and started to beat the dogs with it. This didn't help. Even Speed was so excited he refused to listen. Desperate, I grabbed the fox's hind leg, then swung the animal against a tree. This laid the fox out. I then proceeded to give the dogs a bit of education.

I valued old Speed pretty highly. He was an excellent sled dog and he had a face that made me want to laugh, especially when the going was rough and the snow deep. His face was brown, with a black circle around each eye. Whenever I looked back at him bucking the snow with his pack, his mouth open and teeth shining, he always looked like he was laughing. You can use a little cheer when you are bucking the odds.

Some days in the mountains, when the clouds were lying low in the valleys, it felt like the weight of the world was on my shoulders. There were times I could actually hear the snow, falling with a hiss like a low pressure steam valve with a slow leak. When I first parted from Rutledge, I felt so alone that I was tempted to quit and go home. I missed my family with an almost uncontrollable longing. As the weeks went by I still missed them, but not with the same hopelessness I had at first. I was making a good catch of furs and would have more money in the spring than I had ever possessed.

On the trapline I found a good many books and magazines,

stored with care in tree caches or in oil cans with tin covers to protect them from rodents. Each trapper would save the reading material for the men to follow, remembering his own lonely evenings or the days when it had been unsafe to travel beneath the snowslides. One might be unfortunate enough to become crippled up and have to lay over several days.

In one cabin, I discovered a Bible that someone had packed out to the line – the last thing I read – and I became so engrossed that time slipped away. I started to look forward to getting back to that cabin on every round. I ran out of reading material before the winter ended. At first this frightened me, but instead of reading labels on the Klik meat cans – forwards and backwards – I started to do a bit of writing.

One day in particular was exceptionally hard. The weather was mild and the snow clung to my snowshoes every step of the way. When I arrived at the cabin I was so tired I made a fire, then lay back on my bunk to rest and dozed off to sleep. When I awoke the fire was out and my leg muscles were aching fiercely.

After supper I made an entry in my diary, recording the weather and the day's catch. I sat back, lost in thought. Slowly, words and phrases came to me and by evening's end I had written my first verse:

Beat

I have taken this pen to write and write,
My body feels like lead;
The day's been long, the going rough,
My mind seems blank and dead.

I have sat on this bunk and thought and thought,
My mind cannot inspire.
For every muscle I own must ache,
My legs are pillars of fire.

I'm tired, so tired, so terribly tired,
My pen's still in my hand.
How much? How much? Oh! just how much
Can the human body stand?

I do not know, but these thoughts must stop;
I'll rest here on this bunk.
For tomorrow is bound to be as rough
And I'll have to draw on spunk.

After writing that verse, I never had another lonely evening. I could wile away the hours too quickly, often staying awake until early morning, making the following day tough going.

I always left my siwash camp on the west fork before daylight. It was an easy climb to timberline because the camp was very high. One day, I decided to climb to the top of this rocky peak to see what the country was like to the north and west.

I got to at the top just at daybreak. As the sun rose, it touched upon the higher mountains first, lighting them like candles. The light flowed down their slopes in hues of gold, rose, silver and cream. They lit up like a city in winter at dusk . . . a flash here . . . a flicker there . . . until they were all glittering.

The valleys were the last to relinquish their shadows of mauve, purple, thunderhead black and soapstone grey. They stirred sluggishly like a human from slumber, as if resenting this early awakening. The sunlight gradually crept lower, touching the snow-draped trees, hoarfrost crystals catching the rays and tossing them back in sparkling splendour.

The days passed, stretching into weeks and months, and I started getting bushed. My whole outlook on life changed. I had never much studied my feelings, or my surroundings. Now I asked myself many questions. Life began to make more sense, and then less sense.

When it came time to go home in the spring, I had the feeling I had gone trapping as a boy and was leaving the line as a man.

After Rutledge and I returned to Hudson's Hope, he asked if I would like to go ranching with him. Bonnie and I decided to give it a try. We moved to the farm with Leo and his wife, Ethel. But it didn't take long to decide that I could never stand being at the beck and bawl of a goddamned cow. We moved back up to the Hope after two months, and I worked in King Gething's coal mine for the summer.

Jack Longstreet, who had bought Rutledge's line, asked me if I wanted to go trapping again that winter. I said, "Yes." Bonnie said, "No." She said one winter alone was about all she could take, and put up quite an argument. I put up a better one, using the excuse that I could make more money at trapping than at anything else I could find around town or in the mines. Truth was I wanted another year in the mountains.

Longstreet had never been over the line so we headed for the upper end where I had trapped. I'd show Longstreet the territory, and we would also rebuild a cabin on the west fork of the upper Clearwater River.

The cabin had not been used for many years and had been burned on the inside. The story was that two fellows had come in to this country as trapping partners. After a disagreement, one had pulled out. When the other was away on a trip over the line, the first returned and set fire to the cabin. The supplies burned but the cabin, built of green balsam logs, had been only scorched on the inside. The roof had fallen in, leaving the walls standing.

Earl, Bonnie, Harley and Pat Pollon

Rutledge had siwashed when he was in this part of the country; so had I the year before, but I had taken my best catch off this part of the line and intended to spend more time there this year.

Longstreet and I began working on the cabin, replacing the roof logs and dirt. Suddenly, Longstreet bent over double. "Christ, have I got a belly-ache! Doc O'Brien told me I should have my appendix out before I left."

"Well, this is a hell of a fine time to tell me!" I cried, jumping down from the roof. "Let's catch those dogs. We're getting out of here while you can still walk."

Jack Longstreet weighed about 300 pounds, while I weighed 150. It had taken six hard days travelling to get in to the upper end of the line, loaded down with all the supplies we could carry. On the return trip we made it to the Peace River in less than a day and a half. We left our boat at Twenty Mile and Jim Beattie gave us a ride the rest of the way to Hudson's Hope.

The trip slimmed Longstreet down quite a bit. When we had started up the line he wore the biggest pair of pants he could buy in the country. These still weren't big enough, so he had sewn a pie-shaped piece of cloth in the back and left the top button undone so they'd reach around his belly. By the time we reached Hudson's Hope, he could do up the top button and lap the piece of pie in the back. Doc O'Brien told him the trip was the best preparation he could have had before the operation.

Jack Longstreet, Earl Pollon's second trapping partner.
(Hudson's Hope Museum)

When I arrived back at the Otter Tail (Brewster Creek) it was in the same freeze-up stage it had been in when I had travelled to Manson Creek years before. I didn't yell to Fred Chapman this time, because I thought he might tell me to go to hell after the canoe episode. I walked up the creek about a mile, took off all my clothes and waded across.

Chapman had worked on the Grand Trunk Railroad, then prospected in the Tête Jaune Cache country prior to coming to Hudson's Hope around 1912. I stayed with him for a couple of days. He had spent so many years on the upper river, he could tell by the passing ice floes which jams had held in the water and which ones had flowed through. One morning, Chapman announced that the river had jammed at the Clearwater again, so I packed up and pulled out.

When I arrived at the Clearwater, the jam was heaving and twisting. I watched for a while and then decided to cross anyway. I cut a long safety pole, unpacked my dogs and threw their packs onto the jam across a five-foot strip of open water at the shore. Then I threw my own pack, snowshoes, safety pole and testing stick onto the ice. I picked up my dogs one at a time and heaved them across. Taking a run, I jumped onto the jam and landed spreadeagled. I put on my snowshoes immediately to gain a broader bearing on the surface. I didn't breathe easy until I had reached the south side.

Once inside the cabin, I picked up the kindling that was always laid out by the stove and struck a match. There was a sudden roar. I ran to the window and saw the whole river become a moving mass of ice. It didn't close up again for 10 days.

The next morning I headed up the line, setting traps. When I arrived at Fifteen Mile Creek, I ran into trouble. When Longstreet and I had gone up in the early fall the creek had been high. We felled a couple of trees to cross on, then left them there. They had acted as a dam when the slush started running, backing up the creek until it was spread over the south flat. I was snowshoeing along, whistling happily, when suddenly I was in water up to my armpits. That was bad enough, but my dogs followed me into the open hole. I had been packing 20 pounds of white sugar on the dogs. The water got into the packs, turning the sugar to syrup. I had to put it into jam cans to use on hot cakes and bannock.

My clothes started freezing when I finally got out of the water and slush, but the weather was not too cold so I kept travelling. My moccasins iced up immediately. I was walking along the shoreline when I slipped and fell, hitting my .300 rifle on the rocks.

Back at my home cabin, I decided to clean up my day's dirty dishes. I heated some water and wandered outside to relieve myself when I saw, about 150 yards away, a moose browsing on some willows. I grabbed my rifle and two shells – all I could find among the litter on the table – took aim and fired. The moose wheeled as if hit. I loaded in another shell and fired again. Again it wheeled. I ran back into the cabin and found two more shells among the clutter.

The moose started walking south along my snowshoe trail. I ran after it, noting there was no blood on the tracks. It suddenly stopped. A large tree partially blocked my view, so all I could see was its rump on one side and its head on the other. I aimed at its head, fired and missed. I was sure now my gun had got knocked out of whack from my fall.

The moose started walking away through the trees, toward the willows. About 30 feet ahead on the trail were two trees that jutted from the ground, forming a crotch. I decided to climb them and try to spot the moose out in the willow patch. I had just placed my foot in the tree-crotch when Speed caught up to me. "Get 'em, Speed!" I yelled. The dog made two jumps and did a fast turnabout. The moose had hidden behind a small grove, waiting for me. Speed was fast enough to duck him. I would not have been. The moose, head down, bristles standing, raced after the dog, striking and grunting, his tongue shooting out of his mouth with every grunt. As the animal ran past my tree, I rammed the rifle barrel into its neck and pulled the trigger. I didn't miss that time. It dropped at my feet.

When I stretched out its hind leg to start skinning, I found its gams had been all slashed. It had been in a fight with a pack of wolves and had fought them off in the river right near where I first spotted it.

On the trip back down the line, it started to snow one day when I was away from the home cabin at Twenty-Two Mile. By the time I reached the cabin, snow was piled up 30 inches on my chopping block. The following morning, another 30 inches had collected. Five feet of snow had fallen in 24 hours.

No animal would be able to venture into my ground-set traps now. I decided to spring this line, if I could find the traps. I had made a few blazes on trees along the way, but the snow was deeper than my blazes. I took Speed with me to try to find the traps. "Hunt 'em, boy!" I said, and Speed jumped off the tips of my snowshoes and disappeared into the snow, sinking clear out of sight. I could see the snow bunch up and hear him blowing and sneezing. He found every trap, not missing one.

It took five hours to make four miles, two hours just to return on our broken trail. When we got back to the cabin, it looked as good as the Vancouver Hotel to me. When I came off that trip it was time to go home for Christmas.

On the first trip back up the line after Christmas, I went over to the west fork where Longstreet and I had repaired the cabin. When I arrived at the cabin, it looked like a big hump of snow. Traps I had hung in a tree a good nine feet above ground were now below the snow. I had not set up my stove, so I had to dig a hole for the pipes. I dug down four feet with my axe and snowshoes, then went inside to force the pipes up through the rest of the snow. When I got a fire going, the snow around the pipe melted and ran inside the cabin. By morning, three inches of water covered the floor. It never dried out that whole winter.

One day, my dogs and I caught up to an old bull moose that had stayed too long in a tramped-down clearing in the high country. He had eaten down the willows to one-inch-thick branches. When we approached, the bull started grunting. He couldn't do anything else, because the deep snow was above the level of his back. We made a detour around him and continued on up the draw. When I came back down with the dogs, the moose had started heading for the lower country, following my snowshoe tracks. I hadn't gone very far before I caught up to him. He was rearing up on his hind legs, lunging forward, and then drawing his hind feet through the deep snow. As soon as my dogs saw him in that shape, there was no stopping them. They jumped on his back, bit his ears and pulled hair out of his back and rump. I tried to call them off but they wouldn't listen, and I wasn't going to get in the middle of that mix-up. I don't know what time the dogs returned to the cabin, but the next morning there they were.

I travelled up-river and had to pass the draw where I had seen the moose. I'll be damned if that old bull wasn't out in the shallow water of the creek, browsing the red willows. He stayed there the winter, never leaving that stretch of open water as long as I was trapping. I always hollered a greeting to him as I went by.

I stayed on the line until the latter part of February. When I met Longstreet again, he accompanied me to the Peace River home cabin. We talked . . . well, Longstreet talked and I listened . . . most of the night. Suddenly he said, "I must be getting a cold. My throat's sore."

"No, Jack, it's from talking," I said. "You haven't used your vocal chords for a long time." This is quite true; when you go for months on the trapline without using your voice, your throat muscles become weak and tire easily.

The snow never let up all winter. I had broken new trail almost every day, and my legs were always giving me hell. One day, when I came to my second most important cabin at Twin Creek, I decided to run the spur line as well. It was just a short line, about five miles one way. It was a warm day and the snow was sticking to my shoes. I had to tap each shoe with my axe handle to knock off the snow as I lifted first one then the other. By the time I started up the creek behind Snowslide Mountain, my legs were burning. On my way back down, they grew worse. When I arrived at the main creek, I had to stop and rest.

I sat down and had a smoke. But when I tried to get up, I yelped with pain. I sat down again and pulled up my pant legs. Both legs were swollen and there were lumps the size of goose eggs on each shinbone. I tried to get up and walk. I couldn't do it. I remembered a tale that Jack Pennington had told me years before.

"I was trapping the Clearwater one time and my legs got so sore I couldn't walk," Pennington had said. "I had lumps on both shinbones the size of fists. I had to tie strings to my snowshoe points and lift the shoes with my hands. It took me hours to reach my home cabin, but I made it."

I called Speed over, took the tie wicks off his packs, and tied them to the points of my shoes. I tried walking. It worked. I could not go very fast, but at least I was moving.

When I reached the cabin near morning, I lay down immediately and fell asleep. When I awoke I had forgotten about my legs and tried to stand. I damned soon remembered them. I sat back down on the bunk, swearing like a mad man.

I crawled off the bunk and outside to the snow porch where I had the wood pile. Luckily, I had cut lots of wood with my swede-saw on my first trip to the line in the fall, leaving enough wood at each cabin for the winter. I threw some logs in through the door, crawled back inside and lit a fire.

I poured some water into the biggest kettle I had, which I usually used for cooking the dogs' feed. When the water had heated, I bathed my legs for several hours. They hadn't swollen any more during the night, but they were more painful. I decided to place myself on short food rations, because I didn't know how long I'd be laid up. As it turned out, I lay there for six days. The swelling had not gone down, but I could at least walk.

I still had a lot of line to travel. I never kept any grub in those cabins at all, supplying myself for the trip from the Twin Creek cabin. I knew I would have to save enough food to last me on my trip down to the next cabin 10 miles below, after I had made the circle around the upper end of the line. I travelled slowly, still helping out my legs with strings connected to my snowshoe points.

I made it to a cabin the next day. I had figured on making a cabin a day on my trip over this part of the line; as it was, it was taking me two days. I ran out of food. So did my dogs. I had cut them off food altogether when we left Twin Creek. It took me four days to get to the west fork of the Clearwater, where I still had a short spur line to check. By then I was clean out of grub.

I was skinning out a fisher I had caught in a trap, when I thought about trying to eat it. "To hell with it," I thought. "I'm not that hungry yet." I threw the carcass onto the snow in front of the cabin. Speed looked at it, then went back and lay down on his bed of spruce bows. He got up again and walked over to the carcass. This time he started to chew its front leg. I watched him, thinking, "Well, if he can eat it, I can too."

Speed ate one leg, then lay down. He got up and heaved up the leg. He sat there with a sad look on his face, staring at the carcass. Then he went over and chewed off another leg. Same thing happened. "Well, if Speed can't stomach it, I don't think I can," I thought, changing my supper plans.

I went inside and lay down on the bunk. I had made tea, which I had lots of, but it wasn't very filling. I fell asleep, and when I awoke I was famished. Desperate, I searched again through my dog packs. This time I found a piece of bannock about three inches square in my fur and trap pack. I built up my fire and made more tea. When it was ready, I sat on the edge of the bunk and looked at that stinking piece of bannock. It smelled of wet dog, mixed with the odours of weasel, marten, fisher, wolverine, squirrel, fox and wolf . . . and with an overall scent of rotten fish and beaver castor. But I ate it, and savoured every crumb.

Next morning, I headed over the mountain to Twin Creek. This time I was too fatigued to make the climb to enjoy its solitude and beauty. When I arrived at Twin Creek cabin I had a real feed: a handful of rolled oats with a little sugar on it.

My legs were in good shape again and I quit using the tie wicks. I found out later that trappers call this ailment "Snowshoe Leg." It's the continuous straining of the tendons alongside the shinbone caused by the steady drag of snowshoes laden with damp snow.

That was the last year of the big fur prices, which were still at their peak when I came off the line. Jack Longstreet wasn't so lucky. He came down three weeks later and the bottom had fallen out of the market; he received less than half of what I did for his skins. The year was 1945. It was the last for the big-time trappers who had been the backbone of the north country.

12

Currents of Commerce

In 1948, Hudson's Hope experienced another of its periodic booms. The three productive coal mines (King Gething Mine, Peace River Mines, and Packwood Mine) brought in a number of people who wanted part of what they thought was a sure thing. A hardware store and a Red Cross hospital were built, and Marshall Miller rejuvenated the old Henry Stege building.

On September 25 that year, Bonnie and I were blessed with a daughter, Caroline Eloise. I got carried away and sunk my wad into a building with a carpenter's shop downstairs and living quarters above. I never finished it because I ended up donating my cement for the community hall. I never got enough money together again to replace the cement, so I had no foundation under my own building. Funds got low, so I went back to the coal mines again for the winter.

Next spring, Mel Kyllo came along with a deal. My brother Art had been running Dad's lime kiln since returning from overseas and now wanted to sell out. Kyllo suggested we become partners and buy it.

A lime kiln, when it is burning, is a beautiful sight. A multitude of colours are created as the gasses burn off, and flames dance across the top in flickering waves of gold, yellow, blue, green and rose. The sulphur, forming on the top of the kiln, adds to this enchanting picture. Many a beer bash was held around the kiln in the evenings, roasting moose meat, laughing and telling lies.

We burned off the first kiln of lime in jig time and got it ready for shipping to R.P. Loberg in Dawson Creek. After we had the truck loaded and headed up the hill from the kilns, we stopped at the Old Coffee Pot Cafe that Iva Boynton was running since Ted died a couple of years before. We started in the door, and I noticed that the truck driver had not covered his load. There was a storm brewing; thunderheads were boiling grey and black across the sky.

115

I offered Loberg's driver a bit of advice: "You'd better cover the load with tarpaulins. Quick lime is nothing to fool with."

He didn't respond so I continued: "The minute water hits it, that stuff heats to near boiling and expands to several times its original volume." Silence.

"You're carrying 10 tons," I added.

"Yeah, I'll cover it," he said impatiently.

"Well, you better or you'll wish you had." When we came out of the restaurant, it was raining cats and dogs.

A couple of hours later a truck came in from Fort St. John. "Hey, there's a lime truck on fire just east of Jack Ardill's gate," the man said.

On the back of his truck, in with the quick lime, the driver had placed a 10-gallon drum of gasoline. We figured that the lime, heating and expanding, also heated the gas, causing it to run over and drip onto the exhaust pipes. He lost his truck. The worst thing was he didn't want to pay us for the lime. After a lot of arguing, Kyllo finally got the money out of him – at least the promise of money, although we had to wait until the trucking company received insurance compensation.

We started another kiln right away. It was filled and burning when Kyllo and I got into a row. With no money for our first kiln, we were short of cash. Our tempers were even shorter.

For the first and only time, Kyllo and I got into a fist fight, right on the edge of the burning lime pit. We were giving each other a fair accounting, not considering that if one of us had fallen into that kiln he would have been roasted long-pig in nothing flat. Art was standing on Dad's porch, cheering first for one then the other, laughing and swearing, until he saw my foot go over the edge into the pit. Then he came down to break us up. That fight broke up the Kyllo and Pollon Lime Company before it even got a good start. I bought Kyllo out.

The next year, I fixed up a homemade winch using an old truck transmission to pull the lime cars. I also deepened the kiln so I could burn more at one time. But, as usual, I got over-ambitious and built a continuous-burn kiln out of rock. This cost a fortune. I thought, by dumping rock into the top and drawing the burned lime out the bottom, a lot of money could be saved on fuel; the lime kiln would always be hot, hence the name "continuous-burn."

When it was completed I started to burn with coal. To put it bluntly, it was a dismal failure. I learned too late that steam was necessary to burn lime with the coal, in order to drive the carbon from the calcium.

In 1951, we got trapped in the turbulent current of commerce, tossed like a twig in the canyon waters. For 14 years, we searched for the rainbow's end, only to be finally puked out, branded a failure, richer only in human lore. It all started so innocently.

To help bring in some cash, I built a garage for Gary Powell. At a dance that fall, Powell and I went outside and sat in his truck to have a drink.

"Earl," he said, "I'll tell you what. I'll sell you a sawmill. The one that Marshall Miller brought into the country."

"What would I buy a mill with? I'm so broke after the lime business I couldn't buy a free lunch."

"We could make some kind of a deal."

"Do you know how much money I have right at the moment?"

"No, but whatever it is, it's enough for a down payment on the mill."

I laughed and tossed Powell a 50-cent piece.

"Good enough," he said, pocketing it.

We went back into the hall and I soon forgot about our conversation.

A couple of days later Powell came over to my house. "When are you going to pick up that mill and put it to work?"

"What mill are you talking about?"

"The one I sold you at the dance."

"Oh, yes. Any day now!" I went along with the joke.

"Well, look, I promised Pen I would clear off his timber birth out on the portage. I'd like to get it done right away. I'll pay you by the thousand board feet for sawing the logs he left out there, and I'll take my tractor out to do the hauling. The sawing work can apply against the price of the mill."

"I thought you were fooling!"

"No, I'm not. You can have whatever time you'll need to pay it off, only I don't want to pay cash for sawing those logs that are already cut."

"I can't do it! I haven't got a power unit, I haven't got a timber birth, I haven't got *anything* to log with . . ."

"I'll let you have my motor to give you a start. I think the Peace River Mines want to sell a big team they have there. Pretty sure you could get a deal on them. And you can saw on Pen Powell's limit. He asked me to finish the cut for him."

I was in business whether I wanted to be or not. Funny how the toss of a coin decided the next 14 years of my life.

When I had finished sawing the logs Powell had left, Lloyd Gething and Al Chapple asked me to move the mill to the Peace River Mines and saw for them.

The Peace River Mines had been formed in 1944, over a cup of coffee in my kitchen by Lloyd Gething, Al Chapple, Al Hamilton and I. Later, Bill Currie joined the outfit. I withdrew. There was a pretty heavy gamble involved and I was the only married man in it at the time. The mine was not yet developed, the logistics of transportation still unresolved, and it required too heavy a time investment without a return for several years.

The coal mine was now in the last stages of going broke, although it had made money for several years. The men had given employment to a lot of people and the district had not lost anything by its operation. Over-expansion had run them into deeper debt than they could get out of.

I moved the mill over and sawed for them for awhile. I also bought a big black team, or thought I had. I later found out the original owner had not been paid for them, so I had to pay him. I called the team Sam and Satan. Satan was a high-headed excitable bronc, a big animal and a damned good horse.

After finishing the job for the Peace River Mines, I decided to shut the mill down and cruise timber that winter to see if I could find a timber birth of my own.

Bill Currie had left the Peace River Mines and was trapping on a line that Lloyd Gething had bought from Bill Carter. I stayed with Currie in his old trapping shack while I looked for a timber stand. We were camped at what had been the old Gething sawmill in the early '30s. It had since burned and all that now remained of the original buildings was the old cookhouse. I was using this for a barn, and told Neil Gething, Lloyd's father, that I would feed and water my own horses. He insisted he would feed them while he fed his own, because he was around in the morning several hours before I was.

There was no use arguing with Neil Gething when he had made up his mind. One time Lloyd Gething, Pete Kyllo, Bud Stuart and I had come down from washing gold on the upper Peace. When we were ready to return, Neil was going to cross the portage with his team. The box had been taken off his wagon, so we four had put it back on and loaded it with four barrels of kicker gas. Gething came out, took one look and said, "You boys have put that wagon box on backwards. You'll have to change it."

Now, there was absolutely no difference in the distance the box stuck out, frontward or backward, over the bolsters. The only way you could tell back from front was by the wheel wear on the side of the box, where the front wheels rubbed when turning. I started to protest.

"I'll tell you one thing, fellows," Lloyd said. "We might just as well do it. Dad has his mind made up and we won't move until we do." We unloaded and turned the box around.

When Neil Gething had insisted on feeding my team, I had not argued, although I didn't like the idea of him feeding those high-strung horses.

On New Year's Eve, Bonnie and I planned to take in a dance in town. About eight o'clock that evening, Lloyd Gething and Bill Currie came crashing in without knocking.

"Your horse has kicked Dad and killed him!" Lloyd cried.

"Jesus Christ!" I grabbed my coat and cap.

We ran to the barn and found Gething stretched out behind the horses, which were huddled up against the manger. He was lying on his back and it looked like he was sleeping until you saw the wound on his head. There was no blood, except for a bit around the edges where his skull had been split. Something was strange here. I had killed many an animal in my time by hitting it on the head, and I could not remember one that did not bleed at the eyes, ears, nose or mouth. Then I noticed an oat bundle lying behind Satan, the binding twine still unbroken. I was certain that Gething had been dead before he was kicked.

Neil Gething was 86. I think when he bent over to break the twine, his old heart just stopped and he pitched head-first onto Satan's heels. His daughter, Vesta, agreed with my conclusion. "Dad was lying on the couch before he went out to feed the horses. When he got up, he looked very tired – much different from usual – and he had to grab onto the edge of the table to steady himself."

Lloyd and I stayed with the body while Bill Currie ran to the hospital to get Rose Manchuk, the Red Cross matron. Someone else went to get Mel Kyllo, who was the coroner. After Kyllo examined the body, we laid it on a stretcher and carried it over to the morgue. Rose asked Kyllo and I if we would help her wash and dress the body.

I went outside to have a smoke and think about what happened. I remembered seeing an old mining stake at Manson Creek in 1938, that bore the name Neil Gething. The stake had been there so long it had rotted and was held upright only by the tree it leaned against. I remembered Gething's continued faith in a future market for the high-grade coal in the area, and his prediction that someday there would be a big power dam in the canyon of the Peace River. You came too soon and stayed too long, Neil, I thought. Then I checked myself. Maybe not. He probably enjoyed every minute. I could never recall seeing him upset about anything, unless it was when he was criticizing a political party.

Mel Kyllo's words, spoken as we finished dressing the body, echoed my own thoughts: "We have lost one of our greatest pioneers."

For once I agreed with Kyllo, and said so.

Mel Kyllo and I were often called upon to dress the dead. I remember one case in particular: Fred Monteith.

I had been standing on my upstairs landing one hot day in June, when I saw some people running across town. I ran down and caught Mrs. Ted Vince. "What the hell's the matter?" I asked.

"Fred Monteith is dead! He died in his outhouse!"

Fred Monteith
(Hudson's Hope Museum)

I ran across town to Monteith's place, pushed through the crowd and looked in the door of his privy. Monteith's body was slumped over on its side, still sitting on the toilet seat. His pants were down around his knees and the smell would have driven a starving dog off a gut wagon.

"Holy Christ!" I gagged. "How long has he been dead?"

"Two days, as near as we can figure. He bought some fresh buns from Iva then and there they are, still on the wood pile."

I had a carpenter's shop, so I was asked to build a rough box.

Kyllo and I were given the task, as usual, of helping Rose Manchuk dress the body. When I arrived at the morgue, Kyllo was sitting outside waiting. We held our breath, and opened the door.

We could smell the body before the door was opened, but inside the stench was beyond belief. Monteith's body had bloated to almost twice its normal size, and he was a big man to begin with. I hauled in the box, made two inches larger than normal size, and we began the job. At one point, Kyllo had to straddle the body and hoist the shoulders while I slipped a shirt underneath. As Kyllo bent over, his face within a foot of the corpse, Fred Monteith burped.

"Fred, you dirty old bugger, excuse yourself!" I said. Kyllo didn't say anything. He ran outside and got sick.

When we finally got Monteith stuffed into the coffin, his belly stuck above the top and the lid refused to close.

"What do we do now?" Kyllo asked.

"Step on the lid and force it down, so I can get a nail in it before I get sick!" I replied.

We expected to hear an explosion, but nothing happened. Only the smell became worse.

The funeral service was held outside the St. Peter's Church.

Fred Monteith had come to Hudson's Hope in 1912 and, other than the time he spent overseas in World War I, had not left the area. University-educated, he had taken a number of small jobs requiring some education but little physical exertion, such as mining recorder, postmaster, notary public and ferryman across the Peace. He hated the last job, especially when Lloyd Gething was teaching school at Moberly Lake. When Gething was expected in, Monteith would cry: "Cripes Almighty! Cripes Almighty! Damn! Damn! Damn! Puffpuffpuffpuff. Lloyd will want to cross over after dark. Always does. Always does. Wish he'd come in the daytime. Damn! Damn! Damn!"

Monteith always stopped on his way back from the ferry to "piddle-piddle-piddle." You had to watch yourself, because he was liable to absent-mindedly "piddle-piddle-piddle" all over your boots.

We laid the body to rest, and I recalled an incident that occurred when Monteith was helping Henry Stege look after the mail.

Stege was alone in the post office when I went in. He had dumped one bag of letters on the floor and was emptying the registered mail sack on top of it. This was just Henry's way of balling things up. When he dumped the sack, out poured gobs of letters stuck together, and juice. Brad Angier's wife had a bottle of concentrated fruit juice sent to her, and it had broken in transit. The mail was a mess. Stege watched, unbelieving, as the syrup oozed through the letters on the floor. He bent over and grabbed a handful of letters, which stuck to his fingers. He shook his hands like a cat with water on its feet. He then proceeded to wade through the middle of the letters, cussing as some stuck to his feet. Several that were glued to his hands came off and were now fastened to his pants. He rubbed his hands on his shirt front, leaving more letters stuck there.

"Goddemmit, goddemmit! Vot de hell is de matter mit people dat send syrup trough de mail? Stupid bastids! Stupid bastids!"

Fred Monteith stepped into the post office about that time.

"Puffpuffpuff. What's the matter here? What's the matter here?"

"Demmit, can't you see? Demmit! Demmit! Don't just stand dere. Do someting!"

"Well, sit down in the chair. Puffpuffpuffpuff." Monteith's puffs were almost chuckles. "I'll see if I can pluck the letters off you first. Puffpuffpuff." His belly was bouncing, trying to hold back the laughter that was bubbling up inside him.

Stege noticed that Monteith was laughing inside. This made him madder. "Demmit! Demmit! Stop dat laughing, Fred, and get me out of dis mess! I'll report dese damn fools for sending syrup trough de mail. Stop dat laughing, Fred!"

"Puffpuffpuff. How the hell can I, Henry?" asked Monteith in a tone of annoyance, mingled with mirth. "You look so damned ridiculous . . . like a half-plucked goose!"

The people who stood looking through the wicket were convulsed with laughter.

Fred Monteith always had the feeling that life had slipped away from him and he had missed most of its pleasures. He once told me: "You know, Earl, if I had my life to live over, I would live it differently. Puffpuffpuff. I would live just a little wilder. My life has been wasted. Never got a great deal of pleasure out of it. Damn! Damn! Damn! Yes, I am sure I would live just a little wilder than I have. I'd get married, at least."

During my years running the sawmill I learned many lessons. The main one was that in business, you learn to look every gift horse in the mouth, and if you're smart you go around and peek up the other end as well. I guess I lacked the ruthlessness to become a success. If we made money, along came the birds of prey; if we lost money, along came the vultures to gobble the last remains.

Bonnie moved out to the mill to do the cooking. She also wound up driving skid-horses, tailing the sawmill (taking lumber off the carriage that carried logs through the saw), hauling water for the camp, flipping logs down the rollway, and doing part of the book-keeping. In her spare time, she taught our three children school by correspondence.

The boys, Harley and Pat, were now 12 and 11. They canted on the mill (using hand-held cant hooks to turn the log over so the saw can trim each side), drove truck, skinned Cat, cleaned barns, ran errands and studied their courses in the same kind of spare time Bonnie had. They never failed a grade.

In early November, 1953, I was burning a slab pile when I heard an eagle screaming overhead. The day was cloudy and I could not actually see the bird, but it seemed to be circling for I heard its cries several times. After lunch, Pat and Bonnie came out to give me a hand. As Bonnie approached, I heard the whistle of wings and looked upward. A Golden Eagle was plummeting down through the tree tops, its wings held straight up.

"Look out!" I screamed.

Bonnie ducked and quickly stepped under a large poplar tree. The eagle over-shot her, just brushing her shoulders. It flew across the road and landed on a tree stump, spun around, and raised its wings to take off.

"Face it! Don't turn away!" I shouted, running toward Bonnie and Pat and pulling out my hunting knife. As I ran by my truck I remembered my 30-30 rifle was in it. I grabbed it and raised it to my shoulders as I worked the lever. It clicked. No shells. I grabbed my hunting knife again, and ran toward the eagle. It was only eight feet from Bonnie, who was backed up against the tree, facing it. I could have hit it with my rifle but I was afraid I'd break the stock, so I moved in to stab it. Suddenly I saw Harley coming from the camp, pushing five-year-old Caroline on a little hand-made sleigh. The eagle sprang off the stump and flew towards them.

Harley quickly pulled Caroline off the sleigh. Again the eagle overshot, catching Caroline's coat shoulder with one talon and cutting her cheek with another. I was right behind it. It let go of Caroline's coat and hopped, or I kicked it, over a pile of slashing beside the road. It then flew off with Caroline's hat in its claws.

I picked Caroline up and held her to me. The eagle had slashed her cheek, just missing her right eye. I carried her back to the mill deck and began to dress her cheek, when Harley yelled: "Here it comes again!"

Its wings nearly touched the trees on both sides of the road. My rifle was leaning against the engine room, where I had gone for the first aid kit, so I grabbed a long-handled shovel. Bonnie and the kids ducked under an overhang in the lumber pile and I jumped in front of them just as the eagle attacked. I warded it off with the shovel and it swung away, then swooped again. Once more I warded it off. This time I grazed its wing, causing the bird to veer over the 30-foot high flames of the slab fire. The heat must have stunned it, for it landed beside the mill. I grabbed the rifle, found some shells in my watch pocket, aimed, fired, and missed. I shoved another shell in and fired. This time I was right on target.

The eagle's wing-span was 38 inches. I took it to Dawson Creek to have it mounted, but bad luck still dogged us. Someone stole it off the truck in the dark, no doubt thinking he had found a turkey.

The family and I worked hard to try to make the mill pay, keeping just enough out of production to barely eat and operate. The day before Christmas, 1953, I picked up our mail in Hudson's Hope and found a registered letter. I hated the sight of them. This one was from a man who had worked for me; I still owed him money, although I was paying him as best I could. I had kept back only enough dollars to buy a few things for the kids for Christmas.

On Christmas Eve we sat in our little log shack at the mill, feeling pretty sorry for ourselves. Bonnie and I were trying to put on a happy front for the kids, but it was forced.

"Earl, we haven't anything to cry about," Bonnie said. "Think of Jack and Hilda Reschke. This is their first Christmas without their son, Ernie, and they'll be all alone over at King Gething's mine."

"You're right. We should go over and pay them a visit."

The Reschke's son, Ernie, had drowned in a dug-out while swimming at Fort St. John the previous summer. He was 13 years old, and a very close friend of our children.

When we arrived at the mine, the scene was just as we'd expected. Jack, Hilda and their youngest son, Eddie, were sitting quietly and it was plain to see what was on their minds. As soon as we arrived, our children began visiting. We adults enjoyed our Christmas drinks as we talked about everything but Ernie. With an evening's friendship, we all managed to shed our sadness for awhile.

I had a 2,000-tie contract to take out that winter. We finished it at the end of March, coinciding with the weather breaking up the roads, so we closed down. On April 12, it dropped to 30 degrees below zero. The company still wanted ties, so we started up again. When we stopped cutting, we had nearly doubled our original contract and were almost financially square with the world. But believe me, we had all worked. Even little Caroline had to sit by the slab fire all day, or else in the truck cab, to keep warm as she watched her parents and her brothers become sawmill slaves.

In 1955, I bought a stand of timber on the Butler Ridge near Beryl Prairie containing mostly spruce and balsam. A nice stand to look at but, like some men I have known, rotten to the core, with every defect known to spoil timber: ringshake, starshake, windcheck, conk rot, butt rot and over-mature. I hired Tommy Ardill to build a road into the area.

On August 17, 1956, Bonnie hatched out our final chick. We named him William Roy.

That year, a break came our way, although I did not recognize it at first. I was offered a contract to take out ties for the Pacific Great Eastern Railway, which was building from Prince George through the Pine Pass to Chetwynd and Dawson Creek, with a "Y" connection extending up to Fort St. John. I didn't like the price I was quoted, but then I was informed that "the railroad will pay all the mileage over 20 at one-half cent a tie per mile. You just pay for the first 20 miles out of your price."

"Then write that into the contract."

It was written in by hand, a lucky thing for us. This was the only contract, so I am told, containing this clause.

We moved the camp and mill back to the portage road to our pine timber births. Bonnie's brother, Pete Goodvin, was in the business with us now, working as bush-boss and timekeeper. Bonnie was head cook. Harley was sawing and bossing one mill, and Pat was sawing and bossing another. I was general manager, trouble shooter, master mechanic, spare sawyer and general flunky.

After completing the contract for the first 15,000 ties we got an extension for another 30,000, which we finished by April. We were then offered an open contract on the amount, but with an expiry date of December 31, 1957. Before we finished cutting ties for the P.G.E. railway, we were producing 1,000 to 1,500 ties per day. Our total cut was more than 100,000, double that of our closest competitor.

At the end of the contract, I was harassed, haggard and humourless.

Then we had some bad breaks: construction sales we had counted on didn't amount to a great deal. Wages still had to be met. We had to lay off quite a few men, who had brought in their families when they came to work for us. We made a trip to Vancouver to bid on another tie-cutting contract, but were unsuccessful. The only work that seemed available was sawing export six-quarter lumber.[1] We didn't like the look of the work; prices were not good and the grades very exact. Taking it on meant we would have to expand.

We bought a planer mill, a new edger and trimmer and brought in a larger mill. We then installed slab belts. By the time we had met these extra expenses, we were right out of cash. To get operating funds, we had to mortgage everything we had; down the rat-hole went the properties we had bought in town from the profits of the railway tie work.

Underlying our decision to expand was the fact that a hydro dam on the Peace seemed a sure thing. We hoped to bid to supply the materials that would be needed for its construction.

We had our mill set and were ready to start logging, when an oil outfit drilling above our timber births on the Butler Ridge informed us we could not use the road down Butler Mountain. I had put in that road in 1955. The oil company had simply moved in on my road, upgraded it and extended it to their camp. The fight was on.

The oil company flew in their Calgary lawyer, who told me they did not recognize my road because I had not taken out an easement on it. He threatened me with a court order if I persisted in trying to use it. I informed them that not only was I going to *try* and use it, I was damn-well *going* to use it! They then claimed their maps did not show a road. I made a fast trip to the forestry department in Fort St. John and asked if they recognized my road. They did, and had photos dating from 1955 showing it. Back I went with all hackles standing.

The result was a compromise. The oil company would pay me to stay off the road until they finished their work on the mountain, supposed to be completed in a month. I agreed, on the condition that I could go ahead felling and decking timber on my births. In the spring, Pete Goodvin and I split up the partnership. Bonnie, the boys and I took over all debts incurred by Pollon and Goodvin, and formed Pollon and Sons Sawmills to try and pull ourselves out. Even though we worked all day and repaired all night, we continued to lose ground.

It was a hot, dry summer, and dust from the heavy oil company traffic on the road through my timber births settled in thick layers on the decked timber. The dust caused a set of saw bits to wear out before half a shift was over. Not only was this expensive in bits, it slowed down the sawing, making the over-all operating cost prohibitive.

We still owed on equipment and our payments fell behind, although we made good on many thousands of dollars of debts. We struggled for another year, chiselling on repairs to equipment that, in the end, broke down.

By spring of 1960, we finally reached a state where lumber

sawing was out of the question. Logging was too expensive in the spruce stands, so we moved back to our pine stands. I cut timber for local sales, still paying on debts, but it gained us little. We had no home life whatsoever, and never a dollar we could call our own.

Even our youngest son, Billy, now four years old, was working at the mill. We had very light tie canting hooks (iron hooks with long wooden handles, used for rolling logs) which he could handle to flip tie bolts down the rollway. Bonnie was skidding as well as cooking. We were working day and night, and my sleep was shadowed by nightmares about accidents.

One day I just stopped. "To hell with it," I said to Bonnie. "We've sold nearly all our property and shoved it down this never-ending rat hole. Plus the best years of our lives. They can have the equipment and anything else with a claim against it. But they can't have any more of us!"

We owned outright one small worn-out sawmill, an old truck, two power saws, a couple of skid horses and, between Pat and I, a complete set of tools.

"Well, I started this with a bottle of whisky and a 50-cent piece," I said. "We've got a hell of a lot more than that now. We'll be alright."

We started rebuilding our worn-out junk. When we went to get our old truck, left out by the mill a mile from camp, we discovered it had been vandalized. Everything of value had been stolen: headlights, generator, starter, heater, even the spark plugs.

I began repairing an old T 120 Chrysler truck motor for a mill unit. I had all new parts for it: crankshaft, rings, a new set of bearing-mains and connecting rod, seals and gaskets. It started to snow, so I threw a tarp over the workbench, motor and parts. After a couple of days the snow melted off and I went back up to the mill to continue the job. Everything was gone, including all the wrenches I had been using. Cursing, I headed for the engine room; my worst fears were confirmed: every wrench had been stolen. I was too sick to curse any more. Gone also was our complete set of tools: die sets, compressors, valve grinders . . . everything.

We managed to scrape together a few hundred dollars to buy new parts, but we had to borrow tools from King Gething to finish the repairs. We finally got our junk-heap together and started sawing again, bucking the odds with improper tools to keep up the constant repair work the worn-out equipment demanded.

Then new trouble began: our lumber was being stolen.

In the past, our camp had always been left open to anyone who needed to stop. What was happening to the country? It didn't take long to find out.

Note

[1]Contracting for six-quarter lumber is a method used by the big mills to steal from both the small sawmill operator – the basic producer who is contracted to do the work – and the customer. A 2-inch plank is planed into six quarters. Instead of being paid for a board measuring 2-inches, the sawmill gets paid for 1 1/2 inches, with the re-saw dust coming out of the sawmill owner's pocket. When the customer buys it, he is also cheated, because he is paying for a full 2-inch board but getting only 1 1/2 inches.

13

Burying the Legends

In 1961, engineering studies and plans of the Peace River Power Development Company were taken over by the provincial government from Wenner-Gren. Responsibility for the Portage Mountain Dam project was then assigned to the provincially-owned British Columbia Electric Company. We had read this information in newspapers, and noted increased activity in our area, but suddenly the dam was actually being built. Convoys of trucks were bringing in steel for a new bridge across the canyon; pilot tunnels were being drilled into the rock to find the best channels for river diversion; diamond drillers were testing the riverbed for placement of coffer dams, to be built above and below the dam site to make a dry construction bed. Camps were being set up to house these work crews, as well as the IPEC (International Power & Engineering Consultants) personnel. The Portage Mountain dam, it was said, would be one of the world's largest.

The river's channel was being diverted, the town was crawling with various work crews, and the invasion seemed to have nothing to do with us at all.

I felt at my lowest ebb. Our sawmill was broke, our tools and lumber had been stolen, and our country was changing so rapidly it seemed I couldn't get a clear picture. Were these changes for the best? Or would they forever alter the town we called home, and the people we called friends?

I decided to talk my family into going gold-washing. They had worked so hard all those years in the mill and needed a rest, too. Whether we made any money was not important: we needed time to overcome what had developed into a hopeless situation.

As soon as we moved to Two Mile Bar on the Peace River, I felt the tension drain. I lay by my river, sometimes fishing, other times just dreaming, as I had so many times before. Even though our camp was just across from the construction site, the river hadn't changed, even if everything else had.

The world began to take on its proper perspective. We lived off our rifles and fishing lines, even using leeks, as we had in the past, to flavour our moose and deer meat mulligan. Friends started coming to the bar in the evenings to visit and enjoy a barbecue of moose meat roasted over a Balm of Gilead poplar bark fire.

Bonnie and I slept on a spruce bow bed. The boys were more modern and had brought spring cots.

We were visiting one night with Two-Mile Bob Clark, when Harley suddenly shouted, "Is that a star moving or am I seeing things?

"That star is moving! Look! It's passing all the other stars, travelling east!"

We all looked into the sky. While searching for Harley's moving star, we heard the high-pitched scream of a jet and could see the flare from its exhaust. The noise intruded on the angry hum of heavy equipment working across the river on the dam site. An earth-shaking blast shattered the air, shaking the gravel bar on which we were sitting. We watched the new "star" for about 20 minutes until it dropped out of sight behind the horizon to the north-east.

"What in bloody hell is next, I wonder?" said Two-Mile Bob.

We visited another couple of hours, then saw the star (which we later discovered was the Russian satellite, Sputnik) rise over the mountains again to the south-west.

After Clark had returned home and the rest had gone to bed, I lay beside Bonnie on our spruce bows and gazed at the sky, trying to imagine the future. The past had left records, like the layers of sandstone, coal seams, and fossil beds now being exposed by the heavy equipment whose whine I could hear all night. My river was still as I had always known it. But it would change with the man-made obstruction soon to be placed across its narrows.

Daily, riverboats took engineers and surveyors up and down the river past the bar. Helicopters and airplanes were in the air constantly, hauling men farther upriver and on to the south side for exploration work. The peace of the upper river was ending.

All this would be under water. I thought of the graves that would be flooded, trappers like Jack Thomas, and Ernie Gus, who had died while trapping with Fred Chapman at the Ottertail. Chapman had told me about that. Gus was overdue from his trip over the trapline, and Chapman was alone at the home cabin. Suddenly he heard a rifle shot. He went outside and hollered. Gus answered. Chapman got a "bug" to light his way.[1] He found Gus 300 yards out in the bush, off the trail; he died before Chapman could get him back to the cabin. The cause of death, according to the miners' jury, was exhaustion and exposure. Gus apparently had become lost and panicked. His body was buried near the cabin.

Trapper Harry Holtmeyer died in 1919 and was also buried in land now sited for a reservoir. His body was found in the cabin belonging to him and his partner, Hans Christiensen. It had been riddled with bullets from a .303 Lee Enfield rifle. The man who murdered Holtmeyer had waited in the cabin, concealing himself in the attic, and fired his rifle from above. Ten shots had been fired; nine of the bullets found their mark. The tenth had ricocheted off the corner of the table.

Shorty Webber discovered the body. He got so rattled that he missed the trail in to Hudson's Hope to report it, and instead headed up the side of Butler Mountain. Allen McKinnon, hauling the mail from Hudson's Hope to Finlay, then found the body and reported the murder. Hans Christiensen had disappeared, so it was believed that he had killed Holtmeyer. The theory was weakened when Maurice "Mac" McGarvey discovered part of a skull and hands in 1920. The skull was identified by a dentist, Doc Greene, who recognized Christiensen's dental work. Someone had attempted to cremate the body. The cremation had nearly been successful; the skull and hands were all that remained. However, this grisly evidence placed the bodies of Holtmeyer and Christiensen 18 miles apart.

A few years later, Bill Inesk's body was found shot in his trapping cabin at the bottom of Deserters Canyon on the Finlay River. Inesk's furs were missing, like Holtmeyer's and Christiensen's. He supposedly had once confessed to Shorty Webber to the murder of "the Danes," as Holtmeyer and Christiensen were called. Webber had been the first to discover Holtmeyer's body and the last to see Bill Inesk alive. No other solution was ever offered. Bill Inesk's grave would also be under this new lake.

There was also the body that Donald MacDonald and Guy Robison had buried on the Finlay. This man had drowned in the Finlay River, and they buried him on the spot, using a boat paddle for a headstone.

What would become of the unknown graves near Cust's Landing, and Nigger Dan's? And all the Indian graves? How many Klondikers, whose sluice box tailings were still visible on Two Mile Bar and other bars along the Peace River, would be entombed by the lake? Gone also would be graves of prospectors from the Cariboo Gold Rush of the 1860s.

"What of it?" I thought. "What if there is 600 feet of water on top of six feet of earth? The past is dead."

The new satellite appeared for the third time. "The past may be dead," I thought, "but what about the present? What effect will the flooding have on the animals of the upper Peace River valley? Especially the moose, and the stone sheep?" This valley, containing thousands of acres of willow flats, was a main browsing and calving area for moose during the winter when the snow became too deep in the mountains. Would they be able to get out of the valley without being drowned when the flood came?

One of the main sheep licks was on the Ottertail River about three miles from where it entered the Peace. The lake would reach that far, and would place those beautiful animals within easy reach of high-powered rifles. There were laws against shooting from boats, but give some men the opportunity to shoot one of these trophy animals and, law or no law, if there wasn't a game warden around they would damned well shoot them. Even now, when they visited the lick on the Ottertail, the sheep were being shot. And these butchers were not taking just the rams, but the ewes as well.

I remember reading reports from the 1920s by Constable Ed Forfar of the B.C. Provincial Police, stating strongly that these animals needed protection. As far back as 1921, he reported that the beaver were in danger from being over-trapped by both Indian and white trappers. The Indians trapped in the summer as well as the winter, because they used beaver for food. Forfar was also concerned about the future of marten, lynx, and silver and cross fox, which provided the main winter furs that sold at reasonably high prices. Was his foresight to be ignored?

Art Pollon with pet whiskey jack
(Hudson's Hope Museum)

I lay on my spruce bows, and thought about my brother Art. He was the toughest type of Northerner. Except for his service hitch in the Second World War, he had stayed with trapping until fur prices fell out of sight. Throughout our lives, Art and I travelled in different circles. With the passing of years, we had grown no closer but had become more tolerant of one another. Art never married and had no children, so he doted on ours.

I kind of laughed to myself as I recalled a song that Art used to sing:

"In the spring we spend our fur catch,
In the fall we blow our gold.
In the winter we go bare-assed . . .
Lovely Jesus, ain't she cold!"

Following a pattern set by the early trappers and prospectors, Art had quickly developed into a rugged northern outdoorsman who could survive in the wilderness regardless of the circumstances. When he first went trapping on Jim Ross's line in his early teens, Art had to live off beans an entire winter, eating 150 pounds of them. He joined the army at the beginning of the war and served five and one-half years overseas. He was with the first troops to land at Normandy. When he returned, he immediately bought a trapline on the Liard River, where he trapped and prospected every year. He eventually sold his trapline, but continued to go prospecting every summer in the far northern regions of British Columbia.

What would happen to the Gold Bar Ranch at Twenty Mile? Jim and Elizabeth Beattie had spent many years building that ranch. The large log home was the first in the Peace to have hot and cold running water in the early 1930s. It seemed a shame to destroy their life's work by burying it beneath the waters of the reservoir.

Then there was Two Mile Bob Clark, who had settled in the area to wash gold in the 1930s and remained. He, too, would be flooded out of his home. I had asked him what he'd do when the water began to rise.

"I served me hitch in the First World War and that bloody well cured me of so-called civilization," he said. "I came here to get away, and I'm bloody well going to stay. They're not going to drive me out! I bloody well intend to get up in the mornings and see those mountains as long as I live." Then he had sighed. "But bloody Jesus, you can't argue with rising water, can you? I guess I'll have to move up onto another bench."

Like the moose, Clark and all the other oldtimers would have no choice but to run for higher ground.

Our gold washing that summer provided a great deal more pleasure than profit.

After I had moved the family back into town, I returned to the bar on the river to sit awhile and bid a last and silent farewell to my valley of Peace. One night I remained by the campfire until the small hours of the morning, going over the summer we had just spent. I could only hope the kids had learned something from our time together on the bar, so they would at least get a hint of the way of life that was quickly vanishing.

Note

[1]A bug is a wind lantern made by punching a hole in the side of a tin can and inserting a candle. The light then shines out the top, which is now its front end. It will stand a good deal of wind without blowing out.

14
Lost in Time

Our Hudson's Hope correspondent to the Fort St. John *Alaska Highway News* was Reginald Withers Shaw, who had come to the Hope in 1912. Sometimes called "Deadly," sometimes "Uncle Dudley," Shaw was a man who loved his home and never left it, except to try to enlist during the First World War. He was turned down because of poor eyesight. He returned to Hudson's Hope and stayed. With his colourful language and sparkling wit, he brought an unequalled flavour to local reporting.

Dudley (Deadly) Shaw
(Hudson's Hope Museum)

"Feels noble this morning," Uncle Dudley would write, and go on to describe local events, the size of crops, and the idiosyncrasies of his fellow townsfolk, residents, etc. For over 20 years he provided a window where readers could view our town, from articles about the Board of Trade and Women's Community Club, to notices of the "invasion."

135

"A great deal of aerial photographing of the Peace River canyon has been done lately with a view, we hear, to future hydro development," Uncle Dudley reported on January 2, 1958. That summer, he wrote: "The Canyon Motel is filled to capacity with men from drilling crews. There are five rigs working: three at the upper end of the canyon and two at the lower end." And the following April, Uncle Dudley reported: "Two C.B.C. men were in taking pictures in and around the Hope for television."

In September, 1960, we learned that "Twelve Mile Bob Beattie has just returned from a summer's work on the pack trails north of Gold Bar. He has had out a geological survey party for the last 100 days under the supervision of Dr. Irish, Dominion Government Geologist. The party had 27 horses in the hills."

"We are not building a dam and hydro project yet, up in the canyon," Uncle Dudley reported on September 27, "but we have word that a group of VIPs are arriving to spend a couple of days at the camp and look over the site and take samples, tests and findings in general. Keep your fingers crossed. Cheerio, Uncle Dudley."

We took his advice to "take 'er as she comes," and carried on as though nothing unusual was happening.

"One of the big events of the season was a house-warming party held last Thursday at the home of Keith and Thelma Peck on their dairy farm at Beryl Prairie," Uncle Dudley reported on November 17, 1960. "Keith decided they had to have a new house this fall and as it was late in the season, he had to have it in a hurry. So he gathered a crew from town, took them to his farm, and showed them a pile of lumber, a few kegs of nails, a hole in the ground measuring 25 feet x 50 feet and a plan for a house. One week later he informed the gang that they had better hang the doors and windows as he was throwing a house-warming party in two days hence. And have a party they did. The head carpenter is still scratching his head and trying to figure out why it was all ready in time but he did have a good crew."

Then, in May of 1961 he told us that the power people were back in full force: "Jim Pine, Gordon Spears, John Collis and Bob Markham, Vancouver engineers of the International Power and Engineering Company, Sir Thomas Foy, England world-famous engineer, and three consulting engineers from an English firm, spent two days here studying the proposed Peace River Power development.

"Uncle Dudley Shaw and Bob Birosh took a trip over the portage to see the steel bridge a-building. They sure are making great headway, all skilled workers with most modern machinery and camps. Wonder what the old-timers, Twelve Foot Davis and Trader Cust, would think if they could only see it, eh?"

Uncle Dudley did not live to see the great hydro dam. In one of his last reports he seemed to sense his time had come. "Your scribe, well-furred and prime, comes out of his den to say . . . goodbye." He died quietly in his sleep in August, 1965, and was buried, in a coffin made by his friends, in the little graveyard overlooking his beloved town.

One ray of hope in the hustle-a-buck world that was now racing in to our valley was that the boys and I would likely get jobs Cat-operating or truck-driving on the hydro dam project.

A strange surprise awaited us.

We discovered we weren't going to get any job on the project, because we didn't belong to a labour union. After some arguing back and forth, we were offered short-term jobs in the No. 168 Rock and Tunnel Workers, the only union we were permitted to join.

In the fall I took a job working with my power-saw doing some felling on the service bridge site, which was to span the river at its narrowest point at the head of the canyon. The work entailed hanging over sheer cliffs in some of the most awkward positions imaginable. When I had finished the job, I asked the boss what else he had lined up.

"Take that 'Mexican banjo' and shovel rock with those men down there," he said.

I saw a group of men shovelling blasted rock over the cliff in preparation for bridge abutments. I worked the rest of the week with a long-handled shovel and was laid off. That was it for the year, as far as working on the hydro project.

That winter, Harley went to work for King Gething in his coal mine. Pat was working for the O.K. Garage in Fort St. John.

One night about midnight we heard a knock on our door. We found four men standing on the porch. Their vehicle had become stuck in the 14 inches of snow that had fallen that day, and they had walked about nine miles from the old Peace River Mine site to our place. They asked for a lift to town.

I went out to start the car, wondering if it would make it up the grade to the main road. After the men had eaten and enjoyed a smoke, at my expense, I went out to try the hill. I discovered I had a flat tire and my spare was smooth, so I invited the men to spend the night.

The next morning I got them away, but not before I made a deal with one, who worked for Adco Drilling, to supply some material I had to set their drill on the river ice. We loaded up the material and waited for the snowplow so we could take the road to the mine to deliver it. I was to supply quite a bit of planks and timber to this outfit during the next month.

Several of the local boys went out looking for jobs. They were told that, although Adco needed men to run their drills, they could not employ the locals who didn't belong to a union. The boys stopped in on their way back – a pretty despondent bunch of young men. I took another load of materials over, and confronted the company's head man.

"Why couldn't you have taken those guys on?" I asked.

"We would have liked to," he said. "One of our drills is standing idle because we have no one to run it. But we can only hire who Peace Power Constructors recommends. They tell us who we can and can't hire. They're bringing in two busloads of men from Vancouver for us. So that's that."

A day later, the busloads arrived. The local men stood and watched them go to work. Some of the men on the bus could speak no English and had only been in Canada a short time. Animosity started to build between the local people and the entire dam project.

Adco Drilling went bankrupt and I never received any money for the bedding planks and timber material I had delivered. The one $900 cheque I did receive bounced. I made several trips to Peace Power Constructors' office to try to get the money, without success.

The following summer I took my father, Bonnie and the kids down to the Peace River Coal Mines so Dad could see the work on the dam site. While we were there, Ray Williston, then minister of lands, forests and water resources, came along with a party. I had met Williston many years ago when he was school inspector for Peace River North. At his request, I introduced him to my father; while we were talking I pulled out the NSF cheque, showing him my "personal donation" to the Peace River dam project.

I supplied some material that summer for the re-timbering of the Peace River Coal Mine, so it could be shored up where the east end of the dam would sit. I wound up with another bounced cheque for $2,400.

I had a lot of time to write down my thoughts, but not much peace to compile them. One evening, I left pages of manuscript scattered on the living room table. It rained during the night, and by morning, water had leaked through the roof and soaked my pages.

The floor of our place slanted toward the two bedroom doors; there, the water was over the top of my moccasin rubbers.

"Where's my brace and bit?" I yelled.

"Stolen, along with everything else," Harley said.

I sloshed into the bedroom where I kept my 30-30 rifle, took it off the wall, levered in a shell, walked to where the water was deepest and shot a hole through the floor.

"There, that ought to do it," I said, as water began swirling into the holes.

"No one would believe this," Harley said, shaking his head. "Just like Ma and Pa Kettle."

I had to laugh. Here we were, living like hillbillies, and right beside us was the most sophisticated construction project in the world.

Our flour bin was empty again, so I went out looking for work. I walked over to see Ruben Kilba, who was foreman for Bedford Construction. Kilba had lived in a little cabin of mine with his family when they had first come to Hudson's Hope. His son Jack had felled timber for me when I had been taking out ties, and also when I took out timber for the shoring up of the old Peace River Mine.

"I'll get you on if you need a job, Earl," Kilba assured me.

"How? My name's been in the office for six weeks. I've never yet been called."

"By name request. You gotta know someone, that's all. I can get you on working with your power-saw, burning and clearing."

I went to work, at first using my power-saw to buck down the huge hills of timber that had been piled by the Cats. Then I burned them by hand. Kilba came along one day and asked if I would work with a home-made burner.

The burner was made from a 300-gallon tank with a compressor on it. It was not a regular pressure tank, so I had to watch very carefully to ensure that the pressure didn't become too high or it would have blown to hell. Once when I was under one of the huge piles, directing the torch flame to get a good fire going, I heard a strange "WHUMP." I crawled out and went over to the tank to investigate. The safety valve had frozen and the tank was bulging with pressure. I shut off the compressor and let the tank drain off, then thawed the valve with the torch. This became a regular occurrence. In the morning when I started shift, there were 300 gallons of diesel fuel in the tank. If it blew, it would be a disaster.

I had worked there two months, when I arrived one morning only to be told by the head mechanic that another man would arrive to take my place. I was stunned. I tucked my lunch bucket under my arm and headed for home on foot. I cussed everything with my best long-line skinner's ability: the unions, power projects in general, allied councils, Peace Power Constructors, and B.C. Hydro in particular.

I was stomping down the road, when a truck pulled up and Bud Brenham, the company manager, leaned out. "Where do you think you're going?" he asked.

"I've been fired," I yelled, "but I don't know why. If my work was no good, why didn't you tell me, instead of letting me come to work and watch another man take my job, leaving me standing there like a goddamned fool?"

"Whoa! Whoa! Peace Power sent this union man out. I didn't hire him or lay you off! Your work's fine. Far as I'm concerned, training another man to handle that burning operation at this late date is crazy. There's only a week or so left. I'm taking him back to Peace Power's office."

I found out later what had actually transpired. It was hard to believe, but I had been run off for being too efficient. The gas tank on the compressor was not large enough to run a full shift, so I carried an extra five gallons of gas with me. When the tank got low, I would refill it. I also carried a pair of pliers. Every time we moved, the compressor would quit because the tank had been welded and bronze droppings would plug the outlet. I would undo the gas line and blow the droppings back into the tank. Someone had seen me doing this and reported it to the union. I was not a "115" union man, so was not supposed to use a wrench or even put gas into the tank.

It would have been a lot simpler to put me in the union, rather than run me off. After the burning was finished, the entire crew got their notice.

One day, the boys heard that a large group of men was to be hired for concrete work in the diversion tunnels. This job could last a year or more. The local men wanted steady work, not just short-term jobs, but they'd almost given up trying to get into "115" Operating Engineers, or the 213 Teamsters' Union, for which they were fully qualified.

In the early stages of construction, some of the men employed on the project had stayed in our bunkhouses. They were putting in 10- and 12-hour days, seven days a week, being paid double for overtime, making money at a rate unheard of in Hudson's Hope. Our own people were not offered jobs like this, despite a stipulation that you had to be local to be eligible for employment. What a joke! To be considered "local," you had to reside in the area for not less than 60 days. Many people patiently waited the 60 days, only to find they, too, were bypassed while men brought in from all over the place got jobs immediately. To us, it seemed the unions were emptying their halls in Vancouver and other cities, and the government was getting rid of its bread-lines at the same time.

We were completely disillusioned about any benefits the project might bring to local people. We were used only as a stand-by force for short-term jobs, such as clearing timber or filling the old mine. The main jobs, the steady well-paying jobs, were filled by men brought in from all over Canada and the rest of the world. We locals were starving in the midst of plenty.

The young men looked to me to do something. I had employed men here through thick and thin, providing jobs when there wasn't much going on, just to keep a payroll going. I decided to start soft: I wrote a few articles (printed in the Fort St. John *Advertiser*), that criticized the employment methods.

John Gouge, head of Allied Council, claimed the unions were employing local men in spite of what a little rag of a paper had published. The editor came back with a snappy reply: "Is it in spite of, or because of?" There followed a flurry of short-term jobs for the locals.

One particular case that created animosity involved an Italian employed as powder-man. He was working 12 hours a day, seven days a week. He also cut hair at a dollar a head in his spare time. "Give me two years here," he boasted, "and I'll go back to Italy a wealthy man and start a string of barber shops." The local boys bristled at this attitude. They watched the long lines of working men at the bank on pay-Friday, cashing cheques and sending money back to "the old country." Prejudice had never been a problem at all in the area, but it seemed to us that preference was given to people brought in under the Immigration Act, just to get them off the government's back.

When the concreting work began, a group of local men went to the unemployment office to see about jobs. They were told they lacked the necessary two years' underground experience. It seemed preposterous! Whoever heard of a labourer having to know anything? The foreman tells him what to do. The local men had had enough.

Several carloads of men headed for the Peace Power Constructors office at the dam site, picking me up enroute. I tried to calm them down, but they were determined to bring the situation to a head.

I had the coolest temper of the group at that moment, so I went in first and introduced myself to the man behind the desk. He stood up and told me his name was Bill Wilson. I told him about our problem. He looked at the group standing behind me, and could not help but see their barely controlled rage. Still, he offered no comment.

I persisted: "Are you sure these men you've been bringing in to do underground concreting of the diversion tunnels have the two years' experience that you're asking of our local men?"

He looked at the men, back at me, and then exploded. "Get out! I don't have to answer your questions!"

My own temper nearly got the best of me. My muscles tightened and my right eye twitched. I felt nauseous. Struggling with the effort, I softened my voice and repeated my question.

"No," Wilson said finally. "Two years' underground experience is not asked for by Peace Power Constructors. Tell your boys to go back to the unemployment office and re-apply."

We left the office and headed for town. My mind was in a turmoil. I thought of a comment made by Two Mile Bob Clark, when he heard of the trouble the young men had getting employment. "It seems as if both the government and the unions have placed the glass to their blind eye and refuse to see us! Everyone here is losing: we who love the river and have land that will be flooded, and the young fellows who are seeking work."

No wonder the young men were angry. So was I. At home, the boys let me out and they continued into town to re-apply for jobs. I slumped into a chair in the living room, trying to make sense out of what had become of my valley.

I picked up my pen.

Lost in Time

The campfire's burned to a bed of coals,
The stars above are a glittering maze.
We lay upon our spruce-bough beds
To muse awhile of the bygone days.

On the north side shore we can hear the roar
Of the "turnapuls", saws and Cats,
As they clear the earth for a bed of birth
For a lake on the river's flats.

A jet flies high in the starlit sky,
A Sputnik makes its way . . .
That must be Echo Number Two,
At least so I've heard them say.

Our spruce boughs wince as from a pain.
We hear a mighty roar
As the dynamite blasts the divert shafts
On the Peace's southern shore.

We're lost in time, like tortured souls,
No place for such as we.
I ask you, pardner, friend of mine,
Where can frontiersmen flee?

(1962, E.K. Pollon)

143

Part Two

Prophesies and Prophets

15

Prophesies and Prophets

Explorer Alexander Mackenzie noted the energy potential of the Peace River area in a diary entry in 1793. In the location now named Gething and Aylard creeks, he observed that "one could burn a shoe while standing on certain cracks in the earth, from which emitted heat, smoke and a stench of sulphur." These rose-coloured sandstone areas, caused by slow-burning underground fires, are still visible below the W.A.C. Bennett Dam. Not considering himself qualified to offer "scientific conjectures on this phenomenon," Mackenzie concentrated more on the stratum of a bituminous substance resembling coal, which appeared to be excellent fuel.

Harry Newgord, in a 1914 magazine article entitled "The Last Best West," said that the anthracite coal of Hudson's Hope would rival Pennsylvania's deposits, and the water of the Peace River canyon had the potential to generate more than one million horsepower.[1]

A federal survey of British Columbia's hydroelectric power potential confirmed that "the canyon constitutes a power possibility of considerable magnitude and may some day supply the light and power needs of a large portion of the Peace River district."[2]

But a report by J.W. Bremner and C.R. Crysdale, in the *Pacific Great Eastern Railway Lands Report of Survey of Resources, Part I, 1929-30, Provincial Archives, Victoria*, cautioned that "a market for this power is absolutely dependent on a railway outlet, both to the east and west."

The authors added that "the timber resources of the 30,000 square miles in this watershed would justify the development of a large pulp and paper industry. The numerous streams in the drainage area could be utilized in logging operations and almost any quantity of logs could be safely stored in the reservoir. Recent investigations would indicate that there are extensive mineral deposits northwest of Finlay Forks and it is reasonable to suppose that the construction of a smelter will be necessary when this area is developed. The raw materials required in the manufacture of cement are to be found in the district, and will be adjacent to any railway that may be built in the Peace Valley."

The "almost inexhaustible deposits" of coal were considered among the finest in Canada, with Btu (British thermal units) ranging from 13,500 to 15,000, and of a type that would stand shipment and weather exposure. The area, with "a surprisingly equitable climate," was considered to have excellent development potential.

C.R. Crysdale, engineer in charge of the resources survey, made a surprisingly accurate prediction of hydro development: "A dam at the upper end of the 20-mile canyon, located 100 feet above low water, would create a reservoir extending 50 miles upstream to Clearwater Creek."

Records showed that, at Hudson's Hope from December to March of 1916-17, the Peace River flowed at 4,670 cubic feet per second (c.f.s.). Average flow during these four months, for the 12 years records were available, was considerably more. The minimum flow was established at 4,500 c.f.s. This meant that by drawing 1,700 to 2,800 c.f.s. from the reservoir during this four-month period – lowering the level 20 feet – at least 55,000 horsepower could be generated. A survey from Hudson's Hope to the head of the canyon revealed a rise of 215 feet, half in the upper four miles.

Early reports also predicted that two more dams farther downstream could utilize almost the entire drop in the canyon. Mineral deposits in the Finlay River country were considered to be sufficient to encourage a market for this power, with enough timber in the watershed to justify a pulp mill. An agricultural community could be built, with the large deposits of high-grade coal serving many purposes.

Such optimistic reports were written by everyone from explorers to engineers. It's highly ironic now that Hudson's Hope remained an isolated settlement of log cabins, connected only to Fort St. John by a dangerous route over steep hills.

The Hope had virtually no connection to southern B.C. until 1958, when the local board of trade accepted a challenge from Gordon Moore, president of Fort St. John Lumber, to build a 45-mile connecting road from Hudson's Hope to Little Prairie (renamed Chetwynd in July, 1959). In the fall of 1957, the Hudson's Hope board of trade, which had almost dissolved because of lack of interest, was reactivated. Nine members attended its first meeting; during the winter, membership increased to 23. Earl Pollon was elected president, and Pete Goodvin secretary-treasurer.

A turning-point for development of the country was recorded in the February 6, 1958 issue of the *Alaska Highway News*:

"Mr. E. Pollon and Mr. Pete Goodvin, President and Secretary of the Hudson's Hope Board of Trade, with Mr. Gordon Moore, motored to within five miles of the Hope from the south side of the Peace a few days ago. Unfortunately, though, in order to get here they had to return by way of Little Prairie, Dawson Creek and Fort St. John, a distance of 205 miles. This would seem to indicate we could do very nicely with a bridge up here."

The Hudson's Hope trade board called in other boards and chambers of commerce to solicit their support for a connecting road from Hudson's Hope to Little Prairie. Dawson Creek and Pouce Coupe were supportive, but Fort St. John resisted. "If we support this idea, it would be cutting our own throats. Your commerce would go south instead of north," said a chamber of commerce official. In the end, Fort St. John decided to back Hudson's Hope's proposal.

Board of Trade drive
(Hudson's Hope Museum)

Plans began for a motor cavalcade starting at Hudson's Hope and continuing to Fort St. John, Dawson Creek, Little Prairie and back to the Hope. The cavalcade was reported by George Murray of the *Alaska Highway News,* and Rudy Schubert who took photographs and movies of the event.

"The Hudson's Hope Board of Trade is holding a banquet on Saturday, March 1 in the Community Hall," noted the *Alaska Highway News* on February 27, 1958. "This will be the climax of the road trip by car and truck via Fort St. John, Dawson Creek, Little Prairie, Moberly and Cameron Lakes. The crossing of the Peace will be approximately two miles up river from the village. G. Moore and E. Pollon have crews at work completing the last five miles of road. Good luck, folks!"

"We got off to a roaring start, leaving Hudson's Hope at six o'clock in the morning," says Earl Pollon. "We had a two-way radio with us to keep in contact with the men who had stayed behind to finish the construction work on the new road. It wasn't until we actually reached Little Prairie that we got our first word from the Hope: the Cats had just completed the work.

"By the time our cavalcade had careened over the freshly cut road, we were plastered with mud, having to stop to put chains on several of the vehicles enroute. We had only time to change before the celebrations began.

"We had been given permission to use the schoolhouse for the banquet, and it was a fine occasion. Over 400 people were fed that night. Although our board was heartily congratulated for our work, I felt a twinge of guilt at accepting such accolades. One of our most progressive oldtimers, Tom Jamieson (who had come to the country in 1912) had cut the first road south which came out on the east end of Moberly Lake (whereas ours came out on the west end) and followed around on the north shore to join onto the Jamieson Trail. But our objectives had been the same – to make an outlet to the south for Hudson's Hope."

October 1, 1958, was the date set by then premier W.A.C. Bennett for the inaugural Pacific Great Eastern Railway train to arrive at Little Prairie, via the Pine Pass from Prince George. Gordon Moore of the Fort St. John Lumber Company asked Earl Pollon if the Hudson's Hope board of trade would participate. Dawson Creek, Little Prairie, and Fort St. John had received grants to host a celebration, but the Hope had not gotten anything. The community decided to join in anyway, to promote interest in the new road.

"About the only thing we could see to take over for the celebration was a display of local produce to show what a fertile area Hudson's Hope was," Pollon recalls. "Some of our potatoes weighed up to five and one-half pounds each. We also had award-winning carrots, turnips, pumpkins and vegetable-marrows. Vine-ripened tomatoes had been pulled up September 30 with the vines still green. We also displayed top-quality alfalfa, timothy, sweet clover, oats, barley and wheat, plus a display of big game trophy heads."

Vesta Gething painted a water-colour mural, depicting the first train arriving in Little Prairie against a panorama of the north country. She had indicated the locations of all major cattle ranches, coal mines, oil derricks and, of course, the new road, which still required upgrading. Irvine Reschke had built a model coal mine complete with portals, cars and tracks, in a huge lump of coal from King Gething's mines.

The front of the Hudson's Hope booth portrayed the progress of the Pacific Great Eastern Railroad from start-up to present, with spur lines drawn to Dawson Creek and Fort St. John, then a big question mark at Hudson's Hope, where the town still waited.

Earl Pollon, pres. Board of Trade; The Hon. Ray Williston, Minister
of Lands and Forests; Gordon Moore, pres. Fort St. John Lumber Co.
(Hudson's Hope Board of Trade)

Pollon was invited onto the greeting committee platform in Fort St. John and Little Prairie to represent Hudson's Hope. He and other trade board members used the opportunity to talk to Ray Williston, minister of lands and forests, and Phil Gaglardi, minister of highways. They persuaded the ministers to accompany them on a trip as far as the passable road extended toward Hudson's Hope. When the board members explained why they needed the road, pointing out how many miles would be saved, the ministers agreed. Further, Gaglardi told them that "it was not a hard country to construct in."

In late fall of 1958, Bruce Woodsworth, geologist and site representative for Thomson-Houston Co. (Canada) Ltd., which was exploring in the area, hired Pollon's Cats to plough roads to King Gething's coal mines and down into the Peace River canyon. This would allow Boyle Brothers Drilling into the canyon to drill in search of a suitable dam site. The road into the canyon had been opened a few years earlier, but had sloughed in. The route had been originally built using horses in the 1920s, when the Gethings and the Aylards brought Aylard Mines into production.

Ploughing downhill on these narrow sloping trails was fairly straightforward, because the snow on the blades held the tractor on the path. Coming back up was a different story. Ice formed on the inside of the grade. At one point, Pollon's crawler started to slide over the edge, a 75 foot drop. "I quickly crawled onto the running board and powered only the outside track until I could swing the machine kitty-corner on the trail," Pollon says. "Clawing in that position, I crawled back up over the cogged section with about three feet of the heel of the track hanging over the edge. Scared? You bet."

In February, 1959, Gordon Moore asked the Hudson's Hope trade board to participate in a second cavalcade to be held on the anniversary of the first drive the previous year. The Hudson's Hope's board was expected to get the Peace River crossing ready a second time. "We took our entire mill crew into town and paid them regular wages to do the job, again using our equipment," says Pollon. "We also supplied several thousand feet of 4 by 12 planking to make the ice bridge on the north shore. Other local people, including Noel Verville and Archie Trail, donated money from their own pockets to help bring this venture about."

The second drive proved to be another success. From that point on, it was a go-ahead for the Hudson's Hope to Little Prairie highway, which was finally paved in 1966.

One day during the summer of 1959, Earl Pollon walked into Vaughn Gallichan's cafe in the old Western Hotel that Henry Stege had built in 1932. There sat the premier of British Columbia, W.A.C. Bennett, with his son and an R.C.M.P. constable. Pollon slipped back out without being seen and found Jim Mackenzie, vice president of the Social Credit party.

Pollon and Mackenzie returned to the cafe and started talking with the premier. Bennett told them he had "skipped out on his cabinet at Prince George," to come and have a look at Hudson's Hope before it was completely altered by the development from the construction of the Peace River dam. The two men suggested the premier take a first-hand look at the proposed dam site, which he had never seen.

"The premier was as excited as a boy as he stood on the sheer cut-banks at the Peace River Mines site, gazing at the raging waters 300 feet below," Pollon recalls. "His enthusiasm was contagious as he explained the enormity of the hydro project and what it would do for the entire province. He became so engrossed that time got away and he had to hurry to catch his plane at the little landing strip."

On November 14, 1963 an editorial titled "White Water" by Mary

Humphries appeared in the *Alaska Highway News*. It compared the rage of the river as it was tempered to flow through the diversion system with the frustration of local people shunted aside to accommodate the streamlined business of building a dam.

"Stand at the point where the Peace River pours out from its three tunnels," Humphries wrote, "and you will see a turmoil of raging white water. The water comes out from the tunnels green and smooth, but then the three streams join. As they meet they crash into the ridges of rock which cross the canyon floor. The result is a roaring and tossing of foaming waves, a violent contrast to calm green water a few feet away."

The same contrast could be seen in town. Most noticeable was a grand new hotel built in 1961 at the then extraordinary cost of $300,000. It stood majestically among the few commercial buildings, and dwarfed Henry Stege's once-dominant edifice six feet to its right. The Peace Glen Hotel opened to less than celebratory applause. Jack Scott and Len Norris, in the May 26, 1961 edition of the *Vancouver Sun*, described the decor of the cocktail lounge as "unforgivably designed by Vancouver's Lester Gellen." A green statue of a dinosaur, aglow with black light, rotated on an electric pedestal near a black leatherette bar studded with small pink buttons. "This particular evening," Scott and Norris said, "the place contained but one beer-drinker, a laconic fellow named Art Pollon, who tends the lime kilns down by the river." The Peace Glen stood "like a single gold tooth" among the scattered log cabins and shacks on Hudson's Hope main street, a rutted clay road leading to nowhere. Why was it there at all? The answer, said the reporters, was discovered on match folders in each room: Hudson's Hope is the site of the world's largest dam.

Notes

[1] *Peace River Chronicles*, p. 426.
[2] Ibid.

16

The Dam-Builders

The Peace Glen Hotel, by the fall of 1965, was rocking. The large chromium jukebox by the entrance of the hotel's coffee shop sent waves of Roger Miller's "King of the Road" out the door onto the street, crowded with men and vehicles of all descriptions. A bus stopped by the entrance, emptying its load of 40 swarthy men, who milled about the hotel lobby until a camp bus took them 16 miles up the canyon road to the Portage Mountain dam site.

We, the Mathesons, arrived on a snowy October evening in 1965, exhausted from having gotten stuck twice on the rutted, unpaved road from Chetwynd to Hudson's Hope.

Eyes lowered, I followed my husband Bill through the crowd of men in the hotel lobby, down a hall and into the bar.

The noise level was beyond berserk. Men surrounded every small bar table – more men than I had ever seen in one place. The bar seated 300, but if a customer bought four cases of beer from the off-sales counter, those cases became his chair. The Peace Glen registered more off-sales, at that time, than any hotel in British Columbia.

Bill steered me to the bar. "Tony, meet my wife," he said to a handsome, dark-haired man. He took my hand and kissed it. "Tony works with me," my husband explained. "We'll be living down the hall from him and Ann; they'll help you find your way around."

I looked out at the bar, and 300 pairs of eyes stared back. Then I realized there were only five women in the entire room. The scene was like the Klondike Gold Rush – men with money, and nowhere to spend it. Working men from all over the world were here, making wages they'd never dreamed of, building the largest earth-filled dam in the world.

We had come from Lethbridge, Alberta, following the circuitous path of most newly arrived inhabitants of Hudson's Hope. Bill had worked as purchasing agent for a meat packing company in

Lethbridge. I was a secretary for a car dealership. We had no money. A seven-dollar plumbing bill had to be budgeted over two weeks. The thought of being bound to this nickel-scrounging lifestyle set us on a path that would alter our lives. We sought the goal of others who headed north: a chance for something better.

I had planned to stay in Lethbridge, looking after our two-year-old daughter, Hayley, while Bill found a job and a place for us to live.

"We're moving to Hudson's Hope."

I held the phone for a moment, then asked the inevitable: "Where on earth is Hudson's Hope?"

"Near Fort St. John," Bill said. "A dam is being built here. I've already got a job."

"On the dam? What do you know about dams?"

Bill's tone was evasive. "Well, I'm not exactly working on the dam. The premier has a program to first employ northern B.C. labour, so I have to reside north of Prince George for 60 days before I can get on the project. But I got a job in the hotel."

"The hotel? What do you know about hotels?"

"I'm a janitor."

Long pause. Then Bill added: "I'm getting a promotion real soon. When the beer strike is over, I'll be a bartender."

I have always craved adventure, and this seemed the wrong time to call, "Whoa!" I gave notice, put the furniture in storage, and travelled to Lacombe to stay with my parents and await my husband's arrival. After some friendly parental advice to leave Hayley with them until Christmas because, said my mother, "God knows what he's taking you up to," we left to travel the 600 miles to Hudson's Hope.

Bill had tried to prepare me, but mere words could never have described the colour, sound and sense of excitement we found in the little village on the banks of the Peace River.

Our lodgings were simple: a room on the second floor of the old Henry Stege building, now unoccupied except for a small employment office and barbershop on the main floor. The barber, we were told, had previously lived in a cave near the riverbottom just outside the Lethbridge city limits. The room assigned to us had been used as a store room for extra hotel mattresses. We spent our first night in Hudson's Hope sleeping on a pile of at least six mattresses. I lay on this great mound, recalling the fairy tale of "The Princess and the Pea," and stared at the water-stained ceiling. Raucous noises intruded from the bar next door. I did not feel like a princess, and tried not to think of the strange lumps and hollows that I could feel beneath me.

Henry Stege building left foreground; Peace Glen Hotel behind
(B.C. Hydro/Gunnar Johanson)

When finally furnished, our room contained a single bed, some grey army blankets, a "Roxa-toned" dresser and a cracked mirror. Bill nailed a broomstick kitty-corner for a closet.

"We'll be sharing the bathroom at the end of the hall with five other couples who work in the hotel," he said.

"Well, we're only paying 25 dollars a month. What can you expect?"

The greater shock was to see Bill at his new job. A province-wide, four-month beer strike had just ended the day before he went "on the floor." He was 21, stood six-foot-two and weighed 150 pounds sopping wet. His dark horn-rimmed glasses gave him a studious "Buddy Holly" look, that seemed incongruous with the grizzled faces of the men he served. Business was so constant that the bartenders simply loaded trays with tall glasses of draft beer and raced around the bar until they were empty.

Bill's fellow bartenders were an interesting lot. Alex, (not his real name) of Yugoslavian origin, bore a resemblance to movie star Omar Shariff. He provided my first culture shock to Hudson's Hope.

On Alex's day off I happened to stop in down the hall to visit him and his wife Sue. Alex sat at the table, staring intently at two bottles of

Ne Plus Ultra scotch and one bottle of Mazola Oil. He uncapped the oil and took a big swallow, then tipped back one of the scotch bottles and drank long and hard. He sat back and looked at me. "Good for the stomach," he said, responding to my incredulous store. "Never get sick. You have to coat the stomach!" He sat there for the rest of the afternoon. He was right. He didn't get sick. He told stories: of the old country, of the hard times there and of his arrival in Canada in 1958. At first he had been sent to work in a bush camp in British Columbia. In response to the different food and water in the new country, Alex's body went on strike – for 15 days he suffered constipation. He recalled his father prescribing oil as a remedy; what kind of oil he did not remember. One day he waited near the mechanic's shop until it was deserted, then ran in and took a quart of motor oil. Back in his room he drank it . . . the whole quart, he claimed. It worked, though. His life as a Canadian began, he told me, with a can of motor oil and he hadn't looked back since.

I next met Tarzan. Of French-Canadian origin, Tarzan (René Frigon) had once been a successful contestant in body-building competitions. His nickname reflected his muscular build as well as his acrobatic ability. But a deep scar that ran down one cheek told of another life. That scar was the reason Tarzan no longer lived in Montreal pursuing the Mr. Canada title, but had escaped to the north and found his true destiny: a northern showman. He had married Beatrice, a quiet-spoken Cree Indian woman who made him exquisite beaded moosehide jackets and mukluks and fine fur hats. Their five-year-old son, Archie, was dressed like a young Davy Crockett. When I first saw the three of them riding behind Tarzan's galloping dog team through snowy fields, I knew I had indeed arrived in a world where adventurers were welcome.

Tarzan worked in the Peace Glen bar with Bill, and there he performed many interesting feats. He would grasp a metal pole that ran from floor to ceiling, then hold his body out straight and horizontal. He could do a back-flip with a 90-pound pack on his back, or run, non-stop, the 16 miles from town to the dam.

I then met Chips, who was 49 years old and did 49 push-ups every day. He and his wife, Edna, ran a gamey little place up on the hill in the Thompson subdivision, where there were wilder stories than any reported in the newspapers. Chips' job in the bar acquainted him with potential customers for his after-hours show.

In this male-dominated enclave, the dining room waitress, Ruth Kelly, was a respected anomaly. A smart-looking woman who had been raised in Hudson's Hope, her forthright Northern manner gave her a position among her fellow workers and customers of the hotel similar to that of Miss Kitty of the "Gunsmoke" television series. Kelly was a vital force in the hotel, and held nearly every job, from waitress to manager, during its 20-year existence.

Then there was Bill's boss during the first month, when he had worked as janitor before becoming bartender. Bob Jones, head janitor of the hotel, was nicknamed "the Sheriff." He even wore a sheriff's badge and, on his short fat frame, a western-cut shirt and cowboy hat. At night, when cleaning the hotel, he would play party records by Rusty Warren or Oscar Brand over the hotel's sound system.

I heard stories of other local celebrities – a man who was spending the winter in a stationwagon, raised up on wooden blocks and heated by a space heater plugged into a nearby house. Stranger yet, he had convinced a woman to move in with him! I met Donovan Levschuk, whose black beard and three-cornered felt hat made him resemble Blackbeard the pirate. He explained to me, in great detail, Carl Jung's theory of perfect marriage.

The Peace Glen Hotel seemed the pivotal point from which all people who entered town eventually fanned out. Bill and I ate at the hotel, slept next door to it, and got to know its employees and its customers. Then I went looking for a job myself.

Staff of Hudson's Hope Improvement District (later, District of Hudson's Hope) in front of log-cabin office. L to R: Dennis Geddes, Clerk Treasurer; Shirlee Matheson, Steno; Sandy Kruger, Steno

I applied first at the Bank of Commerce and, unfortunately, was successful. Every pay Friday, there were two-block-long lineups of men, sending vast money orders to their home countries. After working two weeks, wrestling with foreign exchanges, million-dollar payrolls and bank accounts that went up and down like yoyos, I gave two weeks notice and quit.

One day, I was having lunch with Bob McCrae, one of the bartenders, when he asked what kind of job I wanted.

"Well, I've got good typing and shorthand," I said. "I'd like an office job of some kind, if there are any offices here."

"There's always the dam," Bob said, "but it's pretty hard to get on up there. Union, you know. But I hear Dennis Geddes is looking for a secretary at the improvement district office. Why don't you go see him? He works in that little log cabin across from the liquor store."

It was not exactly the kind of office I had in mind. But, armed with a resumé and an envelope full of references, I went to see Dennis Geddes. He was eating his lunch. "Can you type?" he said, ignoring my papers.

"Yes."

"Got shorthand?" he asked, waving his sandwich.

"Yes."

"Start Monday," he said.

The office conducted the business of the Hudson's Hope Improvement District. The one-room log cabin contained a counter where business was transacted, a kitchen sink and cupboards at the back, and – in a cubbyhole the size of a broom closet - a toilet that only worked from late spring until freeze-up.

The chairman of the board of trustees was W.O. (Bill) Findlay, a good-hearted man who put the interests of the town squarely on the agenda. Employed as administrative supervisor for B.C. Hydro and Power Authority, which was building the dam, Findlay nevertheless urged townspeople to form delegations and travel to Victoria to publicize the riches of Hudson's Hope.

In November, 1965, the improvement district was dissolved under section 55 of the Water Act, and the town became an instant municipality. Voters elected King Gething as reeve, four local men (Marshall Ness, Ab Summer, Claude Stubley and Tom Jamieson), and two B.C. Hydro representatives (Bill Findlay and Ralph Spinney), as councillors. The first meeting of the municipal council was held on December 6, but for a time the two boards operated simultaneously, with separate meetings and sets of minutes. Dennis Geddes, former secretary treasurer of the improvement district, was now clerk-treasurer of the District of Hudson's Hope. I continued my role as the stenographer.

Bill Findlay predicted a bright future for the town. He said, at a meeting on December 14, 1965, that he "he would eat his shirt, with mustard on it, if the tourist count by the end of 1966 was not 100,000 to 125,000." Records of meetings detail the proposed local improvements: a new complex holding a proper town office, a fire hall and community hall, ambulance service and a clinic, a $400,000 storm sewer system, street paving and lighting programs, completion of an airstrip to be served by Pacific Western Airlines.

Bill continued working at the Peace Glen Hotel and I at the district office. We had a bird's eye view of local action, and began to feel part of the positive mood. We made friends quickly and through them, Bill was almost certain to get a job on the dam project as soon as we met our 60-day residency requirement.

Bill, born 300 miles downstream in the town of Peace River, felt at home in Hudson's Hope. The river setting reminded me of my childhood home on the banks of the Birdtail River, near Riding Mountain National Park in Manitoba. I had grown up beside the river, been warned as a child of its dangers, learned to respect its hidden currents, understood its seasonal flows.

When snow fell, the country changed. Travel by car became treacherous, so we stayed home and the village was our harbour. We had no television, poor radio reception, with only a province-wide CBC station or a crackling version of the Fort St. John channel.

In the Peace Glen bar, there was a never-ending flow of orange 50-dollar bills; each round included a generous tip for the bartender. In addition to bar sales, the liquor store, in 1966, was selling more than $80,000 of stock per month.

We started looking for a better place to live, and made plans to go home at Christmas and bring back our baby. We no longer feared this wild place. We saw, in Hudson's Hope and the dam, a future of steady pay cheques, a friendliness among people who brought talents and trades from all over the world, and a country of incomparable beauty.

Mary Humphries, in her "White Water" editorial in the *Alaska Highway News*, evaluated the newcomers. "To them, it's a job of work in a lovely setting. They are trying, with good success, to adapt themselves to a strange place and to create for themselves a satisfactory life ... [but] how can people who come here from Vancouver know how a backwoodsman feels?"

I hadn't really considered how the backwoodsmen might feel about our invasion. I had met a few local people, those on council and others who visited the district office to pay their utility bills. But I had yet to discover what was in their hearts.

One day, Bill returned from his shift at the bar in a jovial mood. "Get on your coat," he said, "I've met a man you're going to love."

We walked back to the Peace Glen Hotel, its lights gleaming in the snowy night, and opened the bar door. The warm air turned to a plume of fog as it escaped outside. Bill led me to the back of the bright, noisy room. Sitting alone at a table was a man in his fifties. His long grey hair was combed straight back, curling on his neck. He wore a beaded moosehide jacket, with long swaying fringes. Bill pulled out a chair for me at the table, and the man stood up, holding out his hand.

"Shirlee, I'd like you to meet Earl Pollon," Bill said, and called for a round.

17

Labour Unrest

Earl Pollon had written what he described as the annals of history of Hudson's Hope. His manuscript was partly typed, although some chapters in longhand were stored in various boxes. Earl also had a collection of poems which he asked me to look at. Thus began our friendship.

Earl's words revealed the heartbeat of the Peace valley. I came to understand the lifestyles that had been enjoyed (and in some cases, endured) by the people, and why the hydro project had initially been welcomed.

"Before the dam, making a living in Hudson's Hope was 'catch as catch can,'" Earl admitted. "Then came the dam, which we thought would turn the country around.

"I worked on the dam for a goddamned short time. When I walked off it, I walked off it permanently. I was just being bullheaded of course, but I was highly opposed to it anyhow and the lies they were peddling when they started diverting the river through the tunnels."

Having turned his back on the project, Earl incorporated as a publisher and began to put out a weekly newspaper. It seemed time to publish his "Centennial book of verse and prose of the North," *Beneath These Waters*, through his Hudson's Hope Publishing Co. Ltd. The little book, illustrated by Colleen Smith with a cover painting by Frances Nikon, sold 2,500 copies.

Earl wrote a letter, published in the November 21, 1963 *Alaska Highway News*, that portrayed the clash between old and new cultures in the Peace valley.

> Oldtimers, do you remember the trail from here to Fort St. John? Guy Robison: 'Come on in, put up your team.' Donald McDonald: 'Hoot mon, come in an' hae a bite.' The Ardills: 'Come on in, I'm sure you have the time, you can stay overnight.' Phil Tompkins: 'Put

those nags in the barn, and we'll visit awhile.' The Dopps, Barney and Sadie: 'You're as welcome as the flowers in May.' And of course at Charlie Lake there were the Southwicks, Powells, and the Somans, friendly people all.

West of Hudson's Hope was Jack Thomas: 'Sure, I'll take your boat across the portage; if you haven't got the money that's all right, you can give me a day or two's work.' Gold Bar, end of trail, Jim Beattie: 'You may as well stick around a couple of days until the weather clears; I have to go to the Hope myself. I'd enjoy your company.'

These are only some of the men and women who helped to pioneer this country. Is this the kind of country that they dreamed of building? I think not. A country that is swallowed by a Frankenstein monster called BCH (B.C. Hydro).

The letter complained about everything from the apostrophe s disappearing from the name of the post office (now called Hudson Hope), to the names of nearby mountains suddenly being changed:

> Portage Mountain . . . that name came wandering in here lately from somewhere and jumped onto Bullhead Mountain. Bullhead got excited and galloped across the valley and jumped onto Butler Mountain. Butler got scared, expecting to get the s kicked out of him the same as Hudson's Hope had, and he took off. Anyone knowing the whereabouts of Butler, tell him it is all right to come back.

Earl then worked himself into a frenzy over the rush of dam contracts that did not respect local residents, either in the acquisition of their properties or employing them on the project.

> Throw the land open for purchase or lease. Give us back our rights to barter and trade, the rights to elect by popular vote the men who shall represent our schools, our improvement board, our ratepayers. All this should be without a man sitting there without being elected, yet indirectly controlling the whole district. Is it too much to ask for men who are being pushed, kicked, shoved, ignored, trampled in this mad rush to build this dam? Are the powers afraid the river will dry up?
>
> Mind you, I fully agree with the construction of this dam. It can and will bring industries in here. It, without the least doubt, will bring wealth, and of course that automatically improves the standards of living for all. But I'm damned if I can see where it is necessary to have all this mad rush, rumble and pressure.

The dam was the greatest thing to happen to the town, even Earl said so. So why his anger? What were the lies he spoke of? Why did his poems rage:

God! How I hate it! Yes, hate it!
I wish this dam project in hell!
With all this rumble and racket
I'd sooner hear harness and bell!

And why did they end with a frightened plea:

"I'm afraid . . . I shake like a child.
I long for a silence to last.
My body's arrived at this epoch,
My soul remains in the past.

Dennis Geddes, administrator of first the improvement district (1963 to 1965) and then the District of Hudson's Hope (1965 to 1974), agreed with many of Pollon's points.

"Hydro milked the town," Geddes said. "It was even impossible at times to get a doctor, dentist or the medical clinic without taxing the locals . . . The taxes from the construction of the two schools should have been borne by Hydro instead of by the locals."

Pollon's charge that unelected officials were running the show was true, Geddes agreed. "Once the legislation changed whereby resident-electors (rather than owner-electors) could vote at civic elections, Hydro controlled the voters' list and could pretty well place who they wanted on the council."

The council passed special bylaws to permit temporary accommodation of the transient population during the construction heyday.

The little log St. Peter's Anglican church.
Still used. Built in 1938
(E.K. Pollon)

"Hydro should have left the townsite alone rather than integrating it with trailers and changing the way of life for the people who lived here before the dam days," said Geddes.

"I never felt the powers-to-be intended that Hudson's Hope would benefit to any degree from the construction of the dam. Only a few people felt they could prosper by way of land sales. The promise of a hospital went to Chetwynd, and the railhead was never extended. Basically, everything was pretty well what you would find in an instant town."

Newspapers in the Peace district devoted substantial coverage to Hudson's Hope's plight. A *B.C. Digest* article (reprinted in the February 13, 1964 edition of the *Alaska Highway News*) noted that another historical building was being threatened: St. Peter's Church. "In the December, 1960 cover story we featured a famous northern landmark – St. Peter's log church at Hudson's Hope. Built by volunteer labour in 1936-1938, it is the only church in the community. But progress has arrived at the tiny settlement on the banks of the Peace River. The $600-million Peace River hydro complex is under construction just a few miles upstream, and as part of the project, a new highway is proposed through the community. Apparently the route under consideration cleaves the church grounds, and if approved, the church must go. . . . Stand up and fight, Hudson's Hope! Don't lose your identity completely."

Other stories reported progress on the work, and how proud B.C. Hydro chairman Gordon M. Shrum was of the project.

B.C. Forest Products announced a $60-million pulp and lumber complex for the Peace River area that would employ 3,000 people. Long-term investment plans, including the establishment of a new townsite on the upper Parsnip River, totalled $150 million. The pulp mill and sawmill would begin production in 1968, to coincide with power generation from the dam. Timber logged from the huge 300-mile-long reservoir would feed the mills.[1]

The provincial bureau of economics and statistics, in a 1966 report,[2] confidently foresaw the dam and its reservoir as being instrumental to future industries in the area. The reservoir could offset the high cost of transport associated with a sawmilling and plywood industry, because water transport was considerably cheaper than land transport. Likewise, the Pacific Great Eastern Railway extension from Kennedy to "a point on the Peace River reservoir" would provide access to a vast area containing forest and mineral resources. Demand for Peace River coal was expected to come from offshore markets such as Japan.

A lead-zinc deposit about 20 miles west of Fort Grahame on the Ingenika River had been discovered, but remained unexploited because of high transportation costs. When the Peace River reservoir reached maximum height, ore or concentrates could be barged from the mine to the Kennedy rail extension for shipment.

The bureau's report concluded that the largest and most significant development in the region was construction of the Portage Mountain dam. Apart from the boost to the local economy, and a valuable recreational asset in the form of a 680-square-mile lake, the region would benefit from abundant and cheap power.

In a letter published in the *Alaska Highway News* on February 13, 1964, R.M. Dundas, resident manager for B.C. Hydro, stated that, "in starting development of the Peace River, B.C. Hydro wanted to achieve a maximum of labour-management stability and prevent, as far as possible, any dislocation of provincial economy by labour problems at the project. Peace Power Constructors was formed to meet these objectives. The firm provides the work force for contractors at the project site and handles all labour relations matters.

"Wage rates and working conditions are governed by a 10-year collective labour agreement signed with the Allied Hydro Council of British Columbia (comprised of 18 international unions representing 28 jointly certified B.C. locals and Peace Power Constructors). Peace Power Constructors carries out all hiring through the National Employment Service. The main requirement is that they be competent. It is not a requirement that prospective workers be union members before employment, but they must be prepared to secure union membership immediately after employment." Dundas added that preference would be given to local residents who were union members.

The Allied Hydro Council was the voice for people working on the project. For the first time in the history of B.C. construction, one body could bargain for all trade unions.[3]

But this smooth-sounding system had a rocky beginning. In 1962, local men were put "on permit" to work for Bedford Construction, clearing timber on both sides of the dam site. These were one-to-two month jobs, which the local men dubbed "free manpower standby." In February, 1963, notices went up in Hudson's Hope for a meeting of the "Local Labour Grievance Committee." There, a set of questions was presented to B. Milner, Allied Hydro Council representative for Local 168 (Rock and Tunnel Workers, commonly called the labourers' union). The Local Labour Grievance Committee prepared a report of Milner's responses:

Q: Why are local men not being hired on the Peace Power project?

A: Mr. Milner seemed to be quite unaware that the local men were not being hired. He stated that approximately 250 so-called local men had been hired up to February 15, 1963; to his knowledge, only one Local 168 man had been hired from Vancouver.

Q: Why are local men not admitted to any union but 168?

A: The question was not answered by Mr. Milner because it had nothing to do with him.

Q: Difficulties on joining various unions?

A: Any time any man is working on the project and wishes to join 168, he is to contact his steward or Mr. Milner. He has 15 days to join 168.

Q: Local union mens' problems?

A: Any 168 union questions can be answered by Mr. Milner or the Job Steward of 168. These men may be contacted through the Peace Power Construction office.

Harley Pollon, Earl's son, was hired as a labourer on the diversion tunnels, but fired before he even started work. Management said he did not have two years' cement and underground experience. It was then that, Earl, along with a group of local young men, confronted Bill Wilson, site representative for Allied Hydro Council.

"What about the rule to employ local people?" Earl demanded. "What about the five bus loads of Portuguese that came in last night? We want to see their papers. These mens' last address was Portugal! Some of them were in Canada only four hours before they got here. They were signed up for the job on the boat by the government."

Wilson ordered Earl out of his office.

Harley and 12 others began a protest, firing off a letter to Premier W.A.C. Bennett. Several days later, Harley was told to report for work on the graveyard shift and invited to join the union.

The *Alaska Highway News* reported, on November 14, 1963 that 75 percent of the men hired for Kiewit [-Dawson-Johnson, the general contractors] were from Hudson's Hope, and B.C. Hydro maintained that 60 percent of the labour force was local. But those figures didn't ring true to the residents.

"Lately I keep wishing that I was born Italian so I could really feel at home in Canada," wrote a Fort St. John resident, identified only as "Shortchanged" in the *Alaska Highway News* on November 28, 1963. "If you go to Hudson's Hope and plan to visit a beer parlour, an Italian dictionary is your biggest asset. Otherwise you are at complete loss."

On February 6, 1964, the same publication reported that "a study of the Kiewit-Dawson-Johnson payroll reveals that 75 percent of the men hired in the last month for work on the damsite are local residents (from Hudson's Hope)."

That same month B.C. Hydro claimed that "about 60 percent of all men hired for work at Portage Mountain Dam site last year were residents of the Peace River District." Also, said the company, "of the total of some 2,100 men hired at various times during the year, over 1,200 of these were Peace River District men, who were paid an estimated $2,500,000 in wages."

On March 5, 1964, the *Alaska Highway News* carried a front-page headline: "UNEMPLOYED DEMAND LOCAL WORK FOR LOCAL MEN – 80 Men Sign Brief to Labour Minister." Their appeal went to Leslie R. Peterson, minister of labour. They asked firstly for work, and then for fairness in listing all civil service jobs with the employment service. The men also requested an investigation into the government's minimum wage scale in every category, and into all welfare grants in northern B.C. They called on the federal government to establish a national employment office in Fort St. John. The men asked that the closest labour supply to any project (including the Peace River dam) be utilized. Of the 80 men who signed the petition, average length of residence was four years. Seventy-five percent were union men. Ninety percent were unemployed.

"Within six weeks after the letter was written to the premier," said Earl, "there was not a man left unemployed in Hudson's Hope. After that, local employment became a first. When a local person became 18, he automatically had a job."

A.C. Geddes, Dennis Geddes' brother, came to Hudson's Hope with his family in 1962 in search of spinoff opportunities from the dam project. He and his father had been working in Fort Nelson, but after two winters in muskeg country with a lot of snow and no frost, the oil business was in a slump.

The Geddes' first bought the taxi business, which A.C.'s brother, Gary, ran the first winter while A.C. stayed logging at a mill in Fort Nelson. A.C. described the scene upon his arrival in Hudson's Hope in the spring of 1963:

"Hudson's Hope was a town that had been there for years and years, a coal town. They had Gethings to haul their coal for them. They'd shoot their own moose, some would go out and do a bit of work for a few months in Fort St. John or somewhere, pull in a little bit of money, some trapped, a lot were retired. They put in their gardens and, even if they didn't have anything, life was good. They didn't have any worries. And they looked after each other.

"Then all of a sudden they were putting a dam in. And all of a sudden they've got taxes to pay. And all of a sudden roads were getting paved, and sewers installed, and some of the older people rejected this . . .

"When I arrived they had already let the contract for the diversion tunnels. That was supposed to be a nine-month job and employ 1,200 people, most of them miners. The taxi business got quite busy. Then they let out the next contract that Kiewit-Dawson-Johnson got, plus smaller contracts for diamond drilling and different ones. Basically you had to be in the union to go to work there, or if you had a job you could get in the union, kind of a Catch 22.

"As the job got going there were about 1,500 men working there at one time. Our taxi company would get calls from Peace Power Constructors to pick up people coming in on the bus and bring them into camp, or to go into Fort St. John to get some men at the airport and bring them out to camp.

"Usually the people we picked up were Italian or Portuguese general labourers. I'd ask, 'Where did you come from?' 'Well, from Italy, Edmonton, Fort St. John, and now I'm in Hudson's Hope.' That was the route, or through Vancouver, all within a few days . . . we were told that the men actually knew when they left Italy that they had jobs in Hudson's Hope at the dam. It was ironic because people from Fort St. John or Dawson Creek were having a tough time getting work at Hudson's Hope...

The taxi business got the Geddes family involved in the adventurous spirit that prevailed in the early 1960s in Hudson's Hope.

"We ended up having seven cars, working three shifts, in a little town that had only about 100 people at the beginning, and then just went crazy as contracts were let and more and more men became employed at the dam.

"On pay weekends, we got in our cars on Friday and got out of them Monday morning. It was a hard life. We would go to the liquor store in Hudson's Hope for them, buy a case of Drambui, a case of scotch, half-a-dozen cases of beer and away we'd go. These miners were hard-living people. All my taxi trips were drunk-related. Hardly any miner had a driver's licence. They didn't like to fly; there were a lot of superstitions among miners – like there couldn't be women underground in the tunnels. We even had an Econoline bus to haul their crews, who'd get off on Friday on a long shift-change, and they'd all climb in and want to go to Fort St. John one day and to Dawson Creek for the other day. And we'd have to stay with them the whole time. The bill might be $1,000 for the weekend, but they'd all chip in, no problem. The miners were very honest."

Geddes learned, as I did while working at the bank, that most construction earnings went directly out of the country. Immediately after the dam was finished, there was a mass exodus. "I can't imagine that those people stayed here in Canada after the dam was completed," Geddes said. "They just went back home."

The money that wasn't dutifully sent home was quickly wasted on gambling.

"The people who lived in those camps were very hard people," Geddes said. "Men came from Quebec who didn't even have jobs, but would stay out at camp with friends, sleep in their beds when they were on shift, just so they could work the gambling halls. I can remember seeing thousands of dollars sitting on a poker table, in the rec hall."

The Mounties were often called in to handle situations that turned ugly at the drop of a hat. "There was a fight one night at camp where they just wrecked one complete trailer unit," Geddes said. "The police were called, and they phoned us to go up with them. When they saw the brawl, they wouldn't go into it. They couldn't do a thing, except just contain it to the one wing. Lots of times the police called us to maybe take some miners to town, or send them home. The police were very diplomatic. There would be a disturbance in the Peace Glen Hotel and the police would phone us and say, 'We've got some passengers for you.'"

Geddes said his Hudson's Hope Taxi was always ferrying drunks from the Peace Glen bar. "The hotel was going like crazy, and the first bartenders were pimps. And they had some girls going. The miners decided they didn't like this and they got the bartenders outside the bar – there must have been 100 people outside the bar, everybody – and there were some really bad fights. They had a young policeman there and he didn't even have a gun. He only had his flashlight. He came in waving this flashlight and telling everybody to back off, and

Diversion tunnel outlets
(B.C. Hydro/Gunnar Johanson)

it was pretty ugly. One guy said something and he hit him on the head with the flashlight, and that broke the whole thing up."

By 1965, construction of the project was well underway. An $18-million contract had been completed on the diversion tunnels to temporarily divert the river's flow and allow dam construction on the dry river bed. Three, 48-foot-diameter tunnels had been drilled and blasted about 2,500 feet through a bend in the west canyon wall. The tunnels, carved from one million cubic yards of rock, were lined with more than 160,000 cubic yards of concrete. On September 14, 1963, Premier W.A.C. Bennett had pushed a plunger on seven and one-half tons of explosives, obliterating the last barrier across the mouth of the diversion system.

A low cofferdam had been built to direct the flow into the three tunnels, turning the river away from its centuries-old course. This cofferdam could control the river during the late-season low flow, but contractors had to work triple shifts to beat the heavy spring run-off. A second, larger cofferdam was built at break-neck speed directly behind the first. The second structure ran 1,100 feet across the river channel to a height of 130 feet, and would later become a part of the main dam. The diversion system could handle 320,000 cfs (cubic feet per second). In early June, 1964, the runoff inched toward this mark and continued to rise. Emergency work began to raise the upstream cofferdam another 15 feet. Fortunately, the weather cooled and the river peaked at 311,000 cfs.

Earl Pollon was angry at the rushed, slap-dab construction. "The river came up to the top of the temporary earth-filled cofferdam with the 15-foot dike on top," he said. "They were on television telling everyone there was no danger. But I learned from talking to the men working on the project that they had loaded the top with powder to blow the cofferdam just in case, so the whole river would not come through at once. They found out I was up there taking pictures and they put up a good show so I couldn't get over to the other side of the river. They asked King Gething how high the water could go, and he said it was not as high yet as it was during the 1948 flood.

"They had put gates on all the little creeks to test the water levels and speed for four years, and that's all they were using as an estimate. In 1964 when the water did go high that threw them completely. The man doing the estimates had every truck available hauling dirt to build up that dyke. He was some kind of religious guy and left Bibles in all the hotel rooms. For good reason."

Tunnels were drilled to stabilize the dam's bedrock foundation and canyon walls. Cement and water were injected into each tunnel, filling all the cracks in the rock with a cement, sand and water mixture, called grout. Before the fill was placed, the river bed was sealed with gunite (a pneumatically applied sand-cement mixture, later called "shotcrete").

D-9 Caterpillars at South Moraine pushing fill material
on to 3 mile long conveyor belt
(B.C. Hyrdor/Gunnar Johanson)

On the glacial moraine, D-9 Cats fitted with oversize blades bulldozed fill into portable hoppers, where the material was transported across the moraine on shuttle conveyors.

Conveyor belt
(E.K. Pollon)

Next came the $10-million earth-moving and processing system. This system, 15,000 feet long and 66 inches wide, was the world's longest continuous belt, high-capacity conveyor. The belt, moving at up to 12.5 miles per hour, was driven by four 850-horsepower motors. Every hour, this system could deliver 12,000 tons of material to the processing plant, where it was screened, washed and delivered to the damsite.

In 1965, construction began on the powerhouse (67 feet wide and 890 feet long, located 500 feet below bedrock) and on the 10 giant penstocks, which would conduct the water down from the reservoir through steep shafts. Work also started on a 574-mile, 500-kilovolt transmission line to carry power to Vancouver.

The dam predicted years ago by oldtimer Neil Gething was becoming a reality.

Notes

[1]*Alaska Highway News*, Feb. 6 1964.

[2]*The Peace River-Liard Region*, An Economic Survey, March, 1966, Bureau of Economics & Statistics, Dept. of Industrial Development, Trade and Commerce, Victoria, B.C.

[3]"Hudson Hope – the Past, the Present and the Future" by Trev Schofield, published by Western Canadian Directories Ltd. in cooperation with the Hudson Hope Chamber of Commerce and the merchants of Hudson Hope, 1967

18

Good Intentions

The District of Hudson's Hope was the second-largest municipal district in the province, encompassing 360 square miles. By June, 1966, there were 5,300 to 5,500 people in the area – almost 3,000 of them working on the dam project.

Hudson's Hope's unique status was emphasized in a meeting on April 18, 1966 between the local council and Mr. C.H.L. Woodward of the municipal administration division in Victoria. Woodward agreed it would be difficult to compare the municipality with the standards in the Municipal Act, because the concessions made due to the hydro project were too involved to set out in writing. He stressed that the government was doing all it could to assist the district, and assured the council that Hudson's Hope would not be stuck with a mill rate beyond its capacity.

It seemed, however, that B.C. Hydro would live up to its promises. H.P. O'Donnell, construction manager, assured the council that Hydro would stand by its offer to build a fire hall and office building, on the condition that the municipality obtain the lots, for which Hydro would reimburse them.

Not all corporate suggestions met positive responses. N. Paget, project manager for the general contractors, Kiewit-Dawson-Johnson, attended a council meeting on August 4, 1966. Paget spoke about the necessity of proper zoning and having a "community development plan." Records show that reeve King Gething replied that "it was the intention of council to promote development in Hudson's Hope," and he questioned how long Kiewit-Dawson-Johnson would remain in the area.

Gething, one of the best-known characters in the Peace River country, was a man of few words and soft voice. He had more ability than any one man has a right to, and somewhat eccentric habits. He was an outstanding electrician, radio expert, and river-boat operator.

He knew every path and person in the country, from years of hauling freight and supplies for prospectors, and carrying mail from Hudson's Hope to Finlay Forks and Fort Grahame. Gething walked with a long, over-reaching sway of the snowshoe stride, a mile-eating pace that appeared slow but allowed him to continue hour after hour.

Once, he took a geologist on a trip upriver. The man was in a hurry.

"We really must get going, Mr. Gething!"

Gething continued preparing at his own pace.

"We really must hurry, Mr. Gething! My time is worth 10 dollars an hour!" the man said impatiently.

Gething stopped in his tracks. "By Jove, you're lucky," he said, in his slow drawl. "I doubt if my time is worth over 20 cents an hour, straight across the board. Heh! Heh! Heh!"

When presiding over council meetings, Gething adopted the same pace. His dress reflected his casual attitude. His usual outfit consisted of a plaid flannel shirt, black wool pants held by a strap of leather – knotted rather than buckled – heavy wool socks and moccasin rubbers. During the meeting, he would gradually undress, loosening his top shirt buttons, letting out the tied belt, shucking off his rubbers, and rubbing his socks down his ankles until they lay matted on the floor beneath his feet. But his attention to the agenda never wavered. He was adamant that Hudson's Hope should benefit from the invasion of progress.

The records of the improvement district meetings are riddled with the good intentions of the town fathers to build a future for the residents of Hudson's Hope. On July 15, 1965, for example, "Letters to Dr. Paul C. Trussell, Director, B.C. Research Council, and the Honourable Donald L. Brothers, Minister of Mines and Petroleum Resources, were forwarded, requesting information towards attracting industry to this area to fill the vacuum that will be created when construction of the Peace Power project concludes in 1969-70."

Trussell responded on August 19 that "the Hydro Authority has given quite a bit of attention to the industrial potential of the area and some companies are eyeing it closely – but this does not mean that all possible avenues have been explored." Improvement district chairman W.O. Findlay said some companies were exploring the use of Hudson's Hope's limestone, used extensively in the carbide industry. A discussion arose about the attractive bus-power rates (wholesale rates at the power-generating source, which are cheap because they exclude distribution costs) being offered by B.C. Hydro for industries locating within a 30-mile radius of the power project.[1]

A letter from Dr. Trussell on October 18, 1965, again elicited hope among the board of trustees. Trussell indicated that the Japanese required substantial amounts of coal which could be obtained from the Hudson's Hope area. Chairman Findlay stated that businessmen in town, through the local chamber of commerce, should spend more time and effort in meeting with these people, and encouraging industry *to take advantage of the 30-mile radius, on-site power rates made available by B.C. Hydro for this purpose* (authors' italics).

Finally an idea was presented that seemed to have some potential. General Electric Co. Ltd. was considering locating a heavy water plant in the area. The proposal was hotly debated by council, which had to decide how best to use $150 allocated for luring the firm to Hudson's Hope. Councillor Spinney concluded that "if we send delegations to every company who expressed interest in locating a factory in Hudson's Hope, much time and money would be needlessly spent, whereas if a brief was prepared explaining resources, availability of power, etc. it would be more beneficial to the district."

But reeve King Gething argued that if he and councillor Tom Jamieson travelled to Victoria, it would be more beneficial.

They made the trip shortly thereafter. Both oldtimers, unmarried (Jamieson was a widower) and of thrifty dispositions, they supplied themselves for the journey so they wouldn't overburden taxpayers with high-priced restaurant tabs. Jamieson took along a jug of homemade stew, and Gething a carton of orange pop and a fruit cake.

General Electric eventually chose a maritime location for their heavy-water plant, and another hope was dashed.[2]

From the air, Hudson's Hope was no longer a sleepy little mountain village. Mary Humphries, in the *Alaska Highway News* on December 24, 1963, offered a glimpse of a community being altered daily:

"We don't know what the population was of Bethlehem 2,000 years ago, but we do know that it was a little town set among the hills, just like Hudson's Hope. From the air . . . the town looks so small and the bush so vast. We could see each trailer court laid out like matchsticks . . . the road to Fort St. John winding along the river's edge like a dangerous goat trail.

"Then we came to a great gash in the all-embracing bush, where every stick had been cleared. It was the north moraine, the clearing for the gravel fill which will make the dam. We flew over the damsite, with the water running through the tunnels. Here the hillside is cleared on both sides, showing plainly the outline of the dam-to-be. The KDJ (Kiewit-Dawson-Johnson) camp could be seen close to the work area, and further off on the hillside was the IPEC (International

Power and Engineering Consultants) camp. Winding away west-
wards was the river, and the old road to Gold Bar.

"But there is something new on the scene upriver. There are more
white areas in the bush where Fort St. John Lumber have hauled away
uncounted loads of lumber from the flood area. Drive along the Gold
Bar road and you don't see much of this huge lumber operation, but
from the air the cleared patches show up plainly, and also the size of
the task.

"At the damsite, whistles blow and things go 'boom.' A boom-
town used to be a wild and lawless place. But our little town isn't like
that."

Hudson's Hope quickly took on a new look: attractive subdivisions of bungalows and townhouses replaced open fields of brush
dotted with old shacks. But these houses were not for sale. They were
for the upper-echelon of B.C. Hydro and its contractors. The labour
force lived where they could; trailer parks and skid-shacks
mushroomed

In 1966, the town secured lots for the new municipal office and
fire hall complex. But first the old community hall had to be torn
down and burned. I stood among the oldtimers as the flames licked
toward the sky, listening to them comment on the symbolism of the
burning hall. I had attended several dances there during the past year.
I could envision the glowing pot-bellied stove in the corner, the
counter where the ladies' club sold pop and hot dogs. There was an
outside toilet set off in the trees. With a friend for company, you
would try to negotiate the dark path toward the cold outhouse,
through haphazardly parked vehicles, and past men passing jugs.
Even from there you could still hear the strong beat of butterfly
dances, schottisches, waltzes and two-steps played by Keray Regan,
Claude and Noreen Stubley and the band. Couples danced round and
round on a floor so decrepit you had to wear boots, for fear that heels
of dancing shoes would catch on a broken board.

Construction workers would stand around the dance floor, and
read the names on the walls: visitors from Whitehorse in the Yukon,
Yellowknife, Newfoundland . . . all over the country. A construction
man would ask a local girl to dance and away they'd whirl, the
rhythm the same wherever they learned it. When the set ended, the
girl might sink into an overstuffed chair by the side of the hall to catch
her breath, or watch a fight break out on the dance floor. Claude Stubley, a big man and not to be fooled with, might jump off the stage, pry
the participants apart, fling one out the door, then hop back up on
stage – not missing more than a couple of bars.

We had some good times. But the hall had outlived its usefulness.

So what if the local people had donated concrete for its foundation, and lumber and nails and windows? Even the wavy floor was the result of a "this could happen only in Hudson's Hope" story of a feud between the builders, Earl Pollon and Mel Kyllo. Hydro was paying for a new hall, weren't they?

Community Hall
(Hudson's Hope Museum)

I stood with the oldtimers and watched the flames, with Earl beside me taking pictures for his paper, for his memories.

Our next dance was held in the basement of the new civic complex. The highly polished floor, tile over concrete, amplified the sound of a hundred stomping boots and a hundred clicking heels. "Please remove your shoes," we were asked. "Spike heels cause chips and black marks in the tile." The R.C.M.P. patrolled the parking lot, for it was considered quite improper to be drinking on civic property. The band did its best to excite the crowd into the usual party mood. But it was an effort and we all knew it. At one o'clock, when the dance wound down, we dutifully trooped out to our cars. The northern lights whipped over the hills on the south side of the Peace River. On our way home to Lynx Creek, four miles from town, we tried to figure out what we had lost. Things were moving too fast to keep track.

We had bought a small trailer located, with several others, on a point where Lynx Creek emptied into the Peace. That winter, the river froze solid as usual, and we didn't believe it when we were told this was the last year it would freeze. Bill had grown up on the Peace River; to him, the ice forming in winter and the tremendous break-up in spring were part of a cycle as natural as life itself. Betting pools sprang up to guess break-up date. Earl said the latest he could remember the river breaking in Hudson's Hope was May 11. We watched and listened, but the white silence seemed eternal.

In early May we felt the groans before we heard them – like an animal awakening. We ran to the riverbank. Huge floes of ice from the canyon bumped their way downstream, free-flowing in open channels in the river, piling in mounds high as houses along the sides. Some chunks were grey with rot, some shone silver in the sunlight. They seemed alive.

It *was* the last winter we saw such antediluvian forces at play. After the dam began generating power, the river remained open for many miles, well into the neighbouring province of Alberta.

District of Hudson's Hope staff, 1966: L to R:
Dennis Geddes; King Gething; Shirlee Matheson;
Sharon Findlay; Janet Heard; Roger Porter

I continued working at the district office – now in the new civic complex – and as court reporter for inquests and hearings. The magistrate was Earl's old cohort, Mel Kyllo. His qualifications? Who knew? Who asked? But for the most part he did a good job, based on common sense. Even when all lay magistrates in British Columbia were named judges, and he ruled the Hudson's Hope court as Judge Kyllo, his credentials were never questioned.

Kyllo ordered more inquests than hearings. Some of the deaths seemed obviously due to natural causes. But some that occurred on the damsite were grisly. Sometimes there were two inquests a week, each producing 25 foolscap pages of shorthand notes.

I tried not to think about the man whose demise was discussed so clinically while the doctor's report was read, then so emotionally when the man's friend testified as a witness. Some of the descriptions were so graphic that I expected the body to be wheeled into the court-room as Exhibit A, to be prodded by interested court attendants.

"Just where *is* the body?" I recall asking Marv Young, the attending R.C.M.P. corporal, about one case.

"In the magistrate's woodshed."

"Mel Kyllo's woodshed! But that's awful!"

"It's not so bad," he responded. "They keep the lights on."

When I complained to Earl Pollon about the impropriety of using the magistrate's woodshed for a morgue, he was nonplussed. "Better than it used to be," he said. "We used to keep them in a chicken house."

The young doctor, Doug Jack, was officially employed by the dam contractor. But he also kept a practice in town, because he was the only medical officer within 40 miles. He told me once of his embarrassing experience of delivering a body to the magistrate's woodshed-cum-morgue. There had been a heavy snowfall, and the little hill up to Mel Kyllo's place was just too steep for the doctor's Volkswagen van. It got stuck midway. There was nothing to do but try and carry the body the rest of the way. Rigor mortis and freezing temperatures had left the corpse in an awkward, arm-flung position. The doctor attempted to carry, then drag, the twisted form up the hill through 18 inches of snow. Then the jacket started to come off the body. The doctor grabbed an arm and tugged the corpse along, half-undressing the departed. Only then did he notice the row of trailers, every curtain window parted to reveal eyes peering out in horror at this macabre scene in the snow.

The incident did not, however, affect the doctor's business. At one time he had 200 pregnant women as patients, myself included.

Such tales were commonplace, and each evening of story-telling would end with the comment: "Only in Hudson's Hope!"

"The years went by, on promise and lie," Earl said. Soon the dam was completed and the dedication ceremonies held. On September 12, 1967, we gathered at the dam site and "paid tribute to Premier William Andrew Cecil Bennett whose vision and confidence in the future of British Columbia inspired the success of this great project from its initial conception to its ultimate completion."

The motto on the invitation said, "Every man's work shall be made manifest."

The public relations department of B.C. Hydro and Power Authority could never have coined a more prophetic phrase.

L to R: Premier W.A.C. Bennett and area residents,
Tom Jamieson; Guy Robison; Bill Bradon

Notes

[1]In a letter to the authors from B.C. Hydro dated May 15, 1989, C.W.J. Boatman, vice president of corporate affairs, says the corporation has not located any information suggesting that industry was offered reduced power rates to locate within a 30-mile radius of the Bennett Dam.

In a B.C. Hydro public affairs release dated February 4, 1982, regarding the Site C hearings (for a third dam to be located on the Peace River, approximately 65 miles downstream of the Bennett Dam), Energy Minister Robert McClelland said it was not the government's policy to use cheap electricity to attract industry to a local area, but rather to use techniques such as developing transportation and other facilities.

[2]"The heavy water plant went down the tube," said Dennis Geddes in a letter to the authors dated April 14, 1989, "because the province would not eliminate the sales tax as an incentive to locate at the damsite, [and also] would not exempt taxes from the project. Bob Dundas [resident manager for B.C. Hydro] did a study at the time and indicated that they could not supply the necessary power at a price per kilowatt-hour that was offered down east. The heavy water plant was short-term and presented environmental concerns as well at the time."

Epoch

God! How I hate it, yes hate it!
I wish this dam project in hell,
With all this rumble and racket!
I'd rather hear harness and bell.

The yelps of a dog-teams in winter,
Wolves that bay at the moon,
Trees that smash to a splinter
Felled by a northeaster' croon.

To hear the North's great humming silence
When stillness is grinding her bones;
To live once again by her violence,
Hear cutbanks rolling their stones.

To laze away on a shoreline,
Supposedly mining for gold,
Or bucking my way up an incline,
A black sheep far from its fold.

To hear the hoot of an owl
As dusk closes in with its chill;
From a distance the rapids low growl
When I have just eaten my fill

Of trout I have caught from the stream,
A bannock I've browned by my fire.
It's then that I lay back to dream,
A free man, not up for hire.

Peace . . . you feel it embrace you,
Each year shall pass as a day.
No hustle, no hurry, no worry,
Life softly metered away.

I flinch! The dynamite's roar!
A 'copter whirs low overhead.
Diesel trucks pass by the score,
Their smell and sound fills me with dread.

I'm afraid . . . I shake like a child.
I long for a silence to last.
My body's arrived at this epoch,
My soul has remained in the past.

written in 1964, E.K. Pollon

19

The Political Path

The W.A.C. Bennett Dam was in operation by 1968. The monumental undertaking, from the initial engineering studies by Wenner-Gren B.C. Development Company in 1956, to the commissioning ceremony of the Portage Mountain Generating Station on September 28, 1968, involved world-wide negotiations.

The political path was a maze of high-rolling manoeuvres, bluffs, back room meetings, and chance.[1]

On April 23, 1956, London property developer Jack Roe visited B.C. House in Regent Street. He met for drinks in the Ritz Hotel with Percy Gray, a fellow of the Royal Geographical Society and an architect. Gray specialized in "engineering intelligence," which included aerial photography, large-scale land use planning and power station design. Roe mentioned his upcoming trip to British Columbia in Canada, to inspect some land for sale in West Vancouver. He also planned to investigate potential, large-scale development projects for a Swedish millionaire, Axel Wenner-Gren.

Gray, in a report titled "Central B.C. Development Project, Development Origin Story," wrote that the following day he passed on Roe's information on to his neighbour, Bernard Gore. Gore represented in the United Kingdom, through his firm Gore, Bruce Ltd., several Swedish manufacturing interests. He had asked Gray in the past about recommending Swedish generating equipment, or exploring developments that would tap Swedish financing and products.

On April 25, Gray brought Gore and Roe together for discussions. Gray later reported that "Roe agreed to the idea of mentioning broader potential development areas, and as a result a letter was drafted giving him authority to raise these wider issues with the premier of British Columbia on behalf of Gore, Bruce Ltd."

Gray began an intensive study of every aspect of British

185

Columbia, aided by Harry Smith, B.C.'s representative for trade and industry in London.

Once in B.C., Roe met Ralph Chetwynd, minister of trade and railways, who told him that land would be opened soon in northern B.C. when the railway was extended through the Pine Pass north of Prince George. Roe returned to London, where he passed on this information to Percy Gray on June 12.

Gray, in studying the northern part of B.C., "came to the conclusion that the only region of any geographical cohesion with overall development potential was the area bounded by the watershed line of all the tributaries of the Peace River up to the provincial boundary with Alberta, about 55 miles east of Fort St. John."

Gray wrote a report that Gore forwarded to Stockholm for study, and followed up with supplementary information about the Pacific Great Eastern Railway. The project now had a title: "The Central British Columbia Development Project."

Gray continued preparing an initial development plan, sending reports to Leonard Bruce, Gore's partner in Stockholm. Gray also arranged a meeting between Gore and Harry Smith, to procure Smith's recommendation to the B.C. government.

In his first report dated July 23, 1956, Gray noted the history of Hudson's Hope as a fur trade post in the early part of the 19th century; settlement didn't occur until after the establishment of the Peace River Block by the B.C. Legislature in 1883. The Dominion government was granted 3.5 million acres of arable land in return for its aid in construction of the Canadian Pacific Railway. This was to compensate for alienated and waste land elsewhere in the province. Until the block was selected in 1907, the area from the Rocky Mountains east to the Alberta border had been kept under provincial government reserve which prohibited homesteading. The first wave of settlers from Alberta arrived via the Edson Trail between 1912 and 1915, encouraged by the coming of the railway. In 1931, when the railroad reached Dawson Creek, people trying to escape the Depression rapidly moved into the area.

Gray, however, noted the sad state of the region's economy: "There are three active coal mines west of Hudson Hope, but their production is restricted because of rather poor road conditions, long hauls, and reduction of markets due to the bringing of natural gas to Dawson Creek." A railway would be the only means of transporting the area's developed resources to the coast. Gray further noted that the water systems in the area were highly suitable for hydro electric stations. He concluded that "the area is still largely the domain of the trapper."

Gore had contacted Axel Wenner-Gren and Birger Strid, president of the Wenner-Gren Foundation, and the three were engaged in serious discussions about the railway aspects of the project.

Gore, in his research, had come across a copy of a paper by a Captain G.S. Andrews titled "The Alaska Highway." Smith informed Gore that Andrews was now director of surveys and mapping and surveyor-general for the B.C. government. Andrew's report outlined two possible railway routes into the region.

Route "A" would follow 300 miles of unsurfaced road from Prince George to Hazelton, then parallel the Nass, Bell Irving and Iskut rivers. The route would continue over a 3,300-foot pass, down to the Stikine, then up the Tuya River to Atlin, Whitehorse, Pelly Crossing, Dawson and west into Alaska.

The eastern route "B" would head north from Prince George to the Rocky Mountain Trench, in a straight line to the Dease and Liard Rivers at Lower Post. There, the route would enter the Yukon Territory, continue up the Liard and Frances Rivers, and cross the divide to join Route A at Pelly Crossing.

On July 27, Gore in Stockholm asked Percy Gray to confirm by cable that, in his opinion, the Rocky Mountain Trench was the only sound north/south railway route based on his detailed study.[2]

In a letter to Gore, Bruce Ltd. offices in Stockholm dated August 21, 1956, Gray wrote: "During the ensuing telephone conversation with him (the agent general for British Columbia), he stressed that his government considered the trench route to be the only one they would agree to for the following reasons:

1. it is the only "natural" northern rail route in Canada;
2. snowfall is phenomenally low in the trench as opposed to the coast route (only average of 18 inches);
3. the government wishes urgently to open up the wealth of Central British Columbia by construction of trench rail and road . . . "

There was an added bonus to route "B" through the trench, indicated in the *Alaska Highway Survey* in British Columbia: "Economically the route would offer a western outlet for the famous Peace River farming country by a 50-mile connection down the Peace River from Finlay Forks."

A confidential "Planning Memorandum" was drawn up by Gray in his capacity of principal direct negotiator, following a meeting with the agent general, Harry Smith and the B.C. House Solicitor. The memorandum, typed, for internal security reasons, by Gray's B.C. House secretary, was dated September 15, 1956. The purpose of the memorandum was to present the development aims of the company, and to seek from the B.C. government an exclusive development charter, "which will warrant completion of the arrangements for incorporation of the Development Company."

The object of the Central British Columbia Development Project was "to form a company . . . which will undertake the economic, technical and cultural settlement of areas in the central and northern portions of the Province . . ."

Included was a development plan: first, construction of a rail system which, in addition to the Alaska Railway, would include a branch connection from Finlay Forks down the valley of the Peace River to Fort St. John (the route indicated in the B.C. government's "Submission to the Royal Commission on Canada's Economic Prospects" dated November 28, 1955). Second was a mandate for development of natural resources (including lead, gold, zinc, copper, silver, coal, mercury, natural gas and oil, timber and water power).

On October 17, 1956, Gray was informed that B.C. Premier W.A.C. Bennett had suggested that he discuss the development proposals with Einar Gunderson. Gunderson was financial advisor to the government, executive vice-president of the government-owned Pacific Great Eastern Railway, "and a man generally considered to have considerable influence on government policy."[3]

Gray and Gunderson met on October 19. Gray reported afterward that "the general object was received favourably but Mr. Gunderson considered that the existing developed communities in the Peace River area around Hudson Hope, Dawson Creek and Pouce Coupe, coupled with the total existing oil and gas permit cover East of the Rockies would present considerable complications" in establishing an exclusive area for the Swedish Wenner-Gren Foundation.

According to Gray, "Mr. Gunderson then asked whether the Foundation would be interested in the purchase of the Pacific Great Eastern Railway in order to form a comprehensive north-south railway from Vancouver to Alaska. I replied that I considered that the Foundation would be interested. When asked at what cost, he replied at present share value approximately $62 million, adding that he was sure the government would sell the railway as it was not their policy to run any industry if a private concern was large enough to undertake it."[4]

Gray's final report (dated October 29) to the London and Stockholm offices of Gore, Bruce Ltd. on the outcome of these meetings stated that Gunderson, however, had referred to the proposals as "creating a little empire in B.C."

This "little empire" turned out to be the main stumbling block for

Premier Bennett later, because it looked like one company was gaining a monopoly over a vast area. M. Glover, deputy director of economics and statistics for the province, agreed that the minerals and forestry in the trench area demanded a railway. But the premier argued that if the Swedish foundation continued to insist on outright control of the area, there would be no purpose proceeding with the matter because it was politically impossible.

On October 26, 1956, the government agreed to sell the P.G.E. railway with all rights and land reserves, to construct the Alaska Yukon Railway, and to apply for a forest management licence for areas north of Fort McLeod.

Gray's report concluded: "On October 27, Mr. Gunderson (the government's financial adviser) expressed a desire to be associated with the proposed new company, and in view of his considerable influence this would appear to indicate that there would be a very good chance of a satisfactory conclusion to the negotiations."[5]

The government's offer did not appear to constitute a "Foundation Area," but it would give the Swedish interests considerable control over a large region.

The negotiations paved the way for the "Memorandum of Intention" between Birger Strid of Stockholm and Bernard Gore of London, directors acting for Axel Wenner-Gren, and the B.C. government. According to the memorandum, Wenner-Gren "undertook to construct a railway from the southerly end of the Rocky Mountain Trench adjacent to the Pacific Great Eastern Railway north to the Northern Boundary of British Columbia." The company was named the Wenner-Gren B.C. Development Co. Ltd. Einar Gunderson was named a director on November 21, 1956.

The tentative agreement was amended after discussion with Ray Williston, provincial minister of lands and forests, who wanted to limit the area for development to lands and timber, and exclude mineral rights.

The revised memorandum excluded from development the Peace River District east of Hudson Hope, and struck the word "minerals."

On December 27, Gray wrote to Harry Smith, the B.C. government's industrial and trade representative in London, about the minerals problem:

"When the original agreement was drafted the day before signature, I felt that it would be impossible for the Government to place the reserves on timber, minerals and water over the whole of the Peace River watershed and the Kechika, in view of the settled areas east of Hudson Hope and the complications of oil and gas in the same direction . . ."

"By undertaking to place a mineral reserve," Gray said, "the Government would in fact completely stop all activities in this field, and it was felt that to do so would cause such a public outcry that they would prefer the word 'mineral' [sic] to be omitted from the agreement."

Gray had suggested that after signing the agreement, they quietly investigate and purchase any mineral claims; Gore and Strid were not interested in the minerals, and felt it would be better to have active mining in the area by other investors. But when Gray discussed this with Gunderson, he gained the impression that "they had certainly changed their minds and were extremely interested in the mining."

Gray told Smith that Williston had been adamant about the minerals issue. "Williston told me over the phone that this point was so important to the Government that they had had a meeting and decided that if these changes could not be made they would prefer to drop the whole scheme, as they were firmly convinced the outcry would be so great as to bring down the Government."[6]

Gray was also interested in preliminary studies on hydro power that had been completed for the Nation, Omineca and Peace rivers. But he was concerned about the possibility that the Peace might be dammed, reversing the flow through Summit Lake and generating power through the drop to the Fraser River. Gray wrote again to Williston: "Your investigations along the Peace River seem to indicate a following up of a scheme which I studied from one of the power resource brochures in London, and my only concern at the time was whether reversing the water flow back through Summit Lake would flood any land essential to us for the railway and road section of this scheme to Alaska."

The resulting reservoir would be 240 miles long, with a canal at the south end to drain the reservoir to the Fraser River near Prince George. The proposed dam on the Peace would generate approximately one million horsepower. If the Fraser was also dammed, it could produce another four million horsepower.

Gray felt the scheme introduced two complications that could delay development for years: interference with the fish in the Fraser, which had halted other power development schemes; and problems with the "navigation of the Mackenzie and its reference to Ottawa."

On December 3, 1956, Williston wrote to Gray (following his letter of Nov. 29) and provided the maximum flood levels of the Summit Lake-to-Fraser scheme. Significantly, Williston added that he was "using this continuing survey to direct attention away from your proposals for the time being."[7]

Gray replied: "Your maximum flood level of 2,525 feet certainly confirms my fears as to the extent of the area to be flooded." He also thanked the government for continuing to use surveys of this Summit Lake-to-Fraser project to direct attention away from "our" proposals.[8]

Premier W.A.C. Bennett insisted on secrecy about the Peace project so he'd be able, if everything went as planned, to make an announcement in the legislature. His announcement came on February 13, 1957, although he was nearly robbed of his surprise when The Province newspaper, the day before, published a story about a possible northern development.

The Opposition was outraged, evident in Liberal George Gregory's speech: "I am not prepared to accept the proposition that he (Wenner-Gren) has become a philanthropist whose interest in B.C.'s northland stems from unselfish motives. . . . I do not like Mr. Gunderson's association with Wenner-Gren B.C. Development Co. Ltd.; I do not like Wenner-Gren himself or what the project is or what he stands for. And I have serious doubts whether the project is in the best interests of British Columbia."

Opposition leader Tony Gargrave predicted that the railway would never be completed. But Bennett stubbornly defended the deal: "This could be the greatest thing that ever happened in this province. . . . We have given them (Wenner-Gren) nothing but we have taken their $500,000 bond."

The hard-working Percy Gray was pushed to the background, when Gore revealed that the scheme was the brainchild of Wenner-Gren, and had originated at a cocktail party two-and-one-half years ago between Gore and McAdam in London.[9] Gray, hurt by the slight, wrote to W.A. McAdam, the B.C. government's agent general in the United Kingdom: ". . . It is sad that a project which has been advertised as being of high humanitarian value should start on such an untrustworthy foundation . . ."[10]

Only now did Gray venture forth to actually view the area whose future he had played such a large part in altering. On February 25, 1957, he quietly arranged a trip to the North with Russ Baker, then president of Pacific Western Airlines. Gray told people he was a freight trainee manager for the airline. Finally, he looked down upon the region north of Prince George to Watson Lake in the Yukon, and east to Hudson's Hope down the Peace River.

It is ironic, in view of the massive dam that would alter the landscape, to read Gray's poetic description of the Peace: "Leaving the Finlay Post at night, after a good rum drinking session, to stand alone on the ice-covered river and experience for the first time the silence of the North, and to see a night sky ablaze with stars in such total silence."

In March, 1957, Axel Wenner-Gren travelled to B.C. to meet the premier.

Wenner-Gren was still confident of building a railroad, and plans for his Swedish group's monorail system were announced to a stunned public. Reporters didn't buy it. Wenner-Gren said that he intended to honour his agreement with the B.C. government. But he added that if the resources in the Rocky Mountain Trench didn't justify the cost, he believed the government would not hold him to the plan.

That summer, Wenner-Gren discovered the hydro potential of the Peace valley. On October 7, 1957, Wenner-Gren signed a new agreement with the government for the formation of a company to begin plans to build a hydro-electric project. After signing the agreement, Bennett contacted Attorney-General Robert Bonner in London. With Bonner to receive the news were Bernard Gore, Birger Strid, Gordon Shrum and William Mainwaring, vice president of B.C. Electric.

The following day, Bennett called a press conference for "the most momentous announcement I have ever made." The greatest hydro-electric power project in the world was to be built in the Rocky Mountain Trench. It would produce four million horsepower and create a reservoir 250 miles long that "could change the climate of the north."

Bennett had been considering a two-river policy: power on the Columbia developed by a government agency, and on the Peace by private capital. Ottawa was in favour of the Columbia, although they were not pushing a project because of the complex arrangements that would have to be ratified with the United States. Mainwaring said B.C. Electric was not interested in buying power from the Peace; in fact, the privately-owned company had recently asked Bennett for permission to build a dam on the Columbia River at Mica. Bennett refused to entertain the idea presented to him of buying B.C. Electric, saying "the government would be poor trustees of the people's interests if it did so and thereby jeopardized development of the Columbia." He felt that the only way the two rivers, the Columbia and Peace, could be developed was by the aforementioned combination of public and private financing. The government could not afford to develop the Columbia *and* buy B.C. Electric.

In 1958, Mainwaring suddenly retired from B.C. Electric and became president of the newly-formed Peace Power Development Company set up by Wenner-Gren. The board of directors included Lord Alexander of Tunis, Viscount Chandos (of Associated Electrical

Industries Ltd.), Ralph Chantrill, George Cunningham, Bernard Gore, Einar Gunderson, A.F. MacAlpine, Senator S.S. McKeen, Sir Andrew McTaggart, William Murphy, A. Bruce Robertson (vice president of B.C. Electric), Birger Strid and Lord Tweedsmuir.[11]

In March, 1959, the day after Andrew G.L. McNaughton, (chairman of the Canadian section of the International Joint Commission), submitted a report on the Columbia River development, Mainwaring submitted his plan to the provincial controller of water rights for development of the Peace. The Peace report included a dam estimated to cost $600 million that would generate up to 4.2 million horsepower, which could be delivered to Vancouver for about six mills per kilowatt hour (then the going rate in the city).

The Opposition cried that this was Mainwaring's private gold mine, that a few individuals "would make millions tax-free in stock deals and the consumer will foot the bill." Bennett was supported by Phil Gaglardi, minister of highways, who warned that without dams on the Peace and the Columbia, British Columbians would be walking around with candles in their hats by 1970. Williston agreed, saying that proper power development in the 1960s would have the industrial world flocking to B.C.'s door. There were catcalls about "Swedish Columbia," and warnings that a new line of rulers was being formed in B.C., "The Wenner-Gren line, Axel the First of Wenner-Grenland."[12]

But the province's water controller, Arthur F. Paget, (father of Norrie Paget, who later became project manager for the Peace dam's general contractor, Kiewit-Dawson-Johnson) reported to the government that the Peace project was feasible from an engineering standpoint. Bennett was overjoyed, calling the Peace "an empire crying out for development."

However, Mainwaring could not obtain letters of intent from either B.C. Electric or B.C. Power Commission to buy Peace power. Ottawa favoured power development on the Columbia while Bennett favoured the Peace. A contract from B.C. Electric to buy power from either project could be the deciding factor. If the Columbia was developed, and B.C. Electric had agreed to buy higher-priced Peace power, it might be chastised for making a bad deal. Bennett finally told Mainwaring that if he could get a letter of commitment from B.C. Electric, he would guarantee one from the power commission.[13]

Bennett was being boxed in: nothing was happening about the proposed northern railway and the power plan was in danger of vanishing.

The deadline to begin the 700-mile railway was June 30, 1960. On May 13, Bennett announced that four international firms were joining

Wenner-Gren in building the line. They were A.V. Roe Company; Associated Electrical Industries Ltd.; Cleveland Bridge and Engineering Co. Ltd. of England; and Perini Ltd. of Toronto. Even the press seemed mollified. "Participation of such large companies in development of the new line puts the quietus on the Socialist babble about the 'fantastic position' of the project. . . .," said *The Province.* "British Columbians are not likely to pay any more attention to the cold water Mr. Strachan tries to pour over the plan."

On May 24, the Pacific Northern Railway was incorporated, and asked formal permission from Lyle Wicks, minister of commercial transport, to build a 697-mile line from Summit Lake in B.C. to Teslin Lake in the Yukon. Cost estimates ran about $250 million, and the railway was not expected to ever make a profit. The Alaska International Rail and Highway Commission agreed that it could see no possibility of a railway to Alaska turning a profit in the next 20 years.

A week before the June 30 deadline, Bennett told the railway it could go ahead without Public Utilities Commission approval, under the terms of the provincial Railway Act. The press asked how this was possible, to which Bennett replied: "I am not a lawyer." On June 20, Bennett and Wicks joined Gunderson, Gore and others and flew to Prince George, then to a clearing 35 miles north of Prince George. The clearing was occupied by ten men, four surveyors' tents, eight barrels of gas, an outhouse, and three pieces of brush-clearing equipment. Bennett proclaimed that "the railway which starts construction today is the longest railway of the century," and then helped to hold a power-saw to fell a fir tree. That was all. The Public Utilities Commission dismissed the railway's application, then scheduled a public hearing for September 2. Bennett asked that the hearing be delayed until after the election, which was done. Two weeks after the election, the Pacific Northern Railway halted construction, after clearing a 100-foot wide trail that ran through the bush for several miles. In 1963, the government cancelled all the railway's certificates.

None of the public knew the railway dream was finished. The focus now was on power development.

The Columbia River negotiators had reached an agreement. It involved dams at Mica Creek, High Arrow and Duncan Lake, at a power cost estimate cheaper than the Peace. It seemed Bennett had no choice but to abandon his northern project. On December 27, he asked Gordon Shrum, chairman of the B.C. Energy Board, to prepare a cost estimate of both projects.

The federal government opposed the Peace Power project, because Ottawa wanted cooperation from the United States on shared resources through the Columbia River developments. The government felt the cost of developing the Peace was out of line with expected returns. Also, developing both projects would likely create an excess of power, and the national energy policy prohibited exporting surplus power.

Ottawa had no written approval from the province, but nevertheless prepared to sign the Columbia River Treaty with the U.S. Four days before the signing was to take place, Bennett, in a letter he called a warning to Ottawa, informed the federal finance minister that B.C. would proceed with the Columbia project *if* it proved feasible and economical. The warning was not heeded, and on January 17, 1961, the agreement was signed.

On February 27, Bennett informed an astounded legislature that the government "might" be forced to take over B.C. Electric if it didn't get better treatment from Ottawa. He was referring to a new federal policy that siphoned corporate tax rates paid by power and natural resource companies into an equalization fund shared by all provinces.

On March 1, an interim report by the B.C. Energy Board warned that an unmanageable surplus of power could result if the Columbia River Treaty was ratified before a number of uncertainties had been cleared up. Bennett's offer to the federal government was a second shock: Ottawa could finance the Columbia River project itself, provided it assumed all costs to date, gave a $64 million flood control payment to the province, and turned the dams over to B.C. as soon as they were paid for. Alternatively, B.C. would build the dams, subject to federal guarantee that power could be delivered in Vancouver for not more than 4.25 mills per kilowatt-hour. In addition, Ottawa was to sell any surplus in the U.S. at not less than 4.25 mills. Bennett reminded Ottawa that they had said it was possible to deliver power under four mills; let them guarantee it.

No federal government would accede to Bennett's demands. It appeared, instead of a two-river policy, Bennett might get neither. The official statement from B.C. Electric was that the company would make no plans to buy power until the two governments had reached an agreement.

Shrum's report on behalf of the energy board said that the two dams were the largest hydro-electric projects ever attempted at one time in any part of the world. The Columbia was projected to cost $1.5 billion and the Peace almost $1 billion. Shrum also said they would ensure employment and industrial activity in B.C. for the next 20 years, and prosperity for many decades to come. "In contemplating these gigantic projects, I sometimes think that we British Columbians must be the most optimistic, imaginative and courageous people in the world today," he said. The federal government did not agree.[14]

Rumours then began circulating that Bennett might take over B.C. Electric and the Peace power project, and form a huge, publicly-owned hydro system. In fact, the B.C. government agreed to a motion by Opposition Leader Strachan that it consider taking over B.C. Electric and other private power companies.

On August 1, 1961, one copy was printed of a document whose details had been written in great secrecy. It was handed to B.C.'s lieutenant governor to announce as "a bill concerning the development of electric power resources." Bennett then introduced Bill No. 5, The Power Development Act, 1961, and tabled Shrum's report. Bill No. 5 made B.C. Electric a Crown corporation which, through a share merger, also took in the B.C. Power Corporation.[15]

Shrum's report had said that if the Peace power project were developed under public ownership, it would produce power at the same rate as Columbia power project. The possibility of developing these billion-dollar projects, in a province with a population of 1.6 million, caused even Bennett to admit that "it was too big for small minds to grasp."

Bennett had both his projects going ahead while Ottawa looked like bunglers. "Because the federal government has refused to act in giving B.C. a fair return of the taxes paid by power corporations," the premier said, "it is this government's policy to have basically all electric power and energy that is supplied to the general public under public auspices." On August 3, 1961, Bill No. 5 was passed.

Shrum was appointed chairman of the board of the new Crown corporation, called B.C. Hydro and Power Authority.[16]

On November 29, 1967, Ray Williston, provincial minister of lands, forests and water resources, wrote to Percy Gray in Yorkshire, England.

"This spring my son and I went by canoe from the Parsnip River bridge north of Prince George to the dam. It took us four days and is a trip which cannot be repeated due to the flooding," Williston said.

"You visualized development ten years ago but I am sure you could not have prophesied the change. Instant towns, modern sawmills, pulp mills, and mineral developments are all either in operation or planning stages.

"The dam is finished and the powerhouse is on schedule and will deliver energy next October. Transmission is virtually complete at a voltage once considered impossible to achieve. I still have the original outline for development which you proposed. One day the story will be told with an absence of the fairy tales.

"Ten years is a short time in the life of a province. However, this one project has likely caused as much change as any other single event," Williston told Gray.

On September 28, 1968, a commissioning ceremony was held for the Portage Mountain Generating Station. Billed as the world's largest underground powerhouse at a length of 890 feet, it was 150 feet high and 67 feet wide. It sat beneath a 600-foot tall earth- filled dam, and a 410,000-acre storage reservoir. The powerhouse was equipped with three (eventually 10) 227,000-kilowatt generator units powered by three (eventually 10) 310,000-horsepower hydraulic turbines. The powerhouse was officially named the Gordon M. Shrum Generating Station, the dam the W.A.C Bennett Dam, and the reservoir Williston Lake.

On October 3, a few days after the commissioning ceremony, Williston again wrote to Gray in England:

"The Peace project officially opened on Saturday. I shall send along some of the illustrative material. I am sure you will find this of special interest. I doubt if even you visualized the rapidity with which the frontiers are being pushed back. Personal good wishes, Ray Williston."

A letter from Gray to Williston dated October 25, 1979 offered the assurance that Gray was still going strong on new ventures to change other lands: "Abroad I have prepared a scheme for a new town in Trinidad as well as projects in Australia, Portugal, France, Eire, Belgium and Holland. . . . My next venture may be in Hong Kong if the current negotiations are successful."

However, Gray responded warily to a proposed museum, (to be established at the new mill town of Mackenzie located near the mouth of the Parsnip on Williston Lake), for displaying information relating to the Peace River power project. "With regard to the material for the museum," he continued in the same letter, "I think perhaps it would be much better if you vetted it first just to make sure that nothing of a sensitive political nature is put in for public viewing. . . Best personal regards, Percy Gray."[17]

Notes

[1]Main sources for this chapter:
a. *Bennett*. The Biography of W.A.C. Bennett, by Paddy Sherman, 1966, McClelland & Stewart Ltd., Toronto;
b. archival documents, eg. Central British Columbia Development Project, Development Origin Story by Percy Gray, Concept Planning and Technical Consultant
c. minutes of District of Hudson's Hope
d. personal interviews.

[2]*Central B.C. Development Origin Story*, p. 7.

[3]ibid., Exhibit 29.

[4]ibid., report p. 14, Exhibit 29.

[5]ibid., Exhibit 29.

[6]ibid., Exhibit 64.

[7]ibid., p. 22 and Exhibit 51.

[8]ibid., Exhibit 52.

[9]ibid., Exhibit 66.

[10]ibid., Exhibit 68.

[11]A budget of $1.9 million was presented, which would enable the company to conduct a thorough report of the project. Western Development & Power Co., a subsidiary of B.C. Electric, had 500,000 one-dollar shares; the government-owned B.C. Power Commission had been offered the same. Wenner-Gren B.C. Development Co., Power Securities Ltd., National City Bank, and London and Associated Electrical Industries Ltd. each owned 250,000 shares. The British were taking over from the Swedes. The executive committee of the new company consisted of Gore, Mainwaring, Gunderson and Robertson. (*Bennett*, p. 222)

[12]*Bennett*, p. 226.

[13]ibid., p. 229.

[14]The deals were at a strategic point: Bennett sensed that if the Peace fell through, the United States would be able to drive a hard bargain on the Columbia project, knowing B.C.'s future need of the power. If the Peace went ahead, Bennett would have the upper hand in negotiations. The two rivers would produce a surplus of power, but since Canada and the U.S. both wanted the treaty, this would facilitate breaking the export barrier. Shrum, however, reported that the only potential markets for B.C. surplus power were the U.S. Pacific Northwest, California, or perhaps Alberta. Whatever the outcome, control over the disposition of downstream power benefits must remain with B.C. (*Bennett*, p. 246)

[15]Bill No. 5 said that B.C. Power Corporation, which owned all the common shares in B.C. Electric, would be paid $111 million, the paid-up value of the shares. If B.C. Power felt this was a poor deal, it could ask B.C. Electric to take over all the Power Corporation's shares at $38 (the price just before the premier gave his warning to Ottawa), which would amount to $180 million. Further, $104 million in preferred shares would be replaced by shares in B.C. Electric., which was to take over responsibility for a debt of approximately $400 million. The cost to the government was nothing. B.C. Electric would raise new money by parity bonds; the government would add $684 million to its contingent liabilities, making them $1.3 billion ($850 per capita). Assuming continued growth rate, Columbia River power would cost 4.4 mills; the Peace, 6.42 mills under private financing, or 4.2 mills under public ownership. (*Bennett*, p. 248)

[16]On the board of directors were: barrister Arthur Fouks, Einar Gunderson, B.C. Electric vice president C. Mearns; former lieutenant governor Frank Ross; and lands and forests minister Ray Williston.

[17]*Central B.C. Development Origin Story*, Exhibit 88)

20

Coal: A Historical Headache?

Lloyd Gething was nine years old when he first saw Hudson's Hope coal. He described it as resembling "a chocolate layer cake" protruding from the canyon wall.

Alexander Mackenzie and other explorers had noted the presence of coal in the area. History has it that voyageurs of the Hudson's Bay Company taking the old brigade trails south to New Caledonia carried Hudson's Hope coal in small barrels.

But it was the Gething family who realized its commercial potential in 1908 and prepared to stake it. Neil Gething had been prospecting in the Manson Creek area when he came to Hudson's Hope in 1901 via the Manson, Finlay and Peace rivers and discovered the rich coal seams near the canyon.

The staking procedure involved filing, in person, with the provincial government, an application that contained a full description by section, township and range. But there was a stickler: the application had to be accompanied by evidence to show that the location had been defined on the ground by the locator by planting four-inch square posts not less than four feet above the ground. Each post had to be inscribed with the name of the locator and date.

Neil Gething and his partner Grant Johnson, travelling by dog team in mid-winter from Edmonton via Grouard and up the ice of the Peace River, rushed to stake their claims. They stayed overnight in Old Fort St. John with Frank Beatton, the Hudson's Bay manager who was also the mining recorder. Soon after they had staked out 60 square miles of coal around the canyon area Johnson became ill, so they had to return to Edmonton. Enroute, they stopped again with Beatton. These two stops saved the day in a court challenge by another interested party that arrived the following summer to stake the same claims. The second party argued that no one could have come into the area in the dead of winter. But Frank Beatton's meticulous records proved that "Neil Gething and associates passed through on the way to stake coal claims," and also that "Neil Gething and associates have successfully staked coal claims. One of the men is ill."

Neil Gething
(Hudson's Hope Museum)

The claims were filed by Gething, George Aylard, and W.S. "Steele" Johnson. Senator R.F. Green also bought into the partnership. The claims went all around the canyon, onto a creek later named Johnson Creek (for Grant Johnson), and the little mound on the side of what was originally called Grant's Peak, then Bullhead Mountain, (later changed to Portage Mountain when the dam was built). Gething came in every year to assess the claims until 1919, when they began tunnelling. In 1922 he moved in his wife and children, Lloyd, Vesta, Larry, Quentin (King), Wes and Lillian.

The six-foot thick Grant seam was mined first, and that year the first load of coal was shipped out of the canyon by a raft made of logs – to fuel the boilers on gold dredges near Old Fort St. John.

In 1922, the Geological Survey of Canada made a full assessment of all seams. Their estimate was approximately 600 million tons of minable coal.

A contract for 50 tons of coal, to be shipped 250 miles downstream to the Edmonton, Dunvegan and British Columbia Railway (E.D. & B.C.) at Peace River Crossing, was Gethings' first big order. An analysis in 1923 found the coal to be of excellent quality.

On October 19, 1923, an *Edmonton Journal* headline said: "Satisfactory Test Hudson Hope Coal on the E.D. & B.C. Railway. Officials

Express Themselves as Highly Pleased With the Coal." Train engines usually required 28 tons of regular coal, but a trip using Gething coal had required only 11 tons. But there was a hitch: the railway had to be sure of a steady supply. The Hudson's Bay boat, the D.A. Thomas, came up to the Gething mines for a barge load. However, reefs in the river were too dangerous and the boat had to turn around at an island (which became known as Steamboat Island). Requests to the government to open the canyon passage for barge freighting, by blasting a few of the reefs, resulted in an impasse.

First barge of coal
(Hudson's Hope Museum)

Neil Gething spent thousands of dollars and more than 30 years trying to establish a transportation system to bring this high-grade coal to market. He was still no further ahead in 1935 when his son, Wes, died of a heart attack at the mine. Earl's father, Jack Pollon, was asked to wash, shave and dress the body when it was brought in to town. "It is one thing to dress the body of someone you do not know," Earl said. "But quite another thing to dress the body of a friend."

During the Second World War, dreams of a productive coal mine were re-energized with the need for the mineral in construction camps along the Alaska Highway.

Jack Baker, now living in Fort St. John, was for several years secretary of Hudson Hope Coal Sales Ltd. "We sold coal that was mined at the three mines at Hudson's Hope: King Gething Mines, Peace River Mines (Lloyd Gething's) and the Reschke Mines (the old Packwood Mines)," Baker said. His company sold a lot of coal to the Northern Alberta Railway which ran into Dawson Creek with coal-burning locomotives. "But the railway was beginning to convert over to diesel. The government sold the big airport hangar, they could no longer operate the stoker furnaces. The hospital had stoker furnaces, too, and they modernized. So really the local demand for coal began to diminish."

Natural gas and oil was discovered in the Fort St. John, Dawson Creek and Chetwynd areas, further cutting the need for coal.

A mining inspector named Dave Smith was convinced that coal should have been used as a power source instead of hydro. But even Lloyd Gething admitted that it was not possible to convince others: "Water power is glamorous. It's big. A mundane old coal mine, belching smoke into the air, would have been hard to sell." Most of the coal is still lying, unused, beneath the dam.

The Gethings knew about the potential for a hydro-electric project. Neil Gething had seen such developments throughout the western United States before he came to the Peace. He recognized it, and so did oldtimer Henry Stege with his prediction of Hudson's Hope being "another Pittsburgh."

Lloyd Gething holding sample lump of coal
from Peace River Coal Mine Ltd.

"I guess we were the forgotten people," Lloyd Gething said. "We just happened to own the coal where the hydro development was going to be. There was a time when no one wanted coal, a very brief period of 15 or 20 years, from about 1955 to 1970, when it was thought that coal was something nobody would ever use again. In that period, any good engineer would have gone on the stand for B.C. Hydro to say that coal had no value. In fact, they got one, a very famous one, and one who should not have done so. His name was Victor Dolmage."

Lloyd became meditative as he tried to analyze what happened. "Let me tell you something about consultants. When you hire a consultant, you choose someone that you hope will say what you want him to say. The public has the view of a consultant as someone who is impartial. No human is impartial. So if you know that this consultant has given up on coal, you hire him as the consultant if you want to take over some coal rights. You hire him and he is a recognized authority. A big name. The *Vancouver Sun* newspaper loved him. And *The Province* loved him. Dolmage could say anything and they would believe him. And he said the coal had no value at all, and they (B.C. Hydro) shouldn't give us anything."

Gethings had a partner, George Aylard, who at the time had become very wealthy. Aylard's uncle had left the four children $50,000 each. When George Aylard died, he left his son, Leslie, in charge. B.C. Hydro offered the Gething-Aylard-Green partnership $50,000 for everything, and the Aylard partner favoured accepting the offer.

The undivided interest was split so the Greens owned eight percent, Aylards owned 70 percent and Gethings owned 22 percent. Leslie Aylard disputed the Gethings' argument that the coal was worth a lot more than Hydro offered. Gethings and Greens refused to sign until a better agreement had been reached.

"Strangely enough," Lloyd Gething said, "one engineer will believe another engineer. Aylard believed the engineers when they said the coal had no value. We were awarded $65,000 cash and Aylard got the money. Technically the split should have been 70-22-8. We were the broke people, but we gave him the cash. In exchange we took two-and-one-half square miles of Crown-granted coal, oil and natural gas rights, which became the property of Gethings and Greens. And in addition the Aylard-Gething-Green partnership retained 7,200 acres of their property."

The Gethings' new property of two square miles on Johnson Creek, and one-half square mile where King had been mining on the side of the mountain, was provided in exchange for two square miles appropriated from the Gethings when the dam was built.

"They also took away our rights to mine below a certain depth of Williston Lake, and that cut off a lot of coal. But we have the right to slant-drill under the dam for oil and gas ... It's written right into the agreement," said Gething.

But the agreement was still not completely settled when Hydro was ready to turn on the key to the dam. "Hydro had built a nice bridge across the river near where some seams of coal stuck out. My brother King, who used to get a little bullheaded at times, loaded up some powder and blasting caps and some hand drills and set up over there to start working on the coal seam.

"Hydro roared in, the same way King had got in there, and yelled, 'You can't do this!' King smiled at them and said quietly, 'It's on my property and I can do whatever I want.' So off they went to get the police to order him out of there. The police checked with Hydro officials and sure enough, the area was on our property. Then they came back and this time asked him politely to stop. Negotiations started up again from that point."

But the drawn-out, cloak-and-dagger negotiations left a bitter taste with pioneers whose faith in the country's economy was rewarded with feuds over control. "They hire professional people," Gething said, "and the professional people have it in their heads to get everything as cheaply as possible, without any regard to individuals.

"The only way to improve this system is to improve the arbitration procedure," he added.

Gething said his family had paid taxes on the property for many years. "We had hired a fellow called Milligan in 1913 to survey the property. He brought in a crew of men to survey 60 square miles in one-square-mile lots and it cost $50,000, which at the time was a lot of money. In 1919 we began the tunnel work. Then in 1922 we started plans for opening up the coal mine and building a road. We spent $140,000 building roads and tunnels, so we had a lot invested in this property. Not one cent of that was allowed in Hydro's calculations!

"Between $200,000 and $300,000 of expenses – that may be exaggerating a bit, but not much – could have been produced by identifiable bills against that property," Gething continued. "Not one penny of that could be used. The only value it had was what we could establish by hiring an expert, and B.C. Hydro had already hired an expert called Victor Dolmage, who said coal had no value at all."

This dealing in bits and pieces is how Hydro settled with all the families whose properties were affected by the project. But it was impossible to set up the same businesses on the new land. Gethings and Greens took land they knew contained coal, but it would have required full-scale development costing several hundred thousand dollars to make it productive.

"It was the same with us as with the farmers here," Gething said. "The farmers got raw land in exchange for their farms that were to be flooded out."

Gething sounded sad with remembrance: "The dam project was estimated to cost $600 million. One percent of that is $6 million. If they'd spent even 1/10 of one percent, it would have worked. I expect they paid more to the experts to hold everything down in their settlements, to . . . to say that the coal had no value, to other experts to say farmland had no real value."

B.C. Hydro files indicate that rights were acquired to approximately 14,000 acres, from about 100 owners. Developed land included farms, summer camps and an Indian reserve. Hydro also had to settle with holders of Crown surface leases covering minerals, petroleum and natural gas, timber, and water. Hydro's policy is "not to divulge the terms of compensation settlements," but the total cost of land and rights was in the order of $1.7 million.[1]

The government responded the same way, when the community pushed for a better coal-hauling road to Fort St. John.

"Les Bazeley, a fellow from Hudson's Hope who ran the mail in twice a week and hauled coal in the winter, accompanied a delegation to visit the highways minister in Victoria to explain the conditions here, that if we changed the road to follow the river it would eliminate two steep hills,' Gething explained. "The minister called in people from public works and the highways who brought in a map showing the area from Cache Creek to Fort St. John as being flat. Les Bazeley was astounded. He said, 'It's not flat! I drive it twice a week!' His exclamations met stony silence."

Gething said the community then went to a surveyor, Alwin Holland, and asked if he would conduct a survey of the road. "He refused. Why? It was against professional ethics. Once an engineer makes a statement, no engineer ever disputes it. Even if it's wrong. Alwin Holland lived in this country and knew exactly how it was."

On June 6, 1973, the *Chetwynd Echo* newspaper printed a story titled, "The Development of Iron and Other Smelting Facilities at Hudson's Hope, B.C.," by King Gething. It outlined an encouraging potential for the coal industry in Hudson's Hope.

"Of the exploration work done in the last few years . . . none have been made available by newspaper report except for Cinnibar Peak Mines, which have published results of a two-season program of surface trenching and diamond drilling. The estimate of coal reserves on the Cinnibar Peak Mines is 900 million tons of coal, of which there is about 200 million tons of coking or metallurgical coal and is the closest area being developed to Hudson's Hope. "

"Of the hydro power available, which is also used in some processes for the reduction of iron ore, we have the advantage of on-site power," Gething noted. "B.C. Hydro offered a cheap power rate for any development within 30 miles of the damsite when it was first put on-stream."

Coal, timber, power. It was all there, waiting for development. Just what did construction of the dam at Hudson's Hope provide to the area?

"The construction of the Bennett Dam provided jobs for the sons and daughters of some of the people here," Lloyd Gething said. "One generation of them anyway. But not lasting employment. Not at all.

"There should have been a tremendous push to insist on a rail-road into Hudson's Hope," he added. "It would have paid its own way by bringing in the equipment for the dam construction project. And if it would have been here, then you could have established local industries so you would have here perhaps what Tumbler Ridge and Chetwynd now have, close to 5,000 people in each place, one industry based on timber, the other based on coal."

According to a *Calgary Herald* article dated September 9, 1988, Quintette Coal Ltd. (50 percent owned by Denison Mines Ltd.) has, during its five years of operation at Tumbler Ridge, "experienced ever-increasing troubles in repaying its huge debts and in satisfying the price demands of its coal customers."

Built in the early 1980s at a cost of $1.3 billion to the federal and provincial governments, Quintette (and Teck Corporation's Bullmoose mine) depend on the Japanese steel industry to buy coal on long-term sales agreements. Tumbler Ridge, with a population of approximately 4,400, is located near the Murray River 70 miles south of Chetwynd on the newly constructed Heritage Highway. The mines are serviced by an electrified rail spur line, specifically constructed for the operation. The spur runs from the B.C. Rail line at Prince George, through the Wolverine and Sukunka Ranges of the Rockies, to the Quintette and Bullmoose mines. The question is, why was Tumbler Ridge ever built?

Lloyd Gething is sure there is enough coal in the Hudson's Hope area to operate mines for a long long time – perhaps for 150 years. If the spur line had been built from Willow Flat in the late 1950s, it would have completely changed the development of the area.

"We would have been the new Tumbler Ridge and Chetwynd," Gething said. "Part of the resources in Chetwynd came from our area. We have coal equal to the Tumbler Ridge coal. If there had been a rail-road here, there would have been no need for either Tumbler Ridge or Chetwynd. We just needed 40 miles of spur line ... "

Is there any future now for Hudson's Hope?

Author Earl Pollon and Lloyd Gething
(Shirlee Matheson)

"The future of Hudson's Hope is what always attracted people here . . . tourism," Gething said. "And the only way you're going to have more tourism is to have more dams. Isn't that a statement that will make the people rise right out of their chairs? This is the future of the area, and it's the only future it has. Tell me another? A lake that would form behind the proposed Site C dam would be a perfect recreational lake . . .

"Our chance was missed when no railroad came in," he said. "The engineers building the dam should have thought about that, but engineers don't think. They just think of the project day or the project week. They don't belong anywhere. An engineer has no home. You think about it. He has no home at all . . . He may have a headquarters in Vancouver or Victoria, but his home is not at the sawmill or the dam site. He doesn't plan to live under the bridge. Home is always 'back there.'"

The dam contractors also felt little nostalgia for the area's past. In the *Alaska Highway News* of November 28, 1963, they called the rich coal seams nothing more than a damsite headache:

"The seams are narrow and not merchantable. The best seams, discovered by Neil Gething over 50 years ago, are on the south side of the river, on Johnson and Gething Creeks, but they were never exploited commercially *because of the difficulty of transportation* (authors' italics).

"No coal is being used on the project, where all buildings are heated by propane."

Note

[1]From a letter to the authors dated 15 May, 1989 by C.W.J. Boatman, Vice President Corporate Affairs, B.C. Hydro, Vancouver.

21

Eminent Domain

Moving people out of the way of major projects has a bitter-sweet nomenclature: 'relocation'. The book, *Cadillac Desert: The American West and Its Disappearing Water*, by Marc Reisner, offers a glimpse of how the program began in the western United States:

"The history of 'relocation' started early in the century with the Los Angeles Department of Water and Power, and was embellished a short while later by the New York City Water Department when it drowned the Catskill Valleys to create a new water supply."

This was the first time in American history (except for the 'relocation' programs perpetrated on the Indians) when "thousands of people were dispossessed for the crime of impeding progress."

Reisner explained how the process, now fine-tuned, works:

"They (the owners of the proposed dam project) sniffed through the community, smelling out its most avaricious members, those most susceptible to an offer. They spread rumours; they spread lies. They offered extravagant settlements to the first few who bit, then grew less and less spendthrift with the holdouts, both to punish them and to balance the initial extravagance. They played on the social conscience of communities, accusing them of selfishness, of denying the greater good to the greater number. And in the final resort – judiciously at first, then more threateningly, then like a defensive line blitzing a quarterback – they invoked the prospect of eminent domain.

"They did all this without a sense of shame, because they told themselves they were serving an ultimate good – they were preventing floods, feeding the hungry world, offering power and light to schools and heat and air conditioning to hospitals. They denied – to themselves and to their would-be victims – that the real reason they were doing it was that they couldn't bear the thought of no longer building dams. And the very majesty of their great works made it easier for them to do it."[1]

A local resident of the area where this U.S. project was to be located (the Narrows Dam on the South Platte River in Colorado) described the invasion:

"They were like Jekyll and Hyde. When you met them on the street or in meetings or the coffee shop in Fort Morgan they'd smile and joke with the same people they were trying to throw off their land. They were in here for so long they almost felt like members of the community. You had to keep reminding yourself of the real reason they were here."[2]

Jim Beattie Sr. had come to the Peace country in 1912. Born in England, his ambition was to be a professional pianist. But he was thrown from a horse and landed on a scythe, severing his wrist cords. Beattie was a man who sought perfection in everything he did, so he gave up music and emigrated to Canada to start anew. He was working on the Grand Trunk Railroad from Edmonton to Tête Jaune Cache, packing supplies in with horses, when he and three friends decided to go gold mining. They came down the Parsnip and up the Peace River, eventually arriving at Gold Bar (about 20 miles above where the Bennett dam is now located). He liked the area, and in 1914 he returned to acquire the land.

In 1915, he cut a wagon road across the portage and started a freighting outfit, hauling boats and supplies both ways and transporting prospectors on their way to wash gold along the Peace.

"In the hard times," reported his son, also named Jim, "there were gold miners on every bar along the Peace, and they made a living even when gold sold for $35 an ounce. The gold must have been moving, because they'd come back to wash the same bars every year. It would get eaten off the cutbanks during high water, come down with the high water of the Parsnip and the Finlay, and replenish the bars with about four or five inches of pay dirt after every spring run-off."

In 1919, Jim Beattie Sr. cut another trail up the river to Gold Bar, brought in his wife, Elizabeth, and started a family. They had five daughters: Louise ("Toulie"), Mary ("Girlie"), Clarisse, Olive and Ruth; and three sons: Bob, and the twins, Jimmy Hudson and Billy Hope.

"When we first built up the ranch," Elizabeth Beattie told Earl Pollon, "there was nothing short about our days. We worked as long as we could see to work, or stand to work, in the long days of summer. One time Jim was away with his boat taking a party upriver, trying to earn a few dollars. We had cleared a large tract of land by hand, and had all the brush piled ready for burning when he returned. The day he left a nice breeze came up, just right for burning. As the ground was still damp and there was little likelihood of the fire spreading, I decided to try burning it, although I had never done this before. I kept lighting fires until all the piles were alight. I worked far into the night, turning in the ends of the burned-out piles. When I quit there was not a twig left on our clearing, or a spark left in me.

"When Jim came home the next day he said, 'Jesus! Jesus, woman, how did you ever do it? There was at least three days burning on that job!'"

Beattie home at Gold Bar, now under Williston Lake

On March 24, 1949, Jim Beattie Sr. died. It was a blow to the district, because he had done as much toward developing the country as any man.

The home ranch at Twenty Mile was taken over sons Bill and Jim, while Bob had a separate place at Twelve Mile. By this time, the Beatties had 1,029 deeded acres – including some 300 cleared acres – and quite a bit of leased land, not including the Twelve Mile ranch.

They grew everything at Gold Bar: apple trees, corn, cucumbers, tomatoes that ripened right in the garden, wheat, oats. They raised alfalfa seed and sold it. Theirs was rich land, all river bottom.

The Beatties first heard in 1963 about a dam to be built on the Peace. "But I probably knew for 20 years before that they *might* dam it," said Jim, "because every year the water resources people came in and measured the river; this was done from Whitehorse. My brother, Bobby, would take them out on the boat for a week or so every time they came down. They would run a line across the river at the head of the canyon and perhaps at the Clearwater. They had a big lead weight with fins on it about every 20 feet across the river to measure the depth of the water...

"The first formal visit I had about the dam was from a guy named Charlie Cunningham who was employed by Hydro," Jim continued. "He came in and he was real friendly with one person who was going to sell out. Once they got the first one, then they had the ground floor to go on. Cunningham boarded with my brother Bob and sister-in-law at Twelve Mile; he and his wife stayed right there. So he got one person to sell – I don't want to say who it was – and that broke the wall of resistance. Then everybody had to take what had been paid for the first piece.

"They started off by offering us $40 an acre for cleared land, and we finally wound up getting $70, which wasn't anywhere near what it cost to clear land and get it ready for a seed bed, even back then. They paid as low as $10 an acre for uncleared land. They didn't pay any more for river frontage. And we had the deed on it too.

"They started their negotiations in 1965, and finally settled with us in 1967. At that time, a cleared acre of land around Fort St. John would have sold for $150, something like that. And we had something like 25 buildings on the place. Some were fairly old but some were good buildings, but they estimated a building to be worth $500 and that's what they paid. Not replacement value or anything."

Jack Baker, a retired Fort St. John businessman married to Clarisse Beattie, described the Beattie family's ranch at Gold Bar as fabulous. "Over the years Jim Beattie had built that place up until it was known all over the North... a great big three-storey log home, about another 15 or 20 buildings there, it was beautiful. Just beautiful. It should have been worth around, I would guess, $200,000 or $300,000.

"I don't know how much Hydro finally paid the Beattie family for these parcels of land but I don't think it was very much. I do know that about 10 years before that, a well-known rancher from this area, Bill Pickell, came up there and offered Jim Beattie Sr. over $100,000 for the Twelve Mile property. And that was 10 years before Hydro's offer."

Bill Beattie, at the time, was living in the main house at Gold Bar. Constructed of logs by a top builder, with a water system powered by a hydraulic ram, the house measured 40 feet by 40 feet with a gabled hip roof.

Hydro burned it just before they started backing the water up behind the dam. The corporation's photographer was there to take pictures of Elizabeth Beattie and her son Jim, when they went home for the last time to gather up some things.

Elizabeth Beattie at Gold Bar for the last time

"My brother Bill bought a hunting area and went outfitting over on the Halfway River," Jim said. "And we moved into town, into a building that had been the old telegraph office. After Mother had a new house built she had $4,000 left over, that's all. The house cost $12,000. I think she got $27,000 or $28,000 for the place in total, and it was divided up evenly among Mother, Bill and myself.

"We were never able to set up farming again with what we got out of there," Jim added.

Jack Baker first heard about the dam when Hydro sent in a negotiator to assess the cost of the required land, and Bobby Beattie talked about Cunningham. Baker owned a section of unimproved land at Ten Mile that ran right down to the river. But Cunningham didn't approach him for quite some time.

"He did come to see me, finally, at my office here in Fort St. John," said Baker. "He said he could offer me $4,000 or $5,000 for my full section of land. I said, 'That's ridiculous.' I had no intention of selling my piece of land for something like that. So he came back later and said, 'In view of the fact that there is a spring running through your property, we have decided to increase the offer to $6,000, but that's our final offer.' And I said, 'No, I have no intention of selling this piece of land to you for $6,000.' He said, 'Well, Mr. Baker, I want you to understand that we can and will expropriate the property.' I said, 'Yes, I realize you can do that, but I also realize you don't *want* to do that. Because expropriation procedures are troublesome for anybody . . . so you can make all the threats you like but it's not going to change my opinion.' He stormed out of my office, real mad, stomping his feet."

Eventually another man paid Baker a visit. "He said he was representing B.C. Hydro and he wanted to make a deal with me for my property. He explained how they were putting in a dam and would be flooding my land. 'Well,' I said, 'I'll listen to you because I know the dam is probably going to go regardless, but I think fairness should prevail.'"

After much negotiating, Hydro agreed to pay Baker $12,000 cash, plus the right to trade the corporation any of his remaining land above the high-water mark in exchange for property somewhere else in the province, that he could choose.

"It took a long series of negotiations but I finally got what I wanted," Baker said. "About 19 acres of my land lay above high-water mark on Williston Lake, and in exchange I took two and one-half acres of property at Tutizzi Lake (near Prince George) that had been Crown land."

Several other people were directly affected by the dam's reservoir. They included Ross Darnell, the Kyllos, Ardills, Tompkins, Bill Kruger, Leo Pickell, Clem Brooks and Les Stark, Herb Linley, Two Mile Bob Clark. The Pickells, and Brooks and Stark, only had summer places, but the rest lived on the land.

Ross Darnell had bought Charlie and Madge Jones's place – 320 acres of unbroken land on the point where the Carbon River flowed into the Peace. The Jones's had put in a garden, and Madge's lilacs and perennials made it a place of beauty.

"My dad used it mostly as a place to go in the summer, a fishing camp," said Alene Peck, Ross Darnell's daughter.

Darnell knew that a hydro dam was to be built on the Peace, and figured that sooner or later he would be approached about his property.

"Hydro sent out this Charlie Cunningham, a former photographer and outfitter who was now employed with B.C. Hydro's land division. I think he got Brownie points for making tough deals," Alene Peck said. "He had the same background as perhaps a lot of people in the area. He wasn't a man dressed in a suit and tie, put it that way. He spoke our language. We took him and his wife out hunting one time."

Cunningham offered Darnell $6,000 for his property. Darnell thought it was worth at least $12,000. "People had no idea how to deal, so these offers had met with very little disagreement," Peck said.

"But Dad wouldn't give in. Hydro, of course, went ahead with the dam, and I suppose he was the only hold-out at that time. So Hydro expropriated."

Long before the court case, however, the water started to rise. Hydro burned down Darnell's buildings. "Of course, Dad would have had the chance to go in and take things," Peck said. "They'd warned him . . . but they burned things like the cots and other furniture. Everything."

The court case in Fort St. John dragged on for about 10 years, Peck added. "This was really tough on Dad because he was in his 80s at the time. The courts finally awarded him about twice what he'd asked for, around $20,000 to $24,000. But that still didn't mean that they paid it. So dad spoke to the MLA and through his influence he got the payment through. My dad lived to be close to 90, so he did eventually get his money."

Peck is now facing another go-round with Hydro over land that will be flooded by the proposed Site C. She hasn't yet been approached, but her eight quarter-sections between Tea Creek and Deep Creek that lie along the Peace will be affected. Alene is not personally opposed to the Site C dam, but she warned that "Hydro has to be kept honest."

B.C. Hydro's records show that most of the land and property rights needed for the Bennett Dam project were acquired by negotiation. There were five expropriations, including two that were necessary to resolve problems with transferring title. All expropriations were carried out under the British Columbia Hydro and Power Authority Act.[3]

Two Mile Bob Clark, who had settled on Two Mile Bar to wash gold in the 1930s and had never moved, did not go without a fight.

"I served me hitch in the First World War and that bloody well cured me," he told Earl Pollon. "I came here to get away from so-called civilization and here I'm bloody well going to stay. The bloody bastards are not going to drive me out! I intend to get up in the mornings and see the mountains as long as I live."

He did get driven out, however, and Two Mile Bob became Twelve Mile Bob.

Twelve Mile road was a resettlement road. Hydro gave Bob Clark, the Beatties and Herb Linley each a piece of land there. Linley sold his to Clem Brooks, who still has it. No one, however, is allowed to buy land on the lake.

Mel Kyllo came to the country in 1930, after hearing about gold strikes on the Peace. He hiked around the country with Red Kinsman, looking for land, but found too much bush for his prairie blood.

Instead, Kyllo set up a barbershop. When he couldn't drum up sufficient business in the frontier town of Hudson's Hope, he sold his building to Jack Pollon, and went out prospecting with Kinsman up the Peace, Finlay and Omineca rivers as far as the Black Canyon.

Edith and Mel Kyllo
(Hudson's Hope Museum)

Kyllo's bride-to-be, Edith Edwards, had preceded his arrival in Hudson's Hope by a year. She was the local schoolteacher. After they married, they spent two summers until 1935 washing gold for Bill Mahaffy on Brenham Flats above Gold Bar.

Two of the Kyllo brothers, Ken and Dave, started a boating operation in 1956 called Rocky Mountain River Trips, making weekly or bi-weekly excursions up the river to Finlay Forks. The construction of the Bennett Dam put the Kyllo brothers completely out of business.

"We were usually the first boat up the river in the spring," said Ken. "In the spring of 1957, about the 24th of May weekend, we had a party of schoolteachers from Fort St. John. We figured on camping in the cabin on the Wicked River. The cabin was open, and anyone who came along could use it . . . when we arrived, there were three boats tied up and a survey crew was staying in the cabin."

"That was the first time I heard about the dam going in, about Wenner-Gren's plans," added Dave Kyllo. "We got talking to the surveyors and they told us they were looking for a dam site, that they were going to dam the Peace River and put the water back down the Fraser River. That was the original plan. Back through Arctic Lake and down through the McGregor system. That really shocked us."

In an article in the *Vancouver Sun* on May 25, 1961, Jack Scott and Len Norris describe their introduction to the river: "'Why don't you fellows join us in a little trip across the Rockies by riverboat?' Thus we met the Kyllo brothers, Ken who is 28 and Dave who is 26, a couple of strong, silent types who turned a boy's love for running fast water in long boats into a man's commercial enterprise, and whose journeys up the Peace, Finlay and Parsnip Rivers are an escape hatch we highly recommend for anyone jaded with city life."

Enroute up the river, "planing against the silent, sliding mass of olive-green water" Scott and Norris saw banks "littered with grotesque monsters of soiled ice, the snowcapped pile of the Rockies ahead and herds of mule deer grazing on the gentle slopes of the valley." They passed a "ruin," which the Kyllos explained was once the "split-level log chateau" of Jack and Lucille Adams who, in 1919 had built their magnificent home called 'All's Well,' upstream from the Beatties' place at Gold Bar. The house had featured a balcony overlooking the living room, a huge stone fireplace, picture windows, and the first player piano in the district.

The Kyllo brothers were also featured in a 1964 article, "Adventure on the Peace," in *Beautiful B.C.* magazine: "Dave and Ken Kyllo, operators of the tour, were born in the area and know the river as well as any person. They and their guides are experts on the history and geology of the country which is one of the main reasons almost every tour party includes at least one or two practising geologists on a busman's holiday."

The article described the "rolling hills and beautiful valleys" which could be viewed at each turn of the river, along with abandoned cabins, remnants of old trading posts, and fossilized dinosaur bones encrusting the river banks. The accompanying photographs depict a northern Shangri-La.

But one paragraph carries an ominous warning: "Today at Hudson Hope the stillness of centuries is being shattered by dynamite blasts and the growls of heavy machinery as the Portage Mountain Dam takes shape."

"There wasn't much we could do on the Peace after the dam was built and the lake started filling," said Ken. "There were so many land slides and waves and driftwood."

"Our boats couldn't operate on Williston Lake at all, with the wind and waves," Dave agreed. "We couldn't have base camps then, because the lake kept coming up for years, washing everything away."

Ken used the riverboats for a while on the Finlay arm, until the lake came up there too. "By that time our boats were pretty broke up with log jams," Dave said. "They were just wooden boats, it didn't take too much to crush them.

"Hydro didn't offer help at all," Dave added. "It took years before they offered any kind of compensation. They finally did settle with us, but many, many years later . . . we got a little bit of land there at Finlay Forks bay, about eight acres across the bay from the provincial park, and a little money and that's about it."

Ken was more specific: "Hydro offered us five percent of what we figured we had invested, in time and money. I finally settled in 1978. I thought the NDP government was going to get back in, and their attitude was that 'We own everything,' so I settled when Social Credit was still in. But I finally got only 10 percent. I got some new land at Finlay Forks and $10,000 in cash. We spent $5,000 for lawyers over the years, and the $5,000 left didn't go very far to setting up again. It took us 10 years to get a suitable site from which to work and get title to it."

Dave then went into farming. "And there was still hunting, so we carried on with that instead of the lake trips," he said. "We switched to horses rather than boats. Ken now has some cabins at Finlay bay and a lodge up on the Finlay arm in the Fort Grahame area. Still, it's such a seasonal operation, and it's a short season."

"We've advertised all over Europe and the United States, but it's been limited to small ads," Ken explained. "It's difficult to break into that market, but it's there. It took 14 years to build up that river business."

The Kyllos think Hydro's idea was to eliminate any tourist operations. "I think it was sort of a cover-up for all the drifting timber on the lake," Ken said. "The logs were drifting around for years."

The May 12, 1976 issue of the *Alaska Highway News* chronicles the Kyllos' attempt to get back into business:

"It's been nine years and a lot of problems later, but Kyllo Bros. are finally back in the business of taking people 'across the Rockies by boat.' Dave and Ken Kyllo operated this type of tourist charter service from Hudson Hope from 1954 to 1967 but were put out of business when the slides and debris made the basin behind the dam a hazard . . . "

Jim Beattie still resents the way Hydro treated the longtime residents of the area. "When Hydro gave us this land (in compensation) they said, 'Now whenever you people want hydro power, we'll put it out there for you.' Premier Bennett told this to Mother personally when she was sitting beside him at the dam dedication ceremony. We didn't want power until about four years ago, so we got B.C.

*Jim Beattie at Gold Bar Ranch the day before B.C. Hydro
burned the ranch to prepare for the reservoir*

Hydro officials out from Chetwynd to come and see how many poles they had to put in and all this. When we told them about the old agreement they looked at us rather oddly. 'It's too bad there wasn't something signed,' they said.

"In my opinion," Beattie continued, "the whole dam project could have been handled better. I would say that they should have started logging out the whole reservoir two or three years previous to the dam. There were huge big spruce flats and they all went under. Now they're going 50 to 60 kilometres up the Ottertail River and all these rivers and bringing out muskeg spruce, high country spruce, and they're just poles. Waste. Thousands and thousands of acres. They just wanted that dam finished so soon that they didn't have time to take the timber out.

"Hydro's been lucky these past few years," he added. "Since they put the dam in, we haven't had winters of 40 to 50 degrees below zero for a month or two like we used to. If that happens again, they're going to get all this shore ice build-up, and there's going to be some real floods down the river."

Before the flooding of Beattie's Gold Bar ranch
(Geological Survey of Canada)

After the flooding of Beattie's Gold Bar ranch
(Geological Survey of Canada)

Beattie also stressed that the corporation should have compensated people for what their land was actually worth. "It really wouldn't have cost Hydro much to be fair. Starting from Finlay Forks, there were only about 25 people they had to deal with, counting trappers. They just paid out the trappers whatever they figured the trapline was worth, and that was it. The trappers couldn't re-establish themselves; there were no other traplines for sale."

B.C. Hydro says that compensation was paid to trapline holders affected by the Williston Reservoir, and by the works in and around the damsite, based on the estimated impacts on various furbearers -- especially beaver. Hydro retained a retired conservation officer to do the assessments and determine compensation. Settlements were made in cash. Alternative traplines were not offered as part of the program.[4]

"Most of the trappers were just out of it," Beattie said. "Some of them blew their heads off.

"Jack Longstreet, who lived at Point Creek on the lake, his line was flooded so they paid him out. He had a cabin up there . . . he came to town and sat around down here for a while. Then he committed suicide. He just didn't know where to go anymore.

"Another one was Dick Corless. He used to run riverboats from Summit Lake up to Fort Ware and service the Indian settlement up there. He had three boats, and his riverboats were no good anymore on Williston Lake. So he was finished. He committed suicide too."

Beattie corroborated other residents who said that Hydro offered reduced power rates to industries locating in the area. "But no industries ever appeared. A rail line should have come over from the other side of the Bennett Dam, and they could have brought in everything for the dam. They could have logged that reservoir and taken it out by rail from this end of the reservoir, felled the logs first and as the lake came up, floated them off, and boomed them down to this end of the lake.

"I don't know why they didn't do these things. It's just never been answered."

Notes

[1]*Cadillac Desert: The American West and Its Disappearing Water*, © 1986 by Marc Reisner, All Rights Reserved. Reprinted by permission of Viking Penguin, a division of Penguin Books USA, Inc. (p.441-2)

[2]Ibid., p. 442.

[3]Letter, B.C. Hydro (C.W.J. Boatman) to the authors, dated May 15, 1989.

[4]Ibid.

22

A Lake Full of Logs

Williston Lake was described, in a 1968 B.C. Hydro brochure, as "a catchment area as large as New Brunswick, five times larger than Lake Okanagan." The lake was expected to cover 640 square miles, and contain a maximum 57 million acre-feet of water. It would be ringed by a 1,100-mile shoreline and drain an area of 27,000 square miles. Flowing into this gigantic lake would be spring flood waters from the mountainous country of north-central British Columbia.

If isolation was Hudson's Hope's nemesis, the new dam and reservoir would catapult the community into the modern industrial world, Hydro predicted. The lake would open up development of forest and mineral resources, and provide access to fish and game once denied to all but the "most ambitious sportsmen." Promotion brochures carried artists' conceptions of a northern marina at Hudson's Hope.

The southern arm of the lake would extend "almost" to rail and highway facilities. Politicians foresaw strings of tugboats hauling log booms, and barges transporting mineral ore, through the Rocky Mountain Trench waterway. No longer would the area be solely the domain of trappers and gold seekers. No longer would the Peace area be more closely linked geographically with Alberta than with British Columbia.

Construction of the John Hart highway in the 1950s, from Prince George through the Pine Pass up to Chetwynd and Dawson Creek, had marked the beginning of a B.C. connection. The arrival of the Pacific Great Eastern Railway in Chetwynd, Dawson Creek and Fort St. John in 1958, and the scheduling of regular air flights, also linked the Peace area with the southern part of the province. However, these efforts had not provided cheap transportation to haul the minerals (lead, zinc, mica, gypsum, chromium, mercury, copper and molybdenum) found west of the Rockies. Nor had they helped the coal industry. And residents of the area still could not find steady work in their own region.

The *Peace River-Liard Region Economic Survey*, published by the provincial bureau of economics and statistics in March, 1966, was optimistic: "Extremely high cost of transportation has been the greatest factor in retarding exploitation of mineral deposits in the Peace River-Liard Region . . . When the Peace River reservoir reaches maximum height, ore or concentrates could be barged from the mine to the Kennedy rail extension for shipment in raw form or for further refining using power from the Portage Mountain Dam, if monetary returns warrant."

The forest industry was also in for a boost, the report said. It cautioned that "the existence of a physical resource does not guarantee the establishment of an industry [because] the economies of wood procurement and product marketing must still be reckoned with." But, it added optimistically that "the Peace River reservoir can offset this as water transportation is considerably cheaper than land transport."

The report suggested numerous possibilities for the region: power-related industries such as chlorine and caustic soda manufacturing, with "a plant location near the Portage Mountain hydroelectric site . . . " Or a smelter and refinery, utilizing Peace River power to treat concentrates from a wide area to the north and east. Or a peat moss industry based on the "8,000 square miles of muskeg or bog," which offered the area potential to become the largest peat-producing region in the province. Or vegetable processing, centred on the "500,000 acres of bottom land in the Peace Valley."

The 1966 report also mentioned that survey work had been completed and clearing begun for a 21-mile rail extension from Kennedy to Morfee Lake – near the south end of the lake to be formed by the Portage Mountain Dam – to serve two pulp mills to be built near Kennedy.

But no railway came to Hudson's Hope.

"A rail line in to Hudson's Hope would have been paid for in a very short time," says Tom Roberts, a local resident who was first a logger, and then worked on the Mica and Bennett dam projects. His beautiful home overlooks the Peace River.

"There was nothing here in Hudson's Hope prior to B.C. Hydro's building this dam," Roberts said. "A bunch of shacks, no roads. The employment situation hasn't changed. There should have been a railway . . . It was really short-range thinking to not see that without the railhead into Hudson's Hope, you can't have industry. How can you sell your product? And it was all surveyed."

The reservoir was seen as a panacea for the region's sluggish economic development. But the lake, when it was first filled, was an unsightly and dangerous mess.

Pen Powell, a long-time resident (who married Mary (Girlie) Beattie in 1938), first saw the area to be flooded when he went on a boat trip up the Peace River as far as Finlay Forks in July, 1937. "In my memory it was the most wonderful trip I have ever taken," Powell said. "The only sign of anyone ever being in the area was the odd trapper's cabin, usually situated at the mouth of a creek, and where they had fallen the odd tree to build their small cabin."

In 1957, Powell heard about the building of a dam at Hudson's Hope. He obtained a pilot's licence and bought a float-equipped plane, "as I realized there would be a tremendous amount of activity in the area and this would give me a really good opportunity to watch everything happen." He set up a few fishing camps on the watersheds of the Peace, and by the time the lake started to fill he was well-established.

"Before the lake came up I used to make one or two trips per day, weather permitting, over the area. I used to fly fully relaxed as, with a float-equipped plane, I had a beautiful airport under me all the time. I would often land and visit placer miners working gravel along the beaches, or the natives paddling boats and canoes and camping where the best fishing and hunting areas were. These people seemed to have everything they wanted right on their doorsteps.

"I got to know everyone along the rivers and quite often, when I got tired of flying, I would hope for a storm so I would have an excuse to land and spend the night. Everyone seemed to live along the rivers and I had a perfect landing strip right at their doors, with no debris, snags or waves to worry about."

The construction of the Bennett dam ruined Powell's 'airport.' "First there was a bit of logging done, but apparently that was too slow so enormous-sized tractors were brought in and tied together with heavy cables dragging a large steel ball between them," he said. "They looked to be travelling about 100 feet apart and pulled down thousands of acres of trees a day. Most of the trees would stay down until the water raised, but numerous ones would come back up half-way, leaving the worst mess possible. Even before the water started to cover this mess, it was impossible for moose and caribou to make their way through it. Then as the water started to flood, the animals really got confused and would try to swim through this mess. As I flew back and forth each day that was flyable, the things I saw I often wish I could forget.

"A friend and I were flying one day around the height of the disaster, just north of where the Ospika River enters the Finlay River, and saw a large herd of moose that were trapped on a piece of high ground by floating debris and pulled-over trees. We counted well over 100 moose in about a 10-acre area. The next day we came back over the same area and it was completely covered with water, and we could see lots of dead moose floating among the debris. I don't know for sure whether they all drowned or not, as they float quite low in the water when they drown and are hard to see among the floating logs.

"In a matter of a very short time," Powell added, "the part of the trench that became Williston Lake was transformed from one of the safest, most beautiful areas, to one of the most hazardous and ugly places in British Columbia, in which to boat or operate a float-equipped aircraft."

Tom Roberts, who worked at logging on the B.C. coast for 25 years before being employed by B.C. Hydro, was sent to Hudson's Hope because of debris on the lake. "Hydro sent me up because of the adverse publicity they were getting, little old ladies writing nasty letters to Premier W.A.C. Bennett saying. 'You promised us a nice reservoir for access to this beautiful country, and we were up there and all we saw were logs. You couldn't even see the water.' It was very true. For many years you could walk across the lake on the wood, blindfolded."

A.C. Geddes, whose family operated transportation services in Hudson's Hope since 1963, laughed when he was asked whether Hydro had been concerned about logs in the reservoir. "I can remember when we ran the tour buses for Hydro; they brought in all these engineers from all over the world to look at the dam," Geddes said. "I was on a bus with the press; there was Jack Webster and other newspaper reporters. Dr. Shrum, Hydro's chairman, was the person who did the talking. There was a guide on each bus, who would try to explain what was happening, and then Dr. Shrum would take over. So I remember a reporter asking, 'What's going to happen with all this wood that you're going to flood?' It just so happened that the bus had stopped and, when we looked out the window we could see Kiewit Construction falling trees and logging them off for the conveyor belt-line right-of-way. Shrum said, 'There you go, see? We're logging it off right now.' Well, this was off to the side of the dam. This wasn't even to be a flooded area! But he made them think that Hydro was doing it right now. In fact they hadn't even started."

The first big boat into the lake when the reservoir started to fill belonged to Ernie Krebs, a Hudson's Hope resident since 1962. Krebs had a 24-foot cabin cruiser.

"The greatest part of the sloughing of the banks took place during the first 10 years. That counted for so much debris on the lake. We used to push out through 30 or 40 acres of timber floating in front of the area that is now the yacht club," he said.

"If you were caught in a storm, you just had to have the proper sized boat," Krebs added. "You had to know where the deadheads might be. I hit only one in all the time I was on the lake, but I hit so hard that my first reaction was to look down on the floor to see how fast the water was coming in. It never did come in, but it tore off a strip three feet by four feet square from the fibre-glassing on the hardwood."

Debris on Ospika
(T. Roberts)

Frank Riter, who came to Hudson's Hope in 1962 and set up an electrical business, first put his boat in the lake in 1971.

"The debris was terrible," Riter recalled. "It was expensive on the rigging, but we just battled it out . . . We brought the boat up from Vancouver and put it in at Mackenzie on the southern part of Williston Lake. I had 25 yards of debris to push out of the way with pike poles before I could get into open water. Then we were always fighting logs."

Sloughing of the banks along the lakeshore initially caused some of the most hazardous conditions. But 20 years after the flooding, earth and trees continue to slide into the reservoir.

Terry Curzon, a resident of Hudson's Hope since 1972 and commodore of the Portage Mountain Yacht Club, says it's an ongoing problem. "You can always tell where it's just sloughed because there are trees with new leaves on, lying down on the sand banks, so you know very well that they've fallen down from the bank this year. The sloughing is continuing even though the water is very low. When that water comes up ... there's going to be a lot more sloughing."

A.C. Geddes recalled an unusual experience he had on the lake, one summer evening when he was working on his boat. "I was down changing oil, when all of a sudden the boat started rocking and banging. I was falling all over inside. I didn't know what was happening. There was one big wave, then another not quite so big, then another and another. And this was on a hot calm evening ... My boats were banging against each other – these are all steel boats – and they were dented in on their sides." After cleaning up the mess inside his boats, Geddes walked over the logs to get to shore. "I went to my truck, opened the door and a wave of water spilled out! The waves had come right up onto the shore and flooded my truck, and then gone down."

Geddes suspects that a huge chunk of land had dropped into the water across the lake, creating a big wave. "People used to live down by the river but they eventually moved back up, especially on the Peace arm, because it wasn't stable," he said.

James and Elaine Rhymer trapped on the Carbon River and Schooler Creek, and lived for 10 years at the edge of Williston Lake. They seem resigned to the changes wrought by the reservoir, and were not nostalgic for the river because they had never known the undammed Peace. But they did know an oldtimer, Bill Kruger, who once lived "beneath the waters" of Williston Lake.

"Bill Kruger worked on the river, ran riverboats up and down," said James Rhymer. "I asked him about that lake a couple of times because I was a fairly romantic sort of young guy. I was trying to egg him on: 'Holy cow, Bill, what do you think about them building this lake and destroying all this good farmland?' And he said, 'Well, that river killed more bloody people. There was always someone getting drowned in the sonofabitch. That lake's a lot more normal and more forgiving than the river ever was.'"

Hydro didn't replace the section of Kruger's trapline that was flooded, Rhymer said, because the line went back into the mountains and only the riverbottom portion was under water. "I know Bill never got any compensation. I don't think anybody was compensated right then. They just did it. Most people didn't want to move out but what are you going to do when the water starts coming in the doorway? You've got to leave."

Rhymer noted that he doesn't own any land along the river, "and it doesn't seem to me to be too awfully terrible to flood it and make a nice hydro-electric plant there. I come from England and they have thermal (plants) there, and you can't breathe and after a while everything turns black and it's not good for you. Guys who do own the land and love it, hate to see dams go in. A lot of people hated to see the upper Peace go, but I never saw that river."

Tom Roberts remembers travelling the lake from one end to the other in its earlier years, in search of history and a wilderness seldom found in our settled world. But even since its creation 20 years ago, there have been major changes.

"To me, personally, it is the biggest detriment to this area," Roberts said, adding that he and his wife, Jean, dislike the lake now. "We hate it. We don't go up there anymore. I got rid of my engines. I'm not even remotely interested in going out.

"Jean and I travelled this lake more than any human beings alive, before it was a lake and as it became a lake and the years after it did," he said. "We've got log books of every year we travelled on it; we travelled on it further than the distance from Vancouver to Tokyo and back, every summer for 15 years."

Roberts described what a traveller on the lake might see now: dust on both sides, as far as you want to go, from logging trucks beside the water. At one place, where a fishing and hunting camp is located, he saw five 5,000-gallon fuel tanks, all leaking, spilling diesel oil into the best spawning rivers in the watershed: the Ospika, Davis Creek, Chowika.

"The Ingenika destroyed," Roberts said sadly. "The Omineca destroyed. Garbage from one end to the other." Roberts said he could show a person garbage piles that wouldn't fit into a house, at about a dozen campsites along the lakeshore.

Al Downey poling through debris at the mouth of the Ospika
(T. Roberts)

The Roberts and Downey families spent one summer building picnic tables and placing them in four sites along the shore. They built outhouses and cleared tenting areas that anyone could use.

"They stole all our tools, they smashed the tables up with axes, they dumped their garbage all over the tent sites, and they went to the bathroom on the trail between the water and the outhouse, even though there was a big sign, 'Outhouse,'" said Roberts disgustedly.

The former logger says that logging has destroyed Williston Lake. Wide dusty roads along the lakeshore carry trucks round-the-clock.

"The Omineca is one of the major rivers that runs in about half-ways, right across from Finlay Fork," Roberts said. "We were there a few days ago. The lake is its widest there, 13 miles across. There's a big bay at the Omineca that runs in 11 miles, and there are camps everywhere, logging trucks by the hundreds, skidders and fallers and diesel oil and leakages and nobody cares, nobody gives a damn, there's no policing of it. The fish and game department hasn't got enough money to put on a good lunch, and they never have had, and never will have."

Hydro's attempt at cleaning up debris on the lake has been likened by local resident Al Hamilton to "eating soup with a darning needle."

James Rhymer said the corporation "is cleaning it up. It's gradually disappearing." But he also believes Hydro could have cleaned it up better in the beginning. "They wasted all kinds of stuff, all that wood that's floating around. It's a shame. But I'm a logger myself, and no logger wanted it. If you're clearing for a dam you've got to get it all, even the stuff that's not worth logging."

Boats and driftwood 1984
(K. Kyllo)

Dave Kyllo, whose old wooden riverboats met their demise among the deadheads, thinks he knows why the problem seems to have cleared up a bit. He said that in the last few years of low snowfalls the lake hasn't filled up, so the logs are hung up on the banks. "Hydro hasn't been doing much clearing and burning the last couple of years," he said. "Gave up. Ran out of money."

Tom Roberts doesn't think the reservoir area could have been logged beforehand.

"No pre-logging was done because you couldn't pre-log this," he said emphatically. "You wouldn't make a nickel. The cost of doing that would have exceeded the cost of the entire project, which was in excess of a billion dollars." Roberts said that logging firms, even to cut the merchantable timber in the valley, would have had to build "umpteen miles of roads, which every spring would be gone in the run-off.

"To log it after there was a lake was impossible," he added. "People saw 'merch' timber floating around and they might have thought loggers could just pick up the good stuff and leave the rest. How are you going to do that? Pick one piece out with a magic pair of tweezers from a high altitude and put in on the shore? Here you've got 33,700 acres of debris – and that's an accurate number."

Roberts explained that on September 10, 1968, an airplane flying at 10,000 feet took hundreds of photographs of the entire reservoir. Hydro repeated this survey every year in September, when the air is clearest and stillest.

The worst area was aptly called 'the plug', on the Finlay River at the upper end of the reservoir, where a large bay was crammed with three-to four-foot cottonwoods and mature trees, 150 feet long, and big spruce, poplar and birch. It was so solidly plugged that no boat of any kind, not even a tugboat or dozer boat, could get through.

"You had 34,000 acres of debris floating freely on that lake for many years," said Roberts. "The debris operation I was looking after took out 13,700 acres . . . from just above the Bennett dam, about three-quarters of a mile above the spillway, in a period of about seven years."

Logging companies should have been given the merchantable timber, with no stumpage fee whatsoever, he said.

"How do you get paid for debris? That was one problem we had. How do you measure production? You measure it in smoke. We were burning. You can't go out and scale it because it's limbs and bark and little trees the size of your fist. It was impossible to measure. You see, it was just poor logging volume . . . All you have to have is a piece of paper, a pencil and an adding machine, and in 10 minutes you can figure out there's no way you can make a buck."

Complaints about the clogged reservoir poured in from all over the province the first few years, up to five garbage bags of mail every week. "It showed obvious frustration, but it showed a lot of ignorance too," Roberts said. "There were no letters from loggers; they knew the impossibility of the task. My job was, and I was told by (Hydro chairman) Shrum verbally as well as in writing, to 'get hold of these people who say they have an idea. Get them up here at Hydro's expense, get them to show you the idea. Let's get this solved as quick as we can.' Nobody came. Nobody offered any idea. It was all wind."

Barrie Cornell, who worked at debris clearing on Williston Lake since its creation in 1967, agreed: "I have towed down the Finlay arm with 1,000 feet of tow line, towing a mile of logs, three booms wide, 70 feet each, or 210 feet in total. No debris ahead. All of a sudden the wind would come up and the whole shoreline would come out and it would just snow you. I could tow through it, but it would build up so thick I would have to stop the boat several times . . . "

Rob Scorey, who worked on the problem in the same area said: "I was in the tugboat between the headwaters and the Finlay, with five barges following, hooked together with rope, or boom chains . . . We got 20 miles south of Ingenika when we saw debris on the radar scanner on the tug. It covered the entire lake for as far as the scanner would go."

Ray Williston, provincial minister of lands, forests and water resources after whom the lake is named, admitted there was a problem. In a letter published in the December 20, 1970 *Alaska Highway News*, Williston said "it is true that much debris has floated and collected in various 'pockets' of the lake and this is being removed as quickly and efficiently as possible.

"One can travel a tremendous distance along the waterway without encountering any debris problem," he argued.

"It was devastating what was wasted," said Barrie Cornell. "It was cruel, really. But then you get back to things like your Hydro engineers, who had this stuff planned for the lake. They said, 'Oh, it's going to take a long time to fill up this reservoir.' The goddamned thing started coming up a foot a day and they didn't know what to do! They said, 'This ain't right!' But it was coming. It filled up so fast it drowned forestry camps, with tents and stuff – they didn't even have time to get their tents out! They'd go out for the day and come back eight hours later and there was a foot of water in the tents, and their saws were gone, everything was sopping wet. It filled up 10 times faster than they expected. Then they were stuck with it.

"The big fallers who were logging up there, like Carrier Lumber and Finlay Forest Industries and B.C. Forest Products, were left with cold decks (piled logs) stuck in the bush," said Cornell. "It was crazy. There was more timber felled and left because the rising lake buggered up the roads to get to it, so they just shut the whole thing down, and there's all this timber felled."

Roberts attended a meeting in 1969 where the problem was discussed – briefly. The majority of the 1,700 engineers and designers, from all over the world, agreed that the debris problem at the Bennett dam was not really serious enough to warrant further consideration.

Hydro had envisioned a "northern marina," but there is still not a decent launch site for the public. "Hydro is not responsible for establishing a boat launch," said Terry Peressini, administrative services supervisor for B.C. Hydro at the Bennett dam. "It was not part of the water licence agreement."

However, a section of the Water Licence does say that "the licensee shall provide public access to the reservoir area as may be directed by the Comptroller." Whether the task has been accomplished is questionable. The Hydro-owned launch site at Dunlevy, near the old Twelve Mile area, can be used, if the water rises high enough. If it doesn't, the public has nowhere to go.

The story of the privately owned Portage Mountain Yacht Club is one of hard-won success. A local man, who has been involved with the club from its inception, said Hydro tried to beat out the purchase of the Tompkins land, where the yacht club was located. It was one of the few pieces of lakeshore property that was owned before the dam was constructed. "When they were trying to buy the land our yacht club was situated on, they said they had already made the deal with Tompkins," the club member said. "We found out that they hadn't. Tompkins had told them that the Portage Mountain Yacht Club had preference over anyone else, and if the club could buy it then they would get first choice, and that's how we happened to be able to buy the land. If we hadn't had that, we'd be without a yacht club now."

"I may sound prejudiced," said another club member, "but I think Hydro has got away with murder as far as developing the community is concerned. They could have done a lot more, let's put it that way."

Local residents are sceptical that Williston Lake will ever fulfil the corporation's dreams of becoming a northern marina.

"It could happen, with the right amount of backing," James Rhymer said. "But it gets horribly rough and cold. You can possibly swim in a sheltered bay, but the water stays cold. It's nice for fishing because it's so wild and big. Real wilderness. A challenge for the average boater, too."

Barrie Cornell agreed: "In years to come, perhaps, but not the type of recreational lake like in Florida where you can go on water-skis and that type of thing. This is a little more rugged than that. There's no more beautiful country than the Peace arm to sail in, to go up right through as far as the Wicked River. Even if you never get off your boat, even if you can't get to shore because of the debris."

23

Williston Lake Navigation – An Oxymoron?

The Geddes family first saw the debris collecting on Williston Lake in 1969. They did not view it from an aesthetic point of view; to them, it meant jobs.

Williston Lake then was one-quarter formed; the edge had been taken off the river and silenced forever were the notorious Ne Parlez Pas rapids.

"At that time my dad, my brother Gary, and I were still in the taxi business, the water hauling business, small construction," said A.C. Geddes. "The dam was coming to a close and people were moving away. Having been in the lumber business years before, my dad, grand-dad and uncle could see that there might be a possibility of getting into some sort of business on the lake."

In 1968, before they had started flooding the reservoir, A.C. and his father hauled their riverboat to Mackenzie. They put the boat in on the Parsnip, followed it as far as the Forks, then went down the Peace arm to see what was transpiring. They went back again the first year it started flooding, about the spring of 1969, and a new sight awaited them. The lumber mills, a couple of years prior to the flooding, had started slashing wood, boating crews in at various places along the river. "They were just laying wood down, not skidding it, as there were no roads. They couldn't do this five years previous to the flooding, because wood goes bad within a year or two," explained Geddes.

"They'd brought in three of these tree-crushers from Quebec — there's one sitting at Mackenzie today as a 'monument'. They're enormous, bigger than a house, land machines that ran over the debris on spiked rollers. A thing out front would knock the wood down, then the rollers would run over it and chop it all up. But the machines didn't work because they'd go down a gulley and get stuck. They got a grant from forestry to build these."

When the Geddes' journeyed downriver on their boat in 1969 they saw mats and mats of wood on the water, covering acres. They were forced to spend one night out on the lake, unable to reach shore. "Some people spent longer than that," said Geddes. "Later on it got so thick with mats of timber that you'd get stuck out there for a couple of days, not able to move."

The famous log-crusher
(A.C. Geddes)

As early as 1967, the Geddes' had investigated the possibility of salvage work on the lake-to-be, and had brought consultants up from the coast to look over the job and recommend the type of boats required. Marpole Towing of Vancouver decided to amalgamate with the Geddes', and form a company called Williston Lake Navigation. The partnership included the three Geddes' (Arnold, Gary and A.C.) and from Vancouver, Barrie Cornell, and Jack and John Laurie. Marpole Towing owned some booming grounds near Vancouver, a couple of tugs and a 44-foot wooden boat that they felt would be shaken to pieces if shipped by rail. They did, however send their two, 34-foot tugs by rail from Vancouver.

Williston Lake Navigation, operating independently, began by salvaging and towing logs directly to Carrier Lumber, which operated a small portable sawmill at Finlay Forks. The salvage operation did well in the first few years, but later it became difficult to get bundles of quality wood, and production slowed down. About 1969, Hydro started their debris clean-up program, and Williston Lake Navigation worked under contract.

At first the company had a camp for about 20 people, using six boats. After operating for a year it became evident that the Vancouver partners knew all about tugboat towing, but nothing about the logging part of it. They were only interested in the towing, so a new

Williston Lake Navigation Camp on Williston Lake
(A.C. Geddes)

partnership was formed, consisting of Arnold, Gary and A.C. Geddes and Barrie Cornell.

"My dad had got a contract with Bill Kordyban who owned Carrier Lumber," said A.C.. Kordyban was a successful lumberman from Prince George who had opened up a lumber mill at Finlay Forks. "We were in the process of buying our own crane at that time. Carrier Lumber had bought about 30 barges to put on the lake. Kordyban had an idea about establishing a mill at Finlay Forks to saw the lumber, then bundling it onto the barges and towing it up to the railhead at Mackenzie. He tried that and he ran into debris . . . and then there was the waterline – the water was still coming up.

"The reservoir was supposed to take three years to reach its level," Geddes said, "but even after it got to this mark, you would set up a dock in the fall, say, and in the spring the water would be 100 feet away from the dock, if there was a gradual slope. At Finlay Forks, on flatter land, the dock would be two miles away. The lake would drop in the winter because the turbines were pulling water and of course they wanted to work those turbines, so they kept drawing water."

The Geddes' and Cornell went to work on contract for Carrier Lumber doing the towing with tugboats. They worked the Peace arm, which ran from Finlay Forks to the dam. B.C. Hydro Construction was already there.

"Hydro had bought six cranes and worked double, triple shifts for about six years, and all they did was burn wood," Geddes said. "Our attempts to try to salvage the wood at the Hydro end came to nothing . . . They piled and burned wood for quite a few years. Beautiful wood. We tried to say, 'How about us being in front of your cranes? We'll take the good wood out and sort it, and just throw the debris at you?' No, that wouldn't work either."

The lake had excited a lot of interest. The Peace Salvage

Association had been formed before the dam was flooded. It consisted of Finlay Navigation, Peace Navigation, Finlay Forest Industries, B.C. Forest Products and Carrier Lumber. They were allowed to claim all the wood that was below the flood line, known as "salvage" wood.

"From Twenty Mile down to the dam was actually Hydro's," Geddes said. "We thought perhaps we could put a little mill in there. My dad lobbied in Victoria with the forestry department for permission to take that wood out . . . But we got nowhere. We actually tried to salvage wood and sell it to Chetwynd, which was only 40 miles away. But forestry turned us down."

The *Chetwynd Echo*, on October 11, 1972 corroborated Geddes' view in an article titled "Resources Misused?"

"Regional district directors are concerned that natural resources in this area are being used outside the region," it said. "Leon Thomas of Fort St. John said: 'I have been told that timber from our region is designated to the Mackenzie pulp mill. If we are responsible for economic development of this area we must have control of our natural resources.' Frank Oberle of Chetwynd added, 'They are harvesting trees in our regional district very close to Hudson Hope which are shipped into Mackenzie. Nothing but the pollutants are left behind. Of the sustained yield unit in our area, 80 percent goes into Mackenzie.'

"Williston Lake forest reserve is the area of immediate major concern to the regional district," continued the article. "Daphne Phillips, Dawson Creek, said, 'This is another example of the need for an application to the province to get some organization on zoning of Crown lands. The Forestry department operates like a law unto itself.'"

"When nothing else worked," Geddes said, "we tried to do it politically, get the MLA involved, because it was such good wood. But it was Hydro property and in actual fact they ordered us out of there and we had to stay back at the Twelve Mile limit. Some of the animosity came from the people running the Hydro debris control themselves. They didn't want anybody seeing them burning this good wood."

Geddes said it was then decided the debris would be all right for pulp wood. Kordyban believed there was a market for the wood and started an operation. "We worked all one summer for him, and the pulp mill was really happy with it," Geddes said.

"That summer we did really well, then the next year they wanted to expand, but for some reason they couldn't make an agreement with the government." Geddes suspects that the mill tried to bargain for more high-grade timber above the flood level, provided it took the pulp wood. "The deal fell through. They said, 'Keep your debris,' so we didn't go to work that next summer."

During this period, when the lake was being flooded, Hydro Construction looked after debris control in the Peace arm. Forestry was responsible for the Finlay Forks area and to the north. Hydro subsidized the forestry operation at Cheeko (out of Mackenzie); the department had some boating experience, but nobody had ever seen these many logs on a lake this size.

"I was watching the forestry perform with Hydro's money to control debris, get rid of it, and they were burning wood in much the same manner as Hydro," Geddes said.

Hydro, in the meantime, had scaled down their operation on the Peace arm. They were handling fewer and fewer logs. The corporation's operation had been located in a natural catch basin — prevailing winds pushed debris toward the dam. But Finlay Forks was different. Because of erratic winds, the logs went back and forth from Finlay Forks to Ingenika (approximately 80 miles). Forestry did a lot of chasing after wood.

"At that point," Geddes said, "some fellow in the Hydro engineering department came up with an idea to build what they called a 'burning basket.' This was a huge circular barge shaped like a doughnut, about 100 feet across, with a hole in the middle. Inside that doughnut hole they laid a cable net. They had another barge tied beside it and a tugboat pulling it; the crane would pick up wood and throw it inside the doughnut. Then they were going to burn. They had a floating camp, so no matter where the debris went, they would be able to follow it.

"The only setback with the doughnut was in trying to light the wood on the water. It was like trying to build a campfire over water. How do you keep it going? Your hot coals are sitting on water. They thought the ashes would just drop out the hole, but it was always wet. They'd get wave action and the water would come up underneath it and swish it out. So what they did was set up propane tanks and big torches to try to burn it. They poured diesel fuel on it, everything, because somebody had come up with the idea and they'd spent millions of dollars setting this thing up."

"Barrie and I really laughed at this basket," Geddes said. "Then one night we got talking and thought, 'Why build a basket? Why not just wait until the water goes down in the fall, take the crane and pile the wood on the shore?' Come spring when the lake is at its lowest, that water will have gone down and there will be this 60-foot pile of wood. So I took the idea to Hydro."

After some convincing, Hydro offered a contract for three months' work. "The condition was that I had to do the burning,"

Geddes continued. "They thought it wouldn't burn, and I'd guaranteed that it would. So we had three big long piles; one pile was a quarter of a mile long. There were more than two feet of snow on top of the piles of wood, and Hydro was very sceptical.

"So Barrie and I grabbed some little branches, and the wood was just as dry as could be," he added. "We pulled a lighter out and we lit 'er, and it got going and pretty soon it took off. Just like that. They wouldn't let me light the next one until the first one went out. The forestry picked up on it right away. This was a huge fire! The pile was a good 60 feet high and maybe a quarter of a mile long. Because the water had gone down, the whole thing was now sitting on land. Hydro liked it. They took pictures of it, movie films. It was impressive."

Hydro then offered the Geddes' and Cornell another three to four months' work near the Ingenika River, at the top end of the lake.

"Forestry had a camp up at Ingenika, and they hired university students and they operated some dozer boats," Geddes recalled. "Barrie called it 'Camp Howdy.' You know, 'How d'ya do this? How d'ya do that?'... They had a great big tugboat that stayed there, tied up, that they used a couple or three times a year, and all these dozer boats, and then they had this burning basket ... So there's the forestry sitting with a camp of 20 people or more, trying to run this doughnut and make a fire."

Hydro personnel visited the Finlay plug site to check on everybody's progress, so a competitive spirit entered into the work. This heated up when the forestry operation moved to the same area where Williston Lake Navigation worked. "It just killed them," said Geddes, "because they were doing nothing, even with three shifts going on this doughnut. Meanwhile, Hydro is paying them and us. And our production was just phenomenal, with two cranes, four people (my wife Coby was cooking), compared to the forestry with the double-decker 20 or 30-man camp, with all these little dozer boats and all this make-work effort."

About 1980, Hydro conceived the idea of time-and-motion studies. It started when Williston Lake Navigation won a contract to use a hydraulic crane, rather than an awkward cable-driven grappler, to stack the logs for burning.

"They would come up and count how many swings I could do per hour, and how big the trees were," Geddes said. "It eventually became ridiculous. We were putting up a lot of wood and there was no sense in trying to compare it. What could you compare it to? Nobody else was doing it."

Williston Lake Navigation had prided itself on taking care of its crane barges. Everything was set up and in order: welders, cutting torches, tools, toolboxes. Suddenly, said Barrie Cornell, "Hydro started doing a time-and-motion study with this hydraulic machine, based on hiring it for 20 hours a day, two 10-hour shifts. It was a circus! They wanted this thing to come around full bore, grab wood and throw it, and grab wood and throw it. Jesus! They literally destroyed everything on the barge. Wood was flying out of the grapple, going all over the goddamned place."

Piling debris at Ingenika
(A.C. Geddes)

It got to the point where the crew could stand at the camp, look over and instantly tell if a couple of hours had been lost by the night shift from breakdowns or whatever. But the workers were worried. They didn't like the frantic pace, and the haphazard methods that had to be followed to keep the schedule.

"The way these idiots wanted us to run it, we would have destroyed the barges," said a crew member. "We wouldn't have been standing on anything after a while! By taking a half-second more and coming around with a full load, bringing it over and setting it down – not just clanging it – we would have had control and there wouldn't have been wood flying all over."

The company toughed it out for two seasons, then in 1981 put its foot down. Their progress reports took a bit of a dip, and they had some run-ins with Hydro, but they were adamant that the operation be run using common sense.

"Then they decided to start using Cats," Geddes said. "And they worked quite successfully too, provided they had good weather in the spring and could pile the debris up quick and burn it before the water flooded that area again."

The demise of Williston Lake Navigation occurred when Hydro abruptly decided not to contract out any more debris cleanup. So there the company sat, with a $450,000 hydraulic crane they were still making payments on and no work. They had tied themselves to Hydro, working for them from 1968 to 1981, and had no other job possibilities. A period of odd jobs followed, small tasks for Hydro such as clearing trash-racks, or using Cats at the beginning of the year to clean up the flats. But the work could not sustain a company with an inventory of that magnitude.

"We put a hell of a dent in the debris, though," Barrie Cornell said proudly. "When we worked the top end, the Finlay headwaters, if we'd have kept going the way we were for another couple of years, it would have made all the difference in the world to the Finlay plug."

Burning debris on Williston Lake
(A.C. Geddes)

Cornell fondly recalled one special burn at the top end of the lake, where the mouth of the Finlay flows out into the reservoir. A flat runs out about a mile, straight off the river. They had built piles about 70 feet high in a horseshoe pattern. However, a big blow came up and actually moved the piles. They got all the boats out and, using the tugs, jammed all the wood through the opening in the horseshoe. When the D-8 Cats tried to pile the stuff next spring, the operators couldn't believe it: the knitted wood was piled way above them.

"We lit that sonofabitch, and you talk about Rome burning!" Cornell said. "We lit that one night, the whole works right around, and it took off, and you've never seen a fire like that. It was so hot that I had to pull the camps away from the beach, which were about a city block away. The fire was starting to buckle the aluminum siding on the trailers. We burned all that debris in one shot, about 15 hours, and it was gone. We got over a 90 percent burn-out. It was just phenomenal. It was beautiful, really, to get that much done."

Hydro engineer J.A. Loose, in a March 11, 1987 report entitled "Estimate of Mean Annual Increment Lost as a Result of the Flooding of Williston Lake," refers to a 1975 Williston Reservoir task study document that said 360,000 acres of the flood basin was originally forested with 354,000 acres of productive forest remaining.[1]

Geddes doesn't think the debris problem will ever be licked. "There's always going to be wood coming into the lake from upland logging . . . I would think Hydro should have an obligation to clean up the lake. They said they would clean it up for recreation and I don't think it's anywhere near that level."

A former partner in one of the salvaging companies agreed: "Hydro stopped spending money on debris control because they were only forced to do x amount of cosmetic clean-up. As long as there was no noise they didn't have to sustain a big program. They've always had a program, they still have one this year – playing on the Parsnip, would you mind, with a little T.D. 15 (Cat), pushing debris around on the beach, piling and burning. Which is fine, great, but it isn't going to clean up the lake."

Chris Boatman, vice president of corporate affairs of B.C. Hydro says that the corporation "has spent in excess of $37 million on debris cleanup on the reservoir and the B.C. Forest Service has contributed approximately $6 million more. The expenditures to date would, in 1986 dollars, equal $100 million. Hydro is continuing to clean up debris located in and around high use recreational areas, boat launch sites and other important locations. There is also tractor piling and burning at a few sites where there is a high density of debris on the shore."[2]

Some say the valley was so large that it couldn't have been fully logged and cleaned out. But Geddes still he believes that Hydro or the government could have put in some logging roads, during the 10 years before dam construction actually started. The timber had taken 100 or 120 years to grow and it was just flooded, wasting a phenomenal amount of revenue. "Then when they did take it," Geddes added, "they let the mills almost have it for nothing."

Local companies attempted to establish mills near Hudson's Hope. Barrie Cornell's assessment of that effort sums up the hopelessness and anger of many residents. "Williston Lake Navigation Company tried to put in a stud mill, right here at the end of the pavement. Operate a sawmill ourselves, employ local people to salvage lumber and saw it right there.

"We weren't allowed to do it, because Peace Salvage Association had sanction on the wood. We lobbied for it in Victoria, we did every-thing, but we couldn't get it. It's all political. It's so political it's sick-ening. They've screwed more people on this lake ... "

Notes

[1]Site Preparation and Post-Flood Clean-Up of Williston Reservoir, J.A. Loose, P. Eng., B.C. Hydro Production Department, Prince George, June, 1988.

[2]Letter to the authors, C.W.J. Boatman, vice president, corporate affairs, B.C. Hydro, May 15, 1989.

24

Booms and Busts

From 1966 to 1969, Earl Pollon published a weekly tabloid called *The Hudson's Hope Power News* which began selling for five cents a copy. Its mandate was to provide local news, serialized stories that would tell newcomers of the country's past, and a summary of events at the damsite. In the first issue, April 27, 1966, Earl stated his creed:

"This paper is dedicated to progress, to the men and women of the past who have served their terms and given wholeheartedly of themselves and their time in helping a new country settle and grow;

"To the men and women of the present who are like pioneers of the past, serving their terms and giving the best of themselves.

"Mistakes are the foundation of experience and from them we should learn to guard the future, judging not from appearance, but by results . . . ."

Pollon's attitude was not antagonistic, but his presence – especially with a camera and tape recorder – was not always welcomed at the damsite. It soon became apparent why the press was kept at a distance. Many events at the damsite seemed to follow the maxim that "top administrators too often take the view that complex problems can really only be solved by technical experts."[1]

"For some reason, the people at the top end of Hydro weren't able to calculate that there were going to be great winds on that lake," said one man who had an administrative role on the project. "The chairman, who made such decisions based on what his top engineers told him, and the chief engineer said there weren't going to be any winds on the lake that would be strong or constant enough to warrant any real consideration."

Initially, Hydro proposed installing a main boom at Lost Cabin Creek (near Finlay Forks), at the narrowest gap on the entire reservoir, to stop logs from coming down the Peace arm. The idea was that debris would collect against the boom, and they could then tow it to shore at North Harbour and burn it.

Plans changed, however, when the engineering group decided the wind would not be strong enough to require a boom at Lost Cabin Creek. The engineers thought that as the water floated the logs, they would more or less sit and collect. Hydro finally decided to locate a large boom in the Peace arm at Nine Mile. The boom had been built – using 40-foot logs – before the flooding started.

A.C. Geddes said the corporation eventually installed three booms, four to five miles apart. "I think Hydro spent $1.5 million on them, with cable and boomsticks that they hauled in from Oregon, Sitka spruce," he said. "I thought they could use the spruce we had right here, but nevertheless they hauled them in, all cleaned up, and ran cables through them and set them out. After the reservoir rose, a big wind came up and moved down the debris that had been felled up above the Forks. As soon as the mat of debris — which could have been a couple miles wide and several miles long – hit the boom it stopped, but then some more came in behind it so it was one tremendously big mat. It broke the boom and kept going through all the other booms. That morning we could see the debris right across the dam, which is about a mile-and-a-quarter wide, running all the way up to Twelve Mile, one solid mat. Nobody could move their boats."

Tom Roberts, who has years' experience in logging, thinks he knows why the booms failed. "The logs were put together in a fashion that was haphazard as hell," he said. "There were all kinds of precedents for booms. All they had to do was pick up a phone and call MacMillan Bloedel or any large company on the B.C. coast, or the Americans, and these people would have taken them to see booms that would be able to withstand anything the west coast winds had to offer. But they didn't do that.

"That mickey-mouse boom at Nine Mile cost $800,000 and it lasted eight hours," Roberts added emphatically, "because of its stupid design and the stupid idea of putting it there in the first place. It was like trying to stop a tidal wave. I was sent up because of that boom being destroyed in the summer of 1968. The spillway boom and the intake boom were separate in cost over that. They lasted a bit longer but they were also done by amateurs. The two men who designed the three booms had never seen a tree in their lives before coming to B.C. Hydro."

According to Roberts, the booms consisted of 1 5/8-inch cable strung from shore to shore, 2 1/2 miles in length. This cable was shackled, every 1,740 feet, to a 26-inch steel ring. From each of the rings extended a 50-foot, 1 1/4 inch, holding cable, attached to a can-

Clearing debris from front of trash racks
(T. Roberts)

buoy. The long 1 5/8 inch cable itself rode in a "v" cut into two blocks of wood. In a very short time, it sawed right through and split the block. The holding cable, which was of a type that would not stretch, couldn't be adjusted, so the entire boom disintegrated.

Roberts was sent to do a damage report, and estimate the cost of reinstallation. "I was sent up here for four days, and I've been here 20 years," he joked. Then, he added: "I knew what was going to happen before I left town. The chief engineer was in trouble. The boom cost close to a million bucks and it lasted only eight hours."

Diving operation to retrieve lost boom
(T. Roberts)

Roberts hired a crew of nine divers. They found that the boom had dragged some of its anchors right across the lake toward the Summers' ranch. Thick cables were tangled with logs, up to 300 feet under water. The equipment was pulled to the surface, and stamped on every shackle was the weight it could withstand: 90 tons.

"In my report I basically said that I thought in general the boom was of a poor design and I had 84 different reasons why it was," Roberts said. "It was the fault of the inspectors for allowing them to hook up shackles stamped 90 tons when the (contract) drawings specified 110 tons . . . It took two years to be settled in court."

"The final decision was to not put a boom in at all," Roberts added. "They dismantled that one completely, took away the sections and stored them 'for future use.'"

Roberts said that Shrum asked him about possibly redesigning the boom and rebuilding. "I told him, 'Not if it was my money. I wouldn't put a boom in there because God is just going to wipe you out.'"

The lake proved to be almost impossible to control. Hydro's initial spillway design was estimated to cost $4.3 million (1959 dollars). By the time it was completed, it had cost $32 million (1968 dollars). The main cause of this increase, according to a project summary published in *Engineering Journal* (Vol. 52/10 Oct./69, p.19) was that, "from 1959 the capacity had increased from 80,000 cfs (cubic feet per second), with reservoir at elevation 2,255 feet, to 341,000 cfs with reservoir level at 2,215 feet and including the 16,000 cfs discharge capacity of the nine sluice gates . . . The principal contributing factor in this increase was the lower dam, which reduced reservoir capacity from 88 million acre-feet to 57 million acre-feet . . . As a consequence, the flood storing capability of the reservoir was much less. . . The original studies had been made before the flood of 311,000 cfs which occurred in 1964."

A B.C. Hydro brochure from 1968 described the spillway:

"On the west side of the river, more than two million cubic yards of rock have been excavated for the spillway. Its 100-foot wide concrete-lined discharge channel will extend 2,300 feet from the crest of the dam down the side of the abutment to a point 250 feet above the downstream river bed. Hopefully, it will never be used. Its sole purpose is to protect the dam in the event of an unexpectedly high run-off or any other unforeseen event."

The 'unforeseen event' occurred in 1972, when the lake almost reached its peak and threatened the spillway.

The spillway system included three gates: each arch-shaped gate was separated by a pier nose (a concrete column housing gate apparatus to guide the gate). The gates were raised and lowered with a cable mechanism. When the spillway required repair or maintenance work, a number of fabricated steel stoplogs (53 feet wide and

Spillway discharging ± 60,000 c.f.s.
(T. Roberts)

weighing up to 7 tons) were installed to keep the water back. Each semi-circular stoplog was installed or retrieved by a gantry crane. The electrically-operated crane moved along rail-tracks on top of the dam.

"Any engineer who had anything to do with the design of the stoplog crane should be ashamed of himself, it was so disgraceful," recalled a man who worked for several years on the operation. "To pick up the stoplogs, you had to walk the crane over to where they were stored, while three men trotted along beside it carrying a great big fat electric cable, big around as a coffee cup. Then the hooks were electrically lowered to pick them up. It was so slow you could write four or five paragraphs on a complex subject before the hook got down to grab one."

Power for the crane came from a fixed source at ground level. The cable was so thick it couldn't be rolled on a spool, so the men carried the cable along while the crane hoisted each stoplog. The cable wasn't long enough to reach the power source from the far side. So the men had to disconnect the cable from the crane, go to the other side of the spillway, get another cable, drag it down and plug it into the crane. "Like an extension cord to your weed-eater," explained the worker. "You work from the middle of your house to one end, then when the cord can't reach any farther you have to take it and go the other way."

It took 14 minutes to install one stoplog, sliding it on the pier noses into the water.

"That performance was disgraceful," the worker continued. "And they called that engineering. If you can imagine, you could not move the crane in the winter at all, because the ice froze in the slots of the tracks. There was an inadequate drainage system. They had a half-dozen guys out there with propane torches and little wee bottles, heating up the bloody tracks trying to get the ice and snow out so they could bring the crane out. By the time you got a few feet thawed out, the first part had all frozen up again. A few more feet and the same thing would happen. It was so simple to correct, to design properly in the first place, but they didn't."

Another Hydro worker added, "The problem was with the totally lousy workmanship and materials that were put into the crane. It was originally intended for the diversion tunnels. After final closure the crane and stoplogs were just going to be drowned."

The stoplogs formed a sealed arch, with very little leakage. That part worked. It took 56 stoplogs in each of the three gates to block off the water when the reservoir was at peak.

In 1971, the stoplogs had been put in to do some maintenance work on the three spillway slide gates. Repairs were completed at two of the three gates and the stoplogs removed. But repairs on the centre gate were never finished, due to a delay in getting replacement parts. So all 56 stoplogs remained in the water in front of this gate.

The stoplogs were piled one on top of the other, and several in front of the centre gate became dislodged. Former dam workers said that water surging through the other two open spillway gates, and also up against the piled stoplogs in front of the centre gate, probably shifted several of the beam-like logs. If they shifted by only a few inches, however, the gantry crane would have difficulty hooking onto them and hoisting them out. And once the stoplogs were loose, water surging through the spillway could possible roll them under the gate opening. This would prevent the gate from being closed, causing a problem for dam operators. Sufficient water would have to be drained from the reservoir to ensure the spillway chute stayed dry, allowing workers to go in and retrieve the loose stoplogs. But this much water flowing out of the reservoir would likely cause problems in the river channel downstream, and would certainly upset power generation.

The potential for serious trouble came in the spring of 1972, when the reservoir approached its peak. A concerned Hydro employee notified his supervisor that the reservoir was rising approximately 21 inches a day. The supervisor denied this, relying on instruments which recorded an 8-inch rise. Precious days were lost because of this impasse, until the water was nearly to the top of the spillway gates.

Later, it was discovered that the instrumentation had not been working properly.

The staff recognized that they could have an emergency situation on their hands, because the spillway had not been designed to operate with only two radial gates. The centre gate couldn't be raised until all the stoplogs in front of it had been removed.

But no one knew the exact location of the dislodged stoplogs. They were heavy, of course, and wouldn't travel far. However, the water where they sat was 100 feet deep, very cold, and murky with silt.

On June 15, 1972, the performance of the spillway using two open radial gates was monitored. The water coming from the two spillway gates formed a "diamond" pattern, converging at the narrow part of the trough, hitting, rebounding. At 70,000 cubic feet per second, the flow was fairly violent down the channel, but it didn't appear the water would overtop the spillway.

Then the crew encountered other problems. The stoplog crane's trailing power cable was spliced in three places, and reinforced with rope taped to the cable. Power outlets had been wrenched off their supports, the crane's wheels couldn't make the turn to the stoplog storage bays, and the crane's hooks were bent. A replacement power cable had to be flown immediately from Vancouver.

During the night shift of June 16, when workers had removed two stoplogs of the 56 in front of the centre gate, the crane broke down. One of the wheels running on the outside track rims was badly worn and one rim had partly sheared off. The broken rim was replaced by welded plates. Meanwhile, the rain fell in monsoon fashion, and the water continued to rise. Finally, by 11:30 p.m. the crane was operational again.

In the morning, a supervisor asked a Hydro official in Vancouver to comb the city for two new wheels for the crane. He arrived with them in a specially chartered DC-3 aircraft. But there was no one available at the site to start machining them, because the only machinist on staff was also the day-shift crane operator.

Sunday, June 18, the night-shift – still using the repaired wheel on the crane – removed 10 more stoplogs. Up they came, one by one, dangling like spiders. The first stoplog retrieved by the dayshift came up with one end unhooked, precariously hanging on the lifting beam. A mobile crane was brought in to help transfer the log to the storage bay. The next day, workers snagged another stoplog. When they brought it to the surface, they discovered it was attached to the lifting beam by the crown only. This time, the mobile crane was too short to help. A supervisor decided to close the two spillway gates that had been opened, and call for more help.

Tom Roberts was, at this time, working on Hydro's debris control operation. He was in the office at the debris site when the man in charge called him over. "We've got a real problem," he said, and asked Roberts what he thought could be done. Roberts got his crew ready and waited for permission from Vancouver to move. In about half-an-hour, a telex arrived from head office telling him to use every man and every bit of equipment they had for this emergency situation.

The debris crew brought over their barge and two tugs. The plan was to transfer the stoplog dangling from the crane to the barge, using the barge's winch. A diver was also flown in from Dawson Creek in case of the unexpected. It took almost two hours, but the stoplog was successfully transferred to the barge. The crane failed to latch onto the last stoplog left in the water, however. No one knew where it was, so the diver was asked to take a look.

The diver would call the shots the moment he was in the water; he would decide how the crew was going to hook onto the last stoplog. While the diver was underwater, there was no communication except by one sharp pull on the rope for "go up" and two for "go down." By the time he surfaced, his face was blue with cold. The men quickly got him into a little shack that was heated by a stove and warmed him up.

The diver had located the last stoplog well upstream of its proper location. He had just about hitched it onto the barge's winch cable when his regulator failed. In 10 minutes he was back in the water completing the shackling procedure. The last stoplog was winched up to the barge, and the barge towed to the debris-burning area with its load.

"Operation Stop-Log Removal" was finally completed at 5 p.m., June 19. Removing the 56 stoplogs had taken 85 hours, including 25 1/2 hours for crane repairs.

By now, water was trickling over the top of the spillway gates. Everyone knew that if it came cascading over the top, its force could damage the gates.

"Every brass hat in Hydro was standing on that deck, watching and giving all kinds of orders," said a former employee.

Another worker added: "With all due respect to those operating (the dam) in 1972, good guys and idiots alike, no one on earth had experience operating a God-defying project such as this!"

"None of the engineers or designers were sure what was going to happen," one on-the-scene employee said. "Because what happened next was almost another tragedy. Oh, let a little water through, every-one knows what that's going to do; it's going to run down and spill over the edge. But what happens when you open those three massive gates?

"They had 190,000 cfs (cubic feet per second) running for 12 minutes. The vibration was intense! The deck was shaking so bad it was like an earthquake.

"Another man and I went down into the lower warehouse, which was constructed with steel beams, girders, nuts and bolts. The nuts were backing off the bolts on the steel up high. The vibration in there on that concrete floor was tremendous. We ran out and a rock as big as a coconut was catapulted from the bottom of the river onto the roof of the warehouse, and another onto the roof of his car parked right beside the warehouse door."

The weather helped, in the end, to ward off disaster. The rain eased, and the sun did not blaze the mountains' snow into instant run-off.

After the incident, a B.C. Hydro engineer, who had been sent to the damsite from Vancouver to "render assistance in the speedy restoration of the spillway to full capacity," made some stern recommendations. The stoplog crane had to be completely rebuilt before being used again. The engineer suggested several improvements to the stoplogs, and also made various general recommendations. His final advice was that, above all, the upgrading should not be pushed into the distant future and forgotten.

Stoplog crane hovers over stored stoplogs
(Shirlee Matheson)

The crane was extensively modified in the early 1980s, based on a design instigated by Dave Scorey, mechanical maintenance supervisor for B.C. Hydro. Changes included the installation of an 80-kilowatt diesel generator, thus eliminating the need to carry the heavy cable.

B.C. Hydro is now considering whether to raise Williston Lake another five feet, and is mapping the shoreline to determine how much land would be flooded. According to a Hydro operator, the lake may be raised from 2,205 feet (the initial maximum) to 2,210 feet.

"Hydro is considering raising the lake level to gain more power out of the dam," confirms Bill Davidson, a Hydro transmission supervisor who is also a pilot. He is active with the Hudson's Hope Rod and Gun Club, which is working to re-establish wildlife on the remaining flats along Williston Lake.

Mud flat south of Chowika
(Shirlee Matheson)

We are flying in Davidson's Super Cub airplane, passing over Dunlevy (Twelve Mile) where we can see some of the herd of 130 elk that the Rod and Gun Club has successfully transplanted from the Kootenays. Below us, the Ne Parlez Pas Rapids lie far beneath the waters of the reservoir. We fly past the Ottertail, the Clearwater, and Hole in the Wall high up on the mountain. As I view these sites, I can hear the oldtimers – Earl Pollon and his cronies. Their stories come back, howling like the wind through this inexplicable hole high up on the peak.   We reach Finlay Forks. To our right is the Finlay reach, to the left the Parsnip reach. It is a wide, silent, snow-covered lake.

The mud flats shoulder up through the snow as we near the Ospika. "I've never seen them like this in the 11 years I've been flying here," Davidson says. At Lafferty Creek we see stretches of ground on which nothing grows – brown frozen mud, with stumps sticking out like whiskers over the earth's brown face.

Note

[1]Social Impact Assessment, Theory, Method and Practice, Ed. Frank J. Tester and William Mykes, Detselig Enterprises Ltd., Calgary, 1981, p. xiii.

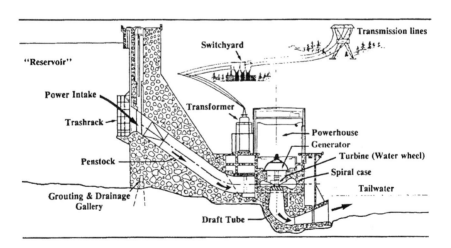

Water flowing from one elevation to a lower one is the source of power in hydroelectric generation. Entering the powerhouse through penstocks, falling water drives the turbines, which in turn activate generators. With 2,416,000 kW capacity, Gordon M. Shrum Generating Station on the Peace River is B.C. Hydro's largest single producer of electric power. (Courtesy of B.C. Hydro)

Portage Mountain Dam

"Oh, River with thy surging jets of power
Who can produce two million kilowatts per hour;
You, whose waters ran so wild and free
Until a man with vision harnessed thee,
Demolishing the glacier's south moraine,
Plugged up your gap, although you strive and strain
To break away.
What sayest thou?"

"Oh, foolish man!
A million years or more I've spent in cutting
Through coal seams, sandstone, fossils laid before.
My waters formed a stream of power
A million years ere man had tried my shore.
The mountains parted by a fault, a fissure,
Through which my waters seeped, to wear away
Until I formed this mighty flow.
Glaciers moved in and tried to bar my way.
But still my endless waters kept on running
Until another gouged-out channel lay
Around the southern edge of Portage Mountain.
What measures time? A million years? A day?

"Then came a man, cherubic face and boyish grin
That well concealed the driving force within.
This puny man,
Standing on my canyon walls, gazed below
Upon my seething waters, formed from melting snow
Of mountains high.

"'Here runs a wealth of power, untapped, untold.
A million horses here, if I can hold
These wild and boiling waters down below!'
He dreamed a while and then he went away,
And still my waters ran.
How was I to know his driving will,
His plan to harness me to be a slave to man?
I continued on, in measured time,
While weak and foolish men wrote in rhyme
Of weak and foolish men.

"Back sent that man, with boyish grin,

Engineers, explosives, clattering drill and pin.
I seethed and raged, but still they augured in
To test my bed, foot by foot, aye, hole by hole
Until they knew the secrets of my soul.
No crevice left where I might seep away.

"Oh! puny man, in months, where I'd take eons,
Demolished my solid walls of stone.
Diverted my wild and raging waters
To run in diverse channels of his own.
After he had channels chopped to lead me
Into the path of concrete-lined diverts,
He started hauling boulders to my shorelines
And poured them from my narrow skirts.
I puked out his boulders as he dumped them!
Like tiny grains of sand they washed away.
But tons on steady tons he kept on pouring
And, like, myself, stopped not for night or day.

"As time went by, my waters slowly halted
To obstinate, persistent, forceful man.
I'd bide my time, for I had time unending,
To overcome his foolish little plan.
When Sol, in springtime, melts the towering glaciers
Increasing all my waters in their power
I'll rip apart this little pile of debris
And wash away, within a single hour.

"I filled his tunnels full, to overflowing,
Crawled up onto the top of this small sham,
But once again mankind had out-manoeuvred
And built another dike upon his dam.
The weather chilled, my raging waters ebbed,
Bested, once again, by will of man.
From endless belts of steel the earth came pouring,
The dam rose up, man never seemed to tire.
The diverts sucked away my surplus waters
While I raged on in wild and senseless ire.

"As time went by my waters slowly halted,
They eddied as my driving force was quelled.
And now, I'm surging through these man-made tunnels
Creating power, unequalled, unexcelled.
With solid walls of steel he lined his penstocks
Through which my raging waters fall away;

Endlessly they'll keep on steady falling,
My time is measured not by hour or day.

"Six hundred feet below he placed his turbines;
Against their spinning blades I vent my wrath.
With all my mighty weight of falling waters
I have tried to shove them from my path,
Without success.

"You asked, what sayest I?
I've tried to tell you.
So please, oh please, be on your way
For I must keep these mighty turbines spinning;
My work's cut out for me, both night and day.
Now man and I shall work in double harness:
For I supply the power, and he the plan.
Aye, our driving wills shall work together,
My endless surging strength . . . the brains of man."

– written in 1966, by E.K. Pollon

25

The Women's Protest

The W.A.C. Bennett Dam had been built, Williston Lake was now part of the landscape, and Hudson's Hope was settling into its familiar "boom and bust" syndrome. Earl Pollon had quit publishing the *Hudson's Hope Power News* after spending four years and four thousand dollars on the project. There simply weren't enough potential subscribers left in town.

The workers had migrated to other projects: the Mica dam on the Columbia River, James Bay in Labrador, or Kettle Rapids in Manitoba. Many went to construction projects overseas, back to the distant places where they came from. A few had remained in Hudson's Hope and built modest homes. These men were looking for work "up the highway" or "down south," or settling for seasonal employment with Hydro, the highways department, or the forestry outfits in Chetwynd – wherever and whenever they could make a buck.

But a rumour persisted that had begun during the Bennett dam construction: there was to be a second auxiliary dam built on the Peace, close to town. Whatever Hydro decided to do, nothing could be as devastating as the huge reservoir that now sprawled up the trench, turning oldtimers' stories of the upper Peace into legends.

B.C. Hydro chairman, Gordon Shrum, in his introduction to a 1968 brochure on the Bennett Dam, talked about how British Columbians had been blessed with a resources heritage second to none, "our birthright that had endowed us with plenty" – especially the asset of a renewable resource such as hydro power. If one dam was good, two would be better. So it was announced that "in addition to the 2.3 million kilowatts developed at the W.A.C. Bennett dam, active investigations are under way at a second dam site 12 miles downstream where studies show an additional 650,000 kilowatts could be realized." Known to engineers as 'Site One,' it would be a 'run-of-the-river' installation, meaning no extensive reservoir would be required.

Shrum retired and a new chairman took his place, carrying forth the same mandate. The *Chetwynd Echo* reported on June 13, 1973: "In an announcement made today by B.C. Hydro chairman David Cass-Beggs, it was stated that the (Site One) project is first on the list of priorities. Tenders could be called as early as 1974 . . . The project would be expected to revitalize the dwindling economy of Hudson's Hope for at least five years."

Site One dam, proposed to be located 14 miles downstream from the Bennett dam (or four miles upstream from Hudson's Hope at the lower end of the canyon), would be controlled by the G.M. Shrum generating station at the Bennett dam. The auxiliary dam would make full use of water already used in generation and now flowing in a regulated fashion down the river.

Publicity for the project went into high gear near the end of 1973: "It may not boom the community the way the construction of the W.A.C. Bennett Dam did, but there is every indication that the big-time construction hubbub will once again ring through Hudson's Hope," said the October 3, 1973 edition of the *Chetwynd Echo,* in an article reprinted from the *Alaska Highway News.* "This week the British Columbia Hydro and Power Authority gave notice that it has deposited a description and site plans of the Peace River Site No. 1 dam and associated spillway . . . and it is the first valid indication that the long-mooted project is on its way."

The first contract, for the initial stage of the powerplant and dam, was awarded to Dillingham Corporation Canada Ltd. on October 29, 1974. Others quickly followed for setting up the construction camp, catering and housekeeping, Hudson's Hope employee housing, office and service buildings, and a concrete batch plant.[1]

The people of Hudson's Hope looked forward to getting jobs on the project. The battles of the Bennett had been fought, and now there would be understanding between the outside and residential work forces. It was not to be.

Again, non-union personnel were brought in on permit from out of town, while a great percentage of local people, who had either not retained union memberships or who had never been employed on the Bennett dam or any other union job, stood idle. This time the women decided to fight.

"It was funny," said Laura Evans. "My husband, Ralph, was the one who started all this. He came home and said to me, 'I think it's ridiculous, all these guys coming here out of Vancouver and the locals not getting hired. All the boys are out of work . . . everybody's boys. If

I were you women, I'd do something about it.' He didn't know that I would act on it, right now.

"I went over to Wanda MacEvoy's and I said, 'Wanda, I need your help. Will you come with me the next morning?' She said, 'Certainly.' We built picket signs on the sundeck all that afternoon."

First the women called on Earl Pollon, who they had nicknamed "the bunkhouse lawyer," for advice on managing the protest. He suggested they see Darryl Knull to get some information. Knull was job steward for local 168, but he told the women exactly how many men were on permit.

"When we called Earl Pollon to tell him what we were doing," Evans said, "Bonnie and Earl said, 'Don't forget to phone Brenda. She would like to be in on this.' So I phoned Brenda (Pollon – Pat's wife), she got hold of Carol Romine and Caroline (Pollon) Stowe and Thelma Peck. Bonnie Pollon, of course, was in on it from the beginning. Bonnie was always very much for the local people. These boys were raised here, and couldn't get work. Bonnie was very outspoken against that. There were six or seven of us the first day, then after that everybody wanted to get in the picture."

The police paid Laura Evans a visit. "How they got wind of it I don't know, but the cop came up that night and said to me, 'Are you planning on a little picket line at Site One?' We said, 'Yes,' and he said, 'Well, when are you going?' We said, 'We don't know yet, we're not even organized.' We were organized, but we weren't telling. He said the only reason they wanted to know was so they could give us protection if it got violent out there. I said, 'I doubt if it will ever get that way because we're not going to be a picket line, we're merely going to protest.'"

The women held a meeting to formulate their plan: to call on women from Hudson's Hope, Fort St. John, Dawson Creek and Chetwynd to form an "information line of protest" at the job site entrance.

But the men, arriving for work by private vehicle or on buses, stopped when they saw the women. None wanted to cross their line. "One guy from the Revelstoke area who was employed on the dam said he felt really badly about this," said Evans. "There was a job close to his home but the union had sent him up here, and he felt badly because he was taking a job from a local person. The women said they were not a legal picket line, and employed men were free to cross."

"I'm not walking over my mother to cross that line!" Harley Pollon said when he saw his mother Bonnie, sister Caroline and sister-in-law Brenda, along with all his women friends and neighbours walking back and forth across the road. Laura Evans laughed as she recalled the scene. "Harley Pollon had been hired on, but he wasn't going to cross that line. We gave him hell. We said, 'Harley, we are not here to have somebody lose his job, we're here to make more jobs for local people! Now get to work!' And he finally did."

But some of the employed men became quite nasty. "My mother doesn't have to get me my job!" one man shouted as the work bus thundered past the rain-soaked women. In general, the men with jobs were sympathetic. When the bus slowed to go through the gates, some of the men threw out rain gear or their lunches.

The Mounties did show up at the damsite, but once they saw everything was peaceful they would come and go sporadically.

Finally, Lyle Girvan, the manager of Peace Power Constructors, declared that it was not a legal protest and the workers should have no problem crossing.

To keep up their spirits in the cold wet vigil, the women's protest line became a chorus line as they lustily sang the words to a new song created by Laura Evans and sung to the country tune of "Give Me 40 Acres:"

"We gals kept on a-walking though it was pouring rain,
Our negotiations didn't work and we could hear this smart refrain:
'If you girls would head for home now, it would be really swell.'
We said: 'Give us 40 sticks of dynamite and we'll blow this dam to hell!"

Someone had brought a nylon pup-tent for shelter, but after a few days it was soaked, too. Brenda Pollon and Caroline (Pollon) Stowe went up to Earl's to change and eat. Earl, seeing his bedraggled daughter and daughter-in-law declared that they weren't going to go back in those wet clothes. They would get sick! So they simply changed into Earl's clothes and returned to duty.

The protest went on for several days and it rained almost daily. At this point, the women decided they needed the media. Earl Pollon came out, accompanied by Rudy Schubert with his big movie camera, and the *Vancouver Province* sent a reporting team to Hudson's Hope. That's when things began to happen.

Brenda Pollon ended up talking to the *Province* and the *Sun* newspapers. The *Sun* ran the following story, headlined, "Women Urged to Picket:"

"Local housewives are urging women from Fort St. John and Dawson Creek to join a picket line protesting hiring practices at B.C. Hydro's Site One power project. About 20 women from this Peace River community have been picketing the project since Thursday, and Brenda Pollon, one of the protesters, said they plan to continue through the weekend. Work on the project has not been interrupted since it is not a union picket.

"Mrs. Pollon said only about 100 of 430 project workers are from the area, and the women want jobs for about 40 unemployed people in the village. She said if the protesters do not achieve results by Monday, unemployed men will be added to the line. 'So far, we've only had women because the police are worried that some kind of hassle might break out if we have men on the line,' she said. 'We're trying to keep it peaceful.'

"She said local conservative M.P. Frank Oberle has expressed support for the protest, and the Fort St. John Labour Council has promised to investigate. B.C. Hydro says it must give job priority to union members, even if they live outside the area."

Brenda said there was some behind-the-scenes action: "The women were threatened with court injunctions. We said, 'O.K., we'll go to jail over this, but remember you have to take our kids as well.' Then Peace Power asked for a list of who we thought should be hired. We gave a list of names of local people who would be eligible for work. At that point, Peace Power asked a number of women to go into the office and talk. If they hired a few men from the list, would we pack up and go home? We said 'No, we wouldn't settle for hiring a few.'"

The protest dragged on. "On the Sunday we had quite a few more women out there – like Ruth Kelly who had to work the other days – and we decided we should take the guitar and sing songs like we'd sing in church," said Laura Evans. "So we paraded up and down at the dam gates, me playing the guitar, all of us singing "Just a Closer Walk with Thee" and "Shall We Gather at the River," and Harley goes by on a bus. It's pouring rain and he throws all these B.C. Hydro slickers out the bus window to keep us dry. The guys all brought extra lunches and threw doggie-bags out to us, because we had nothing to eat out there. The locals on the job thought it was great. None of the union men from outside said anything."

The women stood by their ultimatum to Peace Power Constructors that either the contractor hire the majority, or they would contact other people and it might not continue to be a peaceful protest.

"Mr. Bruce MacMillan (in charge of personnel for Atkinson-Commonwealth Construction Ltd.) was very unhappy with us," Evans said. "He gave me heck for stopping a truck, which I didn't stop. The driver had stopped and asked me what was going on, so I climbed up onto the runningboard and told him, 'It's not a picket line. Everybody's going through. It's a protest because the locals aren't being hired.' So he went roaring down there with his load, and MacMillan came out and started screaming at me, 'You can't stop trucks!'

And oh, he was so mad. I thought he was going to kill me.

"I didn't think Ralph would ever work again," Evans continued, "because MacMillan said to me, 'Is your husband working?' I said, 'Yes, he is working, he was name-requested, no help from you. But our boys aren't working and they were raised here. Why should they go to Vancouver to work, and Vancouver come up here?'

"A few days before he'd told us that we could go in to the mess hall for a cup of coffee. That day we didn't get a glass of water. They were friendly to start with. I guess they thought, 'Oh, we'll be nice to them and they'll go away.' But we didn't. One morning we were going to have breakfast, as they had invited us to do, and then we thought, to heck with them."

The women had a meeting with the Labour Council at the Peace Glen hotel. They expressed their unhappiness about unions bringing people in from other areas or countries to go to work immediately, while local people stood by, without jobs.

"This activated Peace Power," said Evans. "Lyle Girvan, in charge of personnel, said to us, 'Hey, I'm easy to get along with. But this is my job, to get this (protest) settled.' I said, 'You start hiring locals and it will get settled. But we're not going home until you hire everybody on that list . . . before you bring any more guys in from Vancouver.'

"We wouldn't back up. We said, 'We're staying here, we don't care if it rains for a month. We're not going home until you hire everybody.'

"One day when we were out on the protest line, Lyle asked us to join him in the lounge downtown in the hotel when the job was over that day. He would like to talk to us. There were Carol Romine, myself, and Brenda Pollon. Then he asked if the three of us would meet him in his office the next morning at six. We said certainly. He had bought $80 worth of booze during our meeting at the hotel lounge, perhaps hoping that we wouldn't get up that early to make this meeting and it would be all over. Well, we fooled him. We were there before he was. We said, 'Hey! How come you're late?' Then he went down the list, saying: 'If I hire this guy, this guy and that guy, will you women pack it up and go home?' We said, 'No. Everybody on that list gets hired or we're not going anywhere.' The list contained names of males and females of working age in Hudson's Hope. We said they were discriminating in the kitchen – the Greeks would not hire the local women – so (B.C. Labour Federation) came up from Vancouver and we had a big meeting with them in the council chambers over discrimination. We told them, 'They won't hire women in the kitchen, just guys.' And in fact they weren't hiring any local guys in the kitchen either. So after we got done out there, the women went to work: Darlene Koenig, Liz Farrell. Everybody got hired."

After a week of walking in the rain, the women had won.

Several months after it was over, Brenda Pollon got a call from Revelstoke asking how they had organized the protest because the same thing was happening at the Revelstoke dam project.

The April 21, 1976 edition of the *Alaska Highway News* carried five photographs showing progress on the Site One dam. "This tranquil scene on the Peace just upstream from the Hudson's Hope bridge will soon be a hive of activity as the Site One dam construction gets underway this summer," the accompanying story began. Moving back to Hudson's Hope were people who had been away 10 years – ourselves included.

Again the question was asked in the newspapers and by residents of the town: what does the future hold for Hudson's Hope? "The little community, site of the third oldest European settlement in B.C., has seen many changes since Rocky Mountain Portage Fort was set up there in 1798," said the July 19, 1976 *Alaska Highway News*. The newspaper then directed a poignant question to local residents: "Do you feel the community of Hudson's Hope will benefit from the construction of the Site One dam and the increased population that it brings with it?"

The answers were as varied as the people interviewed. W.H. Beckman said that "at least this time the dam is not going to do all the damage that the Bennett dam did. It's not going to take up much more than a half-section of land and there won't be any debris." Barbara Trew, a local school student, felt that "in the short term it may be okay, but after the construction is finished everybody leaves and we're right back where we started." Only a local businesswoman, Carolyn Janzen, felt that it would boost local businesses and bring in more recreational facilities. "When this dam is built there is certain to be even more development of facilities since there will be more money circulating in the community and service clubs can take on bigger projects," she said.

Ethel Rutledge felt the town would never again be the pleasant friendly hamlet she had once known. "Life in the community hasn't benefited one bit even if people do have paved streets and sidewalks. If they keep building more dams it's soon going to mean we're going to have to leave our land and the home we have known for over 40 years."

Rutledge's words turned out to be prophetic much sooner than perhaps even she expected. The August 24, 1976 issue of *Alaska*

Highway News carried an editorial titled "Old King Coal," asking if coal would ever make a comeback in the region. Also, the newspaper noted, "B.C. Hydro has announced plans to push forward sooner than expected in hydro development to meet energy needs of the province with probably early development of the Site C dam on the Peace. Studies are also continuing on the site (E) for a dam further down the Peace near Clayhurst." The writer concluded that "King Coal may be delayed in his comeback if other sources of energy can still be tapped first . . . but it certainly bodes well for the economic future of the area that so much of the province's energy resources are located here."

That same month, the newspaper carried another dam article, titled "Is this the shape of things to come to the Peace?" It described the Revelstoke dam project, scheduled to begin construction in 1977. Already opposition to the project was being reported. "The Fish and Wildlife branch of B.C. has formally objected to B.C. Hydro's application for the water licence to build the dam over environmental concerns – the first time one arm of the B.C. government has opposed another." A local resident said he wanted people to realize that whenever they use electricity, it will cost more than a few cents per kilowatt-hour. It will cost a rainbow trout, a Douglas fir, or a moose – wildlife that will be forced out of the area if the dam is constructed. Emil Melnyk, chairman of the regional district of Columbia Shuswap, said that "unsolved problems with other dams lend some weight to those who are sceptical that B.C. Hydro will deal adequately with the continuing effects of the Revelstoke dam."

Still, the construction force gathered in Hudson's Hope to build yet another project. The Mathesons both found employment on the Site One dam; Bill worked as quantities recorder for Atkinson- Commonwealth, the contractor, and I was secretary to Chris Boatman, B.C. Hydro's construction manager.

I began wondering about the men and women, who, like ourselves, had flocked to this project for work. One winter evening, near Christmas, I paid them a visit.

A strong wind buffeted my car as I steered it around sharp turns on the snow-covered road to the camp. Suddenly, my destination appeared: rows of rectangular trailers, arranged in an "H" formation, their white aluminum siding reflecting my headlights. There was no sound but the wind. The camp seemed deserted. I drove around the back to a parking lot occupied by several snow-covered vehicles, and reluctantly left the warmth of my car for an unknown reception inside.

I was met in the mess hall by an attractive red-haired woman about 50. Her name was May, and she was one of two camp cooks who had agreed to work over the Christmas holidays at this almost empty camp. The only other people in camp were those who had no other home and would not budge, or who did not want to spend $500 travelling to Vancouver to celebrate the season.

May walked me through the dimly lit mess hall. We passed the recreation room where I could see several men watching television or playing pool. We dashed outside to the women's bunkhouse which was back in the trees, separate from the rest. May opened the door to her room.

It measured eight feet by ten feet, and contained a single bed, small bedside table, dresser and built-in closet. Wallboard covered all four walls, reducing the visual size by half. Water stains formed Rorschach blots on the ceiling.

"There's nothing much for the men to do here over Christmas," May said. "They mostly stick to their rooms – identical to this one – reading, drinking. I get to know them pretty good, the ones who stay over."

May lit a cigarette. "Some guys just won't leave," she continued, blowing smoke toward the ceiling. "This is home. These rooms contain all their worldly possessions. If the company tries to close down the camp over Christmas, it's like trying to clean out termites to get them out.

"I worked up at the Bennett dam during its construction. They tried to empty out that big camp over Christmas. Wow! Finally got down to four or five guys – I think one of the Italians we saw in the rec room was one of them – and they just wouldn't go. The R.C.M.P. had to be called in to move them. Know what the Mounties found in their rooms? Food. Piles of sandwiches, cakes, cookies – stashed. They figured that would tide them over if the kitchen closed down. Some Christmas dinner, eh?"

May butted her cigarette in a little ashtray and leaned back. "It's not lack of money. I'll bet any one of these guys has $50-to $100,000 or more in the bank. Ever hear of Salvadore, the cement finisher? He died in his bunkhouse about six months ago. Heart attack. They found out he had $250,000 in the bank, nobody to claim him or his money. Government got it, I guess." She shrugged. "I don't know why they're like that."

We sat in silence. Not a sound from outside, except the wind whining around the corner of the trailer unit.

"Some of them don't care it's Christmas. Others care too much. One kid about 18 was on his way over to the mess hall for Christmas dinner. He stepped outside the bunkhouse and fell headfirst into a snowbank. Drunk. First Christmas alone. He didn't remember much of it."

May has a home, on her son's ranch about 50 miles from Hudson's Hope, near Chetwynd. She is a widow.

"We give the guys whatever they want to eat over Christmas, three steaks a day if they ask for them. It's all we can do." Her voice lowered. "You know, even I got feeling low Christmas night. There was just me and Big George, the head cook, left to clean up in the kitchen after supper. I didn't feel like just coming back here and sitting, so I started cleaning the grease off the underside of the stove hood. Then George filled a bucket, got down on his hands and knees and started scrubbing the floor. I'm working away when suddenly I see a big soapy hand reaching under the stove hood, handing me a glass of rye. 'Merry Christmas, May,' George says. So I sit there on the stove like Cinderella, and he leans against it, and we have a toast. Then we got talking and laughing a bit . . . two lonely people in a deserted camp kitchen, scrubbing grease rather than facing empty rooms. We just howled for a few minutes, then for some reason we didn't feel so sad."

May said she would probably work again next Christmas, if she was asked. She even got two marriage proposals over this holiday. "I bet not many women my age can top that!" she said with a smile.

We laughed together, an easy friendship, made in minutes. Camp life. The Canadian singles. May got up. "Well, you don't want to spend all night talking to me. I'll take you down to the rec room, introduce you to some of our regulars."

"I don't want to talk to no writers, about no Christmas spent in camp." I stood in front of a man introduced simply as "Cadillac Jack." "What's the matter with spending Christmas at home? This is my home."

He looked surly, but motioned for me to sit down on the vinyl chair beside him. May winked, and left us together.

"People expect too much," the man said. "Christmas don't have to be spent around a tree piled high with presents. I'm a religious man. It's our Lord's birthday, and I don't figure he expects me to drive hundreds of miles over ice because of it. I just sit in my room, good bottle of scotch, and think." He paused to light a cigarette. His black hair, sparse on top, matched bushy black eyebrows and narrow dark eyes. I mentioned his unusual name.

"You like that, do you? Cadillac Jack. They've been calling me that since I got into Cadillacs. Used to call me Black Jack, I forget why. I worked at a job over in Saudi Arabia, making 90 grand a year.

Brought back the biggest, whitest Caddy I could find. Thought about buying it for two years straight, sitting in that miserable bloody camp, and I did it. I ain't like old Salvadore, the cement-finisher. I spend, but on important things, not like blowing two grand so I won't be alone at Christmas. I'm not alone here. There were 17 of us at Christmas dinner. Even the Italians spoke that night."

Cadillac Jack turned his back to watch a pool game, indicating our visit was over. I looked around the room and saw a man intently watching me. He beckoned and I went over. He was like a small bird perched on a roost, his slippered feet entwined in the rungs of his chair, and his blue eyes bright with interest. He introduced himself as Sousa Joe. He pointed toward a man sitting alone across the room.

"See that grizzled old bugger over there, pickin' his teeth? That's Jackpine Ollesson. Don't talk to nobody. Piles his fork like he's building a bridge: potatoes, peas, turkey, then dips it in the cranberry sauce and in she goes. And that Indian fellow over there, he was at our table. 'Top of the Mountain' we call him. He's from Bella Coola. Got lost one day and they found him right on top of a mountain." Sousa Joe laughed merrily.

"Then there was those four Italians over there," he continued. "They stick to themselves, spend their time counting their money. Never squander a dime. They like to tell you about Elio, the powder-man who worked at the Bennett dam years ago. Worked seven days a week, 12 hours a day, and you know what he did after shift? Cut hair, a buck-a-head. Stayed two years and went back with enough cash to buy a string of barbershops in Italy."

I asked why he was called Sousa Joe, and his eyes got a faraway look. "Used to be drummer in the army. Everyone's got their memories," he said. The windows of the rec hall filled with the black of night. Sousa Joe stood up, extended his hand, and wished me a happy new year.

The wind swirled in a blast of snow as I pushed open the door of the camp dining hall and made my way through the parking lot to my car.

Inside my car, I looked over at the camp: nondescript trailers, indistinguishable except for a light here, a light there, shining out from the private little rooms. Which was Sousa Joe's? Top of the Mountain's? Behind which bunkhouse window had Salvadore the cement finisher died, clutching his bank book? The rec room lights went out, one by one, leaving trailer A-9 in darkness.

I thought of the men and women all over the country in construction camps, mining camps, logging camps, highways and forestry camps, sitting in the silent bush.

Note

[1]Site One dam (later named Peace Canyon) is a 165-foot high dam containing 515,000 cubic yards of concrete. Its four generating units, made by Mitsubishi Canada Limited at a cost of just over $20 million, can each produce 175,000 kilowatts. The four turbines, costing about $25.5 million and manufactured in the Soviet Union, can each produce 240,000 horsepower. The 1,976-acre reservoir (later named Dinosaur Lake) behind the dam elicited little environmental concern, because it expanded the river only twice its natural size.

26

Beneath These Waters

The history of man in the Peace River country may go back a few centuries, but there was a prehistory that lay in wait for eons to be recorded. This story emerged with the discovery of the bones and trackways of marine reptiles, birds and dinosaurs that had roamed the Peace River canyon millions of years ago.

Hudson's Hope residents had known about the tracks. Any given Sunday afternoon, a party might climb down the bank by the old Grant coal seam in the canyon, pour flour over the tracks so they would show well, and snap photographs of the three-toed prints leading into the river. Some of the tracks were six inches deep, and three and one-half feet long at the middle toe.

Colleen Smith beside dinosaur tracks
(Hudson's Hope Museum)

On May 2, 1973, the *Chetwynd Echo* carried an article titled "Dinosaur Tracks Endangered by Dam." Mel Kyllo, spokesman for the Hudson's Hope Museum and Historical Society, requested the regional chambers of commerce to support efforts to preserve the dinosaur tracks. Kyllo deplored the fact that nothing had been done to save a skeleton which was 30 feet long from being flooded by the W.A.C. Bennett Dam. Further, should a secondary dam be built, all would be lost beneath the reservoir. The chambers of commerce agreed to send letters to government officials, alerting them to the situation.

In 1930, Charles Mortram Sternberg (1885-1981), a vertebrate palaeontologist who had collected many dinosaurs, had come to the Peace valley to study the 130-million-year-old Cretaceous dinosaur tracks from the Lower Cretaceous Aptian to Albian era, and to collect Triassic ichthyosaurs ("fish lizards," marine reptiles that superficially resembled modern dolphins). He observed more than 400 footprints at different outcrops along the canyon. A species of bipedal herbivorous (plant-eating) dinosaur, whose track is now known as *Amblydactylus gethingi,* was named for the Gething (rock-bed) Formation. Neil Gething had accompanied Sternberg on these expeditions. This was only one of several new footprint species discovered in the canyon.[1]

The first discovery of Triassic sediments in the Peace River area was recorded by A.R.C. Selwyn, director of the Geological Survey of Canada, in 1875.

Dr. F.H. McLearn had joined the Geological Survey of Canada in 1913. He came to the Peace valley in 1917, 1920 and 1922 to study what he called his "favourite rocks" located in the Cretaceous rock layers below and above the Gething Formation. McLearn returned in 1937 and 1938 to work solely on the Trias of Peace River. He stayed at the Beattie ranch at Gold Bar, where he had a view of the Triassic hills. Near the ranch house, McLearn collected hundreds of exquisite ammonoids. These are fossils of an extinct group of cephalopods, which means "head-foot," with chambered shells. They are coiled in a flat spiral, and are related to modern squids and octopus. The rocks at the Beattie ledge are the oldest Triassic sediments exposed in the Peace River valley. Farther up the valley, near the Brown and Pardonet Hills, and the ledges of Ne Parlez Pas Rapids, are located the latest (youngest) Triassic sections.

The Peace River area around Hudson's Hope is home to some of the most significant Triassic discoveries of the century. "The Triassic period (a period of 45 million years, which began 225 million years ago) is one for which the Canadian rock sequences contribute important data towards defining and recognizing the time scale," said E.T. Tozer in his 1984 report titled "The Trias and its Ammonoids."

In 1967, when the Williston Lake reservoir was completed, Tozer said, "the Beattie ranch and ledge, and the *Monotis* beds at Ne Parlez Pas Rapids, were submerged to a depth of about 200 yards . . . For the first few years the shoreline was a mess of tangle driftwood. Now there are new shoreline exposures of all of McLearn's old localities and at the site of the Ne Parlez Pas Rapids – with two exceptions: the *Nathorstites* beds of Beattie Lodge, and the *Tropites* bed at Pardonet Hill."[2]

Frank Riter started a boat charter service on Williston Lake in 1978. He said that one of his most interesting parties was Tim Tozer from Ottawa. Tozer's report on the Trias was written after he completed his field research, travelling with Riter on his boat to the Triassic outcrops. A 1981 photograph included in the report shows Riter with his motor cruiser, "Jak."

For years, Riter has ferried geologists and palaeontologists to these hallowed spots at low water, between Hudson's Hope and the Ottertail. Or he takes them to see the fish skulls and bones on the east side of the Carbon River that are visible at high water mark. There are also many fossils under water around the banks of the Ottertail that were first sighted by Bud Stuart and some of the oldtimers.

Years before Riter's operation, Jim Beattie Sr. had taken up various parties. But the fossils at that time were covered with overburden. When the lake water came up, the overburden washed away. Scientists now prefer to make their trips in the early spring, when the reservoir is at its lowest and they have lots of beach to work on.

Pieces of prehistoric relics have been dug up near the damsite.
Shown here is an 11,600 year old Mammoth tusk
(B.C. Hydro/Gunnar Johanson)

The fight to preserve the Peace valley's prehistory had actually begun in 1965, with the discovery of almost 50 percent (skull segment, four leg bones, tusks, lower jawbone, part of a shoulder blade, some joints and two teeth) of the fossilized remains of a mammoth, buried 15 to 20 feet beneath interglacial gravel at the Bennett dam site. Between 1961 and 1968, more dinosaur footprints were discovered upstream from the original site. Members of an expedition from the Royal Ontario Museum quickly made latex moulds of two trackways before they were covered by the earth-fill of the dam.

When work began at Site One, the fight for fossils began anew. Jim Williams found some bones when he was working after a rock blast at the dam site. He reported the find, but no one seemed interested. Harley Pollon, an equipment serviceman at the area, learned of the discovery and asked what was going to be done. The contractor's supervisor said they were merely going to redrill and blast again. Harley phoned his mother. Bonnie, an active member of the Hudson's Hope Museum and Historical Society, was outraged. Here were treasures that had been buried for thousands of years, and they were simply going to be bulldozed and buried forever. Bonnie contacted the B.C. Provincial Museum in Victoria. Then she phoned the historical society in Victoria, and they phoned their federal counterpart in Ottawa.

Within two hours, a stop-work order was issued by B.C. Hydro and the area (between generator unit #4 and the spillway, by the diversion tunnels) roped off. Bonnie Pollon and Edith Kyllo, representing the Hudson's Hope Museum and Historical Society, were there to make sure the site was not destroyed.

An article in the June 23, 1977 *Alaska Highway News* describes the excitement accompanying the find: "The skeleton of an extinct mammoth that roamed North America millions of years ago has been unearthed by construction workers at a dam site on the Peace River in central British Columbia, in a gravel pit 14 miles downstream from the Bennett dam. Tom Lloyd, a spokesman for the provincial museum, said it seems to be a complete specimen, 'and if that is the case, it's very rare.'

"Archaeologist Ross Brand, who visited the site last weekend, said that only the front section of the skeleton had been unearthed, but 'it seems that the rest is lying in the gravel bank and it may be more complete than anything we've ever found before. The skeleton is the size of a helluva big elephant.' Examination of the bones so far indicate it is either a mammoth or a mastodon, two closely related animals from the Pleistocene age.

"Most of the region will be flooded when water begins to back up behind the Site One dam, but the gravel pit the mammoth bones are in is below the dam. Project manager Chris Boatman said the skeleton was discovered by a front-end operator June 9, but the find was kept secret from all but the museum. Boatman said all work in the immediate vicinity of the mammoth was halted as soon as the operator reported his find."

P. McCarthy and Chris Boatman inspect bones unearthed at Peace Canyon
(Hudson's Hope Museum)

The following day, the newspaper reported that the skeleton of the mammoth was found to be at least 10,000 years older than originally estimated. Bjorn Simonsen, provincial archaeologist, said initial geological assessment established the sediment containing the bones was formed 20,000 years ago.

A team of archaeologists, palaeontologists and geologists from British Columbia Provincial Museum, University of British Columbia and Simon Fraser University supervised the excavation and preservation of the bones. Chris Boatman said the area had been roped off to prevent damage, but added that "although the find has aroused some interest among local sightseers, he does not expect vast crowds."

Thanks to the immediate and local effort to preserve the find, original pieces or replicas of dinosaur tracks and plesiosaur bones – along with the famous tusk of the woolly mammoth -- are proudly displayed at the damsites and in the Hudson's Hope Museum.

David Spalding was head curator of natural history in charge of the palaeontology programs at the Provincial Museum of Alberta. He also spent a year planning the spectacular Tyrrell Museum of Palaeontology in Drumheller, Alberta. Spalding has visited most of the major dinosaur collecting sites in British Columbia, Alberta and Saskatchewan; during the last 20 years, he has met most of the active Canadian dinosaur collectors.

"Although we knew of the Sternberg finds (in the Peace River valley) – interesting because so few dinosaur footprints were known from Alberta – the Provincial Museum of Alberta had done no work in the Peace River Canyon, which was, of course, under the jurisdiction of what was then the B.C. Provincial Museum in Victoria," Spalding said in a letter to the authors dated April 12, 1989.

"The potential disappearance of the tracks under the new dam was drawn to our attention by an oil geologist with Imperial Oil in Calgary, who had gone on a fishing trip in the area," he said. "I talked to the director of the B.C. Provincial Museum and ascertained that they had no program able to work on this, and managed to get permission from the B.C. Archaeological Survey and our own department to do some exploratory work."

The Alberta museum's curator of palaeontology position was vacant at the time (Philip Currie had been appointed but had not arrived. Ron Mussieux, Curator of Geology, handled the details on the Peace Canyon exploration until Currie took charge.) William Sarjeant, a fossil footprint specialist (and professor in the department of geological sciences, University of Saskatchewan), joined the first expedition that travelled to the site in September, 1976. The expedition found many more tracks than Sternberg had documented, and several were in excellent states of preservation. With financial help from Imperial Oil, and cooperation and, later, financial donations from B.C. Hydro, the scientists mounted an expedition the following year to document, cast and excavate as many tracks as possible.

From 1976 to 1979, during construction of the Peace Canyon Dam, four expeditions from the Provincial Museum of Alberta collected dinosaur footprints in the Peace canyon – all found in the Gething Formation. The expedition located Charles Sternberg's primary trackway site near Ferro Point, but much of it could no longer be seen because of high water levels. One of the more spectacular discoveries was a single bedding plane, 12 yards long and 5 yards wide, containing over 100 dinosaur footprints. Each year more tracks were found and the scientists, hurrying to complete as much as they could before the dam was finished, mounted two more expeditions.

After the exploratory trip, Philip Currie of the Provincial Museum of Alberta (now assistant director, collections and research programs at the Tyrrell Museum of Palaeontology at Drumheller, Alberta) was in charge of isolating and excavating tracks from the Peace canyon site. The initial scientific papers by Currie and Sarjeant led to numerous publications that dealt with the footprints.[3]

Peace River Site 8 June 4/79

Johnson Creek May 30/79

Location 1, Peace River below mines, September 25/76
(Philip Currie, Tyrrell Museum of Palaeontology)

Currie wrote a paper titled "Bird Footprints from the Gething Formation of Northeastern British Columbia," published in the *Journal of Vertebrate Palaeontology* in December, 1981, in which he indicates the age of the beds to be Aptian to early Albian (Early Cretaceous, 130 million years ago). The Gething Formation, which measures 1,640 feet thick, represents a time span of between 10,000 and 15,000 years. The 200 slender-toed footprints discovered there were less than 1 1/2 inches long and differed profoundly from the more than 1,500 dinosaur tracks found in the canyon. The concentration of bird footprints was so high it was difficult to distinguish among more than 30 actual trackways (the longest having seven footprints). The birds which made the tracks were small, and the water in which the tracks were made was only a couple of inches deep.

"The discovery of bird footprints in the Aptian strata of the Peace River Canyon extends our knowledge of the existence and behaviour of shorebird-like forms into the Early Cretaceous," Currie said. "Fundamental differences in track and trackway characteristics distinguish bird footprints from those of dinosaurs as readily as osteological (skeletal) features."

The Provincial Museum of Alberta returned to the Peace River canyon in 1977 and 1978, and made rubber moulds of some dinosaur trackways and individual ichnites (footprints). Other trackways were mapped and photographed and, where possible, actual specimens extracted. During a trip to Grant's Flat, the expedition discovered a "tremendous" number of dinosaur tracks in front of the abandoned coal mine. During the last expedition (June, 1979) emphasis was on removing the original footprints rather than attempting to cast moulds: scientists used a 10-inch round diamond blade, hammers and chisels. Over 50 original specimens were collected and transported out of the canyon by helicopter.

The excitement of discovering tracks of baby hadrosaurs (duck-billed dinosaurs – *Hadrosaurid ornithopods*) was heightened by the fact that so little had been known about young dinosaurs. These discoveries taught scientists much about herding habits of these herbivorous reptiles. Some of the longer trackways provided remarkable information on behaviour: evidence of hadrosaurs travelling in herds, and at one point, carnivores approaching a herd of hadrosaurs which then veer away. "At one site in the Peace River Canyon, parallel trackways show a herd of 17 hadrosaurs walking in the same direction. At one point, four animals were walking so closely together that when one lurched sideways it bumped its neighbour, initiating a chain reaction that affected all four," wrote Philip Currie in the "Dinosaur" section of the *Canadian Encyclopaedia*. This herd behaviour and fast reaction has been considered indicative of "hot-blooded" (as opposed to cold-blooded or reptilian) behaviour by some scientists.

A total of four expeditions were made to the canyon; 90 dinosaur footprints and more than 200 casts were obtained for the collections of the Alberta and British Columbia provincial museums. Almost 1,700 dinosaur footprints were observed, greatly surpassing the 400 seen by Sternberg in 1930. Of the 1,700, more than 1,000 were mapped and almost 1,000 (in more than 100 trackways) measured.

Scientists also discovered a holotype. A holotype is a unique specimen on which a new species is based, and which will thereafter be used as the reference in discussions of that species. The holotype of the species, *Amblydactylus kortmeyeri* was named for Karl Kortmeyer of Dawson Creek, who drove the jet-boat that transported the crews to the various sites. The specimen was found on a riverside bench of rock on the north bank of the Peace River, about 275 yards upstream from where Aylard Creek flows into the canyon, in the "Gething Formation of Bullhead Group, Lower Cretaceous."

With all this palaeontological action occurring during construction of the two dams on the Peace, Chris Boatman of B.C. Hydro says, in a letter to the authors dated May 15, 1989, that "no records of the fossils uncovered near W.A.C. Bennett and Peace Canyon dams have been found within Hydro."

Boatman recalled, however, that "fossils that were not displayed at either of the damsites for public viewing were turned over the provincial government for safekeeping. Mr. Rick Kool of the Royal B.C. Museum advises that the dinosaur footprints are presently on display at the Tyrrell Museum of Palaeontology" in Drumheller.

Financial grants and notification of changing water levels provided to the palaeontologists by B.C. Hydro were extremely important in allowing last-minute retrieval of the fossils. However, there is a strong irony in the emergence of tourism as a major industry in the west shortly after the tracks were buried. "This beautiful and scientifically important site would have been a major tourist attraction if the dam had not been built," said a member of the original expedition to the Peace valley. "The huge success of the Tyrrell Museum as a tourist attraction underlines the new importance dinosaurs now have. As a palaeontologist and environmentalist, I was appalled that the dam was being built without apparently any environmental impact study in which palaeontology was taken into account. As a civil servant in the next province I could, of course, say nothing which could be implied as criticism of a neighbouring government, and particularly which might have jeopardized our rescue attempts when the dam was going ahead anyway."

Judging by the now sanctified collection of original specimens, photographs, moulds, scientific papers and films recording the palaeontological discoveries, the Peace River canyon gave up its last treasures at the time of its demise. "When we first ventured forth into the canyon on that sunny September morning in 1976, we were truly doubtful whether the expedition was worthwhile," Dr. Sarjeant said in his article in the *Explorer's Journal*. "Certainly we never dreamed that we were to be rewarded by such a scientific bonanza!"

But his article ends on a note of quiet resignation, common among scientists who hear of exquisite sites which have awaited discovery, only to become suddenly inaccessible at the moment the find is made:

"It is sad to reflect that, apart from those taken to the museums, all these scientific riches are now hidden under the waters held up by the Peace Canyon dam and that, at the end of the four expeditions, only four miles of the 17-mile-long canyon had been thoroughly searched. On the other hand, if the area had not come under the threat of 'drowning,' those riches might have remained unperceived (by scientists) for very much longer."[4]

Notes

[1]To date, over 1,500 tracks have been found along the Peace River which are believed to have been made by members of different groups of dinosaurs, travelling alone or in pairs. These include herbivorous hadrosaurs, horned dinosaurs (ancestors of Triceratops), coelurosaurs (small carnivorous dinosaurs that hunted in packs) and carnosaurs (the large meat-eating relatives of Tyrannosaurus rex). Evidence of their existence has been discovered in deposits preserved in rocks found in the Peace valley; the rocks were formed in the delta region on the margin of the then-Cretaceous inland sea. Tracks are described as different kinds of ichnospecies, or "species of tracks." Fifteen ichnospecies have been recorded from the Peace valley. Scientists caution that, while it is not always possible to be certain when attributing tracks to species – or even families – of dinosaurs, in this case attributions were made fairly confidently.

[2]"The Trias and its Ammonoids: The Evolution of a Time Scale," E.T. Tozer, Geological Survey of Canada, Ottawa, 1984 (Misc. Report #35, 1984).

[3]Sarjeant, William A.S., "In the Footsteps of the Dinosaurs," *Explorers Journal*, Vol, 59, No. 4, December, 1981.

[4]The authors are indebted to David A.E. Spalding of Edmonton for providing knowledge integral to this chapter, and for reviewing and correcting early drafts of the manuscript relating to the palaeontological aspects.

Further information on Sternberg's discoveries can be found in the following book:

Sternberg, Charles Hazelius, 1985. *Hunting Dinosaurs in the Badlands of the Red Deer Valley, Alberta, Canada,* 3rd edition. Edited and introduced by David A.E. Spalding. NeWest Press, Edmonton. 235 p. (Charles H. Sternberg was the father of Charles M. Sternberg who collected in the Peace valley).

A manuscript in preparation is: Spalding, David A.E.: Altogether Wonderful, The Discovery of Canada's Dinosaurs to 1950.

The authors thank David Spalding and William Sarjeant for providing copies of Sarjeant's article (referenced above) and Sarjeant's and Currie's paper, "Lower Cretaceous Dinosaur Footprints from the Peace River Canyon, British Columbia, Canada, *Palaeogeography, Palaeoclimatology, Palaeocology*, 28(1979) 103-115, Elsevier Scientific Publishing Company, Amsterdam.

We wish to thank Dr. Sarjeant for also looking over the material, and forwarding his comments.

We further acknowledge the assistance of Monty Reid of the Tyrrell Museum of Palaeontology, Drumheller, Alberta, for providing copies of Philip Currie's papers, including "Bird Footprints from the Gething Formation of Northeastern British Columbia," published in the *Journal of Vertebrate Palaeontology* in December, 1981, and slides of the Peace canyon expeditions for our use.

27

River Girl

The fight for the dinosaurs was Bonnie Pollon's last. In May of 1977 she was diagnosed as having cancer. The town rallied to support the stricken family, collecting over $2,000 to enable Earl to take Bonnie to a Vancouver hospital for treatment, and later, when no hope was given, to the Hoxie Clinic in Mexico.

The plane ride was a nightmare. Bonnie was too sick to comprehend where she was going, and Earl and son Pat had to hide her condition from airline personnel for fear they wouldn't let her on the flight. The clinic offered hope and six bottles of brown medicine. Spiritually lifted, they made their way home to Hudson's Hope with the woman who was their wife, mother and teacher. Their efforts were to no avail. Bonnie died July 26, 1977. Their children, and the townspeople, were desolate. For Earl, it was the end of his hopes and dreams.

"I just don't give a damn anymore, you know," Earl would say, over and over.

The residents continued with their support, donating toward a Bonnie Pollon Memorial Fund set up at the bank to help others in time of illness.

Bonnie's death caused Earl to evaluate his life. It had all been for the family, hadn't it? The business of the sawmill. But what, in the end, did it get them? The children taking school lessons by correspondence, taught by Bonnie, later attending classes in town, but hurrying home after school to work like men, feeding logs into screaming saws. Young Caroline diving in after her grade three class to help her mother peel mountainous bags of potatoes, scrape carrots, stir gravies for the evening meal for the 20 men living in camp. The youngest, Billy, being tended by two cranky old grandfathers.

"Ten babies would have been easier to handle than those two old beggars," Earl said. "We couldn't leave them alone, and we couldn't take them with us. They wouldn't join in conversation, they'd just complain about why we weren't going home. So it got so we just stayed home, or had people over. Fifteen years we looked after them. Fifteen years!"

Earl recalled a comment Bonnie made just before she died. It told him that Bonnie did not feel their lives had been in vain.

"We were in the kitchen one day, having coffee, and we knew she was dying. We were talking about all the goods and the bads of our married life. I said, 'Jesus Christ, honey, I feel badly because I could have made your life so much easier than we had it.' And she said, 'I wouldn't have wanted it any easier.' She said then that the most fun we had was when we were working our asses off, skidding logs and sawmilling. I had to agree with her.

"We'd go home from work at nights so tired we could hardly stand up, and just fall into bed. One night the bed collapsed under us, and I was too tired to get up and fight with it. Milton Vince came in the next day. He said, 'Boy, you guys must have really been cutting the mustard last night!' Bonnie and I laughed about that."

But for all their work, in the end they had nothing. Trying to keep the sawmill going had cost them all their savings, their property investments in town, almost their health. The wind now whistles through the broken windows of the abandoned bunkhouses of the little sawmill. The rusted mill sprouts alfalfa and Indian Paintbrush. The great bronze blades sit idle, allowing young poplars and spruce to sweep their branches against the metal teeth. When the Pollons left the sawmill behind they had no home; they rented an apartment in town from Mel Kyllo. It was the only time Bonnie ever had a home with running water.

One day, a referendum on a money bylaw came up, on which only owner-electors could vote. Tom Jamieson, an oldtimer who had come to the Peace in 1912 and who had made some solid investments in land in Hudson's Hope as well as Dawson Creek and Pouce Coupe, asked Earl what he thought of the bylaw.

"I haven't thought about it," Earl replied. "I can't vote."

"You can't vote on it? You who've been here 35 years? Why not?"

"I don't own any land."

Jamieson just looked at him for a moment. He thought of the years Earl and his family had worked out in that bush; of Bonnie cooking, cleaning bunkhouses, weeding a big garden, butchering chickens and turkeys. He remembered Harley and Pat working like grown men, standing on boxes to boss crews. Jamieson also thought of the earlier years: Earl's father, Jack, coming to the Peace country and setting up his lime kiln on the banks of the river, shipping lime that now supported plaster and foundations in towns along the Peace. Landless pioneers. Settlers without homesteads.

"You can vote, Earl," Jamieson said quietly. "I'm selling you one of my acre lots."

"Can't afford it, Tom, thanks just the same."

"Got a dollar?"

"Yes."

"You're a landowner then."

Earl Pollon lives on that one-acre lot in the Jamieson subdivision to this day, in a house that was once a restaurant – procured for the cost of skidding it away.

Earl took to sleeping out on the couch, hating to go into the bedroom even to hang up his clothes. He would rather lie on the couch, watching television until three or four in the morning.

"You know, we've been richer and we've been poorer than most anybody else in this town," he said. "God, we had some good times! On our honeymoon it was raining cats and dogs, we hung a tarp to keep the rain off the bed, down in that old cabin of McGarvey's. Then, suddenly that tarp gave way and splash! We were screaming, thrashing around in water up to our . . . well, Christ that was funny.

"I guess Bonnie wouldn't have minded being married in the church. Just built. We'd have been the first couple married in it. I said no way, I wasn't a church-going man and I wasn't a goddamned hypocrite, so we got married by the justice of the peace. Married just the same. Her funeral was in that church. I still didn't want to go in. She wasn't there.

"I remember that summer we spent on the river, washing gold, just like it was yesterday. We'd take the boat out and float down the Peace, just a few miles, then put the kicker on to bring us back to camp. My river girl. Always, my river girl."

Earl never thought he'd live beyond Bonnie. "The thought never crossed my mind. I've had bad lungs since I was in my twenties. You remember that piece I wrote, "Memorabilia?" It was about 50 below zero when I got stopped by that avalanche and had to go back and around, 10 miles out of my way. Snow up to my waist. That's when I got snowshoe leg, when I had to tie the rawhide strings to the toes of my snowshoes and pull them with my hands. I guess my lungs got frozen then, but I didn't know it. Years after, I went to see a doc in Fort St. John and he examined me, thought I had pneumonia. 'When did you freeze your lungs?' he asked me. 'Damned if I know!' Then I got thinking back and it must have been then. I was huffing and puffing that last 10 miles, breathing through my mouth, so I guess that's when they froze . . . the first time anyway."

Earl didn't have much to say about the Site One dam project. The dam was not considered highly controversial, except for the fossil fight, which was over. He wrote no more letters to the paper, but viewed the bustle of the town from his position as bartender at the Peace Glen Hotel. For eight years he served the wave of humanity that had come to town to cash in. At my urging, his book of poems, *Beneath These Waters*, went into second printing. It sold out its 1,000 copies – resurrecting the stories of prospectors and trappers; of wood-nymphs and summer days; of moose running for their lives through six-foot snowdrifts to the safety of the river where the wolves would not follow them; of rivers that ceased to be; of crazy horses and men and the strong women who put up with them.

But Earl seemed worn out: "These books of mine that you're doing – well, honey, it's more for you than me that I agreed to get them printed again. I don't give a damn. I don't need the money, never did, and I don't need people coming into the bar to get me to sign the goddamned things. Sure it's nice to meet them, some of them I used to know years ago. But as far as the book goes, I just don't care about it. It means a lot to you, and you mean a lot to me, so we got it done. But that's it."

Earl's strength and interest in his writing was waning, but mine was increasing. I felt he had something valid to say, and that his memories of life in one of the most beautiful and remote parts of the country should be recorded. The school system agreed, and several readings and visits in Hudson's Hope and at other schools in the district were arranged. Earl had this to say about that idea:

"I don't want you setting me up with any more schools! I like the kids, I don't mind telling them about what it was like here 50 years ago. But most of them could get the same thing from their grandparents. And that last trip to the school in Fort St. John ended up costing me 200 bucks."

"What?!"

"First it cost me the gas, 65 miles there and 65 miles back," he said. "I filled up my car at Pete's and it came to 30 bucks! So a neighbour hears I'm going in to (Fort St.) John and she asks if she can get a ride, so I say okay. Then another couple want to come so I said fine, there's lots of room. So I dump them off downtown and I go off to the school.

"The kids were fine. They were interested and all that. But what I'm saying is that I really didn't need the trip.

"I picked the neighbours up and we went to the Legion, and who should be in there but this old friend of mine I hadn't seen for 40 years. She used to teach school, years ago. Well, she came over and we got talking about who's here and who's not. I told her Bonnie had passed away and that cut her up pretty badly, because Bonnie and her were friends when they were young. So I buy a round, and another. You don't get by with less than $20 a round. So anyway then we go up for supper. We had Chinese food, which I personally can't stand. But anyway, that came to 30 bucks and I paid it. What the hell, I hadn't seen Irene McClelland for 40 years and we were having a good time. So anyway I paid the bill and then I had to drive Irene back to her car at the Legion, so we went in for just one more. And by the time I got home to Hudson's Hope, which I never should have left in the first place, it had cost me 200 bucks.

"So don't go lining me up to speak to any more schools. You may think you're doing me a favour, but I can't afford it."

With Bonnie gone, Earl's feisty spirit was flickering. I tried to get him interested in writing again, but it was an uphill struggle. He just didn't give a damn, he'd say. He thought he should be dead, too. "I look around at these friends of mine, now bald-headed, toothless, grizzled old bastards, and I don't want to be counted among them!" And for that I had no answer.

River Girl

My River Girl, companion,
My loyal and loving wife,
You're the finest thing to happen
to me, in all my life.

I built a house, or hovels,
Your love made them a home.
Our children turned to you for comfort,
With you near, they weren't alone.

Our village here, too, loved you
And your identity.
My darling, I shall love you
Throughout eternity.

This poem I dedicate to my wife, Bonnie, whose love,
understanding and patience I have had the pleasure of
enjoying and sharing for thirty-eight beautiful years.
Written in 1977, E.K. Pollon

28

Death of a Delta

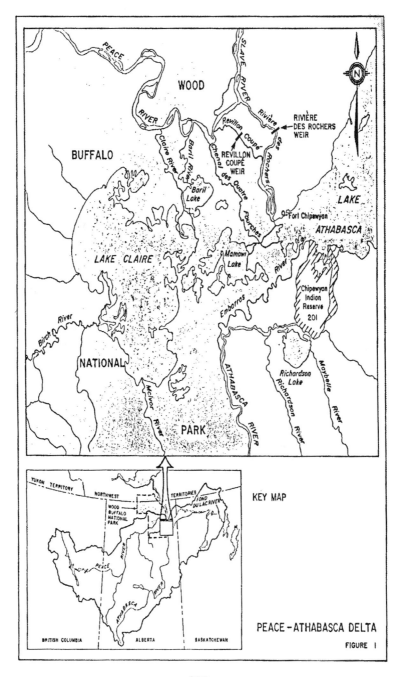

KEY MAP

PEACE-ATHABASCA DELTA

FIGURE I

Fort Chipewyan, Alberta., is a picturesque community of 1,200 to 1,500 people located on the northwestern shore of Lake Athabasca. It is 90 miles south of Fort Smith, N.W.T., 150 miles north of Fort McMurray, Alta., and approximately 750 miles downstream (north and east) from Hudson's Hope. Yet a dam built near the headwaters of the Peace caused such drastic changes that, according to a Fort Chipewyan native, "even the frogs left town. No water."

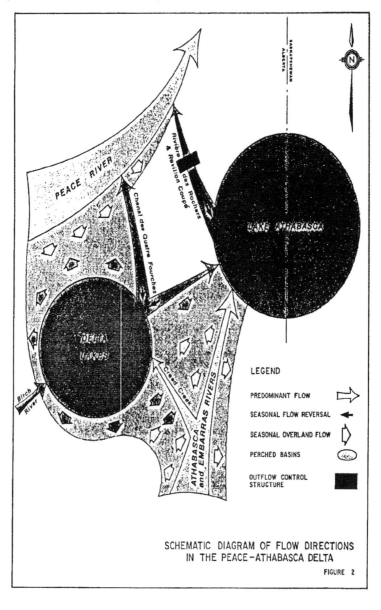

LEGEND

PREDOMINANT FLOW

SEASONAL FLOW REVERSAL

SEASONAL OVERLAND FLOW

PERCHED BASINS

OUTFLOW CONTROL STRUCTURE

SCHEMATIC DIAGRAM OF FLOW DIRECTIONS IN THE PEACE-ATHABASCA DELTA

FIGURE 2

Fort Chipewyan claims to be the oldest community in Alberta (a bicentennial honour lately shared with another Peace River community, Fort Vermilion). The establishment of a post at the boundary of the Cree and Chipewyan territories in 1778 by Peter Pond's North West Trading Company opened the Athabasca-Peace- Mackenzie basin to the fur trade.

Ten years later, explorer Alexander Mackenzie's brother, Roderick, moved the Pond House from the lower Athabasca River to the shore of Lake Athabasca and founded Fort Chipewyan.

Wood Buffalo National Park was established in 1922 north of the Peace River near Fort Chipewyan; the government transported 6,600 wood bison by train and barge. Forty-six species of mammals and 227 species of birds have been recorded in the park, which occupies 80 percent of the Peace-Athabasca delta (and was designated a World Heritage Site in 1985). It is the second-largest national park in the world and has the world's largest herd of free-roaming bison. The other 20 percent of the delta includes the Chipewyan and Cree Indian Reserves and Alberta Crown land.

But it is the river system that distinguishes the area. The river occupies wide, flat valleys, constantly meandering and cutting new channels, abandoning old channels that become narrow lakes and swamps. Where the silt-laden waters of the Peace, Athabasca and Birch rivers meet, there is the still expanse of Lake Athabasca – one of the largest inland deltas in the world, measuring 1,475 square miles.

The Peace-Athabasca delta is spectacular. According to a 1972 summary report prepared by the Peace-Athabasca Delta Project Group, few other deltas in the world, including the Nile River delta and the Florida Everglades, compare with its continental or world significance.

The delta is home to a native population whose ancestors in 1899 signed Treaty Number 8 between the federal government and the Cree and Chipewyan bands (the Beaver/Slavey Indians were chased out by the others). There is also a Metis population whose Scottish ancestors came from the Orkney Islands to work for the trading companies. It is an isolated area in a unique location, and the lifestyles it supported were strongly independent.

Water controls the delta's environment. The Peace River is particularly important because it flows along the northern edge of the delta and regulates the rate at which water flows northward, away from the delta. Here the sediment is dropped and the shallow lakes, marshes, sedge meadows and meandering channels are extremely productive. They support bison, moose, woodland caribou, black bear, wolves, beaver, muskrats, and many fish species. The surrounding forests shelter fox, lynx, mink, ermine and red squirrels.

"We would move to the bush in late September, with dogs packing, to live off the land," recalled Fred Marcel of the Chipewyan band. "We hunted for moose, deer, caribou. At the end of October when it started to snow, we built shacks and stayed there for the winter. The men trapped and hunted, not to make big money but to survive in a good way in the bush. We stayed until long after the ice was frozen, then we went to Fort Chip to buy supplies, taking in our furs. Three different companies would send their men back to our camp to buy our furs.

"The young generation would not know how to survive like that. I worked for the Hudson's Bay Company in 1937 to '38 for one dollar a day, seven dollars every Saturday. You could smoke for three whole days for 15 cents. Then I worked for the Indian Affairs, then on the boats from Fort McMurray to Fort Chip. We had lots of good times, lots of hard times, but we didn't care."

Then, in 1968, the natural flooding of the delta stopped and the delicate balance of the ecosystem began to undergo drastic change.

In January, 1971, the governments of Canada, Alberta and Saskatchewan established a co-operative study group to investigate the cause, effect and extent of low water levels in Lake Athabasca. The Peace-Athabasca Delta Project Group published their summary report in 1972.

"In 1968, after reaching a peak of 684.6 feet, about four feet below the estimated long-term average for mid-July, the waters of Lake Athabasca began to recede without any appreciable flooding of the delta," the report said. One season of minimal flooding was not a catastrophe, but the situation continued for three successive years, with peak heights of only 685.8 feet in 1969; 684.6 in 1970, and 686.5 in 1971.

Due to lack of flooding, an estimated 38 percent of the surface water and 36 percent of the shoreline disappeared on perched basins north of Claire and Mamawi lakes.

"By 1970, as water levels declined in the delta lakes and perched (closed or restricted drainage) basins, more than 125,000 acres of mud flats became exposed and the inevitable process of plant succession was able to progress unchecked," said the summary report. It predicted that "without the age-old balance of low levels being followed by years of high water, the delta will become a very different place indeed."

The cause of persisting low water levels in Lake Athabasca was the crucial focus of the group's hydrological study.

"Clearly the problem must be largely attributed to the reduction in flood flows in the Peace River since 1968," the report said. "Just as clearly, this reduction in Peace River floods *is the direct result of the regulation of river flows by the W.A.C. Bennett Dam*" (authors' italics). One-quarter of the Peace River drainage basin, which contributes 50 percent of the river flow, is located above the dam some 700 miles upstream of the delta. So *"the Bennett dam effectively controlled 50 percent of the flow in the Peace River"* (authors' italics) long before the river had its natural regulating effect on Lake Athabasca.

"Since 1968, this reduction in flows has been particularly severe, due to the initial filling of Williston Lake, created by the dam." the report noted. "During this time 50 million acre-feet of Peace River waters have been stored in this lake. Flood flows on the Peace River at Peace Point were reduced by as much as 200,000 cubic feet per second, and river levels were 10 to 12 feet lower than usual at flood time. At such low levels the Peace River no longer provided a natural barrier to the outflow of water from Lake Athabasca during the flood season."

The ecological edge (the area between water and land) of the delta's perched basins is marshy and swampy, offering a wide variety of habitats in a small space. The greater the amount of edge, the more productive that habitat is; therefore, a lot of small basins are more productive than one large basin because of increased edge. The delta was the perfect environment for muskrats and nesting waterfowl, which thrived in the environment.

Vegetation responded very quickly to the sudden alteration: grasses, sedges, willows and many annuals appeared and were, in turn, taken over by denser willow growth. Thirty-six per cent of the waterfowl breeding areas in perched basins and their shorelines dried up. The effect on the muskrat population was devastating. During the winter of 1968-69, after the first season without midsummer flooding, the muskrat catch in the park portion of the delta was 38,000 pelts. In 1970-71 it decreased to 8,000 and the 1971-72 harvest in the park was less than 2,000. A large number of the marshes had become too shallow for the animals to over-winter successfully, and the perched water bodies froze to the bottom.

The period of unusually low water levels between 1968 and 1971 was marked by very low population numbers in the delta, agreed Susan Bramm of Amica Environment Information Services, in her Peace-Athabasca update report of February, 1983. Restoration of a more normal regime between 1971 and '74 brought increases to the muskrat population, and peak numbers were observed in the fall of 1975. However, "since 1976 the water levels have been relatively stable, with the maximums insufficient to cause recharge of the perched basins and the minimums creating flood conditions at the lower levels. This modified regime has brought an overall reduction in suitable habitat and therefore a decline in the muskrat population, to approximately 70 per cent lower than that observed in 1975."

Frank Ladouceur, Metis trapper, and author
Shirlee Matheson, at Fort Chipewyan, September, 1988

"The delta is muskrat country," said Frank Ladouceur, a Fort Chipewyan Metis who narrated and starred in a documentary film titled "The Man Who Chooses the Bush." "The people who had traplines inland were not affected by the Bennett dam, but we who had traplines in the reserve, the park and along the lakeshore were affected a lot. Now the lakes where we used to trap are all poplar and willow. Over 200,000 to 300,000 muskrats came out of the delta every season. I used to get 50, 60, up to 100 muskrats a day. Only one year did I have to go on social assistance. I have 11 kids and there was nothing in my traps."

Since the Bennett dam was built, the number of muskrats trapped annually has dropped to 50,000 to 80,000 pelts, Ladouceur added. "Even the frogs left the country. No water."

Records indicate that the earned income from trapping among

the 370-man labour force in Fort Chipewyan in 1965 was $180,000; in 1970 it had fallen 40 percent to $110,000. Trapping accounted for approximately 28 percent of the community income in 1965. In 1983, some 200 of the male labour force still trapped to some degree, although there were probably only a dozen men who earned $2,500 or more.[1]

According to information compiled by ecologist Deirdre E. Griffiths for the Canadian Wildlife Service, the Peace and Athabasca deltas began their evolution several thousand years ago, converging at Mamawi Lake. The Athabasca River continues to extend its delta eastward into Lake Athabasca. Claire and Mamawi lakes remain connected to Lake Athabasca by wide channels, and their summer levels fluctuate with those of the main lake. The important Fort Chipewyan fishing grounds are on Athabasca, Richardson, Claire and Mamawi lakes.[2] Fish studies carried out in 1971 and 1972 focused mainly on goldeye and walleye, and to some extent lake trout. The 1971 spring and fall water levels (684 to 685 feet in Claire and Mamawi lakes) appeared to be the lowest absolute minimum to allow the migration of goldeye. Walleye could have trouble entering Richardson Lake for spawning until after breakup, and this was expected to severely curtail production.

"I've been fishing these waters for 47 years," said Frank Ladouceur. "Where the spawning grounds used to be in three to four feet of water, now there's three to four inches of water. It backfilled the lake. Nothing but mud flats. Where high water level was 50 years ago, now there is a seven- to eight-foot difference.

"Where there used to be three feet of water in the lakes, they went dry as a bone. A moose could run across the mud and sink in only two inches where it used to be a lake. Now there's brush and willow and poplar where there used to be lakes."

Navigation was also affected: a significant increase in dredging operations was necessary at Big Point Channel on the Athabasca River. According to the 1972 summary report, "between 1958 and 1967, dredging in the channel averaged 95,000 cubic yards; between 1968 and 1971 this increased to approximately 201,000 cubic yards . . . Nineteen additional more navigational aids were required at various locations on Lake Athabasca to indicate shoals which became dangerous at low levels." Shallow-draft problems were also experienced in the Chenal des Quartre Fourches, especially at the confluence of this river and the Peace River. Shifting sand bars at low water held up barge traffic, and the reverse-flow conditions shifted the deep-water channels from one side of the river to the other. It became difficult to safely dock at Fort Chipewyan and several other points.

The 1972 summary report concluded that, with flows in the Peace River modified by the Bennett dam, Lake Athabasca summer levels could be expected to average about 686 feet – about one foot lower than the average summer level under the natural regime. Average summer maximum levels with the dam were expected to reach only 686.5 feet – two feet lower than the average natural level of 688.5 for the summer peaks. And such lake water levels were simply not sufficient to flood the delta.

The delta was destined to die slowly, "as continued absence of flooding, permanent reduction in lake levels, and persistently low summer peak levels will result in significant decreases in the acreages of habitats that support the wildlife of the delta," the report said.

Various remedies were suggested: a removable ice dam, rockfill dams, gated control structures and weirs, even the possible release of water from the Williston reservoir to partially restore the historic flood peaks on the Peace River. However, because this latter solution would require releases of about 200,000 cubic feet per second for a minimum of five days to significantly affect the level of Lake Athabasca, the sheer volume of water rendered the scheme unfeasible.

The delta was not the only downstream area to feel the effects of the Bennett dam. The Fort St. John *Alaska Highway News*, on September 30, 1970, published a story that "Alberta authorities are really roughing up B.C. over the Peace River dam." A lawsuit was pending by the town of Peace River, another being contemplated by the Alberta Metis Association and much attention being paid by the *Edmonton Journal*. "Not content with roasting us over the dam, the *Journal* now points to plans to flood the Skagit valley as part of B.C.'s 'scorched earth policy'," said the *Alaska Highway News*. "Worse, they point out that the sale of four Christmas trees per acre would give the same return per year as will flooding the valley to provide power for Seattle."

On December, 1970, the Fort Chipewyan natives filed a claim for damages against B.C. Hydro. But Thomas Berger, the natives' lawyer, was appointed to the bench and the case lost momentum.

The Town of Peace River claimed that the Bennett dam had eliminated spring flood peaks and this had caused the Heart River, a tributary of the Peace, to scour its river bed. The town's water intake pipes were exposed by the scouring and were damaged by freezing. According to a letter to the authors from Peace River town manager J.W.D. McLeod, P. Eng., dated April 4, 1989, the Town of Peace River sued B.C. Hydro and lost. "The trial was held in the Alberta Supreme Court in the spring of 1974, before Justice J.H. Milvain. The Town had successfully taken the issue of jurisdiction to the Supreme Court of Canada and the trial was held in Alberta rather than British Columbia."[3]

According to McLeod, the town of Peace River continues to experience environmental effects. The water levels in winter are higher because the river often stays open later into the fall; before the dam, the entire river froze; now the water flows openly year-round until the river begins to freeze upstream from the town near the B.C.-Alberta border. "When the river does freeze up," said McLeod, "there are large volumes of ice produced as, due to the high (winter) water level, the upper river surface is much wider and provides a much larger surface area."

In pre-dam years, McLeod said, the town would construct a winter ice-road across the Peace River from the present museum site at the mouth of the Heart River to the lower west Peace. "But the high winter levels, uncertainty of winter flows, rough ice conditions and shorter ice-cover season now make a winter crossing of the Peace River impractical."

A committee has been formed comprised of Alberta Environment, B.C. Environment and B.C. Hydro to monitor B.C. Hydro's actions and to provide a liaison between the two provinces, with one of its major functions to open – and keep open – a line of communication between B.C. Hydro, the Town of Peace River and the Province of Alberta which had been pretty well lost following the court case, McLeod said. "Alberta Environment, each year since, works with B.C. Hydro at freeze-up in the fall, in an attempt to establish and set an ice level of sufficient height that will prevent ice jamming in the spring. This operation has been successful."

According to Joan Freeman's report titled, "Summary of a Surprise: The Unanticipated Effects which resulted from Developing the Peace River for Power," unexpected environmental changes occurred because some basic properties of ecosystems were either not investigated or misunderstood. "The Peace River has been, since 1967, experiencing aggradation downstream from the mouths of tributaries, while tributaries are undergoing accelerated bed and bank erosion (B.C. Hydro, 1976. Peace River Sites C and E. River Regime and Morphology Studies, Report #783). This phenomenon was the basis for the town of Peace River's lawsuit. The possibility that the allegations were legitimate caused B.C. Hydro considerable concern. The surprise was caused primarily by a lack of understanding of fluvial dynamics."

Who is to blame for these problems? Is it possible to anticipate and plan for all consequences resulting from such a large-scale project?

Legal and jurisdictional concerns were carefully documented in the 1972 Peace-Athabasca Delta Group summary report, which noted that the matter went far beyond pointing a finger at any one corporation or consulting one act of legislation. "The question of management and use of these Peace waters manifestly transcends the strictures of provincial borders and the special interests of any one province. It is a vital concern of the provinces of British Columbia, Alberta and Saskatchewan and of the government of Canada. Use of Peace River waters by one has relevance for all," the report said.

Depending on how Peace River water is to be used, approval is subject to various provincial or federal laws under the Canadian Constitution. Navigation and transportation, regulation of fisheries, and anything affecting Wood Buffalo National Park or migratory birds, is federal jurisdiction. But uses for domestic or industrial water supply, or for the generation of electric power, are subject to the legislation of the province where such use is made. "Such varying uses to which the

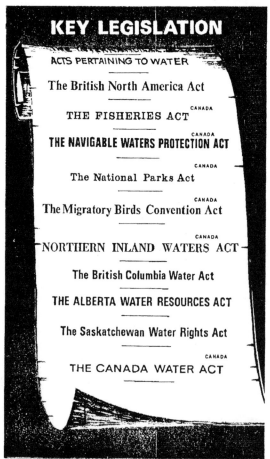

KEY LEGISLATION

ACTS PERTAINING TO WATER

The British North America Act

THE FISHERIES ACT
CANADA

THE NAVIGABLE WATERS PROTECTION ACT
CANADA

The National Parks Act
CANADA

The Migratory Birds Convention Act
CANADA

NORTHERN INLAND WATERS ACT
CANADA

The British Columbia Water Act

THE ALBERTA WATER RESOURCES ACT

The Saskatchewan Water Rights Act

THE CANADA WATER ACT
CANADA

same water may be put, together with the division of lawmaking authority between provincial and federal jurisdiction relating to that water, creates a most complex legal framework within which conflict of interests must be judged," the report said.

The legal can of worms was opened when the British North America Act of 1867 divided legislative jurisdiction between federal and provincial governments. "When the western provinces entered Confederation, their existing water laws (based on English common law and statutory law) were continued . . ." the report said, "So it is that the Provinces of British Columbia, Alberta and Saskatchewan all have the heritage of the common law, as modified by local courts and legislatures, regarding the rights inherent in, and the use and enjoyment of water within, their borders.

"Since the western provinces were granted ownership of land and natural resources within their boundaries by the Constitution, and since they also had the authority to pass laws in relation to 'property and civil rights in the province,' they asserted ownership in the water flowing over the provincial land. The federal government, holding ownership of specific properties in the western provinces, used similar legislative authority to assert the same rights of ownership to water flowing over its property."

The legal tangle gives each level of government the ability to pass different laws that may affect the water rights of other governments for the same water.

"The British Columbia Water Act appears to repeal the common law with respect to water. All ownership in, and the right to the use of all water in the province, belong to the Crown in the right of the province," said the summary report.

The Bennett dam's effect on the delta is complicated by this legislative labyrinth: "The generation of hydro-electric power and its use within a province is a matter within the scope of the legislative jurisdiction of the province," the report noted.

"On the basis of these points, it may be said that the regulation of the flow of the Peace River within British Columbia, for the purposes of providing water for the Gordon M. Shrum Generating Station, was within the legislative jurisdiction of the Province of British Columbia. Further, it appears that the planning, construction and operation of the project was carried out in accordance with all the requirements of the law of the Province of British Columbia."

On the other hand, the report added that the Peace River is a navigable stream, so the provisions of the federal Navigable Waters Protection Act apply to this river. "Therefore, approval was required by the Federal Minister of Public Works before a work such as the

W.A.C. Bennett Dam could be constructed on the Peace River. *Neither the British Columbia Hydro and Power Co. nor its predecessors did, in fact, obtain such approval* (authors' italics). Similarly, there is uncertainty as to what extent the requirements of the Fisheries Act of Canada were met by the developers of the W.A.C. Bennett Dam."

The questions could be debated for years. Can a province, acting in accordance with laws it has passed, authorize the impoundment of water within its borders even though this will affect the flow and quantity of water in another province, or impact upon federal lands?

According to the 1972 summary report, "Anyone planning to bring his case before the courts regarding his claims about the adverse affects of the regulation of the Peace River by the Province of British Columbia would be faced by two formidable questions: in the courts of which province would he bring his law suit? Which law would that court apply in a determination of his action?"

After the cooperative study group completed its studies, the governments of Canada, Alberta and Saskatchewan signed, on September 16, 1974, the Peace-Athabasca Delta Implementation Agreement. The pact set out cost-sharing arrangements for construction of remedial works (ice dams and rockfill weirs), and established the implementation committee to oversee construction and monitoring programs in the delta. Between September, 1974 and December, 1983, the committee supervised the building of weirs on Rivière des Rochers and Revillon Coupé, implemented monitoring programs, and created sub-committees to monitor flora and fauna, fisheries and hydrology.

Alberta Environment and Environment Canada developed a hydrologic model to simulate and analyze flows in and out of the delta, and also monitored sediment and water quality.

Parks Canada kept watch on vegetation in the delta area of Wood Buffalo National Park.

Ducks Unlimited (Canada) monitored waterfowl populations between 1971 and 1974, with funding from Canadian Wildlife Service. The service in turn conducted aerial surveys of breeding, moulting and staging waterfowl, and recorded the population and distribution of harvested furbearers – such as muskrat numbers for 31 lakes and perched basins.

The implementation committee's status report confirmed that "the Bennett dam has altered the natural regime of the Peace River. Its immediate effect on Lake Athabasca and the Peace-Athabasca delta occurred during the filling of the Williston Reservoir when 50 million acre-feet of water were stored, and is specific to the period 1968 to '71. . . . During the filling of Williston Lake, spring floods were greatly reduced, by as much as 200,000 cubic feet per second. As a result, peak summer lake levels were an average of 2.5 feet below those which would have occurred without the Bennett dam."

The status report went on to note that "future flows in the Peace River will be modified by the Bennett Dam and Shrum Generating Station which, when in full operation, is scheduled to release an average annual flow of about 38,000 cubic feet per second."[4]

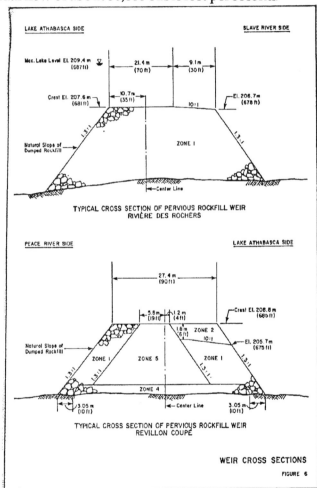

Three weirs (rock dams) were built to hold water back by partial damming and constriction. The first experimental weir, consisting of two submerged wings, was installed in 1974 and completed in September, 1975, at the Rivière Des Rochers (Little Rapids) site. It was intended to reduce the summer and fall outflow from Lake Athabasca that was occurring as a result of the lower than natural levels on the Peace River. Additional weirs were completed in March, 1976 on the

Revillon Coupé (built across three-quarters of the channel, causing water to flow around and sometimes over it), and a temporary rockfill dam – later removed – was built on Chenal des Quatre Fourches. Records since 1976 suggest that they appear to control outflow when Peace River discharges are less than 141,000 cfs. Peace River flows are now below this level for 10 months of the year; in May and June, when flows exceed this, the weirs are 'drowned.'

Another plan considered, to create a temporary blockage on the Peace's lower branch at Rivière des Rochers, was the construction of a man-made "ecological" ice dam.[5]

"The weirs installed in 1976, although performing as expected, have created their own set of impacts which ultimately can also be attributed to the Bennett dam," said Dan Frandsen, park warden at Wood Buffalo National Park, in a letter to the authors dated January 23, 1989. "Some of these impacts are restricted fish movement (particularly goldeye) over the weirs, reduced amplitude of water level fluctuations and timing which has narrowed the bands of vegetation around the open drainage system which rely on frequent flooding and exposure to the atmosphere for their survival, and scouring of the Chenal Des Quartre Fourches," Frandsen said.

The weirs did raise water levels. However, high *water* levels were not so much the concern, as peak *flood* levels, which had been lowered by approximately one foot by the Bennett dam. But in the delta area, that one foot meant the difference to flooding or not flooding the lower basins.

"The Bennett hydro-electric dam clearly demonstrates that changes in one area can cause impacts far downstream," said Deirdre Griffiths in her brochure issued by the Canadian Wildlife Service. Griffiths is an ecologist whose studies of the Bennett dam impacts relate to wildlife and vegetation and their responses to the altered hydrological regime. "Since 1971, 75 to 85 percent of the mountain snow-melt has been held back every summer to recharge the dam's huge reservoir. Only 24 percent of the Peace watershed area is controlled by the dam, but [750 miles] downstream, at the Peace-Athabasca delta, June and July river *flows* are depressed 40 percent or more. Another [270 miles] downstream the decrease in Great Slave Lake summer levels is noticeable. The stored snow-melt water is released over the winter to generate electricity, but it is the loss of the June flood that affects wildlife so much. This peak was responsible for short-term flooding that extended over much of the Peace-Athabasca Delta every three to five years, maintaining its diversity and productivity."

The 1983 status report agreed: "During the period of Peace River peak flows (mid-May to mid-July), water would overflow into the delta and Lake Athabasca, and, *more importantly, the Peace River would act as a dam and retard the outflow of water from Lake Athabasca and the delta* (authors' italics).

To assess the hydrological performance of the weirs, simulated water levels were compared for a common period (1960 to 1984) for three scenarios: natural conditions, Bennett dam without weirs, and Bennett dam with the weirs. The findings, contained in the April, 1987 *Peace-Athabasca Delta Water Management Works Evaluation* (final report), were that "weirs constructed on the Rivière Des Rochers and on the Revillon Coupé in 1976 generally restored normal lake levels to Lake Athabasca and the delta, although the amplitude of their fluctuations has been reduced somewhat. However, nothing has been done to restore the apparently reduced frequency of ice jams on the Peace River.

"The lack of ice jams on the Peace River since 1974 has resulted in the higher perched basins (normally very productive) on the north and east side of the delta not being flooded. These basins are undergoing rapid vegetation succession toward willow and other shrubby habitat which is much less productive for wildlife (especially muskrats) than the original vegetation associations."

Park warden Frandsen emphasized the importance of the ice-jams that used to occur in the delta before the Bennett dam was built. "There are two main mechanisms by which the Peace Athabasca delta is normally flooded," he said. "Overland flooding from either or both the Peace and Athabasca Rivers as a result of ice jams occurring during spring breakup (late April to early May). And (secondly) high Lake Athabasca water levels (consequently, high delta basin levels) which tend to peak in late July each year. The Bennett dam seriously disrupted both mechanisms."

For example, at Rocky Point (where the Peace joins the Slave River), water would once flow from the Peace River into the delta channels running south. Resulting ice-jams caused a good flood to occur every three to five years. There have been no ice jams in the delta since 1974.

Ken East, superintendent of Wood Buffalo National Park, agreed that there was a definite effect from the Bennett Dam on "three million acres in the area that had been dependent on traditional flooding patterns. For three to four years during the flooding of the reservoir, we received lower flows. In the early 1970s they discovered that the effect was permanent."

The fact that the Bennett dam has caused permanent loss of some wetland habitats is substantiated in the biological assessment of the Peace-Athabasca Delta Implementation Committee's final report. Although the weirs were constructed to mitigate long-term impacts, it was recognized that they could not return the delta to its natural condition.

During a Fort Chipewyan-Fort Vermilion bicentennial conference (held in Edmonton on September 23 to 25, 1988, and organized by the Boreal Institute for Northern Studies), area problems, both past and present, were discussed. Carl Granath, manager of the fish plant in Fort Chipewyan, said the local people have to worry about a lot of things affecting their waterways. In 1980 there was an oil spill which set back the fishing industry. They also worry about toxic dioxins being dumped into the river systems from various plants to the south. For example, from the pulp mills that discharge waste water contaminated by dioxins.

In 1972, Alberta Environment opened an office in Fort Chipewyan, under the administration of the technical services division. Its purpose is to monitor fluctuations in water levels and flows throughout the Peace-Athabasca delta, and to measure the continuing effects of the Bennett dam. Working within a 50-mile radius of Fort Chipewyan, environment technicians record water level changes on 12 automatic water level gauges which operate year-round and one automatic gauge which operates during open water season. Data are also obtained on precipitation, ice thickness, break-up and freeze-up dates, and water colour, odour, salt, algae, scum, nutrients, metals and organic compounds.

Leigh Woton, of Alberta Environment's water quality control branch, said upstream waste from plants in Fort McMurray, Whitecourt and Edson has definitely affected water quality in the delta. The department's function, he added, is especially important with the announcement of new and expanded pulp mills along the Peace River system at Hinton and Whitecourt, and at the town of Peace River. (Further, a huge mill is going in at Athabasca). The new development at the town of Peace River "could result in a five-to-six times increase in pulp effluent contamination in the river system," Woton said. "Some companies have suspended their plans pending results of tests for water quality levels, as they may require secondary or tertiary treatment facilities."

The changes to the once undisturbed ecosystem are expected to continue. According to the 1983 status report, the projected long- term effects of the modified flows in the Peace River are lower water levels in Lake Athabasca (1.1 feet lower in summer and annual maximum

Fort Chipewyan, Alberta, September, 1988

levels 1.8 feet lower), with fluctuations expected to be 0.8 feet compared with a natural fluctuation of 1.5 feet. The delta's perched basins will be filled less frequently, and the shoreline (edge) will decrease by about 50 percent. Waterfowl production is expected to decline by 20 to 35 percent because of habitat loss, and the muskrat population by 41 to 66 percent. Blockage to Richardson Lake for spawning walleye is expected to occur more often, and there'll be a decline in the food supply (zooplankton) for goldeye. The delta, an international key link in the four North American flyways for waterfowl, is dying.

"Trapping and fishing are important to the local economy and are an integral part of the lifestyle of the local native people. Any reduction in muskrat population, or increased hazards to successful spawning of walleye and goldeye, will further compound the already undesirable social and economic problems of the area," warned the implementation committee's 1983 status report.

The report concluded with a comment that "the existing federal statutes available, ie. The Navigable Waters Protection Act and the Fisheries Act as presently framed, are ineffective instruments for dealing with the complex environmental problems which can occur on interprovincial rivers."

It is, without doubt, an understatement.

A final report issued April, 1987 recommended that additional long-term work in the delta be co-ordinated by an inter-governmental body. The Peace-Athabasca Delta Group was terminated, and responsibility for implementing their recommendations transferred to an "information exchange mechanism" called the Mackenzie River Basin Committee.[6]

The Peace-Athabasca Delta group's 1972 summary report had ended with a sad and inevitable statement: "The Peace River Power project was conceived in the late 1950s, and executed in the 1960s. The concerns of the 1970s were not within its purview. Water was then seen, apparently, only in terms of its economic value as a source of electric power. It was not seen as the very artery of life to an amazingly complex ecological system outside of the Province of British Columbia."

Frank Ladouceur still smarts from the insult of being kept in ignorance about the dam: "There were no meetings with anybody. They just went ahead and built the Bennett dam. A Frenchman came up to me one day and said, 'What do you think of this dam?' I hadn't heard a thing about it. Nobody knew from Chip. It affected the fishing and trapping, both.

"Now I'm told there's going to be another dam, on the Athabasca River. If this new dam is going to come, I hope they have a meeting with the trappers. We have no education – I graduated in grade three and I could not talk English when I started to school, I picked up French and English in school – but I still want to be consulted. It's our living. This is our home."

Notes

[1]*Peace-Athabasca Delta, (Status Report)*, Peace-Athabasca Delta Implementation Committee, Canada, Alberta, Saskatchewan, 1983, p. 32

[2]Four large shallow lakes are located in the Peace-Athabasca delta: Claire, Mamawi, Baril and Richardson. During most of the year, the general direction of flow through the delta area is northeast: water flows into Lake Claire via the Birch River and other tributaries from the west, then into Mamawi Lake, then either north via the Chenal des Quatre Fourches, or into Lake Athabasca and north through one of its two major outlet channels, Rivière des Rochers or Revillon Coupé. Baril Lake, and areas north, drain into the Peace River. Richardson and other lakes of the Athabasca delta drain into the major channels of the Athabasca River.

[3]Information obtained from sources such as letter to authors dated March 31 and April 4, 1989 from John W.D. McLeod, P. Eng., Town Manager, Town of Peace River, Alberta; "Summary of a Surprise: The Unanticipated Effects Which Resulted from Developing the Peace River for Power," Joan Freeman, April, 1979; Review of the Literature and Miscel-

laneous Other Parameters Relating to Water Levels in the Peace-Athabasca Delta Particularly with Respect to the Effect on Muskrat Numbers, W. Thorpe, Wood Buffalo Park Warden, January, 1986.

[4]According to a report prepared by Susan Bramm, Arnica Environment Information Services, February, 1983, under natural conditions Peace River flood flows averaging 311,000 cubic feet per second or greater, lasting for at least 10 days, prevent flow out of Lake Athabasca. During the period 1960 to 1967, the Peace River added an average of one million acre-feet to Lake Athabasca. Between 1968 and 1971, peak flows in June were much less, (150,000 to 200,000 cfs) and the mean monthly flows were reduced by half. The river's water levels at the delta were 10 to 12 feet lower than before 1968.

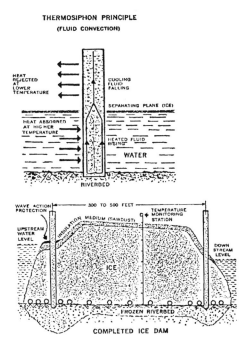

THERMOSIPHON PRINCIPLE
(FLUID CONVECTION)

COMPLETED ICE DAM

[5]Based on the thermosyphon principle of fluid convection, pipes called thermopiles are half-filled with a fluid like freon, and stood up a series in the water. This fluid, taking heat from the water then going to the cold air, gives off steam. The bottom of the pipes gets so cold they begin to freeze, eventually creating an ice-dam. This ice would be protected with sawdust to maintain the mass until the summer's peak water levels are attained. Field tests in 1972 proved the concept was feasible for producing the ice required for the dam. Its chief value was that it could create flooding on demand, or could be removed. However, it would have to be rebuilt every year that high water levels were desired. Also, such ice dams work only in winter.

[6]The Mackenzie River Basin Committee was established by the governments of Canada, British Columbia, Alberta and Saskatchewan under a 1977 memorandum regarding water resources of the Mackenzie River Basin. The committee was charged with exchanging information on water and related resource activities and intended developments in the basin; determining the need of studies; recommending such studies to ministers and carrying out any approved studies; planning and implementating recommendations contained in the 1981 Mackenzie River Basin study report. Further information on the Mackenzie River Basin Committee (MRBC) can be obtained through Alberta Environment, Planning Division, 9th Floor, Oxbridge Place, 9820 – 106 St., Edmonton, AB T5K 2J6

29

The Site C Question

When B.C. Hydro first announced the possibility of building a third dam, capable of producing 900 megawatts, on the Peace River about 55 miles downstream from Site One (now called Peace Canyon), local residents reacted immediately. Some were for the project, welcoming the opportunity for more employment after the lay-off when Peace Canyon was completed. To others, the project was a sacrilege.

Leo Rutledge found himself at the forefront of a group opposing the Site C project. Rutledge, Earl Pollon's former trapping partner on the Clearwater and a longtime Hudson's Hope resident, lives with his wife Ethel in their home on the banks of the Peace River. The Rutledges stand to lose the homestead portion of their river land if Site C dam goes ahead. Rutledge is involved in several wilderness-oriented organizations: he's president of the Northern B.C. Guides

Leo and Ethel Rutledge, and Earl Pollon
(S. Matheson)

and Outfitters, director of the B.C. Wildlife Federation, and a member of the Sierra Club of Western Canada and the Peace Valley Environmental Association.

"First it was rumoured that they were going to build Site C," Rutledge said, "and then Hydro started having their little softening-up meetings. We said, 'Hold it, there's got to be a forum.' So the first thing we went after, some of us, was a hearing. We formed the Peace Valley Environmental Association and it's still active."

In 1980, the British Columbia Utilities Commission Act was passed, which compelled Hydro to produce demand and supply forecasts for power, conduct environmental and social impact assessments, and have power rates examined at public hearings.

"So, reluctantly, through the minister of energy, we got a hearing," Rutledge said, "and we only got a hearing because they felt it was going to be a push-over."

It was not quite that simple, as it turned out.

A protest seemed untimely after the creation of Williston Lake. What was the difference if a few more acres were flooded downstream between Hudson's Hope and Fort St. John? The $3.2- billion (1984 dollars) dam project would provide employment to an area that was once again feeling the pinch. Fort St. John certainly needed the extra boost, and was gearing up for it. The town was building new motels, houses, apartment buildings, and a shopping mall, because the Site C dam would be located just five miles from its boundaries. Hudson's Hope residents, who would have the choice of commuting 55 miles or renting a place in 'John' and coming home weekends, were basically out of work again.

The timing of the Site C announcement was typical of B.C.'s energetic young premier, Bill Bennett, the son of W.A.C. Bennett. The premier unveiled the project when he was attending the ceremonial opening of the 1,800-megawatt, $2-billion hydroelectric dam in Revelstoke, which had taken eight years to build and was second only to the generating capacity of the Bennett dam on the Peace.

"The days of dams, their construction and their contribution to the B.C. economy, rather than being over, never looked brighter," Bennett said. It seemed an optimistic statement in light of the fact that contracts had not been signed with California for power sales. Also, the Bonneville Power Administration, a U.S. federal government agency which controls more than 80 percent of the transmission lines in the northwest (including direct access between California and British Columbia) and is therefore crucial to transmission of power into the United States, had not made a deal with B.C.

An article titled "The Electric Jungle" by Michael Anderson, published in *Sierra Report* May-June, 1988, outlined three basic market areas in international electricity trade: the U.S. eastern seaboard (served by Ontario Hydro, Hydro-Quebec and Nova Scotia Power), the U.S. northern midwest (served by Manitoba Hydro), and the Western Systems Co-ordinating Council, covering almost one-third of the United States (served by B.C. Hydro).

According to Anderson, the west coast electricity market is a "jungle" of competing interests. "California utilities have long wooed B.C. Hydro, and this relationship led to open conflict when BPA (Bonneville Power Administration) shut down firm transmission access between B.C. and California. After two failed court challenges by the City of Los Angeles, B.C. Hydro was left with considerable surplus generating capability and insufficient sales to pay the costs of construction. The result was wholesale lay-offs in B.C. Hydro in an effort to contain costs and power rates." Basically, said Anderson, "Bonneville Power's objective was – and is – to prevent B.C. Hydro from competing for the California and Pacific northwest markets for surplus power. More recently, BPA has been actively seeking a long-term agreement with B.C. Hydro to 'cooperatively' manage the joint power system on the Columbia River. The present goal is nothing less than a Northwest 'superutility' to control the market for surplus power."

Leo Rutledge, in his article titled "Blueprint to Bondage" (published in 1981 by an Terrace, B.C. environmental group) that dealt with B.C. Hydro's *Energy Blueprint 1980,* listed the facilities already producing electricity within the province: 31 hydroelectric installations, four large gas turbines, 13 stationary diesel generators, 68 mobile diesel and small turbines, the Seven Mile dam project in the Kootenays and the Revelstoke dam to shortly come on line. There were also hundreds of privately owned generating facilities entirely removed from Hydro's systems. All this in a province with a population of only two and one-half million people! The supply-demand ratio seemed completely out of whack.

In a four-page brochure titled, "To Dam or Not to Dam: The Site C Question," the Peace Valley Environmental Association outlined the pros and cons of more dam construction. Each point was illustrated by a drawing of a beaver. There was a beaver thinking, a beaver reading a book called "Truth and ?," a beaver playing with a box of "killowatts" [sic], and a beaver trying to replant trees, escape from landslides, and protect its young against the impact of floating debris.

The environmental association's 1987 brochure blasted Hydro's reasons for building Site C: "To date, B.C.'s potential for conserving electricity has barely been scratched. Indeed, within a stone's throw of the proposed Site C facility's dam site, the forest and petroleum industries are both allowed to blithely blast their 'waste' heat off into thin air, day and night, year in, year out. Among other civilized options for generating electricity, B.C. has unlimited hydro and thermal potential. All it needs to generate electricity is the political sagacity to distinguish civility from incivility – to tell the difference between right and wrong."

"B.C. Hydro and assorted politicians enthusiastically tout electricity derived from mega-projects as an unqualified 'clean' source of electricity," the brochure continued. "On the switch end of the power-line, immaculately clean it certainly is. So quick, so quiet, so clean and beautiful. But at the line's other end may lurk ultimate ugliness and desecration. The 640-square-mile Williston Reservoir with its 1,000-mile long unusable shoreline is a case in point."

But Site C would bring employment, wouldn't it?

"We have had 25 years of first-hand experience with boom-to-bust Peace River dam-building scenarios. As a job-creator, Site C dam leaves much to be desired," the environmental association said. "At $3.3 billion borrowed dollars, at 10 to 12 percent interest, the price for, say, 3,000 temporary jobs seems awfully high. $3.3 billion divided by 3,000 equals $1.1 million per temporary job."

The W.A.C. Bennett Dam, after construction, provided permanent jobs for 65 people, plus up to 10 seasonal temporaries. Peace Canyon resulted in 20 full-time personnel and up to four temporaries. Hydro Force Construction added another two employees for smaller construction projects and minor modifications.

A report by Vancouver consultants Thorne Stevenson & Kellogg said that if Site C went ahead, the project would involve a $3.2 billion investment (1984 dollars) and create 5,400 man-years of construction employment. B.C. Hydro estimated that 2,400 man-years of employment would go to regional residents, for a $128 million (1981 dollars) payroll. In the peak year of employment, approximately 800 of the 2,000 workers would be regional residents. Nearly seven years from the date of agreement would be required to bring the project on-stream. Once built, it would provide 20 to 25 permanent jobs.

But the Peace Valley Environmental Association was sceptical:

"While much is made of the proposed Site C dam project as a 'job creator,' we should be reminded that so were the pyramids of Egypt ... and the Great Wall of China. In the ultimate reckoning, they didn't really amount to much – except to mollify someone's monumentally bloated ego," the group's brochure said. "With the proposed Site C facility in place, the power fleeing south of the border, and the money lenders skimming the top of sales, (it) means that there may be precious little left for us and our children's children but the eternal mortgage and one more valley foregone."

Adrienne Peacock, coordinator for the Peace Valley Environmental Association during the Site C hearings, is a board member of the West Coast Environmental Law Association. When Peacock wrote an article, "B.C. Doesn't Need Site C," published in the June, 1986, issue of *The Democrat*, she was running as an NDP candidate in the Vancouver-Little Mountain riding. "The Social Credit government has a history of making bad power deals with the U.S.," she said, referring to a 1961 deal where B.C. sold 30 years' of power from the Columbia River to the U.S. for the lump sum of $273 million. The money sounded more than adequate, but it cost the province half-a-billion dollars to build the three dams required under the Columbia River Treaty. Peacock suggested alternatives to building Site C, including following a conservation plan, using waste wood products from the forest industry, linking up with a thermal system, or developing small hydroelectric power sites.

Vic Gouldie is a Hudson's Hope resident who originally worked as a chuck-tender, then miner, on the Bennett dam, and has since become the owner of a trapline that would be affected by Site C. Gouldie said he intervened in Hydro's application for the water licence to construct the dam "because the proposal was to give Hydro the water rights *before* studies and compensation and all that had been done. I just stepped in and said, 'Don't you think we should check all these things before we give them the water rights? And then what we discover will determine whether they get the rights or not. You don't give it to them first and then look into it.'"

Newspapers carried articles about problems that had plagued Peace River residents since the creation of Williston Lake. The people, it seemed, had memories. They were no longer buying the propaganda.

Site C would flood the 50 pristine islands in the Peace River from Hudson's Hope to Fort St. John, destroying the best family recreation sites in the country. The Peace Valley Environmental Association pointed out that the downstream Peace River stretch between the proposed Site C dam and the Alberta border would inevitably receive whatever effluents originated from Dawson Creek, Fort St. John, Chetwynd, Taylor's town and industrial complex, Tumbler Ridge coal project, as well as the entire region's agricultural sprays and fertilizers. The lower reaches (extending 700 miles to Fort Chipewyan) were not suitable for future family water recreation, said the association. "With the proposed Site C facility in place, recreationists and the people of the Peace must be expected to endure several years of smoke, din and unsightliness while B.C. Hydro's machines clear and torch the 50 islands and the valley's lower levels, several more years of debris-clogged pondage, sloughing of the banks, an 'eternity' of tributary streams contributing drift and debris, wind-tossed waves, and ultimately a sluggish river meandering across a flood plain plugged with mud – the legacy of our time to posterity."

Not a pretty sight, but when the association's brochure described the wildlife problems that would be encountered, even the most hard-hearted person would be moved.

"The lower levels of the Peace Valley that would be flooded are critically important to moose and deer for their wintering habitat – the time the animals are most vulnerable . . . The Peace Valley's 50 islands and innumerable river flats provide feed and sanctuary at the time of giving birth, and when under seige by predation. At the Site C hearings, B.C. Hydro evaluated each of the Peace Valley's 19 wildlife classifications as 'insignificant' in the provincial context. B.C. Hydro further took the position that the Peace Valley's wildlife consisted of a 'standing crop', measurable in dollars. If it could get on with Site C dam construction, B.C. Hydro has let it be known that it would like to do something nice for the Peace Valley's wildlife by way of 'mitigation.' To 'mitigate' for the Williston havoc, why not do something nice anyway, Site C or no Site C? Like retroactively?"

Local people remember what occurred when the Williston reservoir flooded, and they don't want to see it repeated along the valleys from Hudson's Hope to Fort St. John if Site C is approved.

"The Bennett dam flooded the winter range for the moose," Leo Rutledge explained. "In the winter when they came down, the bottom lands that they depended on weren't there anymore. You can't say to game, 'We need this space, go over there.' There's no use them going over there, because there's another moose there already. That niche is already full. So they just die out, one way or another . . . The small animals and birds are territorial, too; there's only room for so many. There were millions – billions – of deaths resulting from the flooding behind the Bennett dam, if you count little things."

B.C. Hydro, in a public affairs release dated May 3, 1982, noted that John Waite, the corporation's compensation and mitigation witness, appeared before the B.C. Utilities Commission Site C hearing on April 27. Waite assured the commission that Hydro's fish, wildlife and water quality studies provide adequate information on which to base a decision whether or not the Site C project should proceed. Also, Hydro had offered to develop the recreational potential of areas surrounding reservoirs and to operate the parks and facilities it created.

But the Peace Valley Environmental Association maintained that the Site C dam is just not safe. Two massive landslides, both large enough to plug the Peace River, had occurred near the proposed damsite in recent years. Lesser slides were an annual occurrence. In 1957, a spectacular slide of soft shale led to the collapse of the Peace River bridge at Taylor. The Pacific Great Eastern Railway engineers said that the ground on the south side of the Peace was still geologically 'alive.' The first suspension bridge that was built across the river in the proposed Site C dam area had cables embedded in the riverbanks; one side failed and the bridge collapsed. When the first railway bridge was being built across the Peace in the Site C area, a 1,500-ton pier shifted and had to be blasted out. According to the environmental association's brochure, professional engineer Nigel A. Skermer, wrote in 1979 that "one of the worst landslide areas in B.C. occurs east of the Rocky Mountains in the Peace and Kiskatinaw River valleys where clay shales predominate." Information Canada said the proposed Site C damsite is in an area where 'moderate damage' from earthquakes may be expected; quakes were felt during the Site C hearings and an average of one per year have since been recorded.

A B.C. Hydro public affairs release dated March 1, 1982 said that Dave Cathcart, a project development coordinator, told the hearings commission that all major structural components of the dam would be founded on bedrock. Earthquake factors had been accounted for in the design and the spillway and reservoir could handle any conceivable flood situation, Cathcart said.

Alan Imrie, Hydro's geological supervisor, added that the proposed damsite is in a low-risk earthquake zone, and that Hydro's conservative design approach could handle any geological problems.

The project's geological consultant, Graham Morgan, further noted that he saw no possibility of waves overtopping the dam and the reservoir would have a limited effect on the banks of the Peace River. The area near Hudson Hope may be affected, but it could be protected, Morgan said.

The environmental association acknowledged that B.C. Hydro 'owns' a substantial portion of land that the proposed Site C reservoir would flood. "It 'owns' it because after spending several years creating a state of angst among the Peace Valley settlers, the utility company was able to buy it from them. In other words, B.C. Hydro relieved the people of their anxieties by relieving them of their homes and lands," said the association.

Hydro estimates that about 35 households, or about 135 people, would have to move their homes if Site C proceeds (public affairs release February 15, 1982).

The Mathesons owned land on the banks of the Peace River in Hudson's Hope that would be affected, and Hydro offered to relieve us of our burden. Along with other residents with property on the riverbanks, we quickly formed the Riverbank Property Owners Association. Members contributed to a fund to hire lawyer Andrew Schuck of Fort Nelson (now of Prince George) to take our concerns to B.C. Hydro. None of us sold out, even though we were issued maps showing Hydro's 'safe line' running across the back end of our properties. We would stand on our doorsteps and watch surveyors tramp along our riverbank, cutting swaths to mark the proposed high water lines.

The Peace Valley Environmental Association's view is that the government of British Columbia erred by allowing B.C. Hydro to negotiate land-buying transactions with the residents *before* receiving approval to construct the dam. The association saw this as intimidation – buying, then bulldozing down and burning buildings as former owners and neighbours watched. It was a 'play one against the other' tactic, of land deals made under a shroud of secrecy, even though public funds were at stake. 'Confidential' became the buzz-word. Despite efforts of the year-long Site C hearings to pry them open, Hydro's land acquisition files were never fully divulged.

In a May 15, 1989 letter to the authors from Hydro's Chris Boatman, he says that "the land B.C. Hydro owns for the Site C project was acquired at market value after the owners indicated a desire to sell – ie. B.C. Hydro had a responsive land acquisition program in effect. A new Provincial Expropriation Act, to which B.C. Hydro is subject, became law in 1987. This Act sets out a procedure to be followed for the expropriation of land and provides for the establishment of an Expropriation Compensation Board. B.C. Hydro will continue to attempt to acquire property rights it needs by negotiation and, when expropriation is necessary, it will be done in compliance with the Expropriation Act."

"It was a divide-and-conquer thing," maintained Leo Rutledge. "The dam builders had gone through this before in the States. They knew exactly how to approach the people. And it worked quite successfully. When they felt they had some of the people sufficiently frightened and softened up – and this took quite some time, a year or two at least – then they circulated a letter to every landowner who would be affected. The letter said, in effect, 'If you are interested in selling, come to such-and-such a place at such-and-such a time, and we'll negotiate.' Well, by that time a lot of the people were frightened so they did go. Some of the people sold quickly, and parted with quite a bit of land. But some wouldn't negotiate at all."

"Corporations live longer than people," Rutledge added. "One engineer said to me, 'Leo, as long as there's a river running, there's always the potential for building a dam.'"

The Peace Valley Environmental Association wasn't fighting the battle alone, however.

"The Vancouver office of the Society Promoting Environmental Conservation got involved and at the time they were the most active environmental group in B.C.," Rutledge said. "The West Coast Environmental Law Association helped too. We took the position that if money was going to be spent proving the point why the dam should be built, surely some money could be spent for a hearing telling the other side..."

The choice of location for the hearings surprised even the local residents. "Instead of having the hearings in Vancouver where we wanted them to be, next to the media for good exposure, they dragged it up here to Fort St. John, as far back in the hinterland and boondocks as they could," said Rutledge. "They went on four days a week, and every weekend all those connected with it – and there was an army of them – migrated back to Vancouver for the weekend, so it cost a bloody fortune."

For the town of Fort St. John, the protest over Site C hit at a bad time. Inflation had climbed out of sight and money was nervous. Investors wanted a haven and the town had seemed a likely place. Oil drilling continued in the area, the Mackenzie Valley pipeline would come down from the Beaufort Sea, there was timber and agriculture, Site C was going in – everything seemed to converge at Fort St. John. So the town was over-built, and then came 20-percent interest rates. A 10-year moratorium was placed on the Mackenzie pipeline project by Thomas Berger pending resolution of native land claims and environmental concerns. Development in Fort St. John ground to a shuddering halt. Newly constructed 150-unit motels never opened, and builders of housing subdivisions simply boarded up the windows.

Notable at the Site C hearings were Fort St. John businessmen, who promoted the project for all they were worth. Nigel Hannaford, editor of the *Alaska Highway News*, said the dam was the best scheme to meet the province's power needs. Hannaford produced 48 letters from local businessmen who supported the project. Gerry Tucker, long-time Fort St. John resident, said he could remember what it was like to use coal and coal-oil lamps, and asked how many of those protesting the dam had ever lived without electricity? He urged the protesters to sign sworn affidavits that they would be the first ones to have their electricity cut off if a shortage occurred. Wally Gentles, another long-time area resident who would lose part of his land if the project went ahead, said he had always found Hydro to be cooperative and above-board.

Jack Baker, a now-retired Fort St. John insurance agent, told the authors that when he was in business, he supported new developments. "Now I'm retired, I'm more inclined to share Leo Rutledge's position and think to myself, well now, these transient money-making things are maybe not all they're cracked up to be. When I say transient, I mean that when the boom is gone people have to get by on less money, government hand-outs, and many can't stand it, so they leave. That could happen quite easily with Site C."

Baker recalled the upper Peace as it was, when he owned land along its banks that Hydro bought for Williston Lake. "The upper Peace River is no longer a river, it's a lake, such as it is, with all its drawbacks. Whether it's fair to continue building dams on the Peace, I don't know. What my contention was, since the Peace River was spoiled as a river, as a beautiful part of our Northern heritage, rather than Hydro going up into the Liard and Nass and Stikine and building dams up there, let them continue with the Peace River. Ruin it all they want."

B.C. Hydro continued to report details of the fight that was occurring, neighbour against neighbour, at the Site C hearings.

"In one of the largest mass meetings ever held in Fort St. John, more than 500 people enthusiastically voiced support for the proposed Site C hydroelectric project," said a Hydro public affairs release on April 22, 1982. "Two people who tried to speak against the project at the pro-dam rally were drowned out with boos. Posters and bumper-stickers were distributed proclaiming 'Stop the Hearing, Start the Dam.' Hydro was praised lavishly by some of the speakers while anti-dam groups and the hearing process were vilified at the meeting organized by the Fort St. John Chamber of Commerce and the local economic development commission. . . . Brian Palmer, mayor of Fort St. John, said the province needs power now and will need it in the future."

On May 15, provincial energy minister Bob McClelland promised "a cheering crowd" of about 400 Site C supporters in Fort St. John that he would take their request for a speedy decision on the project to cabinet and report as soon as possible.

Finally, on November 9, 1983, the following statement was released by the cabinet in Victoria: "(That) the report and recommendations of the Utilities Commission to the Lieutenant-Governor in Council, on disposition of British Columbia Hydro and Power Authority's application for an energy project certificate for Peace River Site C hydroelectric generating station, together with its appendices and the Site C Division's report on the review procedures and recommendations for future reviews, be made public, and *that the energy project certificate applied for be refused*." (author's italics)

"Site C was turned down in 1983 because the need for power was not persuasive in the down-turned economy, and also because a couple of studies, including one on fisheries, were not complete," said Lorne March, director of environmental services for B.C. Hydro. "Re-applying for the water licence is not a complicated deal . . . and the hearings have already been conducted. I would be very surprised if there was another hearing."

In the meantime, there are the Liard, Stikine and Iskut rivers, the Kootenay diversion, and the Keenleyside project on the Columbia. Perhaps even plans will be resurrected for what Leo Rutledge called "the light sleepers": Site E (a fourth dam on the Peace River, downstream of Site C, near the B.C.-Alberta border at Clayhurst); the McGregor diversion (diverting water from the McGregor River through the Fraser into the Parsnip, thereby bringing more water into Williston Lake and through the Bennett dam); dams on the Homathko River (near the province's south-west coast); the Nass River (northeast of Stewart) or the Taku River (south of Atlin Lake).

Has anything been learned to prevent the environmental destruction that happened at the Bennett dam?

"No, we haven't built on information, and it's a shame in a way. Most of the people who worked on the Bennett dam are not still with B.C. Hydro," acknowledged John Kelly, environmental studies coordinator with B.C. Hydro. "There were not a whole lot of reports and stuff done. 'Environment' was not considered in exactly high esteem at that time and it was largely a government- sponsored project, so the premier's main drive was to get the dam going and the power generating."

"I guess we are not as bad today," Kelly added. "If you look at Williston Lake, it was a result of the times. Now when we are assessing projects, even at an overview level, a lot of the information we have learned is now being applied. The gap is being closed."

Adrienne Peacock's article in *Sierra Report* (Feb.-March, 1988) noted that former Social Credit environment minister Rafe Mair had been quoted as saying that the premier – by announcing Site C as a "must" to develop for power export – "made it obligatory" that other river systems, including the Stikine, Iskut and Liard, will be dammed.

Peacock added that the Canada-U.S. Free Trade Agreement seems logically to point to integrated U.S.-B.C. system planning. "A Gibson Economics study for the Pacific Northwest highlighted the problem that joint system planning would give to B.C. 'One region would necessarily become an exporter, raising for it questions of resource exploitation and environmental damage to support another region's or country's energy consumption,'" Peacock said.

Michael Anderson, in an article titled "The Electric Jungle" published in *Sierra Report* (May-June, 1988), said conservationists are worried that the preoccupation with surplus power sales and new hydroelectric projects will delay commitments to energy conservation and least-cost planning principles in both the U.S. and Canada. "Canadian environmentalists have good reason to worry that provincial and federal governments bent on the short-term gains (both political and financial) from mega power development will accept the sort of long-term environmental destruction no longer tolerated in most U.S. jurisdictions," Anderson said.

In a 1988 power demand forecast, Hydro predicted that Site C would not be required until the year 2001 ." . . unless long-term contracts were obtained from utilities in southern California." To gain those contracts, B.C. Hydro needed guaranteed access to transmission lines owned by the Bonneville Power Administration.

On May 27, 1988, the *Alaska Highway News* reported that B.C. Hydro was now able to sell electricity to the U.S. on a firm contract basis because of a new policy announced "this week" by the Bonneville Power Administration. Hydro spokesman Chris Boatman, said the policy change certainly represented a "crack in the door," because to date B.C. power exports were dependent on the Bonneville Power Administration giving Hydro access to its transmission lines on a "spot" basis.

The *Peace River Block News,* on June 22, 1988, published an article headlined, "Hydro Consumption is Growing Fast."

"'Electricity consumption is growing so fast that British Columbia Hydro may run short of power unless it brings forward its dam construction schedule,' says a spokesman for the Crown corporation.

"'Our actual load growth for the past two years has exceeded our forecast, and again in 1988-89 we have already achieved a load increase about equal to that forecast for year-end,' Ray Hunt, Hydro vice-president, system development group, told the consulting engineers of British Columbia on Monday. 'Recognizing these uncertainties, B.C. Hydro has decided to maintain a contingency plan which will enable us to meet either domestic or firm export requirements . . . by bringing forward either Site C on the Peace River, or Keenleyside on the Columbia River."

Hunt said a "prime hydroelectric engineering consultant" should be chosen from the private sector by October, 1988 and some field exploration work could be done in 1989, to reduce the lead time for developing the next hydroelectric project.

In the same issue, the *Peace River Block News* reported that "B.C. hydro had set new sales records in the last fiscal year, with total revenues for the year ended March 31, 1988 rising six percent to a record $2.1 billion, resulting in operating income of $93 million, an improvement of $133 million over the operating loss of $40 million a year ago.

'The rise in operating income was due to net earnings of $110 million on interruptible electricity exports to the United States, plus $17 million on gas operations and $2 million from Hydro's rail division,' Hydro Chairman Larry Bell said in a news release. The turnaround allowed Hydro to transfer $38 million to the rate stabilization account and finish the fiscal year with net earnings of $55 million, the third-highest in B.C. Hydro's 26-year history."

The *Alberta Report* (June 20, 1988) also carried an article on "California's Northern Powerhouse." It said that B.C. Hydro had developed a 15-year plan to expand output by nearly 30 percent; the largest project would be a thermal plant at Hat Creek (100 miles northeast of Vancouver) expected to produce 11,800 gigawatt (one gigawatt equals one billion watts) hours annually – more than one-seventh the province's total output. "Not all the power will be for domestic consumption, however. B.C. Hydro, with 33 existing plants and 72,500 gigawatt hours of production last year, is eyeing the American market."

The projected growth of California from 36 million to 40 million people by the year 2000 apparently has "softened the opposition of the Bonneville Power Adminstration (BPA) which has a hammerlock on power transmission in the region, to B.C. power being 'wheeled' through its systems to California," said the article. "The Free Trade Agreement will move B.C. up to the same priority level on the BPA grid as Nevada and Montana. More important, however, was the BPA's announcement in May that it will guarantee access for B.C. power to California customers, thus allowing long-term contracts."

California's great need could also involve a deal with Alberta's TransAlta Utilities Corporation, said the *Alberta Report*. Because Alberta's thermal plants have idle capacity at night, which the company would like to use to generate power for export, "sending Alberta power to the U.S. at night would give B.C. Hydro an opportunity to close the sluice-gates and build up higher heads of water behind its dams. During the day the dams would open up to supply the Americans' peak demand period. 'The synergy is excellent,' observes Walter Saponja, TransAlta's senior vice-president of generation. 'Together we can put out a better export product than B.C. can alone.'"

On December 13, 1988, B.C. Hydro announced the launching of POWEREX, the British Columbia Export Corporation, to assume responsibility for the province's electricity exports. Key positions in the new company will be filled by senior Hydro officials including Chris Boatman as president, Doug Forrest as vice-president of marketing and Ken Epp as vice-president of operations.

Already, public interest groups such as the Mackenzie River Basin Committee are alerting their forces to possible new development. The committee's annual report (1987-88) says that "a joint study involving B.C. Hydro and U.S. Utilities has concluded that development of the Site C Hydro-electric Project is economically viable as a power source for Oregon and California. ... The next step involves further negotiations and the fulfilment to environmental impacts of the dam and the transmission facilities. The earliest date for a start to construction is 1989."

Local residents who don't oppose Site C still see it not only as a distinct possibility, but also a benefit. They are thinking about the construction jobs during the building of the dam, and of the recreational lake they envision in the fertile valley between Fort St. John and Hudson's Hope. Supporters of the project focus on building an economy based on tourism. Yet the Kyllos are still struggling to create a viable operation on debris-strewn Williston Lake. It is tough going, even with lodges located on land they received as settlement or owned prior to the lake.

Dinosaur Lake, the reservoir created behind the Peace Canyon (Site One) dam, does not have a debris problem. It is banked and protected from winds by the high cliffs of the canyon. There are still several problems, such as sloughing and the fact that Dinosaur Lake runs up to the business end of the Bennett dam.

"I put two booms across Dinosaur Lake, upstream of Gething Creek and one right next to the Bennett dam powerhouse," said former B.C. Hydro employee Tom Roberts. "Idiot people in small aluminum boats, one with a boy about 10 years old and two men – no life-jackets in the boat – came right into the powerhouse of the Bennett dam, into the manifold! There were signs, five feet by eight feet, I put them up myself, saying 'Don't go beyond this point.' Some people disconnected the boom."

"As far as other travel on Dinosaur Lake, there's the business about the slide," Roberts continued. "I went onto the slide area on Dinosaur Lake with big pumps, three or four years ago, and strung pipelines in there with a chopper; put a big generator on a steel float, took it up the lake and pumped water into the giant holes and cracks in the ground. I spent three weeks there, pumping water round the clock. And it was determined by geophysicists, geologists and engineers in general that, after we had finished saturating it, it would not move any further. If it was going to slide, it would have gone.

"But, just like the Halfway Slide that is the scare for the Site C reservoir, there is a material down at a certain depth much like soap. When you introduce water to it, it becomes slippery. At the Halfway, water coming into the ground got it to the point where it became like quicksand. Little ball-bearings of water got in there and actually created an envelope, a level, between the soil above and the rock below. When it reached a saturation point, away it went. It's the same at Dinosaur Lake. And so the danger from a slide there has not passed, and never will."

Terry Peressini, administrative supervisor for B.C. Hydro at the Bennett dam, said Hydro is not responsible for accidents that occur on the lakes. "There are signs up all along the river saying it can rise x number of feet. Hydro pays a water fee to the provincial government to use the water to turn it into electricity. Hydro owns access to the lake in certain areas. The provincial government owns shoreline except for the area around the dam . . ."

Hydro reaffirmed their position in a letter dated April 6, 1988 from K.H. Lashley, supervisor of property management, to an applicant who wanted to occupy Crown land on Williston Lake. "B.C. Hydro has a flood reserve to the 2,225-foot contour level on Williston Lake . . . " Lashley wrote. "We advise that structures placed within this flood reserve shall be entirely at the owner's risk. The reservoir level is subject to large and sometimes sudden fluctuations which can occur between the drawdown low of 2,100 feet to a present temporary maximum storage level of 2,206 feet. Winds and waves may increase storage levels on occasions. Sudden water level changes may be more severe during high precipitation or rapid snow melt conditions. Varying water levels may cause problems for boat launching, mooring, storage, etc. The shoreline of Williston Lake is still in the process of stabilization (20 years later – authors' comment) and some areas are experiencing severe sloughing and erosion. You should be aware the reservoir contains some stumps and floating debris. If Williston Lake is raised, as is being considered, further sloughing and more debris is likely to result."

When a local resident, Terry Curzon, tried to establish a boat tour business on Dinosaur Lake, he encountered a strange reception from Hydro.

"I put my boat on Dinosaur Lake with intentions of taking tours and fishing trips when the fishing was finally opened," Curzon said. "When I did start, in 1984, Hydro, to cut a long story short, told me I had to move off. I have my own opinion on their reasoning, but I heard they didn't like the idea of an entrepreneur taking advantage of what they classified as their water."

Curzon said that a Hydro superintendent told him to move his docks downstream. "Well, downstream was just a sheer bank, and the water there was so shallow that I couldn't bring my boat close enough to shore to allow people to board. That being the case, we said we'd build enough docks to get 100 feet out into the lake and we made up all these docks – at quite an expense of money and time. After we got them built, we hadn't even got them in the water when Hydro said no, we couldn't do that either. Then they brought out a tug, towed my boat away, and tied it to the boom that goes from the anti-vortex dam across to the other side."

"I couldn't fight anymore," Curzon said. "I just put it into the hands of a lawyer. It ended up costing me a bunch of money and I didn't get anywhere. I haven't been back since."

Len Kidder, senior production supervisor at Peace Canyon, sees the incident differently: "Curzon asked to dock his boat on Dinosaur Lake. Hydro said yes, until the park opened and tourists arrived and it became a hazard. B.C. Hydro had not made provision for private enterprise on Dinosaur Lake."

The situation apparently changed when the municipality made a deal with Hydro to take over the park grounds around the lake, operating them in conjunction with Parks Canada.

But Curzon said the situation "has gone too far" for him to reapply to the municipality to use the lake for tours. "It's no longer possible to buy the big boat I had intended to use when the tour business built up," he added.

Curzon thinks the same problem with establishing private enterprises around the lake will occur at Site C. "Unless land is given as a settlement, there is no such thing as privately owned land along the lakeshore. Nowhere, as far as I know."

Curzon also isn't optimistic that Hudson's Hope will benefit if Site C proceeds. "They went through some fiasco in Revelstoke about what Hydro had to do for the town, for tourism, to help the area. Revelstoke learned from us. As far as I'm concerned, Hydro has done nothing compared to what they should be doing. They've got two dams here now, and the money they've put back into this town is minimal . . . On the Williston Lake they don't even have a decent launch site for the public, after all these years. And that, I think, is disgusting."

But Hydro's Len Kidder maintains that Site C will be different: it will have more recreational areas built into it.

Dave George, who first came to Hudson's Hope in 1973 with Pentagon Construction to put in the number nine generating unit at the Bennett dam, then returned in 1977 to work at Site One, has worked on construction jobs all across Canada. He has made his home in Hudson's Hope, doing temporary work for Hydro while waiting for Site C to begin.

"They've got a lot of money invested to date in exploration drilling," George said. "Work-wise, I'd like to see Site C go in. I would maybe be a little more careful of my money this time around."

Ernie Krebs, who lives on the banks of the river in Hudson's Hope, also hopes Site C will go ahead, although he's beyond the age where he would work on the project.

"If Site C dam goes ahead, there would be a lake at the bottom of my lot and I could have my boat on it. We have water flowing through two dams already. While the reservoir may cover up some land, we cover up thousands of acres every year in our cities, putting concrete on them, and they never grow anything," Krebs said.

Ken Kyllo has mixed feelings about Site C. "I don't think it will make that much difference now," he said slowly. "There isn't that much land that will be covered. But I don't think it's going to do much for anybody in the country."

Lloyd Gething's estimation of Site C's value to the community is based on his long-term knowledge of the area. "With Site C, you would have the perfect outdoor lake for people to romp around. This is the future for the area, and it's the only future it has. Tell me another? I see no chance of industry here. That chance was missed when there was no railroad."

Barrie Cornell agreed. "The only salvation I see for Hudson's Hope is if the Site C dam goes and we go for the tourism bit. That lake would be a definite asset. You're talking cream of the crop here because with these little lakes like Dinosaur and Site C, you're not going to have any weather to contend with."

"If people get on the bandwagon and put proper facilities in here, it might entice tourists," he added. "This lake would be cleaned out first, like they did in Revelstoke, because Hydro has had enough shit with Williston Lake – they don't want any more of that."

Cornell noted that the valley at Site One (Peace Canyon) was logged before the reservoir was filled. "And this one, Site C, is going to be similar. They've already designated three areas they're going to let out to contract to three different people for clearing, and it's going to be wiped clean same as Site One, which is the way it should be done."

James Rhymer thinks Hydro will likely go ahead with Site C simply because "flooding agricultural land doesn't seem to be a big drawback to anyone with lots of money. And I'd far sooner live next door to a hydroelectric dam than to a nuclear power plant, and I think that anybody would. The moose and deer and bear and stuff will just move back when the floods come up. There's a lot of people on the Save The Valley Committee who say it will be a terrible blow to the country to put another lake down there, but I say it could actually prove to be quite the opposite. It could be quite a tourist attraction."

But Elaine Rhymer has sympathy for residents who knew the area before the Bennett dam was built, and who were not treated fairly. "Probably a lot of the reason that the Save the Valley movement came into being was because there was so much resentment about the Bennett dam, and fear that it's all going to happen again. People remember how they were treated."

Jim Beattie says he doesn't like to see Site C go in, "but I guess they need the work . . . I think they're giving people a better deal now than we got. About six years ago, one guy who lived along the river got around $130,000 for eight or ten acres and a house. He got more out of that house than we got out of the whole ranch at Gold Bar."

Dave Kyllo views the prospect of Site C cautiously. "The Peace River Valley is something that cannot be replaced, so I guess I could say that I'm not for it. It's one of the most scenic places in the country, it is historic, there are settlements along the river, farms and things like that. But at the same time, I guess if they have to build a dam somewhere, if they have to build one somewhere, I guess it makes more sense than flooding out a whole new area. Site C doesn't need a big pondage area, it already has that up at Williston.

"But if they're building Site C just for jobs, I don't agree with that at all. There's got to be a need for the power. The result of the dam is forever, the jobs won't be."

The Northerner newspaper of Fort St. John reported on February 1, 1989 that Hydro would re-open the old Site C tunnel. Several instruments had been left in a tunnel on the north bank of the Peace when original studies were halted in 1981. Investigators will be taking a careful look at the instruments and what effect almost eight years of underground 'life' have had on them, in order to provide information for creating a geographical model of the site. Klohn-Crippen Consultants Ltd. will be compiling information from the drilling projects in the region affected by Site C – which now carries a $3-billion price tag.

"Hydro has already started looking for suitable office rentals in Fort St. John during the eight-month period while doing the studies," said *The Northerner.* However, Hydro's project engineer Lachlan Russell cautioned that people shouldn't take this as an indication that work is about to commence on Site C. "He declined to support one popular theory that the work on Site C will have to start no later than 1992, so Hydro can be prepared to meet power commitments by the year 2000. And whether it's 1992 or 2000, that won't be a time Fort St. John will forget."

The possibility of Site C has some Hudson's Hope residents poised for another round of protest. Others are packing their lunch buckets, renewing union memberships, and hoping for high wages to lift them from their economic slump. To those who want the work, the wait is the main irritant. Others, whose lands will be affected, or who simply do not want to witness the destruction of one of the most beautiful and fertile valleys in the province, pray it will never be built.

30

Squatters on Their Own Land

The Sekanni (sometimes spelled Seccani, Sekkanni, Sekani, Sicanni, Tsekani) Indians of the Athapaskan nation once hunted, trapped and fished throughout north-central and north-interior British Columbia. Now, the 685 remaining Sekannis are concentrated along the Rocky Mountain Trench in the area of McLeod Lake (near the point where the Pack River flows into the Parsnip), and at Ingenika Point and Fort Ware on the Finlay River.

It is the Sekanni language, a form of the Beaver-Sarcee-Sekanni branch of Athapaskan, that gave the poetic names to the rivers of the trench. Jean Isaac, whose people have always lived along the Finlay, explained the meaning of some of the names: "The Ingenika was named after the red berries that you see on the ground in the summer; there's a lot of them here. Ingeni is 'red berries', and ka, 'by the river.' Ingenika therefore means 'by the river of red berries.'

"Mesilinka actually means, 'where the waters flow out to the main river,' by the river that flows out. Chowika . . . the mountain that's right by the river."

Sekanni means 'people of the rocks and mountains.'

Described in 1810 by North West Company trader D.W. Harmon as "a quiet and inoffensive people, whose situation exposes them to peculiar difficulties and stresses," [1] and in 1833 by Hudson's Bay trader John McLean as "reputed honest, industrious and faithful"[2], the Sekannis' history is one of being pushed around.

When they roamed to the west side of the Rocky Mountains, said Harmon, they were attacked by the Tacullies (Carriers) and Atenas; on the east side, they were attacked by the Beavers and Crees. "They are compelled, therefore, oftentimes to subsist upon the roots, which they find in the mountains, and which barely enable them to sustain life; and their emaciated bodies frequently bear witness to the scantiness of their fare," he wrote.

Pete Toy was a Cornishman who, starting in the summer of 1862, washed gold on a bar of the Finlay River that became known as Pete Toy's Bar. In the winter, he trapped on Manson Creek. He also kept a free trading post (competing with the Hudson's Bay Company). Toy's principal customers were the Sekanni Indians, whom he described as "although gamblers, strictly honest."

This story was told about Toy and the Sekannis by J.C. Bryant, a gold-seeker who headed to the Omineca country in 1871: "Pete had an understanding with them that if at any time they came to his cabin in want of supplies, and he was absent, they were to help themselves to whatever they were in need of, such as sugar, tea, or ammunition. They always did this, and would leave a statement behind them of what they had taken, which would be perfectly legible to Pete. Pete told me he had never known them to take advantage of this privilege."[3]

A Presbyterian minister, Rev. Daniel M. Gordon, said in his book, *Mountain and Prairie: A Journey from Victoria to Winnipeg via Peace River Pass* published in 1880, that "The Indians appear to be throughout this district (the lower end of McLeod Lake) quiet, trustworthy and industrious."

In 1897, Inspector J.D. Moodie of the North West Mounted Police described the Indians of the Finlay as "a miserable lot, half-starved most of the winter, and utterly unreliable. . . . One bad feature of these Indians is their proneness to fire the bush, this they often do from sheer mischief, without giving a thought as to the destruction of the game caused by it. Their morals are of the lowest, their anger easily aroused and they are very vindictive. I have been assured, on good authority, that the murder of the aged and helpless and any supposed to be bewitched is no uncommon occurrence..."[4]

As the years go by and the Sekannis are more exposed to white civilization, positive reports on the Indians became fewer and fewer, and what evolves is a sad picture indeed.

In 1916, Paul L. Haworth, an American professor of history, made a journey into the Finlay River area. In his book *On the Headwaters of Peace River*, he wrote:

"The Indians (who live near the Hudson's Bay trading post of Fort McLeod, where the McLeod Lake empties into the Pack River) belong to the Sekanni tribe. In view of the fact that they have been under white influence for more than a century, one might reasonably suppose that they would have made considerable progress in the arts of civilization, but they still prefer to lead a primitive existence. Though they are fond of potatoes and other products of the soil – when they can beg them of white people – they have made little effort to raise these desirable articles themselves. For the most part they are still meat-eaters and hunt and fish the year round."[5]

In January of 1989, Susan and Ralph Klassen, journalists and photographers, accompanied a film-crew to the Ingenika. Susan interviewed the people, and also studied the Sekanni history. A three-part article that Susan published (in February and March, 1989) in the Mackenzie *Times* newspaper offered some information about the Sekannis' claim to land that was to be flooded by the Bennett dam. Indian reserves in B.C. provided approximately 20 acres per family, much less than the 80 acres per family allotted in the prairies. In 1874, Ottawa challenged B.C.'s Land Act as unconstitutional because it denied Indian land rights. The province argued that the Royal Proclamation of 1763 (which had confirmed native title) did not apply west of the Rockies. "Clearly," said Klassen, "the Sekannis' troubles began long before the flood."

In 1912, the federal government proposed a Royal Commission to settle disputes between native groups and the B.C. government. In 1914, five federal commissioners visited the Sekannis at Fort Grahame and Fort McLeod (communities with 57 and 75 members respectively); 800 acres were set aside at Fort Grahame and the existing 286-acre reserve was affirmed at Fort McLeod. The reason for the small reserves was, according to the Commissions' report, "because (the Indians) are nomadic." In the mid 1940s, a group of Sekannis also settled at Fort Ware, and in 1958 built a school there.

In 1962, Charlie B. Cunningham, an employee of B.C. Hydro's land division (and former big game hunter, outfitter, guide and photographer), made a trip up the Finlay prior to construction of the Peace River dam. Travelling with Art Van Somers, who ran supply boats up to the Indian settlements on the Finlay, Cunningham kept a journal of the visit. He found the Ingenika settlement to be "a very lovely setting," surrounded by "lovely clear water that was so good to drink." After watching Van Somers open the trading store, buy furs, sell supplies and conduct commerce with the Sekannis, Cunningham wrote that "the Indians at the Ingenika seem to be a nice bunch, and their honesty is borne out by the fact that the store is left for weeks at a time – just locked up, with a fairly good stock of groceries – and it is not molested while (Art) is away. The trust is mutual."[6]

Cunningham wanted to talk to the Indians about the rising water that would come with the construction of the dam. For the most part, the Indians seemed to stoically accept the fact. 'I guess I go someplace else when the waters rise,' he quoted several as saying, although they expressed sadness that they would lose their good beaver traplines.

Cunningham reported that there were about 25 to 30 people at

Ingenika and 200 at Fort Ware, at the extreme north end of the Finlay River. At Fort Ware, he showed the Indians maps of the forthcoming lake, depicting high water lines, and said that these maps were very helpful in explaining the situation. "So far, I have not found anyone hostile to the flooding," Cunningham wrote in his journal. "Some have natural regrets that they are going to lose some very good fur country, but are in hopes they can find some more. Those trappers that live around the fringes of the flood area are very hopeful that their trap lines will be better, and even wished the Company were going to flood right away."

Despite what Cunningham reported, the flooding ultimately caused such misunderstanding and misery that Susan Klassen, in her article "The Heart of Ingenika," described Williston Lake as "a primary source of hydroelectric power in the province and a primary source of sorrow for the Sekanni people."

Before the reservoir was completely filled, government surveyors put in red flag tape where the actual water level would be. These flags were put along the banks of the reservoir wherever a person could land a boat or an Indian group could establish itself. This way, the Indians, or anyone else who planned to build a cabin, knew it had to be located above that line.

Tom Roberts worked for B.C. Hydro when the Indians were being advised they would have to rebuild their cabins farther up the bank. "The surveyors and Hydro and forestry people said to them, 'When are you going to move? You're going to have to move by next spring. See those red ribbons there? The water's going to come up to there. And you're not going to have a chance to get a new cabin built then, unless you get out and build it now.' But they stayed perched there and waited until the water came up over at Finlay Forks and flooded the burner out at the mill, Carrier Lumber. When the mill moved out, the Indians were still tented there. Then they moved in to the mouth of the Omineca."

Pen Powell, a Hudson's Hope resident who operates Carbon Lake hunting and fishing lodges, watched the scene from the air, flying his plane over the rising waters. "The natives seemed to be as confused as the animals," he said. "I often tried to explain to them what was about to happen, but they just couldn't seem to understand. The only and biggest dam they had ever seen or heard about was a beaver dam, and when I would try to explain to them that a whiteman was going to build a dam the other side of the mountain that would fill the whole valley, they seemed to think I had had a few shots of whiskey along the way. The Fort Grahame band to me seemed to have the hardest time of all, trying to understand that they were going to be moved to an area where they would have to give up their boats and not be able to live off the land. Their whole life-cycle had been waiting for spring next year, when they could put their boats in and move anytime from berry patch to good moose pasture and fish holes as they wanted to."

Powell said the Fort Grahame band was moved to the northern head of Williston Lake near the mouth of the Ingenika River, but couldn't get into the upper Finlay due to a three-mile jam of debris blocking its outlet into the lake. "They had just gotten partly settled when the logging companies arrived and removed nearly all the timber near where they had been relocated. Then the next thing to happen, during the winter the generators lowered the lake some 30 feet and when the ice went, it left miles of silt-covered lake bottom exposed to the prevailing south winds, which in turn caused the valley to become a dust bowl until the lake started to fill again. There were numerous times when I would fly over the Indian camp and I couldn't see a thing for dust."

A.C. Geddes and his father arrived by riverboat at a camp on the Finlay in 1968, just as the lake was starting to fill. They stopped at Finlay Forks and camped for the night. Bud Stuart was set up with the Kyllos at the Forks in a general store called "Uncle Bud's" which was in a tent. The store had to be near the water, but the water was coming up so fast that they had to keep moving it back. They kept setting it up and moving, and finally moved it to the inside of North Harbour where it sits today.

There were Indians camped at the Forks, and A.C. and his father visited their camp. "The Indians said to my dad and I that this was the biggest flood they'd ever seen, and this is springtime. So my dad proceeded to tell them that this wasn't an abnormal flood, it was because they had a dam down there. So the Indians said, 'Well, we should go down and break up that dam.' My dad proceeded to tell them how big this dam was. They said they'd never seen a dam that big. And it became apparent to us that we were taking about a hydro dam, and they were talking about a beaver dam . . . They didn't speak very good English, they weren't educated people, they just didn't know."

A.C. said the Indians had been repeatedly moving their camp up to higher ground, but each morning they'd be flooded again. "So they kept moving back. There was no game. Fish and Wildlife had said, 'We're going to flood the dam, we're going to lose moose pasture,' so they put open season on game there for two years, all year round. With all this flooding and no animals, and all this debris, it looked like the end of the world."

Geddes said that after the water rose, the Indians would try to cross the lake in their old riverboats. "The debris is knocking the props off their boats, they're stranded out there on the water, trying to build a little fire on those mats. They'd get trapped there in their little boat, and they'd be there for days."

Susan Klassen, in her newspaper article, said that even if the Sekannis had fully understood the implications of hydroelectric development, if their band leaders had understood the language of politicians and developers, and if they had been able to assert that they had never relinquished aboriginal title to the valley, it is unlikely they could have influenced their fate.

"It is clear that the decision-makers of the day considered a few hundred Indians to be of minor concern in a major project," Klassen said. "Then-Cabinet Minister Ray Williston remarked that the area of the reservoir 'was an absolute wilderness and there were no people there, no nothing. Outside of Fort Ware, where there were a few Indians and so on, there was nothing in the whole area.'" (*Mackenzie Times*, "The Heart of Ingenika" part three, March 7, 1989).

Williston, in a letter published in the December 23, 1970 edition of the *Alaska Highway News*, contended that the Finlay Forks region was never designated as an Indian settlement. "No tribe regarded or occupied the area as its 'headquarters' or permanent place of residence," he said.

Williston maintained that Indians and their families from Fort McLeod, Fort Ware and Hudson's Hope converged on Finlay Forks when construction of the dam project started, in hopes of working in lumber mills.

He added that a year before the Finlay Forks area was flooded, the Indian families involved were offered several settlement areas "all of which they rejected. The matter was left in their hands . . . to make their own decision."

The Indians were offered two reserves in lieu of their flooded lands at Fort Grahame, Finlay Forks and Ingenika; they were called Tutu and Parsnip and were located near the proposed site of Mackenzie. But the Sekannis stayed there only three years and went back home. But they had no home. Reverend Father Brian Ballard, O.M.I. (Oblate of Mary Immaculate missionary priest), who has been serving the Fort Ware and Ingenika communities for the past seven years, said the Sekannis at Ingenika are now squatters on their own land. The people whose home was Fort Grahame "no longer had a past. Their memories had no place to touch," Father Ballard said.

I travelled to the Ingenika and spoke with the people myself. Bill Davidson of Hudson's Hope flew me in his Piper Cub on a cold crisp day in April, 1989. On the west side of the Finlay reach is the mouth of the Ingenika; the Sekannis are squatting on land called Ingenika Point. It looked isolated and dirty, with mud shining through snow patches.

Jean and Francis Isaac at Ingenika Point
(S. Matheson)

Jean Isaac is an attractive and well-spoken 44-year-old Sekanni, now living at Ingenika Point with her husband, Francis. Jean was born in the area and grew up at Fort Grahame.

"Before the Bennett dam we resided at Fort Grahame, past the Chowika, about three or four miles below Factory Ross," she said. "We had a reserve there, it was quite a size. The people used to do their own farming, growing potatoes, carrots, peas – peas grew real well up here – turnips, cabbages. Very rich soil, in the flats – all under the water now. It's not doing us any good now. We went hunting and fishing from that area because it was our 'stomping ground,' so to speak. So we hunted and did our thing there in the summer, and in the winter everyone went trapping, brought in furs and sold them to the Hudson's Bay. The post was right at Fort Grahame. The trader's name would have been Larry Campbell. We were very self-sufficient people. That was around 1940-45."

Isaac said her people first heard rumours of a dam about 1964. "Around 1966, we started hearing a little bit (more). My dad, Thomas Toma, who lived up here all his life, never moved out of this area, saw surveyors coming in and surveying around. He went and asked them, 'What are you doing?' They told him they were surveying for timber-cruising. And he said, 'What do you want to do up here?' But they were very evasive. None of them cared to explain to my dad what they were doing."

Most of the people had temporarily left Fort Grahame at that time to work at Finlay Forks, Isaac said. "In Francis's generation, the young boys used to go out in the summer to work and come back in the fall with what money they made and go trapping. They used to go out by riverboats right from here (Ingenika) and from Fort Grahame and Fort Ware all the way down to McLeod Lake for jobs in the sawmills, or whatever. So they had an idea about sawmills and all that when Cattermole Timber moved to Finlay Forks in 1965. We lived in Finlay Forks for a couple of years, with the men working in logging camps."

Albert Poole at Ingenika Point

Albert Poole, a quiet-spoken 41-year old Sekanni, recalled hearing talk of the forthcoming dam about 1963. At that time Poole was 14 or 15 and didn't know what it was all about. "I thought it was exciting," he said. "They were talking about jobs and stuff. But we never knew what would be the long-term effect of a dam. We figured it wouldn't affect us here, up at the Ingenika."

Poole didn't recall anyone from Hydro visiting his community to tell people about the project. "There was never an impact assessment done by any of them, Hydro, or the Indian Agents, or you may as well say the B.C. government. Nothing. Not of this area."

"No one ever came to explain," agreed Isaac. "They never said anything to that point until the day that they came, in 1965, around that area. The DIA (Department of Indian Affairs) went to certain people, and it was only the people whose traplines the water was going to affect. They told them, 'There's going to be a flood and we want to give you so much money. Twenty-seven hundred dollars to each head of the family.' And then what they did was, they didn't give the money to the people. They told them, 'We'll hold it in the office for you.' This was Mr. Preslosky at the time, the Indian Agent. He didn't give the money to them, he gave them maybe $100 or $200 for spending money. Then what he did with the rest of it, he bought bedrolls and motors and power saws for the older people, who owned traplines down below in the south part. They were older men, really old, old men. So the older men didn't mind getting new bedrolls, new power saws, yet they didn't realize they were paying for it themselves. Then all of a sudden they had no more money, because they'd got it paid to them with these things. And no trapline to boot."

Isaac said her family was living at Finlay Forks. She said no one ever imagined the river would just disappear.

"Then in the year 1968, in the month of May – I remember because my son was born in December of 1967 and in May he was five months old – what happened was we saw the water rising and we thought it was just from the runoff. Then it started to go over the banks and come quite close to our homes. Then the DIA called John Harvey, a DIA helper, and he came down and he said, 'We're going to move you people out because the river is already rising and you have no chance to do anything.' So what he did was he just hooked up our houses, those that could be moved, and he started moving them. He moved the whole thing. On skids. Some people weren't as lucky; they could only take the bare necessities. The rest of their stuff they left for overnight, and by the time overnight came, the houses were floating away."

Isaac said the water was undrinkable for a while because of all the "junk, logs and bits of trees" floating in it. Then people started seeing animals getting drowned, including moose and bear. "We actually saw them drown. Because they were trying to manoeuvre through the debris and they would just get sucked in by all the gasses and stuff coming up out of the trees that are down below. They just get pulled under, and they have no hope."

Beavers used to make their homes along the river banks, when the water was high in the fall, she said. "Then come the middle of winter, the water started going down, from the dam. What happens to the beaver, they die without water, their food is frozen solid to the ground – they eat willows and poplar, mostly. So they try to make new houses. Some places you could see where a beaver has come out between the broken-up ice, at pressure points, and if you follow them they're trying to find another place where they can live for the winter. .. I think most of the beaver perished that way."

Even squirrels were affected, Isaac said. "Do you realize that the flood came right in the spring of the year when the animals were having their young?" she said sadly. "Just imagine how many must have been killed. When I think about that, I think that's the thing that really breaks my heart. The waste . . .

"We watched things like that, and we were afraid. We were cut off from our own home town, which was Fort Grahame. Only then did we realize why the men were getting large contracts to cut down the timber in the trench and top it, to be floated down for the mills to pick up."

Isaac said that her husband Francis travelled by riverboat to Fort Grahame, to see how far the lake went. She said the Sekannis were told their houses would be burned, but their belongings would be put in a safe place where the men could pick them up. "Francis went up the trench to see, and when he got there he saw that they were burned all right, but there was nothing outside. They burned our houses with everything in them. Some of the men had guns and stuff underneath the floorboards, so nobody would know where they were, and all that was burned. And our pots and pans. Everything. There were five houses, our church and everything, burned in Fort Grahame, and another five or six houses burned – six houses to be correct – right here in Ingenika Point." Some people received compensation, but some didn't, she said. No one received a new house.

Albert Poole's father was a trapper. Half his old trapline is underwater now. He was one of the people who found his house burned with everything in it, Poole said. "He came home one day to find his cabin burned. I was in Finlay Forks at the time that happened. Everything was burned: guns, pictures, all that. It was all gone." Poole said his father received $2,700 compensation for his flooded traplines, and that's all.

Isaac said the Sekannis have been promised a new reserve, to bring their people together again. "That's what they're saying. Up at Hydro Lake, about another four or five miles from here. It's relatively flat, a swampy place, so I believe that we could grow certain things."

"At least we will have a place to call our own," she added. "But then again, we'd still be depending a lot on the way we lived, and the lake is still our big enemy.

"I was born up the river, Francis was born here. Most of us were born in Fort Grahame or somewhere in the immediate area. So after the seven years we were (living) in Finlay Forks for work, when we came back up, do you know what the DIA – who should know better – and the government people were saying? We were just Indians who happened to move to this area. So we had to prove we were born in this area! That's stupid, isn't it? When the name of my dad was on the trapline list, Francis's name above dad's trapline. How could people turn around and try to make it sound we just moved in? It was in the news one time, it said nobody knew where we came from. We were living here even before they came!"

Isaac said that the lake which flooded people's homes also changed the Sekannis' way of life. "With that lake came a lot of things that our people never saw before. Like the winds are a lot stronger. And the sand that gets blown into this area is just something else. When we try drying meat around here it just fills up with sand. And you know that's not good for you . . . You saw some places where the banks are slipping? That's where the sand comes from. I'll tell you, you couldn't go even close to the edge when there's a strong wind, because the sand gets in your eyes, ears, everything. And then our people have a lot of skin sicknesses, that come out in little welts and different ways; it could be just something from . . . a psychological problem too, I don't know. You know, when a person thinks too much, they could break out in a rash, they could have stomach cramps, they could have anything. So we don't know which is the real sickness, or which is in our minds. But it didn't used to be.

"Long ago when I was a young girl, the only major sickness we used to have was a headache or a cough, and that was it. But today you see our people having stomach problems, chest problems, eye problems, skin breaking out sometimes with boils and stuff. I think that has come about from the pollution brought about by the lake, as well as the oil spills that have been happening on the ground all over wherever the industry goes."

The people who live at the head of the Finlay, at Fort Ware, are part of the Sekanni tribe also. Isaac said they have a pretty good area, but logging is happening there, also. "And alcohol causes a lot of social problems."

Isaac said there's no question that logging in the area brought more harm than good to the Sekannis. "None of our men are working in any of the camps. It's only the workers who come from the outside in . . . They just don't deal with us. We helped them to flood our land, then after that when the going got good then they said, 'Oh, forget Indians.' Then they just started to cut trees around us and then pretty soon our men are out of a job, then (on) welfare. That's what the situation is now."

Albert Poole is not optimistic about the immediate future of his people. "For one thing, you can't enjoy the river, you just see a lake, logs. I used to work in the sawmills. It's too far away, in the Mackenzie area, now. I did a little bit of fighting fire. When the logging companies started moving up here, I would go logging. But it's such now that the natives can't get on." Then he adds with a resigned laugh,

"Even the dogs here are unemployed."

Cameron McCabe is a schoolteacher who has been at the Ingenika since November, 1988. "I was amazed and angered by what had happened to the people here and I thought that they could use somebody who was qualified to teach the kids how to read, for openers," he said. McCabe, who has an undergraduate degree in history and a teaching certificate from the University of British Columbia, is probably the most qualified teacher the Sekannis have had for some time. The College of New Caledonia in the community has classes from Grade 1 to 8.

McCabe said that from what he has learned about the history of the Sekannis, he fully agrees with the view that the people did not believe technology like that existed to flood them out. They also didn't think anyone would be so cruel.

The tribe's history indicates the Sekanni's have always been treated badly by other tribes. But McCabe said that "they could understand that. That's real to them. A dam and high-tech and flooding a whole valley, how is that possible? That's the word I get from the elders I've talked to; they couldn't understand or relate to a lake flooding them out."

"I teach kindergarten to grade eight," he added, "and the parents are desperate to have their kids educated. Their kids represent the hope for the future." McCabe is quite happy with the participation and response he has received from the community. "First of all, the attendance is excellent. I've never worked in a school where the attendance was so good. And the parents are very, very supportive, which is also nice. I've seen some real improvement since I've been here . . . They said it's the first year, ever, that the kids have learned how to read."

Nevertheless, McCabe thinks it will take the Sekannis a long time to recover. "They really are lost. They are traditional hunters and trappers, in every sense of the word. Williston Lake not only pushed them off their main settlement, but it split the people up into different groups and it separated them from their traditional hunting and trapping. They were thrust hundreds of years into the future, totally unprepared, no choice. There's a lot of walking wounded here. That they can function at all is amazing, that they're good people is amazing. You know, you can always cut people down, but there's strength here."

Susan Hatfield, who teaches basic adult education in Ingenika Point at the College of New Caledonia, agreed. "It's easy to come in here with our standards and say there are social problems. But you have to look at it from their point of view. I think if you took a group of white society from the same socio-economic background, the same educational background, and put them in a place like this, they probably wouldn't do as well as these people. I'm fond of them. Like Cameron says, there is honesty. There is a great deal of shyness, and I think a lot of that results from the fact that they can't come to grips with themselves, deal with a lot of their personal problems. But they don't have the skills. I have three women who are really tops in the town; they're probably at a reading level of grade 8 or 9. But the average, the younger people who have quit school in grade 4 or 5, don't even remember what grade it was they quit school in. One thing I've discovered, the people here have a deep, deep feeling for this country that is so innate that they can't even talk about it."

Teachers Susan Hatfield and Cameron McCabe at Ingenika Point
(S. Matheson)

Health facilities at the Ingenika are about as good as can be expected for a sparsely populated, isolated community. There's a community health nurse, and a resident who can dispense medicine.

Hatfield guessed that the population of Ingenika Point was about 100, including adults and children. Another 487 or so Sekannis live at Fort Ware, she said, and about 10 or more families at the Mesilinka River (off the Omineca arm), and some in Prince George or Mackenzie.

Albert Poole does not feel his people have been singled out to be treated badly by B.C. Hydro's dam. "It's not only us, but I heard a lot of stories about what happened to other people who were living down the trench, or along the Peace River." However, very few Sekannis trap anymore – maybe three or four trappers at most, Poole said. Not only did the dam destroy the old lifestyle, but there's nothing to take its place.

Poole stretched his legs under the table and gazed outside the window. "I read an article once about our dealings with the DIA (Department of Indian Affairs), the Finlay River people and B.C. Hydro," he said. "What I can't really comprehend is this: the B.C. government and B.C. Hydro started planning this dam a long time ago, back in 1956. And nobody knows about that. You would think the DIA would have known about it, since they work for the government. People heard about it here around 1963 when it was too late to do anything. The dam was part way built, plans were done, about that time."

Chief Gordon Pierre at Ingenika Point
(S. Matheson)

The day I visited the Ingenika, a reporter and photographer from the *Vancouver Sun* newspaper were also there. In the living room of Susan Hatfield's trailer, we conducted a group interview with Chief Gordon Pierre, Albert Poole, Jean and Francis Isaac, and the schoolteachers. The chief explained how logging has affected his people's trapping livelihood.

"Six people have traplines now from Ospika up to Pesika," he said. "That's all our band members' traplines . . . Most have lost their traplines in recent years because of the logging. They've all been logged. They haven't done any active logging up this way this winter; they're on the Ospika now. But like I said, next year's going to be up this way. It's going to go fast. I've been hearing rumours that maybe five, six contractors are coming up here next year. So it gives you an idea of how much logging that's going to be."

Albert Poole recalled the years when Williston Lake was filling up, and how the beaver died when the lake dropped. "They didn't do any impact studies, environmental studies, anything like that," noted

Chief Pierre. "They just went ahead and done it. I don't think they even realized themselves how much damage they'd done. I don't think they ever dreamt it would flood such a big area. I honestly believe that. We cry about the logs, a natural resource like that, billions and billions of cunits of timber just flooded out, left to rot."

The chief questioned whether Hydro really needed all that water to produce the electricity. He maintained that he never saw Hydro's red flags designating the high water mark. Pierre said the Sekannis should have been treated similarly to the people in the Arrow Lakes area, where they got new schools, a new airport, and compensation for relocation. "Same with Hudson's Hope. I think they got better compensation. You look at our situation, it's like day and night. We did research on what revenue B.C. Hydro makes per year off that dam there, and it's something like $735 million a year." Pierre estimated that "it's going to cost the federal and provincial governments somewhere in the neighbourhood of $10 to $12 million to relocate us. That's what we're negotiating now."

Ten million is exactly what has been allocated for a fish and wildlife study, related to the project's aftermath. "Why would they spend so much money, $10 million on animals, and $1 million on people?" the chief wondered. "The move is going to cost $10 to $12 million, and the province has offered to put in $1 million."

Barrie Cornell and A.C. Geddes witnessed a sad desecration imposed on the Sekannis by the waters of Lake Williston: "Barrie and I were flying in to Ingenika," said Geddes, "and we looked down and saw all these people standing around at the end of the runway. Then we could see, down the cliff, that a piece of land had broken off and slid into the lake. It was where their graveyard was, and there were coffins, some whole and some broken up, bones and bodies, strewn all down the bank."

Cornell continued the story: "The bank had eventually sloughed back far enough so it interfered with the graveyards. Pretty soon you could see the ends of boxes sticking out of the cliffs, crumbling and falling down, bones all over the place. Naturally the Indians, with all the right in the world, got upset. So they went after Hydro to go in with machinery and move the gravesite quite a bit farther back."

Jean Isaac completed the story of the graves: "At the Point here, we have a graveyard. That graveyard was sloughing in when we moved up, so what we did was move our dead farther inland. And it sloughed some more. There again, they told us they were going to take the bones out and take them down to the Parsnip reserve and rebury them. I think they just made a mass grave there, of all the bones of our peoples. We don't know who's where or anything. Anger! I

mean, nobody likes their dead to be desecrated. Because the graveyards are sacred places."

The Sekannis had already said farewell to the graves of their
ancestors at Fort Grahame, now flooded beneath Williston Lake. "I
don't know what they did there," Isaac said. "I don't even know if
they exhumed all the graves that they said they would. I think they
just covered the whole place with a cement block. I'm pretty sure
that's what they did, because at that time they were just using riverboats, and if they were removing any kind of remains we surely
would have known."

The Sekanni tribe is scattered throughout the trench, from one
end of Williston Lake to the other. For Isaac, who was born on the
Ingenika River, this is home. "My parents were buried here at the
Point. And some of our people that we lost last year are buried here.
Once you've been through so much, a country, a place, sort of grows
on you. I mean, it's part of you. You can't deny it. And that's the reason why I really felt bad about Fort Grahame because I can remember
when I was a young girl, it used to be such a nice place. Mom and dad
used to just watch us play out in the fields, and sometimes we'd go
berry picking."

The saskatoon berry-picking areas are now all under water. The
community discovered some high-elevation huckleberries, but there
is another problem: the herbicide spraying programs carried out by
the forestry department (and to a lesser extent, by B.C. Hydro along
their transmission lines).

"The air brings it," Isaac said. "It just doesn't stay in one area,
when they spray, especially when they spray with planes. It goes all
over. Then there are air pockets that bring certain amounts here and
there, and it's falling all over. And think of that stuff, too, that goes
down into the ground, goes into the drinking water, then goes into
maybe the other little willows, and grass gets a hold of it, which the
different animals eat, then they get affected by it. They said its not
dangerous, but I don't believe them."

There is one chief and three councillors at Ingenika (there used to
be four councillors but one resigned), elected by the band members.
John Pierre, a handsome man of 26, is a band councillor and cousin to
the chief.

"We've had a problem for 20 years with this lake and it's not settled yet," John Pierre said. "Hydro doesn't want to settle with us,
because they know what they did to us. And they don't want to admit
to the world what they did to us. When they made the Bennett dam, it
was just going to create a little lake, eh? They didn't even tell the people here, they just flooded it. They didn't take the trees out of the

whole trench. They never explained to the oldtimers. They said, 'Oh, we're going to raise the water a little ways.' They didn't tell them they were going to raise it five miles across. My father, my older brothers and sisters, all lived at Fort Grahame."

Pierre said that the Bennett dam "may have benefitted the world, but what did it do for us? We're the people who got no money out of it, but we suffered with it. It's not only the people, it's the animals also. When you look at the lake now, it's polluted; the trout don't spawn anymore. Our water is polluted. There's a lot of things to worry about with the lake. You can be out there in a boat, and 10 minutes later, 5 minutes later, you can't get back to shore. They are spraying the trees, the leaves fall off into creeks, and all the poison, it all comes back."

Isaac's husband, Francis, was hesitant to talk about the problems the Sekannis have experienced. "To my own knowledge, it was white people who started the whole mess. Then there's the ones who come behind them with books and stories. They make money, we get nothing. We got nothing out of the dam. If you had been used – if you had been in my shoes and been used – as a native person, you would know."

Teacher Cameron McCabe sympathizes with the natives' plight. "Strange things are still happening. The B.C. government has offered to help them with a commercial fishery off this lake. They're not a fishing people!"

"And with contaminated fish," Isaac added. "Nobody's going to buy them."

Chief Pierre said that the fish, although making up part of the Sekannis' diet, were never considered to be a prime source of income. "We live off the land," added Francis Isaac, "and the best land is down by the river. We lost it."

Hunters have also invaded the area via a logging road that comes in from the Mackenzie area, the Indians say.

"The hunters come in, and the fishermen," said Francis Isaac. "They over-hunt and over-fish. In the river across here, I remember guys taking out tubfuls of fish, and dumping them out in the lake."

Francis became angry. "When I saw this, I reported it and they caught these guys at the dam. They were partying right at the creek there; they had five boats. They caught two boats, and the other three, I don't know what happened. They took their boats and everything."

"Up at Grassy Bluff we have another settlement," Jean Isaac added. "People have been going in with jet boats and taking stuff out of the houses."

Francis, a well-built man, got up from his chair, his eyes flashing with anger. "I'm willing to get an AK-47, and if I ever catch these guys . . . 60 shots per clip!"

"This is not Prince George or Mackenzie," he said. "This is an isolated area. We need all that we have." After sitting back down, he added: "But that's where you really get a bad name. I told one guy who questioned me on what we are doing, I said, 'I never come to your city and ask you what you are doing. Stay out of my country! We are not a violent people, but pretty soon we are going to be.' They are going to teach us to be violent. It's true."[7]

Pilot Bill Davidson and I left Ingenika as the sun was beginning to set, flying up over a group of kids playing soccer on the landing strip. Below us, the buckskin logs ringing the Ingenika shoreline gave an untidy, dirty look to the pristine rivers and mountains.

"Over the rock pile"; Rocky Mountains
(S. Matheson)

We turned east, over the 'rock pile' – the snow-covered peaks of the Rockies. Twilight had left the valleys in shadow. Davidson pointed out Wicked Lake at the bottom of a steep valley. At the Ottertail, we saw log bundles ready to be towed to Mackenzie. He tilted the plane so I could get a photograph, with the Peace Reach stretched in the background. We spotted a deer kill on the bay, the wolf tracks leading up to it, blood spattered on the snow and the black hulk of a partly devoured body. I thought of Earl Pollon's poem: "this is a tale that I saw on the trail . . . ."

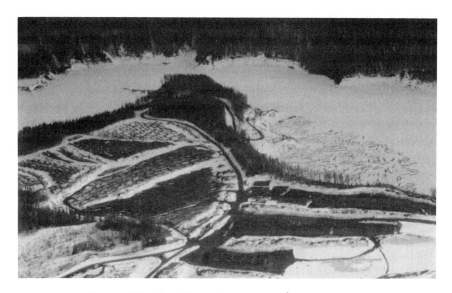

Ottertail; log bundles ready to be towed to the Mackenzie

Notes

[1]*Sixteen Years in the Indian Country, 1800-1816,* Daniel Williams Harmon, edited with introduction by W. Kaye Lamb, Toronto, 1975, copyright 1957, reprinted in *Peace River Chronicles,* p. 33.

[2]*Notes of a Twenty-five Years' Service in the Hudson's Bay Territory,* John McLean, London, 1849, reprinted in *Peace River Chronicles,* p. 51.

[3]J.C. Bryant, as recorded by Dr. W. Wymond Walkem, in *Stories of Early British Columbia,* Vancouver, 1914. Reprinted in *Peace River Chronicles,* p. 77.

[4]Inspector J.D. Moodie, N.W.M.P., Report dated January 14, 1899, North-West Mounted Police, Part II – Reports of Northern Patrols, Canadian Sessional Papers No. 15, Vol. XXXIIII, No. 12, 1899, Ottawa. Reprinted in *Peace River Chronicles,* p. 199-200.

[5]*On the Headwaters of the Peace, a Narrative of a Thousand-Mile Canoe Trip to a Little-Known Range of the Canadian Rockies,* New York, 1917. Reprinted in *Peace River Chronicles, p.330.*

[6]*C.B. Cunningham, extracts from an unpublished report to R.W. Gross, Manager, Land Division, British Columbia Hydro and Power Authority, June, 1962. Reprinted from Peace River Chronicles,* p, 534.

[7]An article in the *Calgary Herald* dated December 22, 1987 tells how it is in the Ingenika 20 years after the flood:

"The Sekanni Indians are thankful this Christmas following two decades of hardship – most of it unnoticed – after deciding to ask for aid last year. Food shortages, unsafe drinking water, poor housing and 100 percent unemployment have been the daily lot for the 92 residents living in the remote village 350 kilometres north of Prince George, B.C."

The article told how the band was flooded out of its traditional reserve 20 years ago, when the water began rising behind the W.A.C. Bennett Dam. "Without consultation, the Indians were moved to a reserve close to Mackenzie, B.C. But the boom town atmosphere brought alcoholism and social problems that threatened to destroy the band so the Sekannis moved back to the mountains. They were safer, but ineligible for assistance because they were not on reserve land. The people are still squatting on Crown land, as the reserve they want is farther north where the Finlay flows into Williston Lake."

The Sekannis were 'thankful' because they received $180,000 from the B.C. government toward improving living conditions. The Indians converted a trailer into a learning centre (now occupied by the College of New Caledonia), purchased two skidders (for promised work with local forest companies) and made other improvements they could afford.

31

The Birds and the Bees, the Fish and the Trees

"Science without conscience is the death of souls," said geneticist and broadcaster David Suzuki, "yet a humanist without the knowledge of science cannot hope to control the physical elements that impinge on his very existence."[1]

How does the sudden creation of a 640-square-mile lake affect the fish and wildlife population? Where could scientists and humanists have met to ensure the least possible ecological damage?

Spillway; fence to prevent animals falling in is on the left side
(S. Matheson)

"Unfortunately, there were no studies carried out by fish and wildlife before the construction of the W.A.C. Bennett Dam, or the flooding of the reservoir now known as Williston Lake," said B.P. Churchill, acting section head in the Peace sub-region of the provincial fish and wildlife branch. In a letter to the authors dated

December 28, 1988, Churchill said: "Consequently, I have no reports to forward to you. . . . The only identified direct wildlife impact to my knowledge has been the loss of a number of mule deer into the spillway at the W.A.C. Bennett Dam, and this situation has been corrected by B.C. Hydro through the construction of a fence."

The layperson who tries to make a judgement about wildlife losses to the dam hears conflicting views. On one hand, conservationists, wildlife biologists and local residents may feel that losses have been severe. On the other hand, variables such as weather, biological cycles and fading memories of 'the good old days' undercut the feeling that things have gone terribly wrong.

'Controlling nature' is based on the view that nature can be arranged to suit man's convenience. Yet insects, birds, fish, and small and large mammals also share this space, and have been here for eons before man's arrival. Is Leo Rutledge right in thinking that the dam and its lake caused "millions of deaths, if you count the little things"?

Fish are 'little' things. The first change people noticed after the dam was that they weren't catching grayling anymore. Whitefish seemed to multiply and the Dolly Varden population improved, but Arctic Grayling began to disappear from Williston Lake about 1978 to 1979, and are now nearly extinct.

The grayling, once called "the flower of fishes" by Saint Ambrose[2], may weigh as much as four pounds. Similar to trout in its habits, the grayling is more slender, graceful and active, and its scales are larger. Its beauty lies in its fins: a high dorsal fin coloured grey with dark blue spots and a red edge, and lower fins which are streaked purple and white.

The whitefish has a long body, a cone-shaped snout and a forked tail. Its mouth is toothless and its upper jaw protrudes from the lower. It feeds on insects and shellfish and usually lives in deep water. To people in the Peace area, whitefish are considered as common and unchallenging as cattle.

The Dolly Varden is the native char of Pacific coastal waters; it's a slender-bodied fish with red spots on the back and sides. The larger 'Dollies' are two to three feet long and can weigh up to 20 pounds or more. They are caught in swift, cold streams and are game fighters. An aggressive member of the trout family, they are sometimes called 'bull trout' by local fishermen.

The rainbow, another member of the trout family once commonly found in the Peace, is brightly coloured with a rosy band. Highly prized as game fish, it fights long and hard for its freedom.

According to local resident Terry Curzon, "after the lake was created, when we caught a rainbow trout you could see that it had tried to spawn, and wasn't able to; there were old eggs inside. So obviously these fish were not able to go in the creeks, or use the creeks properly for spawning. Maybe the fluctuation of the water was too much."

"Hydro is doing a study on the fish to find out what caused the changes in population, finally, after all these years," Curzon added. "I took them up in my boat a couple of times when they were doing studies in the 1970s, taking water temperatures because they thought the lake temperature might be too low. But nothing came out of those studies. Hopefully this time they'll find something conclusive. It's not good."

Hydro spokesman Chris Boatman says that the corporation paid the recreation and conservation department (now the environment ministry, fish and wildlife branch) $10,000 in 1962 to study the effects of the project on fish and wildlife and to identify compensation measures. "It is known that winter flights were taken to estimate the moose, wolf and other large mammal populations. No reports or compensation proposals were ever made to Hydro based on these studies," Boatman said in a letter to the authors dated May 15, 1989. "A report on the impacts to the fishery was prepared by Mr. I. Withler in 1959 (copy provided to authors); however no compensation recommendations were forthcoming. No pre-project inventory of beaver numbers was undertaken; neither has there been a post-project assessment."

Boatman said that B.C. Hydro initiated post-project studies in the early 1970s, to assess the impacts after the reservoir was filled. "In 1984 a final report was issued. However, its value was minimal because of the substantial passage of time between the studies and the preparation of recommendations, due to the changes to the biophysical landscape adjacent to the Williston Reservoir."

Ken Kyllo doesn't put much stock in Hydro's studies. "Hydro did a survey of the fish in Williston Lake in 1974 and 1975, but they didn't publish a report until 1984," he said. "Now they're doing another study, but they're finding mostly suckers and squaw-fish. They seem to be setting up their nets and depth-sounders in the wrong places most times, but they're finding some fish. I don't know when they'll publish the new report."

The June 28, 1989 edition of *The Northerner* reported that some 5,000 to 7,000 fish taken from the Peace and its six tributaries between Fort St. John and Hudson's Hope will be tagged and released. Up to 60 sportfish will be equipped with radio transmitters and monitored from small aircraft during the next year.

The monitoring of fish in the Peace between Fort St. John and the Peace Canyon Dam is the first environmental study to get underway. Additional studies of the impact of the proposed Site C project will go ahead after 1989. Other aspects of the study will include counting anglers along the river, checking fish for mercury levels, water quality analysis and temperature monitoring at selected sites including the proposed Site C site and the Peace Canyon Dam tailrace. The project is intended to meet the recommendations of the B.C. Utilities Commission, which reviewed and rejected B.C. Hydro's application for Site C between 1980 and 1983, after lengthy hearings.

Ice-fishing around the dam intakes
(T. Roberts)

Kyllo said that after Williston Lake flooded, the fish population exploded. "But its gone downhill again, mainly from over-fishing. Up here at the dam in the winter time, there will be 150 people ice-fishing all day long, and they aren't the same 150 people all day. They've eliminated the rainbow."

Ernie Krebs is also familiar with the change in fish population: "We used to get all kinds of fish when we went up to the Carbon River, all kinds of grayling, and we'd smoke them. Beautiful fish. Now they've pretty well disappeared. Now you get mostly Dolly Varden, some Kokanee (a landlocked species of Pacific sockeye salmon)."

"The Kokanee weren't there before the lake formed," Dave Kyllo noted. "The Arctic Grayling were the dominant fish before, and now they're practically extinct, compared to the old numbers. They claim that the grayling, when the area was first flooded, were not oriented to lake spawning and as long as the water was coming up they wouldn't spawn. They'd carry the eggs full term. We'd catch them in

August and they still had their eggs. After they carried them so long they started eating themselves internally. After a few years they seemed to become oriented to the lake and started spawning again, but by that time all the boats were getting up there, into all the creek mouths where the grayling hung out, and they were just slaughtered.

"Now the most numerous fish would be the whitefish. They're a good enough eating fish, but not a sport fish. There's still Dolly Vardens and rainbow. They didn't stock Williston Lake at all; they said it was too big a lake to consider stocking it."

In a letter to the authors dated May 15, 1989 Hydro spokesman Chris Boatman agreed that the fish species in Williston Reservoir are different from what existed in the Peace River prior to the project. "One of the riverine species that has not been successful in the reservoir is grayling, however it should be pointed out that this species did not simply die as a result of the reservoir formation," Boatman said.

"The grayling, along with mountain whitefish and rainbow, have declined in numbers relative to the pre-project situation, because of the loss of suitable habitat. These species have been replaced by Dolly Varden, kokanee, lake trout, ling and peamouth chub, species that were present in the Peace River, that have thrived in the lake situation. Also, lake whitefish, a minor species prior to reservoir creation, have greatly increased in numbers and now account for approximately half the total fish population. They are the main prey species for Dolly Varden, lake trout and ling. In total numbers of fish there are likely more fish in the basin today than prior to reservoir formation, which is due to a major increase in aquatic habitat. Access to the area has also improved since the project was undertaken so that more people can now fish in this area than before."

B.C. Hydro built a fish hatchery at Peace Canyon, which started operating in 1981 when that dam was completed. In the brochure describing the hatchery, Hydro admits the flooding had detrimental effects on the fish population, and therefore the hatchery was developed "as a *product of mitigation* (author's italics) between B.C. Hydro and the Ministry of Environment as a *partial compensation for the social opportunity costs* (author's italics) of the construction of the Peace Canyon dam." The hatchery's goal is to raise 50,000 yearling trout to 20 grams in weight (or five inches in length) each year, and release them into Dinosaur Lake in May. The adult spawners are captured by "angling, electro-shocking, seining and trapping."

"Quite a few of their trout are surviving," Terry Curzon said, "so it's got potential. The water temperature, after it's gone through the generators of the Bennett dam, is a degree or two warmer than Williston Lake, so that likely helps. One of the problems was finding enough spawning rainbow trout to use in the hatchery. I spoke to the biologist and he said they can't take fish from other areas because they might bring parasites in, so they have to try to catch the fish within these lakes here and use them for spawning. I'm hopeful they'll keep up the program and perhaps start stocking Williston Lake too."

Hydro's Boatman said that the Peace Canyon hatchery "was constructed as an experimental facility to determine the potential of a hatchery operation on this type of run-of-river reservoir. The hatchery was able to reach its goal in terms of fish numbers; however it was not successful in two other areas. The cost to run this facility has been $146 per kg (kilogram) of fish whereas other provincial hatcheries cost $17 per kg. The second problem was the lack of use of the fish by anglers. Only about one percent of the fish stocked were caught by anglers either in the reservoir or in the river downstream. More fish were angled in the river downstream than in the reservoir. Costs to operate the facility total about $125,000 per year. When capital costs are included, B.C. Hydro has spent over $1 million on the hatchery up to 1988."

In a story in the June 28, 1989 edition of *The Northerner*, B.C. Hydro chairman Larry Bell admitted that the hatchery was a flop, with fish costing more than $100 each to produce. "It made no sense for us to continue spending for such minimal returns," he said. Bell announced that an interest-bearing fund is being set up by Hydro to help pay for a yet-to-be-identified alternative to the Peace Canyon hatchery.

Bell also said that recreation facilities at Williston Reservoir will receive $100,000 for development; an additional $1.5 million will go toward rehabilitating Williston viewpoint. He promised that Hydro would meet local residents' long-standing demands for a new boat launch.

Williston Lake reservoir affected the Peace valley's indigenous animals in ways that are only beginning to be realized.

The moose population has dropped by more than 75 per cent, according to Jim Beattie. "They used to come down to the river flats for winter pasture. Along the Finlay and Parsnip rivers there were big willow flats up to 20 miles wide; now there are no moose there. At the head of the Ottertail and Ospika where my brother Bill's hunting territory was located, there were old moose trails a foot deep, worn in on the mountains. Now they're all mossed over. They can't go back, it's all spruce, there's no feed in it. They had to go down to the river flats for their feed ... but there was no river flat any more."

Beattie said the moose hunting season was left open for two

years, to reduce the animals' numbers. Some local residents saw the decision to leave the season open as the only practical alternative to the moose starving, but some could not accept that reasoning. Noreen Stubley of Hudson's Hope gave her position in a "Voice of the Canyon" column in the September 20, 1972 *Chetwynd Echo*:

"It was reported that up around Williston Lake area game is very scarce. This, I believe, is caused by a foolish mistake of the Game Commissioner for allowing a no-limit, no-sex mass-massacre for six months of the year on moose in that area. This was sponsored also by some local sportsmens' clubs. Their reasoning seems to be some moose may drown so we'll open the season and let the bloodthirsty ones kill them all. What a way to protect and conserve our game, wouldn't you say?"

Hydro's Boatman said that "the decision to implement the extended moose hunting season and increase the bag limit to two moose per hunter was made by the (provincial) Fish and Wildlife branch. B.C. Hydro, to our knowledge, was not privy to the decision. As you noted the plan was meant to utilize moose that would be permanently displaced by the loss of habitat caused by flooding. It was probably believed a larger impact to the overall population could be minimized by reducing the standing crop immediately prior to the actual flooding. The extra harvest was implemented for the 1967 and 1968 seasons."

Ken Kyllo recalled the situation with sadness: "The moose on the Finlay died out after about 1973. They lived for a few years on the tops of the trees that were still sticking out of the ice, but when the trees died, the moose disappeared. There's very few moose compared to what there was. Their ranges are gone. Hydro was supposed to make a bunch of money available for improving the habitat other places, to offset what was flooded, but to date they haven't done anything."

Dave Kyllo said there was a possible solution to preserving the numbers of moose and other animals. "There wasn't too much timber left in the new areas for them to go to. What we would have liked to see them do was burn off large chunks and make areas for them to winter in. But they didn't want to do that in heavy timber country. Too much value to the trees. More value to it than game.

"The lake simply pushed any animals that were left back into the bush. A lot of them were drowned in the lake, in log jams. There were deer along the hillsides in the Peace area, and that was one of the major areas where it sloughed, because this end was the highest. And the same with the bear."

Lorne March, director of environmental services for B.C. Hydro, refers to what happened at the Bennett dam as the bad old days, when the words 'ecology' and 'environment' weren't in our vocabulary. As Dave Kyllo said "There were a lot of environmental changes being made by people who didn't know what they were doing. Or care. Build the dam and get the power going." But the problems, most of which still exist, will only become more complex as Hydro forges ahead with plans for Site C, which will eliminate the last remaining valleys and about 50 islands in the river.

"The animals' main reason for crossing the river would be coming from the islands where they had their calves," Kyllo explained. "After the calves were born, they'd take them back across the river. There was no real migration route across the Peace; down the Finlay River there was more. The moose haven't increased because of the access roads into logging areas; when an area gets opened up, the animals get killed off."

Jim Beattie saw firsthand how the moose tried to cope with the changes: "I sometimes would see moose trying to go through the debris on the lake up at the Carbon, having a heck of a time getting across the Carbon Bay, just plunging through the debris. And it's less than a quarter of a mile wide there. They made it, but they had a heck of a time. The moose are more plentiful now around the town-site. They have drifted down onto the Butler Ridge and into the east there. This is the only river flat left between Site One dam and Fort St. John. They come really close to town on the bottom-lands, along the roads. I work for the highways department and we've pulled all kinds of them off the roads, road-kills. You didn't used to see too much of that."

Beattie said that the deer population seems to have increased, "but that's because of the mild winters we've been having. I don't think they ever had to open the season on deer." He added that the bears weren't affected too much, "but I guess the lake took away a lot of the saskatoons they ate."

Local resident Dave George who's a hunter has not noticed a change in big game numbers resulting from the lake itself, as much as from the access brought about by the lake and the associated industry. The improved access brings an influx of hunters from out of town – something the Sekanni Indians also said.

"You meet more hunters now from Vancouver or the lower mainland," George said. "Word of mouth, I guess. There's roads and cutlines, seismic lines, transmission line, all over this country now. The oil companies have put in a few roads, the logging has increased so there's more bush roads. And with bush-buggies and three-wheeler all-terrain vehicles, people can go pretty well anywhere they want."

One situation that occurred in Hudson's Hope because of Hydro's lack of foresight was so bizarre that no local resident would have dreamed it. People heard Hydro might poison them, and the howl of protest was heard right across Canada.

"Hudson's Hope on the Boil over PCBs," said a headline in the Fort St. John *Alaska Highway News* on November 29, 1982. And what a boil that was!

The first inkling residents had of Hydro's plan was a 'leaked' corporation memo dated December 15, 1981. It was to H.J. Goldie (vice president, electrical operations, central interior region), from E.T. Davis (division manager of the region). The memo said that Hydro planned to move 1,100 leaking electrical capacitors to the Peace Canyon warehouse (located 75 yards from Bull Run creek that flows directly into the Peace River), with other containers "dribbling" in later from the central interior areas of the province.

"I suggest that the site be chosen carefully," Davis's memo said, "and undoubtedly the NIMBY (not in my backyard) syndrome will result in a careful study. If a major concern is possible contamination of people, the storage in a densely populated area would be inappropriate. Central storage might be re-examined in terms of transportation of most of the PCBs since that is a time of maximum risk. I recognize remoteness does not guarantee minimum risk of exposures since if leakage occurs and it reaches a watercourse that exposes much population or food supplies to PCB contamination, we will have chosen a poor site. My own NIMBY syndrome said I don't want it in my region but, at risk of repeating myself, we do need to study all possible options. Perhaps several smaller sites would be a better solution."

Jim Gemmill, superintendent at the G.M. Shrum generating station at Bennett dam, responded in his own handwriting: "Not happy with storage of PCBs there, but may be best for Hydro."

When the memo hit the streets, Gemmill hastened to assure alarmed residents that the capacitors would be encased in four-inch thick containers which would then be stored in large bins. The bins would be sealed and painted with two layers of epoxy-based paint to prevent any rusting. Also, the concrete floor of the warehouse would be coated with another layer of paint. "Any sort of leakage would result in nothing more than a three-foot wide puddle in the building, and there will be monthly inspections so any leakage could be cleaned up according to regulations," Gemmill said. He added that Hydro had received environment department's approval for the storage plan, and had been working closely with the municipal council. But Hydro had postponed the October moving date for the capacitors until the debate died down a bit.

The town went wild. An ad hoc committee was formed, leaders appointed, and committee members given specific jobs. The authors of this book were among the first to join. Local residents who were employed by B.C. Hydro wondered what to do, and whether their jobs would be on the line if they protested. But they thought of the impact – PCBs stored in their territory, right beside the river – and they joined in. Soon, information was pouring in on the hazardous effects of PCBs, which most people had never heard of.

Polychlorinated biphenyls, or PCBs, are synthetic fluids used as a coolant in electrical transformers and capacitors. Their resistance to chemical and biological breakdown means they accumulate in the environment and concentrate in the food chain. Long-term exposure to PCBs has resulted in adverse reproductive and tumorigenic (cancer-causing) effects in laboratory animals. Symptoms of excessive short-term exposure include digestive disturbances, eye, nose, throat and upper respiratory tract irritations; liver injury and harmful reproductive effects may also occur.

A B.C. Hydro policies and procedures manual dated December 6, 1979 contained information on PCBs. "A common or designated name for PCBs in the electric industry has been 'askarel.' There is also a wide variety of manufacturers' trade names for PCBs. These include Asbestol, Chlorintol, Inerteen, No-Flamol, Pyranol and Saf-T-Kuhl. Regardless of the trade names, almost all fluids used in North America were manufactured by the lone North American manufacturer – the Monsanto Co." Under a section called Hazards, the manual said that PCBs "persist in increasing concentration as they accumulate in each step of a food chain. This increase is termed bioaccumulation. Within the past 10 years, PCBs have been identified throughout the global environment in water, air, soils, sediments, fish, mammals and birds."

Local politicians quickly got on the bandwagon against Hydro's storage plan. "Since this carcinogenic chemical doesn't break down, but builds up in the food chain, a spill cannot be treated with an attitude of 'dilution is the solution to pollution,'" said Elmer Kabush, a Hudson's Hope schoolteacher and North Peace NDP candidate. "Hydro has a corporate responsibility not to store PCBs on a major watershed, threatening communities downstream. It is B.C. Hydro's responsibility and duty to ensure that these cancer-causing substances are completely destroyed."

The major fear was that a spill might pollute the entire Peace-Mackenzie river system, all the way to the Arctic Ocean. Earl Pollon dashed off a letter and sent photocopies to newspapers and magazines from one end of the country to the other: "This makes no sense whatsoever! Surely they must know this area lies near the upper end of the longest watershed in North America . . . and the fourth longest watershed in the world! It would appear that B.C. Hydro does not give a damn about north-eastern British Columbia, a large part of Alberta, and all the Northwest Territories. I request the opinions of the Alberta and federal governments, as well as our own B.C. government, on this matter, for it is definitely of concern to a great many more people and places than just Hudson's Hope. There must be a better and safer method for a cure to this infectious problem than this band-aid method chosen by B.C. Hydro."

The municipal council asked Hydro's Jim Gemmill to attend a meeting on October 6, 1982 and explain the matter, and a public information meeting was scheduled for November 30.

Five hundred signatures were obtained on petitions objecting to the storage. Phoning committee members called people in the local area and outside, at their own expense.

Four hundred and forty people showed up at the November 30 meeting in the community hall – more than for a hot municipal election, noted one oldtimer. The media, complete with television cameras, also attended. The agenda included two Hydro presentations on PCBs, and one on environmental concerns by the provincial environment ministry. Rebuttal was by Dave Joslin and Gabe Hannon, spokesmen for the Hudson's Hope Citizens Action Committee. Joslin, as he was mounting the steps to the platform, tripped across an electric cord. He regained his balance and stepped up to the microphone. "You see, accidents can happen," he said.

The secret ballot vote on Hydro's scheme resulted in two 'yes' votes for storage at Peace Canyon. The rest – more than 400 – said 'no.'

Hydro's PCB storage plan at Peace Canyon was not a one-time situation, either. "In future, Hydro expects each year to store approximately three to five additional bins each containing 26 failed capacitors," the corporation said in an information sheet dated November 30, 1982.

On December 7, the *Alaska Highway News* reported that the Hudson's Hope municipal council had passed a resolution requesting the provincial waste management branch to enact a bylaw "regulating and prohibiting the storage and disposal of hazardous substances within the district's boundaries." The council also asked the federal environment protection agency to exercise its authority to prevent the proposed storage. The resolution emphasized that council would seek support for its cause from politicians at all levels, and from other municipal governments, and would also actively lobby for the construction of a permanent PCB disposal facility.

The new Waste Management Act was proving to be a can of worms. "Not only has the government failed to pass special regulations regarding hazardous wastes," Elmer Kabush said in the December 8, 1982 *Alaska Highway News*. "But the act itself could override local government by-laws refusing PCB or other hazardous waste storage. This may mean that PCBs could be shoved down the throat of local government by this act."

Federal environment critic Jim Fulton (NDP-Skeena) reported the information he had obtained at many national and international conferences on PCBs, had led him to take a strong stand opposing PCB storage on major watersheds such as the Peace-Mackenzie. According to the December 8 *Alaska Highway News*, Fulton "also pointed out that the B.C. government was notably absent at a recent PCB seminar sponsored by the Ontario government, which dealt with the effective treatment of the toxic waste." Fulton sent a telegram to the citizens of Hudson's Hope supporting their protest.

The December 15, 1982 edition of the *Alaska Highway News* published Hydro's response to allegations that the corporation was not acting responsibly in this case and had not done so in the past with other PCB-related incidents. D. Panaioti, production manager for the central interior region, denied that Hydro had ignored a supposed PCB problem at McLeese Lake. Panaioti said that Hydro had been informed (of the charge that a McLeese Lake family's food and livestock had been contaminated by PCBs between 1974 and 1976) at the end of November, 1976, and did everything possible at that time to alert local residents. The problem was investigated and the findings – made public – were that "no further restrictions (because of contamination) are necessary on the consumption of locally produced food or fish from McLeese Lake."

However, the same edition of the newspaper carried an article that said PCBs were a definite dilemma for Hydro. The corporation had admitted to a two-week delay in cleaning up leaking chemicals at it's Kennedy capacitor site on the Parsnip River near Mackenzie. "Hydro pollution experts blame the delay on 'lack of proper supervision' at the outdoor site where 16,000 capacitors containing PCBs are stored. . . . 'During the snow removal at the end of April, one dozen capacitor cans were inadvertently damaged by a bulldozer, eight of them severely enough to cause them to lose most of their free insulating liquid,'" a Hydro technologist said. But another Hydro official assured the public that the messy spill caused no environmental damage. Andy Grikis, senior pollution control officer, noted that Hydro has 58,000 capacitors and 70 large transformers containing a total of

306,000 litres of PCBs — one third of all the PCBs in the province. "Grikis said Hydro is caught in a Catch-22 situation: it cannot destroy the PCB capacitors at Kennedy and it cannot store them indoors because of opposition from local residents. 'Nobody wants these things in their backyard,' said Grikis, 'but everywhere is somebody's back yard. It's a real dilemma.'"[3]

Like the problem of debris on Williston Lake, no one seemed to have a solution to the PCB predicament.

Finally, the *Alaska Highway News* reported on December 15, 1982, that "the Hydro board of directors bowed to pressure from incensed Hudson's Hope residents and scrapped plans to store 1,100 damaged PCB capacitors from Kennedy in an empty warehouse near the northeastern B.C. community."

Rumour had it that the capacitors were eventually stored near Ashcroft, in central B.C. However, according to Terry Peressini of B.C. Hydro, PCBs originally slated for Hudson's Hope were stored at the Kennedy sub-station near Mackenzie. The capacitors may be moved to Vancouver for treatment soon, Peressini said.

Other hazardous chemicals are being legally – and invisibly – used in the Peace region as an indirect result of the dam. These are poisons contained in sprays used to control foliage on the Hydro transmission lines that swing out of Hudson's Hope overland to Vancouver, and (by the forestry department) to encourage marketable timber growth.

New industry on the southern and eastern parts of the lake has brought a good living to those who work in sawmills or reside in Mackenzie, (an instant town created to accommodate the sawmill industry that resulted from the lake). But development comes with a negative side. Hudson's Hope sits quietly, with a high percentage of its residents unemployed, but at least the air in town is clean.

"On the Osilinka there was a big noise made recently by contractors about Finlay Forest Industries and B.C. Forest Products using Roundup to spray," said former logger Tom Roberts. "Some people said it killed the animals, it killed the fish. I don't know the extent of it, but there's lots of evidence of their spraying program at Germanson Landing, through the community and up for another 24 miles. We were told that Roundup was used to spray timber so just the spruce would survive. The small stuff would die off."

"But if the big animal eats the willow," Roberts added, "and another animal eats grass, and the little animals eat whatever, they're going to be affected by it. And the fish, and the birds."

In a January 16, 1989 letter to the authors, A.R. Pakrastins, resource officer for the provincial ministry of forests, says that "Vision is the same chemical formulation as Roundup but the name has been changed for administrative reasons."[4]

John Kelly, environmental studies coordinator for B.C. Hydro, said that "we do use herbicides but we've changed our approach radically over the last number of years. We historically used aerial spraying, but we have not used it for years. Most of our treatment is done by using nylon capsules of Roundup mixed in gel base (like handsoap) where they are screwed into the base of the stump, so there is little spillage. Or we cut the stem off and carbo-paste is layered on the surface with a little squeeze dispenser; or (there's) the 'hack and squirt' method using machetes to put cuts into the stem."

Hydro employs these methods when it uses Roundup, a glyphosate manufactured by Monsanto, along its transmission lines. Lorne March, B.C. Hydro's resident animal physiologist and director of environmental resources, said that Roundup does not affect the brush that the animals eat, but only the tall species like alders and aspen. So the herbicide would not be a problem in feeding areas, he said.

A catalogue issued by Alberta Agriculture, "Guide to Crop Protection in Alberta, 1988," says that Roundup controls brush "weeds" such as alder, birch, maple, poplar, raspberry, snowberry and willow. Such growth is called weeds by those whose business is selling and applying chemicals. But in the economy of nature, the natural vegetation has its place, providing food, cover, and nesting areas for birds, and homes for many small animals. There's a concern that chemical companies don't understand the value of proper habitat for the preservation of wildlife. Perhaps scientists that develop chemicals don't realize that moose, deer, caribou, elk, and other starving animals rely on willow for winter feed. If Roundup does kill the tall tree species, then what food is left poking out of the two or three feet of snow that covers the flats in winter?

A Vision pesticide use permit application of November 3, 1987, and authorized by the provincial ministry of environment and park's pesticide control branch on June 23, 1988 for the Kobes Creek area near Hudson's Hope, lists the target species as grass, aspen, balsam, poplar, alder and raspberry. The method of application? Aerial (fixed wing or helicopter). The purpose? Forest brushing and weeding.

B.C. Hydro's Boatman maintained that "Roundup has passed every safety test to date. Furthermore it binds tightly to the soil colloids and organic matter in the soil, with no detrimental effect on other vegetation. The ultimate breakdown products are phosphorus compounds which act as fertilizers . . . Our ultimate goal is to reduce the use of herbicides by means of biological controls – low-growing vegetation. Considerable success in this regard has already occurred."

The 1983 *Herbicide Handbook* of the Weed Science Society of America describes glyphosate as a very broad spectrum herbicide, relatively nonselective (ie. it affects many species – author's comment) and very effective on deep-rooted perennial species and annual and biennial species of grasses, sedges and broadleaved weeds. It is absorbed through foliage and spreads throughout the plant, with visible effects normally occurring on annual species in two to four days and on perennial species in seven to 10 days. It is corrosive to iron and galvanized steel. The substance did cause 'slight' irritations to rabbits' eyes in the laboratory, and was 'moderately' irritating to their skin. But "no relevant gross pathology was noted when they were sacrificed and autopsied 10 days later." No cases of poisonings have been reported or observed since the herbicide was first introduced in 1971. It is now registered for use in several crop and non-agricultural uses in the United States, Canada and many other countries.[5]

Not everyone is convinced that Roundup is benign, however. Elmer Laird, president of the Back to the Farm Research Foundation in Davidson, Saskatchewan, stressed (in a letter to the authors dated February 4, 1989), that there are *no* (Laird's italics) safe agricultural chemicals. First of all, he said, all tests done under the auspices of the federal Pest Control Products Act are based on the LD-50 concept – Lethal Dose 50 percent.

The 1989 *Farm Chemicals Handbook Pesticide Directory,* (p.C-174) explains LD-50 as the median lethal dose. The lower the LD-50 value, the more poisonous the chemical. LD-50 indicates the amount of toxicant necessary to effect a 50% kill of the pest being tested, and is used to measure the acute oral and dermal toxicity of a chemical. Environmentalist and many scientists say that such an arbitrary testing method cannot prove anything about the effects of long-term exposure to low levels of such chemicals, or what happens when several chemicals enter the environment at the same time.

Laird noted that chemical companies also refuse to make their production data available because they claim this would reveal trade secrets. There is no testing of chemicals on animal embryos, and very little research of the genetic effects.

In a February 18, 1987 presentation to the House of Commons legislative assembly on the environment, the Canadian Organic Producers Marketing Cooperative Limited of Saskatchewan said that "in the spring of 1986 the agricultural section of the Nielson Report on Government Efficiency said 'most of the 4,936 pesticide products registered for use in Canada have never been evaluated for environmental effects. Most pesticide products do not meet modern data for registering new chemicals.'"

The trappers of the Hudson's Hope area think that fears about these largely unknown substances are not foolish. The problem came to trappers' attention when the forestry department scheduled a meeting in Hudson's Hope, and sent letters to all persons who might be interested – including James and Elaine Rhymer.

"They wanted to spray this chemical, Roundup, on the logging slashes," said James. "The people from environment and forestry said the only way they could ensure a good regrowth of loggable timber was to spray this stuff to hold back the poplars and give the spruce a chance. They call it 'silviculture.' In actual fact, it should be called acid rain."

The Rhymers' love for the wilderness area they call home prompted them to speak up at the meeting. "I pointed out to these guys that right now the three- or four-square-mile area they were talking about was of specific interest to me," said James. "It was on my trapline. Right now it holds a really good population of white-tailed deer, mule deer, moose, bear . . . everything. I said, 'The animals living there, all they eat are those poplars. They don't eat spruce trees. You're going to lose all the animal population. I'm going to lose all that animal population on my trapline. And being a trapper, my business is trapping fur-bearing animals which follow big game animals."

An April 19, 1989 article in *The Northerner* quotes B.C. Trappers Association president, Mike Green, saying that trappers are "society's wildlife mangers, front line troops [who] usually have a better idea about fluctuations in wildlife than most of society."

Rhymer noted that Williston Lake is the main watershed in the area, and any creek will flow into the lake, eventually. "They say the quantities (of herbicide used) are so small that it wouldn't have any effect on anything, but I'm sceptical," he said.

"If I had a little more time and a little more money I would protest every damn herbicide program they're doing in B.C., or anywhere in the world, because I don't think a person should spray chemicals in order to grow trees. It's not the right way. These people learned their jobs from a course, and nobody questions their knowledge. If some great catastrophe happens, they'll rewrite a couple of courses and the new guys will learn it a little bit different. In the meantime the environment suffers."

Hydro's environmental spokesman, Lorne March, acknowledged that "it takes years to prove you've done any damage, and then it's too late." However, he is optimistic about the 'sustainable development' mandate of B.C. Hydro's current chairman, Larry Bell – to ensure resources are there for the next generation. Hydro spear-headed a conference on energy and the environment in Vancouver in May, 1989.

But Rhymer thinks that if the forestry department wants to thin out the bush, they should pay wages for people to go in with power saws, not just roar over the area with an airplane – blindly spraying chemicals.

"The forestry people were insisting they could spray the area with pinpoint precision, which I know to be a complete fallacy," Rhymer said. "Then they said this stuff was not harmful anyway. Maybe it's not, but I don't think a person should use it liberally without any care and attention. A few years from now they may find out it is VERY harmful. Everything here seems to be experimented upon. Who knows the impact it could have 50 years from now?"

One Hydro employee, who applied the spray from helicopters along the transmission lines, laughed when asked if sensitive areas such as creeks and ponds were avoided. "Oh yes, someone might say, 'Hold it, there's a creek.' But you couldn't hold anything. And the wind would blow it all over anyway."

John Kelly, Hydro's environmental studies coordinator, maintained that "the problem is being handled much better now. I am not saying the record keeping is ideal – I am working now on 14 or 15 different projects – I simply can't keep as good a records as we should."

As far as right-of-way clearing and herbicide restrictions around spawning streams are concerned, "if that information is not passed on to operations, all the efforts during the construction phase is lost," Kelly acknowledged. "We're nowhere near being perfect, but Hydro has taken great strides toward being a more environment-conscious organization.

"Game animal habitation is a cost, and we recognize that," Kelly added. "The willow that grows only five to six feet tall, we leave. For safety purposes, what we don't want are tall-growing species like alder and aspen under the lines. We recognize that it is a kind of trade-off, but we're still providing a level of food to moose and deer and elk. We're trying to get the best balance between what nature requires and what we require, and serve our customer load. We're working with it as best we can."

Both Hydro employees and ex-employees who have been involved in the spraying programs agree that the corporation is safety-conscious. Hydro ensures that employees are familiar with how to handle the herbicides, and makes every attempt to not jeopardize employees' safety. Still, some people object to the spraying.

Len Kidder of Hudson's Hope became aware of it when he was travelling the hunting area at Farrell Creek, and found white residue on the leaves. "I was told it was not due to spraying," said Kidder, "but I found an airplane and a mixing station for herbicides close to a watershed, which I knew was wrong. I questioned the fellow there, and he didn't want to say anything about it. I don't know what spray company he was with. There was no company name on the plane – it was a helicopter with spray bars. They were mixing; one of the cans said "Vision" on it, and they were mixing that with water and spraying. The amount of area they were spraying would do a fair amount of damage not only to the larger wildlife, but to the smaller wildlife and to the birds. All your berries and the small things they spray, which the forestry feel are detrimental to their planting new trees. The rodents can't feed, and if the rodents don't feed, then the owls, eagles, and osprey can't eat, and of course it affects the whole food chain. Also it kills green foliage for the moose and deer to eat."

Kidder asked to see the application for permit, which was for spraying over a three-year period (copy provided to authors.) "(The map accompanying the permit said) they were actually supposed to be doing 33% per year. In the first year they did about 87% of the spraying in the total area," Kidder said. "So I wrote to Mike Smith, the president of the Hudson's Hope Rod and Gun Club, with a copy to Tony Brummett, MLA for Peace River North. A board was set up to investigate this . . . I think why they're spraying is because when they log, they don't do any cleanup at that time. They should go in and clean up, then plant new trees the following year. They let it go three or four years, because of economical reasons, then the broadleaved trees grow faster than the coniferous trees. So this is why they try to get rid of the trees that feed the animals, such as moose."

Kidder is concerned that the spray programs will change the entire ecology of the area, although he noted that B.C. Hydro has stopped aerial spraying. "Aerial spraying is a lot faster, a lot more economical, but you do have drift problems. It's got to be perfectly still when you're spraying. There can't be any wind whatsoever, and you've got to stay well back from the creeks and watersheds. Then you're still going to get surplus runoff. With any of the pesticides or herbicides used, you have to be very careful and look at how long they are going to be sustained in the soil. The longer the life, the more chance they have of getting into the waterways."

Kidder is happy with the local rod and gun club's response to his letter. "The rod and gun club took my letter to a meeting and I got 100% support to carry the fight forth," he said. "It was not only my concern, everybody's concerned with the area. You have to protect the environment. The forestry told me – and I have also been told by people who would not be affected by the spraying –that it would not damage the meat of wild game. The game could eat the foliage. But it's dying and there is no nourishment. My objection is that we've taken the habitat away from the animals to start with by building up roads and farms, and that's for human survival. I'm not against forestry, but I am against management by dumping chemicals somewhere so we can manage the environment."

Hudson's Hope people maintain that the stated purpose of the forestry silviculture program – "to promote growth for future timber industries" – is not believable.

"They say it takes 100 years to grow a spruce tree that's 10 or 12 inches in diameter. But the way the forests grow now, it takes longer than that," said James Rhymer. "If you have a burn in the bush, first of all it grows poplars, then gradually the pines take over and then the spruces take over. It probably takes 500 years to grow a tree out in the bush the regular way. Now these people think they know everything about the eco-system, that they know how to grow trees a lot quicker and a lot better than God knows. I kind of disagree. I don't think they know shit. And it's hard to have any kind of meaningful conversation with people who know they're right."

A hundred years from now, it's anybody's guess what will exist in the Peace Valley," Rhymer said.

"These guys are interested in that timber growing back in 100 years. There won't even be a lake there! What's the life expectancy of that dam? One hundred years, from when it was first started. All dams are known to silt up, then there isn't enough head to run the generators and they have to do something else. A beaver just moves away downstream and starts another pond. I don't know what people do."

On July 26, 1988, the *Chetwynd Echo* reported that B.C. Hydro had announced a major program to enhance local fisheries and wildlife in the Williston Reservoir area. The five-year, $10-million program will be carried out by the provincial environment ministry and Hydro. Hydro will provide the funding to compensate for impacts to the fisheries and wildlife from the creation of the reservoir in 1968.

"This program is consistent with provincial policy for encouraging sustainable development in a sustainable environment," B.C. environment minister Bruce Strachan said at the time. "For both residents and visitors to the region, the enhancement activities should result in dramatically improved sport fishing, hunting and wildlife viewing." The first year's activities, scheduled to begin in the summer of 1988, would include "identifying areas where immediate enhancement can proceed for moose, elk, deer and other species; mapping and inventory of wildlife habitat and populations; testing and inventory of fish habitat and populations to determine the potential for fish production in the reservoir and its tributaries, and identifying suitable enhancement sites."

The plan sounds great. The only problem, say Hudson's Hope residents, is that it's about 20 years too late.

Notes

[1]"The Titan's Return: Science in the Modern Age" Suzuki, David, 1977, lecture delivered at University of Waterloo.

[2]Saint Ambrose (340 to 397 A.D.), bishop of Milan, became one of the most influential figures of his time; he wrote books on scripture, morality, dogma and asceticism.

[3]The federal government has banned the import of PCBs into Canada, and their use by utility companies is gradually being phased out. However, facilities are still needed to get rid of the stuff. Swan Hills in Alberta is the only plant in the country that can do this.

[4]A June, 1988 report, titled "Vision Use in Forest Management," issued by Province of B.C., ministry of forests and lands, states that Vision is identical to Roundup. The name Vision was adopted by the manufacturer, Monsanto, in 1987 for the product used in forestry. "In Canada, Vision, (also known as Roundup) has been used for forestry purposes since 1984; in the U.S., since 1979." Manufactured by Monsanto Canada Inc., Roundup/Vision is a glyphosate, "consisting of a salt of glyphos, water and a surfactant, a soap-like chemical that allows glyphosate to adhere to the leaves. Glyphosate is an organic chemical made up of carbon, hydrogen, oxygen, phosphorus and nitrogen."

[5]Herbicide Handbook, Weed Science Society of America, fifth edition, 1983.

32

20-20 Vision

The 20th anniversary of the Bennett dam occurred September 8, 1988, and was marked by a celebration – complete with birthday cake. B.C. Hydro chairman Larry Bell, although unable to attend, sent a congratulatory message: "It's too bad we can't bring every single British Columbian to see this superb project so they can appreciate what is behind the power they take for granted." His memo to the 'staff and family' of the G.M. Shrum generating station ended with the comment, "Have a good party. Thanks for the light."

What might people have thought about as they celebrated the 20th birthday of the generating station, dam and reservoir?

If they came from out-of-town and wanted to camp near the site, they might have wondered about the park and recreational facilities that were supposed to be located near the Bennett dam. Proposed in March, 1967, to be developed by Hydro and the provincial department of recreation and conservation, the facilities are still conspicuous by their absence. In December, 1968, a Hydro memo from H.K. Pratt (International Power and Engineering Consultants Ltd. chief design engineer) to J.P. Ottesen (project manager) said the original plan for recreation sites could not take into account "the actual extent of debris accumulation and sloughing of the shoreline which has occurred . . . The public should not only be discouraged from gaining access to the lake and its shores, but should be prevented from doing so."

However, as soon as the debris had been cleaned up and the banks had quit sloughing, the recreation areas would go ahead. These sites would include a picnic or camping area at the 'Old Trappers Cabin,' on the road from Hudson's Hope to the damsite, and a boat launch. A letter to W.R. Redel, provincial director of lands, from the District of Hudson's Hope on July 15, 1970, again raised the subject of a park and "marina type ventures," to take advantage of the promised recreational lake; the development would include a boat launch and confectionary, beach area for swimming, and perhaps a golf course. The municipality offered to manage the facilities.

Twenty years later, there are no parks, camp ground, usable public boat launch, marina, swimming area, confectionary or golf course to enhance Williston Lake. Hydro chairman Larry Bell (as noted in the previous chapter) has promised money for recreational facilities and a new boat launch. But who knows? Perhaps Dennis Geddes, administrator for the District of Hudson's Hope, was right in his thinking that Hydro never was interested in developing the town. A plethora of letters over the years from the municipality, begging for these developments, proves his point.

It's not that the Bennett dam hasn't been a money-maker for its owner. A memo issued by Dennis Knight of B.C. Hydro on August 29, 1988 – a week before the 20th birthday party -- included some figures on the 'golden calf'.

"Burnaby Mountain has pulled together the figures for total generation from (the Bennett dam) since we began generating in 1968," Knight said. "The total to July 31, 1988 is 2,440,391,815 megawatts. Average selling price of this power at transmission levels today is $20 to $25 per megawatt, making this power worth about $40 to $50 billion. The nominal rate for residential electricity is almost $50 per megawatt. Income for all of this power if it were sold for residential today would be almost $100 billion.

"Plant Accounting informed me several years ago that the cost of building the dam, generating station, switchyard and associated equipment was $682,437,000. Operating costs for the fiscal year ending March 31, 1988 were $7,539,000. This cost does not include water licence fees, provincial or federal taxes nor the cost of transmitting or distributing electricity."

Despite these figures, Hydro is considering 'raising the pool,' or raising the normal maximum water level of Williston Lake by an additional five feet to a level of 2,210 feet. A B.C. Hydro memo dated July 16, 1987, says the studies have been completed (including overview, environmental and preliminary study of properties cost).

"In general, the study results indicate that the raising is feasible; no socio-economic or environmental issues were identified during the study that would preclude the raising," said the memo. "The principal concerns are related to the effects on the forest industry caused by the loss of productive forest land, the flooding of infra-structure and the effects on native Indians. A major obstacle is the absence of suitable mapping to accurately define the area that would be inundated by the raising and hence the impacts . . . *In addition, there appear to be unresolved issues remaining from the original project and it is expected that these will be raised if we proceed with the proposed raising of the reservoir* (authors' italics). These issues include reservoir debris, property erosion, exchange of Indian reserve land, and fisheries and wildlife compensation." The report recommends that more detailed studies be carried out. Raising the reservoir, of course, would allow Hydro to generate more power – and income.

Ron Fernandes, an engineer employed by B.C. Hydro at the Bennett dam, says that raising the level of Williston Lake will require careful study. "I would say if they are going to raise the pool they'd better do a lot of homework – a complete environmental impact study – to see what effect it will have on everybody in that reservoir. Will the costs, whether social or financial, of all the upstream effects justify the extra power they're going to get? If so, fine, do it. I think all the impacts have to be considered very carefully . . . And I am sure that Hydro will not do it without doing that."

Fernandes was optimistic that the $10 million recently allocated to assess fish and wildlife would result in a thorough study. "I think, as Hydro engineers, that Hydro recognizes their responsibility to the environment. I would be very disappointed if they were to do something like that and not completely and honestly study it . . . not just start off with the premise that it's okay and work their report to do it. Study the thing honestly. See if what you lose is justified by what you gain. Then the decision has to be made by the government; that's what they're there for."

Some people say the climate has changed with the creation of the 640-square mile reservoir. Hydro believes that's not true, but the corporation can't be sure. "Climatic changes have not been documented for the area adjacent to the Williston Reservoir " said Hydro spokesman Chris Boatman in a letter to the authors dated May 15, 1989. However, Boatman noted: "No pre-project climate studies were carried out with which to determine a 'base case' for future comparison and therefore post-project data is of no value in this regard."

One thing that Hydro employees and ex-employees agreed on is the poor record-keeping of construction details. "The record-keeping is terrible," confirmed Terry Peressini, administrative services supervisor at the Bennett dam. "If you wanted to find out how much was spent by Hydro in Hudson's Hope, it would likely take a full man-year."

Ron Fernandes agreed: "Complete records are non-existent. Technical information about installation and alignment of the original turbines are somewhere, but not accessible." Fernandes also criticized the awkward design of the powerhouse building. "The maintenance floor is 500 feet above where the work is to be done – it should be right on the turbine floor. This was originally going to be a remote station where a few people could work but be run from Vancouver."

There's an indication that the Bennett dam may indeed, some day, be operated remotely from Vancouver. An April 17, 1989 letter from Fritz Sabean, president of Modern Systems Management Ltd., to the assistant supervisor at GMS (Bennett dam), says: "We are ready to roll with the first phase of automation for the Central Control Building." Perhaps in the not-too-distant future, the staffing at the dam will be reduced to basic maintenance, and even the promise of continued local employment from the mega-project will disappear.

Hydro chairman Bell's mandate is "demand side management," which mean that people are being urged to minimize energy costs through efficient use of energy. The goal of the three-part program is to delay the need for additional generation and transmission, by making the most efficient use of facilities, and planning for the gradual and orderly development of new projects.

Hydro has formed a new power contracts unit, responsible for long-term power purchases. An information memo dated August 19, 1988 informs employees that "Hydro's strategy, as outlined in the Twenty Year Resource Plan, has changed significantly from previous years." The corporation intends to look increasingly to non-utility sources of supply – seeking purchase agreements with other producers – for both the integrated domestic system and non-integrated areas. Also, projects built for the export market will likely be undertaken by the private sector.

The ongoing challenge – ensuring the safety of a 20-year-old dam – is never far from people's minds. The failure of the earthfill Teton dam in Idaho Falls, Idaho in June, 1976 send shivers through people who operate, own, and live beneath the dams.

"There is no direct correlation between the serviceability of dams and the age of dams," said Hydro's Boatman. "Long-term durability is a characteristic of all materials that are normally employed in the construction of dams. Careful design and construction minimizes other changes such as settling and obstruction of drains.

"In keeping with modern practices, B.C. Hydro's dams are monitored throughout their life for the detection of changes which may be indicative of deteriorating performance. Methods of repair are available for the correction of almost any conceivable deficiency that is found.... The W.A.C. Bennett dam is still very young."

A paper titled, "Embankment and Foundation Monitoring and Evaluation of Performance of a High Earthfill Dam,"[1] confirms that the dam is holding up, even though minor earthquake tremors have been felt and a big 'quake occurred in the immediate vicinity in 1985. An earth-filled dam is much more pliable and less susceptible to major damage from earthquakes than a concrete structure. Inspection tunnels and instrumentation devices for embankment and foundation monitoring are located beneath the Bennett dam. Because of earthquake action, in 1988 there was increased surveillance by B.C. Hydro crews. A computerized system was installed for measuring shifts and pressures in the dam.

Switchyard and central control building for Peace River Project are located at east side of W.A.C. Bennett Dam, directly above underground powerhouse. At right are intake structures and at far left, spillway.
(B.C. Hydro and Power Authority)

In case of "dam breach," emergency evacuation procedures have been designed and practised in the town of Hudson's Hope. Evacuation procedures have been printed on bright yellow cardboard notices, available to all residents through the district office. Inundation maps were prepared in 1985, that provide flooding information in case a breach at the Bennett dam occurs simultaneously with the maximum predicted inflow into the reservoir and peak flows downstream of the dam. On April 4, 1989 an emergency plan exercise was conducted in the event of "the aftershock of an earthquake measuring

7 on the Richter scale, in the Fort St. John area." Procedures in a real emergency would include advising site personnel, ensuring evacuation was underway in low-lying areas, opening two spillway gates, and evacuation of non-essential personnel from the site.

The Bennett dam is a monstrous structure, surrounded by bush, rivers and mountains, and backed by the great lake. World-wide (ranked in *Water Power & Dam Construction Handbook*, 1989) it is the twentieth highest embankment dam, has the ninth largest capacity reservoir, and the fifteenth largest hydro plant classified by present capacity (2,730 megawatts).

I toured the *monstre sacre*, accompanied by engineer Ron Fernandes. We stood in front of the portal access. A 400-foot rock wall towered overhead, hung with aprons of steel curtain like webs to prevent rocks from tumbling down and damaging the access. The rock pile called the W.A.C. Bennett Dam loomed above us. We stood watching the flow of water from tailrace tunnel #1 back into the river. It had a hypnotic power, and this very day a woman had apparently thrown herself in, to end it all. The PEP (Provincial Emergency Program) people were out, with the R.C.M.P., and were dragging the river (Dinosaur Lake) between the Bennett and Peace Canyon dams.

"The rock pile called the W.A.C. Bennett Dam ascended above us to the blue sky."
(S. Matheson)

We entered the powerhouse through the access tunnel and walked toward the manifold viewing gallery. We could not talk because of the loud roar of water thrashing within the concrete walls. Each of the two groups of five generating stations discharge 35,000 cubic feet per second into its own manifold chamber.[2]

"When we take down a unit, the bottom of the scroll case (a

snail-like water-funnelling device leading to turbine pit) used to be covered with dead fish, at least two feet deep," Fernandes said. "Now we just get a few. Eagles stay around, to eat the chopped up fish as they are discharged."

I wandered the length of the powerhouse, a structure that's as fossiliferous as the rocks along the river, containing the memories of the men who built this great edifice.

I recalled an advertisement by B.C. Hydro in the October, 1969 *Engineering Journal* that triumphantly declared, "The Mighty Peace Has Been Harnessed!"

"This project *was* a monster," confirmed George Metcalfe, who worked for Northern Powerplant Builders as field engineer and party chief. "Thousands of men put in real efforts here. Some men put in everything they had. Seventeen men died."

I remembered from the inquest reports I compiled: the young miner on his first shift who, while scaling in the area that I toured (manifold #1), was killed when an automobile-sized rock fell on him. And the carpenter who plunged to his death from the scaffolding down a penstock shaft, a black hole about 20 feet in diameter, and just over 800 feet long. He cried out the name of his workmate as he fell. And the man whose nylon jacket caught in the running conveyor belt that carried the fill from the moraine. I can still see the burnt offering of the jacket entered as an inquest exhibit.

View of powerhouse chamber looking East, 1966
(B.C. Hydro/Gunnar Johanson)

I recalled the close calls, like the time when a 12-foot roc-stabilizing bolt fell from the powerhouse roof, spearing like a javelin into the muck floor in an area filled with workers. Or the time a four-wheel mobile crane flipped over while lowering an airtrack drill into the manifold, but was miraculously hung up on a rock-bolt protruding from the wall and thus spared from plunging 30 to 50 feet. The cable hung, spinning the one-ton airtrack like a yo-yo at the end of its string. The operator climbed out of the dangling rig, walked out of the tunnel, and immediately started his vacation.

George Metcalfe has vivid memories of building the powerhouse. He arrived in Hudson's Hope during Easter of 1966. The powerhouse excavation was just beginning and the engineering department was in total disarray, he said. "You see, 'the Finn' had taken almost all the instrumentmen to Vancouver on an unauthorized holiday and Peter Schultz, with a few chainmen left, was going crazy. Into this void I stepped, or fell. I was now a party chief. Records show 17-hour, 20-hour, 14-hour shifts on successive days. The cold was intense. We had an influx of new people, some good, some terrible. Somehow we got through this period, but it was a war within a war: department versus department, trade versus trade, shift against shift. Day-shift was swamped by demands far exceeding their manpower. Night-shifts were largely wasted, by doing work not required or for which they had not been briefed. Surveys were done over and over again, errors compounding errors."

The *Engineering Journal* (October, 1969) said that "there is no resemblance whatever between the proposed 1959 powerhouse and the 'as built' powerhouse." The journal detailed the problems: the successful low bid left $22 million 'on the table' (the difference between the successful bid and next higher); the unstable rock had to be excavated over the designed excavation line; the extra work cost more.

When the job was completed, the contractors sued B.C. Hydro and Power Authority, over 'changed conditions' in the powerhouse roof and other areas. The plaintiff companies were Northern Construction Co., J.W. Stewart Ltd., Morrison-Knudsen Co. of Canada Ltd., Perini Pacific Ltd., and J.A. Jones Construction Co. (Canada) Ltd. The trial began September 14, 1970 with the plaintiffs suing B.C. Hydro and Power Authority on 51 claims. The claims, for a total of $55 million, arose from a contract of June, 1965. The plaintiff companies claimed that mismanagement by Hydro caused them extra expenses in hiring men and equipment to finish the project on time.

It was a long battle that dragged through the courts for 10 years – the longest trial in Canadian court history. It was finally settled about

1980 – pending appeal to the Supreme Court of Canada – with the contractors being awarded about $36.1 million.

Metcalfe noted that several problems were encountered during construction that had not been covered by the original contract. "To mention a few: the coal-seams, which greatly hindered rock excavation, the very dangerous methane gas pockets, and the very hard sandstone encountered in the turbine pit areas."

When it came to excavating the powerhouse roof, the dimensions of the required rock-cut were set out as the 'A' line, to be paid for as noted in the contract. A 'B' line was marked nine inches outside of 'A' line, which workers could excavate in case of soft rock, and this would also be paid for. But any excavation beyond the 'B' line would be classified as "over-excavated" – no payment. When the actual work was being done, workers found they had to excavate to 'B' line, and in some places go beyond that because the rock was so faulty. This entailed hours of extra work and many extra tons of concrete. Hydro refused to pay.

Metcalfe, whose shift had kept detailed records of the excavation, felt under tremendous pressure when it came time to testify; the work had occurred seven years before his appearance in court. "The powerhouse excavation was much like a class-action in a court of law," he explained. "If we won here, then Hydro would have no recourse but to pay all the other excavating quantities also, such as for the draft tubes, penstocks, galleries, manifolds, and tailraces."

Metcalfe has worked on dam projects across Canada, including seven after the Bennett dam; he was project manager on the last two. "In concept, in scope, in construction expertise, in personnel – even considering all the errors and inefficiencies – Portage Mountain's (the Bennett dam) total picture was far superior to any that I came in contact with afterwards," he said.

"I have been back to the beautiful valley several times. In the powerhouse, walking along the corridors to the hum of the turbines, my mind harks back to the vast, dark cavern full of dust and smoke, ringing with the shouts of hundreds of men and the roar of scores of machines. I feel like the survivor of a war, but of a war which we won."

Notes

[1]"Embankment and Foundation Monitoring and Evaluation of Performance of a High Earthfill Dam," Commission Internationale, Lausanne, 1985, by H. Taylor (manager of geotechnical department), V.S. Pillai (senior soils engineer) and A. Kumar (civil inspection engineer) for B.C. Hydro and Power Authority describes the embankment and foundation monitoring of the W.A.C. Bennett Dam over a period of 16 years. It concludes that the monitoring instrumentation system in the Bennett dam continues to perform satisfactorily, and performance of the embankment and foundation of the dam is not at variance with the design specifications.

[2]The two rectangular manifolds collect the water from the two groups of five generating units. Each manifold discharges through a tailrace tunnel to a transition section where the two flows join to feed a common tailrace channel.

33
Other Dams

The work of conservationist Sir David Attenborough has been acclaimed throughout the world. His message, through his books *Life on Earth* and *The Living Planet*, emphasizes that we can no longer afford to senselessly change the environment. In an interview published in *Maclean's* magazine November 30, 1987, Attenborough offered this opinion on hydroelectric mega-projects:

"By and large, I am in favour of hydro electricity because it is one of the least polluting sources of power that the world has, so far. What you have to do is make sure you know enough about the consequences. You have to have a very detailed ecological survey and be prepared to spend some money to reduce the environmental impact. The naivete with which we have gone into some of these hydroelectric schemes is mind-boggling."

Protests continue against other dam projects, by people who know what has happened before. Empirical research on dams is fragmented, and most is not carried forward to other projects. B.C. Hydro admits that most of their construction personnel were laid off between projects, and its record-keeping on environmental and technical matters has not been ideal.

Meanwhile, other projects are being pushed ahead across the country, with the same political drive as was done "in the bad old days" of the Bennett dam.

A supplement on the topic of water, published in *Alberta Report* in 1988, made light of protests against the Oldman River dam in southwest Alberta, under construction near Pincher Creek.

"Last year's political war over construction of the $350 million Oldman dam north of Pincher Creek appears to have died, but ongoing remarks in the press point to a lingering resentment among some Albertans . . . It's the reservoir backing water into the upper Oldman, Crowsnest and Castle rivers which has caused the most extravagant objections by anti-development lobbies. Last summer a group calling itself FOR (Friends of the Oldman River) financed by the Canadian Environmental Defense Fund of Toronto, launched a blistering attack on the work, which was by then already underway. It succeeded only briefly in a court challenge to halt the project but in the process disseminated some alarming allegations of irreparable cultural and environmental damage."

The article ridiculed FOR's fears: the amount of land the reservoir will cover is *negligible* (authors' italics); the loss of rainbow trout is *being taken care of* by Alberta Fish and Wildlife, which has announced that *new mitigative techniques* above the reservoir should actually increase trout stocks; fears about adverse effects on wildlife, which FOR has insisted 'could not just pack up and move elsewhere,' are *'simply wrong.'* "Most mammals and birds move readily to new areas," claims the article, "and the addition of 400,000 acre-feet of water will have a vast beneficial effect on sustainable wildlife population along the entire Oldman basin." Further, "the Committee on the Status of Endangered Wildlife in Canada, has confirmed that no endangered species live in the flood zone." The article ignore's FOR's concern, which focuses on "endangered wildlife" rather than endangered species. Many of the issues echo the controversy that dogged construction of the Bennett dam. The article also noted that the Peigan Indians, whose reserve is a couple of miles downstream of the damsite, "tried unsuccessfully for two years to have the dam's location moved downstream to the middle of their reserve so they could receive public compensation for land loss." A story published by the *Calgary Herald* on June 14, 1988, said that "nearly 50 Peigan Indians vowed to continue their fight against the Oldman River dam." A conflict between environmentalists and the Indians had to do with methods of protest, not whether the Peigans wanted the dam. Then Peigan chief, Peter Yellowhorn, (new chief is Leonard Bastien), said: "I've spoken out against the dam for the past five and one-half years, but absolutely no one came forward back then to help me. . . . I think our people are being used by FOR and I wonder how many of these FOR people will be looking after our economic well-being when the dam issue is settled." Yellowhorn added that the Peigans voted to seek a court injunction halting dam construction until a decade of legal wrangling over ownership of the Oldman River ends.

The dam is expected to flood "hundreds of burial sites, artifacts and ceremonial grounds used for centuries," according to the Peigans.

"I wish white people would realize that taking away that land is like taking away the holy chalice in the Christian religion," said band councillor Nelbert Little Moustache, a spokesman for the band. "It will be just like the Waterton dam (also in southwest Alberta). When it was built it killed 70 percent of the vegetation downstream. The same thing will happen here on our reserve, on the river bottom that we used for our ceremonial grounds." The Peigans say they own the Oldman River as it flows through their reserve; the river below the dam site is being diverted into a canal operated by the Lethbridge Northern Irrigation District. Little Moustache said that about half the Peigans are opposed to the dam, while others are more interested in attempting to gain water rights and payment from farmers if the court rules in favour of Peigan ownership claims (from an 1877 treaty that the Indians say gave them rights to the Oldman). The Alberta government argues that more recent legislation gives all Albertans rights to the river.

The *Alberta Report* article argued that the man-made lake was necessary, because "there are virtually no large natural lakes of recreational quality in southern Alberta. Nor are there significant wet-lands suitable for wildlife, especially nesting waterfowl." It's worthwhile recalling the response of the Fort Chipewyan people to a dam's benefit in "managing" wetlands. It would also be worthwhile studying how the wildlife has "managed" to survive very well for centuries without a large lake, which, the article said, "will be great for wind-surfing, water-skiing, sailing and sport fishing."

Cliff Wallis, head of the Friends of the Oldman group, noted that "instream uses for fish, wildlife and riparian environments are just as economically important as water for municipal and agricultural uses. We do not expect agriculture to use water at the expense of domestic and industrial needs and there is no reason for the environment to suffer because of irrigation, industry and municipal growth."[1]

Quebec is also surging ahead with hydroelectric schemes, with an announcement that Hydro-Quebec will proceed with a $7.5-billion plan for a new hydroelectric project (James Bay 2) by the end of 1988. But an article in the *Calgary Herald* (March 10, 1988) indicates that native people have concerns about that project, too:

"Quebec native leaders don't share Quebec Premier Bourassa's jubilation over plans to proceed with new hydroelectric construction at James Bay, but they admit there is little they can do to stop the pro-ject. 'My land is being flooded,' said Matthew Coon-Come, grand chief of the grand council of Cree in Quebec, which represents some 10,000 Cree in northern Quebec. 'Premier Bourassa says he is so proud for the youth and so on. Well, the trapper cannot pass down what is most vital to him, his way of life, to his son and to future gen-erations, because it will be under water now.' Scientists say the developments included in Bourassa's $7.5-billion plan will flood at least 600 square miles of land in northern Quebec. The James Bay area is the size of France, with lakes covering about a tenth of its surface. The region is inhabited by some 10,000 natives, mainly Cree and Inuit, and supports a wealth of wildlife, including the largest caribou herd in the world."

The people in northern Quebec retain images they would rather forget: rotting carcasses of 10,000 caribou that drowned in the Caniapiscau River (approximately 90 miles south of the Ungava Bay town of Kuujjuag) dammed to create a reservoir to feed hydroelectric stations on La Grande River. Inuit leaders blamed Hydro-Quebec for the mass drowning by releasing too much water from a reservoir 240 miles upstream from Limestone Falls, but fault was denied by Hydro-Quebec and James Bay Energy Corporation officials. "We're more or less saying it was an act of God," said Jacques Perrault, the energy corporation's director of engineering and environment, in an October 4, 1984 *Calgary Herald* story. However, such disasters were envisioned years ago, according to testimony given at a court hearing on the disaster. The fluctuation of the water was predicted to have detrimental effects on the flora and fauna in 1973 – when an injunction hearing took place regarding the $15 billion James Bay project – because the caribou traditionally used the Caniapiscau River area as a western migration route from Labrador to grazing grounds near Hudson Bay. The Makivik Corporation (representing the Quebec Inuit) demanded that the provincial and federal governments conduct an impartial and independent inquiry into the disaster, and called the Quebec government officials' denial that there would be an impact on the caribou herd "utterly irresponsible and premature." (*Calgary Herald*, October 6, 1984) But then premier René Levesque refused to hold a public inquiry, agreeing with Hydro-Quebec's assumption that it was, indeed, an act of God. (*Calgary Herald*, October 15, 1984)

In southeastern Saskatchewan, two dams are scheduled to be built. The Rafferty dam, six miles upstream from Estevan on the Souris River, would create the main reservoir. The Alameda dam, to be built later on Moose Mountain Creek, would provide a water supply for the Rafferty reservoir and maintain the flow level of the Souris. According to the Saskatchewan Environmental Society, this flow level maintenance would allow "an adequate amount of water to be passed along to our American neighbours. The Americans have even pledged $11 million to help pay for the scheme."

According to a *Calgary Herald* article on June 23, 1988, the resulting reservoir will provide some irrigation plus water to cool the $500-million Shand coal-fired generating station under construction. (Water from the Rafferty reservoir will be pumped 12 miles to the plant, converted to steam and used to turn the turbines). But its construction met with protests and allegations of wrongdoing before the project even began. "Simon de Jong, the New Democrat MP for Regina East, suggested that Saskatchewan essentially blackmailed Ottawa into issuing the dam-construction licences," according to the *Herald*. "Environmental Minister Tom McMillan denies there was any connection, but environmentalists are not convinced. Environmental issues are quickly becoming the new battle ground in the federal-provincial war of jurisdiction, (environmentalists say) and the provinces are increasingly blackmailing Ottawa into submission. Many believe that federal environment minister Tom McMillan was pressed into approving a licence for construction of the Rafferty and Alameda dams, and that Saskatchewan offered to proceed with a final agreement on the proposed Grassland National Park as payment for the permit."

A report compiled and forwarded to the authors by the Saskatchewan Environmental Society in March, 1989, outlined the conflict connected with the Rafferty-Alameda-Shand project.

"There are real concerns about the environmental ramifications of the project and the process used to assess it. The Canadian Wildlife Federation is about to take the Canadian government to court over the issue. SCRAP (Stop Construction of the Rafferty Alameda Project) has, by virtue of a court order allowing them to search the Souris Basin Development Authority files, just unearthed a collection of documents which substantiate long-held suspicions regarding the physical-environmental aspect and the assessment process."

According to an article by Bert Weichel in the February-March, 1989 issue of *NeWest Review*, the fundamental flaw in the scheme is the lack of water, a fact poorly concealed in the environmental impact statement "where the hydrological modelling ignored low flow records from the mid 1980s and even assumed the Rafferty reservoir would begin its existence full." There is a chance it will never be full. Natural evaporation will claim nearly one-fifth of all water that would (over a long-term period) flow across the border into North Dakota. Additional evaporation would be forced by cooling the Shand and Boundary thermal power stations (each year they consume an amount of water three times the current combined municipal demand for the region's two cities, Estevan and Weyburn). According to Weichel, the plan is to lose and use water at such a rate that in 42 out of 100 years there wouldn't be any left for a river at all.

Weichel also maintained that "hidden within the environmental impact statement was information that despite promises about irrigation, recreation and other benefits, Rafferty is to be used primarily as an industrial reservoir dedicated to power plant cooling. The secondary uses are to be allowed only when the water exceeds a 'working supply level.' Environmental impact statement graphs indicate that the water level will lie below that level 20 percent of the time, and can continuously remain there for as long as 12 years."

The third major problem cited by Weichel was the quality of the reservoir water, considering there would be high nutrient levels and associated algal growth that would hamper any efforts to stock the lake with fish.

The fourth concern was loss of valley land due to flooding, and the detrimental effect this would have on wildlife, and farming activities such as valley hay crops. The dam would destroy 56 miles of valley land, and drain 40,000 acres of permanent and semi-permanent wetlands in the upper reaches of the Souris Basin, which had not been drained in the past because of fear of increased downstream flood risk. Downstream impacts in Saskatchewan, Manitoba and North Dakota were predicted to substantially alter growing conditions for plants, and damage a $4-million annual fishery resource in Darling, North Dakota. There are also concerns about 9,000 acres of wetland habitat in the Upper Souris and J. Clark Salyer National Wildlife Refuges, in addition to fears about downstream water quality and quantity.

The political path of the Rafferty-Alameda project is as convoluted and complex as that behind the W.A.C. Bennett dam. The cloak-and-dagger process of obtaining approval brought about the formation of SCRAP (sometimes referred to, by those opposed to their views, as "Sneaky Conniving Radicals Against Progress"). SCRAP's objective was a moratorium on construction of the Rafferty dam until a more thorough assessment of the project had been done. Court action against the Saskatchewan government was launched in the spring of 1988, even as bulldozers began work at the Rafferty site. In June, 1988, the required federal licence was issued by then federal environment minister, Tom McMillan. Construction continued through the summer of 1988, even though concerns in North Dakota and Manitoba had not been settled. In September, 1988, the Canadian senate started hearings about the Rafferty-Alameda project. A suit against the federal government was launched by the Letzeff brothers, ranchers in the Moose Mountain Creek valley. The Canadian Wildlife Federation began legal action against the International Rivers Improvement Act licence to Saskatchewan. SCRAP received their court order allowing them to search the Souris Basin Development Authority.

One of the documents the group found – excerpted in the

Saskatchewan Environmental Society report sent to the authors – was a letter from George Hood, director of planning for the basin authority, to Robert Walker, then director of the coordination and assessment branch of Saskatchewan Environment: "The undeniable fact is that the Rafferty dam is a very controversial project with the potential, if not managed carefully, to attract significant opposition on both sides of the 49th parallel. . . . The project, given its complexity both in terms of hydrology and jurisdictional inter-dependence, will have a far greater chance of success if the principals (Saskatchewan, North Dakota, the Army Corps of Engineers and the city of Minot) have the chance of building a consensus on the most difficult aspects of the project. It will come as no surprise to you, I am sure, that a number of federal officials have in the past expressed their aversion to this particular project. Given that a number of these individuals are still working in related areas, the distinct possibility exists that if given the opportunity, they would deliberately attempt to scuttle the project. Our strategy has been, and will continue to be, to take the project as far as we possibly can on our own and build as much momentum behind it before we open the process up to other governments."

Another significant quotation comes at the end of a five-page review of the first draft of the environmental impact statement, by Saskatchewan Environment's Robert Walker:

"A preliminary review of the Shand-Rafferty-Alameda (environmental impact statement) shows the document to be of poor quality and unjustifiably limited. It fails to address many of the guidelines in accordance with which it was meant to have been prepared. Most importantly, it does not facilitate meaningful technical or public reviews. This impact statement will be carefully scrutinized by a sophisticated, organized, international public who are unlikely to buy the argument that there wasn't sufficient time for the proponents to address all of the pertinent environmental issues fully, or to conduct an assessment properly. Under such scrutiny, this document is likely to place the government and the credibility of its review agencies in a very awkward position. In short, this (impact statement) does not present a good case for the proposed development."

The Canadian Wildlife Federation's court case against the federal government began March 30, 1989. The Saskatchewan Environmental Society asked the federal environment minister, Lucien Bouchard, to issue a stop work order on the construction pending the court hearing. They were successful. Mr. Justice Bud Cullen of the Federal Court agreed with the environmental groups and ruled that the federal licence issued to permit construction of the $125 million project was invalid, because Ottawa had not conducted a proper environmental impact assessment. This assessment has now been ordered by

Bouchard. The project, meanwhile, has ceased for the time being. Both the Saskatchewan and federal governments are considering appealing.

The implications of the decision were widespread, giving momentum to similar protests where federal jurisdiction was involved: oilsands projects, the Husky oil upgrader in Lloydminster, Alta., the Oldman dam in southwest Alberta (in a recent court case, the judge ruled that as no federal land was involved in the Oldman River project, the federal government had no obligation to conduct impact studies; the ruling may be appealed), the proliferating pulp-mills in northern Alberta . . . against Goliaths from coast to coast.

A proposed $8-billion dam on the Slave River in northern Alberta, originally planned by TransAlta Utilities Corp. and Alberta Power Ltd., is another project to watch for. It is predicted to have severe consequences for the Peace-Athabasca delta – which has already been affected by the Bennett dam. TransAlta has vowed it will be built some day. In its initial stages (1978) the dam was to cost $1.5 billion; $40 million in engineering work was approved by then provincial utilities minister Larry Shaben, even though the project had not been approved by the Energy ources *Conservation Board (ERCB). According to a Calgary Herald* article on March 19, 1983, the proposed project's transmission lines would run through Wood Buffalo National Park, disturbing breeding grounds of the last wild flock of whooping cranes, and affecting one of six known colonies of rare, white pelicans. The dam would alter spawning areas for goldeye, whitefish and pickerel, and in the Peace-Athabasca delta the remaining muskrat and beaver populations would suffer. Again.

By March of 1984, the projected cost of the Slave River dam had dropped by $2 billion to $6 billion; it would produce an estimated 1,800 megawatts. Gordon Pearce, coordinator for the project, said "the government is still committed to bringing the dam on stream in the mid 1990s." Pearce also said that the two owners and the Alberta government were forming a task force to see if Alberta could sell some of the power to outside markets such as California and the Pacific Northwest of the United States. By August of 1985 project plans had come to a standstill because of the slowdown in Alberta's economy and dwindling power needs.

But projects put on the shelf temporarily have been reactivated. B.C. Hydro announced, on October 31, 1988 that Kloh-Crippen Consultants Ltd. had been appointed as the corporation's prime consultant for hydroelectric engineering work. "Hydro expects to spend more than $7 million over the next year to complete unfinished studies and investigations for the proposed Site C and Keenleyside projects on the Peace and Columbia Rivers," said a Hydro statement. E.J. Klohn, president of Klohn-Crippen, said: "With Canada moving rapidly into its important position as an industrialized and creative world leader in energy matters in the 21st century, British Columbia will assume a leadership role in western Canada. It will also serve as a marketing focus for the entire Pacific Rim area. (Klohn-Crippen) and Team B.C. will create a world-class hydroelectric engineering company in Vancouver for the benefit of the whole province and for Canada."

An August 14, 1989 *Alberta Report* article titled "Water Worries Return" discussed the effect the U.S.-Canada free trade agreement might have with regard to Canadian water exports to the United States. "Canada's worries over its water heading south of the border are nothing new," the article says. "Since 1959, various schemes for diverting massive volumes of water to parched regions in the U.S. have been discussed. One of the grandest was the 1964 plan to divert flows from the Mackenzie and Yukon rivers down through the Rocky Mountain Trench in B.C. to the U.S., at an estimated cost of $100 billion." The article adds that, "like other giant diversion projects, this plan never left the drawing boards of the engineers who conceived it."

Site E . . . the Liard . . . Stikine-Iskut . . . all are projects on B.C. Hydro's shelves. Other provinces have similar schemes. And the dam beat goes on.

Note

[1]"Water Conflicts in Southern Alberta – Can Water Conservation and Fair Pricing Provide Relief?" Cliff Wallis, Cottonwood Consultants Ltd., Calgary, Alberta.

34

In Accordance With the Great Spirit

Vic Gouldie has lived in Hudson's Hope since construction of the Bennett Dam, which brought him and his parents to the Peace River country from Manitoba. Working first as a chuck-tender and then as a miner on the Bennett dam, he left the Peace area when the dam was built to work on other construction jobs around the country.

"Suddenly I realized that every time I wanted to go back home, I came back to Hudson's Hope," he says. Gouldie met local trappers, and worked on others' lines for several seasons. That led him to the conclusion that he wanted a trapline of his own.

We are sitting in his yard, located high on a cliff three miles from Hudson's Hope. It overlooks the Peace River and his trapline, which stretches 20 miles from Hudson's Hope to the Halfway River, then south to the Moberly River. The sun is shining on this July day, as we sip our coffee in a three-walled picnic shack he has rigged up in the yard – with the open side toward the river. The sounds of his children splashing in a small plastic pool merge with the songs of birds as they flit from tree to tree. The scene is peaceful, and Vic Gouldie looks like a peaceful sort of guy, with his ready smile and twinkling blue eyes. Then he begins talking about his trapline and a way of life that is quickly vanishing.

"I hunted all over the country for a trapline for sale. I walked up and down the street and anyone who looked like a trapper or a farmer – wearing suspenders, you know – I just stopped him and said, 'Jeez, I want to buy a trapline. Do you have one, or do you know anybody who has?' I chased down a lot of things."

Through a chain of coincidences, Gouldie was informed that an Indian from Moberly Lake, Fred Courtoreille, had a line that he may want to sell.

"I walked in, and here was a real nice house. There was a little sign over the door that said, 'Christ is an unseen guest in this household, the silent listener to every conversation and the silent guest at every meal.' They're real nice people, Fred and Mary Courtoreille, remarkable people, you could see that right off the bat. Then this Indian came out and he just gave me the old eyeball. He checked me over pretty close, made me kind of nervous. I said, 'Have you got a trapline for sale?' 'No, but I have one I might sell you.' 'Oh, O.K.' Very subtle little difference. So we sat at the table and looked at maps for a little while and, oh my God, I couldn't believe it. Here was the trapline right at Hudson's Hope, the one I wanted. After all this, it was just like a gift from God or something. I talked to him for about 20 minutes and: 'O.K.,' he said. 'I'll sell you my line.'"

Gouldie bought the line and moved onto it in 1975.

Only a small amount of his line would be flooded if Site C was built – a strip of land along the bank of the Peace River about a quarter- to a half-mile wide. But it would have a significant impact on the beaver.

Beaver house
(E.K. Pollon)

At Williston Lake reservoir, beaver become isolated from their food supply as the water level drops lower and lower as spring approaches. The level may measure a 50-foot fluctuation, but this can be translated to 150 feet when one considers the slope of the bank. The beaver is forced to leave the safety of the water and travel up the bank to the edge of the bush to get something to eat, with bears, wolves and wolverines just waiting for him to make the trip. "The beaver," said one trapper sadly, "just gets skinnier and skinnier, not being able to get to food supplies, having no protection. The houses they've built in the fall are away up on the bank when the water drops, so they dig little shelves – scoop out a little hole – in the ground on the bank, line it with some chewed-up stuff, and do this over and over as the water goes down, trying to keep near the water's edge." Traps may cause a cruel death, but the sight of the beaver frantically trying to make sense out of what has become of his environment seems even more cruel.

"Dam reservoirs hurt the beaver," Gouldie agrees. "The water fluctuates so much, they never survive very long. Site C lake won't be as volatile as Williston Lake, but it will still likely fluctuate 10 to 20 feet."

A few years ago when Site C was a hot item, Gouldie decided to phone Hydro and ask what was going on. They said they were glad he had called and would come up to see him. They hired Pen Powell to fly them to where Vic and his wife were living on the trapline.

"We sat on the porch and discussed things," says Gouldie. "They told me they had a trapper's compensation package, a little booklet officially done up and everything. They left that with me and I read it over. They came back in a couple of days and asked me what I thought of it. I told them what to do with it.

"It was a bunch of bullshit. It was a trick, simple as that. They proposed to pay me a maximum of about $2,500 if I did a bunch of work on my trapline. I said, 'Now, wait a minute. This is my trapline, not yours. What you are proposing to pay me to work on my own trapline is $7.50 an hour. Pardner, when I want to go to work, I'm already a tradesman. I don't make $7.50 an hour, I make $20 an hour. If I go to work somewhere and I make a few thousand dollars, then I can quit and come home and work on my own trapline for free. That makes me a millionaire. If I quit that good-paying job somewhere and work for you guys at $7.50 an hour on my own place, that makes me an underpaid slave. I think I'll keep being a millionaire, and you guys go back home. How's that?'"

The booklet Gouldie refers to is titled "Registered Trapline Program," issued by British Columbia Hydro and Power Authority, properties division. It states that the trapper is the principal participant in this voluntary program, and that "it should be considered separately and independently from any possible mitigation or compensation agreements made between B.C. Hydro and the Fish and Wildlife Branch for conceivable population or habitat loss to the furbearer resource due to the impact of Hydro's activities." B.C. Hydro would determine the level of impact for each trapline.

The work Gouldie was asked to do was outlined in a section called "Trapline Improvement Component." To improve the "remaining areas" of the trapline, the trapper is paid at the rate of $7.50 per hour to cut trails, build cabins, caches, and cubbies (permanent trap sets). The 22-page document concluded with a table of figures – a compensation formula based on "reasonable harvest densities for British Columbia furbearers."

"They already had experts estimate the loss for me," Gouldie says. "And it was nowhere near the truth. They had some wildlife biologists, employed by Hydro, do the estimating. When I went to the trappers convention in Prince George, the wildlife biologists there were quite willing to admit that there are all kinds of things they don't know about the wild animals. So how can Hydro hire biologists who pretend they do know? They don't believe us, because they say we're padding it in our favour. Just like I'm sure they pad it a little in their favour. Otherwise they wouldn't have had that idea.

"When they came out to my trapline, I put all my fanciest food on the table. I had an airplane sitting in my yard there, and I'd flown out and got fresh tomatoes. I fed them all my good stuff. And while we were sitting there at the table having lunch I said, 'Well, here you guys are. I knew you were coming so I made it a point to go and ask other people – who have already dealt with you – about you. And do you know what they told me? 'Whatever you do, don't trust them bastards.' That's what everybody told me. So now here you are, sitting in front of me, and you seem to be real nice guys. But now what am I supposed to think about this?'

"So there was a little silence. I just said, 'See you guys later. I'll be here when you're gone, and I'll be here when you get back.' They weren't too happy when they took off. They didn't get what they wanted. But the whole problem is, they leave people with the feeling they've been cheated."

When Gouldie intervened during the Site C hearings, he says he was not fighting the project – if it goes ahead, he will likely work on it – but he was fighting for fair compensation for what he would lose.

"In my opinion, it's my personal place, my trapline. I won't lose it all, just a half-mile strip off one side, a very important half-mile because it's right on the river and the river is where the best trapping is. Two years ago I went down there and got 100 beaver in two weeks. It would be pretty difficult to do that once there's a lake there. When James Rhymer first went to the Carbon, there were lots of beaver; the shore was lined on both sides with beaver houses. But within a couple of years they weren't there anymore. This year he got two beaver out of Schooler Creek, and they were skinnier than rails. So I'll be losing a certain amount.

"But on the other hand, the lake is a very nice thing. I've seen some of the lakes down south behind dams, full of fish, full of tourists, and they're good. They're actually nice places. I think the tourist industry in Hudson's Hope would just boom because a lake is a way easier to navigate for a person who's not used to being in a boat on that river. That river's dangerous ...

"Plus the people who will come to work on the dam – they're just like me, they've got a wife and kids at home and they've got to buy supper with something. I can't say, 'All you guys can't go to work down there because I want to save my beaver.' I can't be that selfish. But I want fair compensation. I don't want to be ripped off."

Gouldie has so far refused Hydro's offer, and they haven't approached him since. The information that promoted him to reject the offer was the case of his neighbour, Frank Napoleon.

"He went for Hydro's offer, and built himself a new cabin beside his old cabin. He needed a new one anyway. He got compensated for that cabin. Then Hydro put a powerline across his trapline, and over to Taylor Flats to feed the pulp mill and whatnot at Taylor, and he got compensation for that. I don't know exactly how much, but I do know it was less than $5,000 for a 100-yard right-of-way across his trapline.

"It's quite interesting to note – and I saw this because I'm a pilot – after those guys came and visited me that time and I told them to go back home, then they put that powerline in across Frank Napoleon's line. That powerline just takes a big dog-leg and bypasses my line entirely. They made sure they stayed right away from this guy. But they went across this old Indian guy's place. He might have been a bit easier to fool than me, you understand."

According to Gouldie, a transmission line running through a trapline has a definite effect on the business. The animals gather on the right-of-way where the brush is kept short, and the hunters follow, "hunting the powerline."

"They spray the powerline with 2,4-D or Roundup, or whatever it is," Gouldie says. "Poison never did impress me much. I don't think it's good to poison things. I haven't seen any effects of it, but it's an unknown to me. But I do know that with the powerline going through, there is a highway through the bush for hunters to travel on, simple as that."

Gouldie feels if he would have accepted Hydro's offer, he would now be the one who has the powerline across his trapline. "I got quite a kick out of seeing that dog-leg, to tell you the truth. I thought, 'Jeez, I didn't think they listened to me that much!'"

Gouldie wants the freedom to build himself a cabin on the shore of the new lake, without fear of Hydro stopping him. "If they own the land, they could kick me out. If they build Site C, what I want to negotiate with them is the fact that I'm going to be allowed to have my own piece of property on the shore of the lake, where I can have my cabin, and keep carrying on with my life. I've started renting out my cabins on the line to German wilderness survival groups. I want to keep on doing that. If they own the lake, they might tell me I'm not allowed to have a boat on the lake, or live on the lake, or rent out my cabins. It's their lake. Right now, it's my river."

Legally, Gouldie owns the right to trap the land, and own five acres around his main cabin and one acre around every line cabin. It's not a deed, but a registered agreement. If he sells the line, those privileges go with it. But as long as he is the registered owner of the trapline, nobody can come in and "log it off, or push my cabin over with a Cat or whatever."

In the meantime, he sits at his house overlooking the flowing Peace River, his trapline dark green with trees as far as the eye can see, and tries not to think of the fight he may be facing.

"Well, you know, some of these people in high places can do anything they want," he says quietly. "Look at what happened to the Beatties. They were ousted off their own private property and they had a stronger hold on it than I do on a registered trapline. So if they can oust them, they can oust me . . . but they're not supposed to be able to. According to . . . according to . . . the Great Spirit." And he laughs.

35

Philosophies and Futures

Drive in to Hudson's Hope on Highway 29 from the south, through Chetwynd, or from the northeast through Fort St. John. On each side of the road you see space . . . acres of trees, hills, fields, valleys, lakes and rivers. All is serene and pastoral.

Along the hedgerows grow saplings of alder, poplar, small pines and spruce, skirted by wild rose bushes that seem to be in bloom every year on Earl Pollon's birthday, June 10. You may see someone picking berries: cranberries, saskatoons, raspberries, strawberries. The tall white blooms of Queen Anne's lace stand regally above the red slashes of Indian paintbrush, bluebells, wild violets and buttercups.

If you stop your car at the Moberly River, or at Bear Flats, you'll find trails where you had not supposed there might be foot traffic. You wonder what has made these trails, cut deep enough to eliminate the grasses. Suddenly it is no longer quiet. Birds are sending messages about your presence. The grass rustles and you think you see something move – a flash of fur, the bend of a blade of grass. A porcupine waddles down the bank toward the river.

Because you have been quiet, there is movement again: two mule deer that have been standing beside the trees, so still that you had not noticed them at all, lower their heads to eat. In the dark forest, you know there are moose and bear and lynx.

If you are on the cliff at Bear Flats, you can see the green waters of the Peace flowing to the Arctic. You know the river has been tamed. There are two dams upstream and another scheduled to be built downstream, so this part of the river, too, will become a quiet lake. But today it is swift and sure.

If you are on the Moberly bridge, you may have heard of this wild river that flows beneath your feet, pouring from the lake, cutting through land that only trappers and wild animals know intimately.

Approaching Hudson's Hope from the north, you see in the distance the snow-covered peak of Portage mountain, and as you wind down the hill toward the village, a picture on an old Christmas card comes to mind.

Approaching the town from the south, you curve down a long hill and see – shining in the wilderness – the high steel spans of a bridge. It is a precast concrete suspension bridge, 680 feet long, spanning the canyon. It's presence is shocking. You cross, and from its lofty bench you see a startling sight. A dam. The four generating units of the Peace Canyon dam churn out their waters, four ruffles that merge quickly with the flow of the river. Your gaze follows the flow downstream beneath the bridge toward the Glen, marking the lower end of the once-feared canyon. You cannot believe this pathetic river once dashed explorers to their deaths. Rocks poke up from each shore to the deep middle channel, rocks that would not be visible if the river still raced unhindered through the canyon, spilling through rapids created by its own mad energy. So tamed now, so different from what you'd imagined this river to be . . .

The town of Hudson's Hope, high above the banks of the Peace, is quiet and smaller than you'd thought. Some of the buildings appear shabby – a few stores, houses, trailers supporting sagging porches. Some dwellings are abandoned, with wild grasses growing up to the doorsteps. You drive past Hydro subdivisions where modern bungalows squat on landscaped lots.

Hudson's Hope Museum
(E.K. Pollon)

Then you see the little red-roofed museum, and the log church of

St. Peter's beside it. You stop the car, enter the museum, and its historical secrets surround you. There are artifacts – gold dredging and coal mining equipment, animal traps, household and farming implements, rocks, moulds of dinosaur tracks and fossils. There are the photographs of people you feel you know: the Beatties, Pollons, Kyllos, Gethings, Fred Monteith, Henry Stege, Uncle Dudley – trappers and miners and drifters and dreamers, families who lived here when the river tossed its mane as it bucked through canyons and rapids with romantic names.

You become engrossed by the legends contained within this museum, and by the unsolved mysteries whose answers are buried forever beneath the waters of the great lake – in the bones of prehistoric life-forms encased in the river's cliffs, in the black coal seams and the shimmer of placer gold.

You close the door on this cache of memories and drive up the winding hill, up the old Portage road, now paved but still treacherous with sudden curves that hug the hills above the flat. The road straightens and heads toward a mountain that resembles the head of a bull-buffalo, and you know that this must be Bullhead Mountain. Or is it Portage? The sun is setting behind its peak, casting a pink glow over the meadows.

The Bennett dam comes unexpectedly: first the look-out, soon to be a $1.5-million tourist centre, then the great blue tower controlling the hydroelectric operation. You can see Williston Lake, its choppy waves and dark water warning those not familiar with its changing moods. You imagine the furious roar as the water surges through the power intakes (three at the 2,000-foot level and the remaining seven at the 2,100-foot level), down the ten penstocks, through the tightening curls of the spiral-cases. You can almost feel the 17,700 cubic feet of water per second spinning the turbines, spouting through the draft tubes to the tailrace manifolds and the tailrace tunnels, and then the transformation to Dinosaur Lake below the dam. This performance is repeated 16 miles downstream at the Peace Canyon dam, before the once-mighty Peace finally has the freedom to run unhindered in the channel it has carved in the valleys, north to the Arctic Ocean.

The Peace country has attracted all types of people: explorers, prospectors, farmers, loggers, dam-builders, those who wished for a better life free from the confines of the city. But the country has been changed by progress, and so have the people.

"The dams changed the attitude of the North," says Earl Pollon. "For one thing, there are more unemployed people in Hudson's Hope than there were before the dam. The dam brought them, but there is nothing for them to do anymore. Between the mines and the sawmills

– we kept people working, if they wanted it. Some would work in the winter and build up a bit of a stake; some would work just long enough to buy binder-twine to get their crops off."

Al Hamilton, another oldtimer, agrees. "There have been a lot of changes to the town since the dam," he says morosely. "They took the cowbells out."

Hamilton was referring to a time when the Gethings and the Kyllos used to have a corral in which they kept a few cows. In the evening they'd take them down to drink from the spring, not far from where Jack Pollon tended his lime kilns. Cowbells and lime kilns, steam boats and gold. All are gone.

"I don't know if there is a future for Hudson's Hope," Ken Kyllo says. "The dam is being run from Vancouver, and Hydro keeps moving their personnel out of here. There's some farming. They'll have everything logged out of here before long. I can't see them developing the coal fields unless gas prices go sky-high. There could be a tourist industry built up. That's about all there is."

Lloyd Gething feels that, aside from "the nice farmland we're going to have here someday when the dam all silts up," the future of Hudson's Hope is what has always attracted people: the beauty of the land. "I suppose the biggest criticism is how things have changed," he said. "But if it had remained as it was – a town of 200 people – the young people would have had to leave anyhow, so that wouldn't have changed. And in the 25 years of construction here, whole families grew up."

But Pollon's view is that the dam jobs took a generation of kids and stopped them from getting further education or skills. "Big money, too fast, stops kids from doing anything else," he said. "Sure, there were 20 years of work available, but not steady work – high pay and then lay-offs, just like hockey players who have a limited number of years to pursue their careers."

Frank Riter has his own ideas about why Hudson's Hope "missed the boat" – from being a place featured daily in newspapers to reverting to the little village that time forgot.

"If Premier W.A.C. Bennett would have left Axel Wenner-Gren alone, we'd have something here today," Riter said. "He was more interested in developing the north, with his railway proposal and everything, and I think he would have got more co-operation from the oldtimers.

"This is a Hydro town now. The oldtimers fought B.C. Hydro tooth and nail when they came in. Hydro was almost a four-letter word around here. Dr. Shrum just threw his hands up and said, 'I'm finished with Hudson's Hope.' They brought in a planner for six weeks to plan the town; there was no main street or anything. They had planned to put the highway through, but they would have had to move some buildings around, and everybody got up in arms about that. There's still no main street in Hudson's Hope. Now the highway cuts the town up, runs directly in front of the little log church.

"The oldtimers still wish they'd never heard of the damn dam. Before that time, if someone was going to build a barn, everyone was there to help him. After the dam started, one person got a trailer court going, another opened a store, a few of them started making a bit of money, then jealousy set in. They started to get at loggerheads with one another. Jack Reschke said several times, 'It's not the same.'" And will never be the same again.

Then Shall We Rest

We weep for her, not because she has been raped
by the normal lust of progress,
But for the reason that women weep when they attend
the wedding of a young maiden,
Or the funeral of an old and ailing friend
whose time has come.

We know the river shall never be again,
Nor the things we've seen while walking in these forests.
For her ever-restless, rippling waters are now
harnessed for the use of man.

We weep for secrets buried beneath those waters,
For obstructions being placed across her narrows,
And wish it did not have to be.
We are not ashamed of our tears. Why should we be?

We have watched the death of our old and trusted friend.
If we mourn for her, it is but right,
for we have known her as intimately as a lifetime mate.
When her past is dead, so shall it be with us.

How can strangers who have just arrived
know her as we did?
They cannot, nor shall we expect them to.
But can they not respect our grief?

Mingle our ashes with her soil, and over us
place not a stone, for it is a dead thing;
but plant seeds of grass, flowers, trees,
and we shall become a part of her, forever.
Then shall we rest.

Written over the years by Earl K. Pollon

(Arlene Arlow, "The Northerner")

About The Authors

Earl K. Pollon came to the Peace River area in 1931 and still makes his home in Hudson's Hope. He made his living by hunting, trapping, dredging gold and operating a lime kiln and a sawmill. Through his presidency of the Board of Trade, he spearheaded building a road from Chetwynd to Hudson's Hope and was editor and originator of *Hudson's Hope Power News*. Pollon's main interest is writing and his collection of poems and prose of the north, *Beneath These Waters*, is in its second printing.

Shirlee Smith Matheson lived in Hudson's Hope for nine years while her husband (who was born and raised in Peace River, Alberta) worked as a surveyor on the Bennett dam project. Matheson was employed with the District of Hudson's Hope. She learned first-hand that the project which had brought her family to the town, along with thousands of others, was having grave effects on the people who called Hudson's Hope their home. Matheson has published her stories in many anthologies and literary magazines and has won numerous awards for her writing. Her first book, *Youngblood of the Peace*, was published in 1986 and her second, a novel entitled *Prairie Pictures* in May 1989.

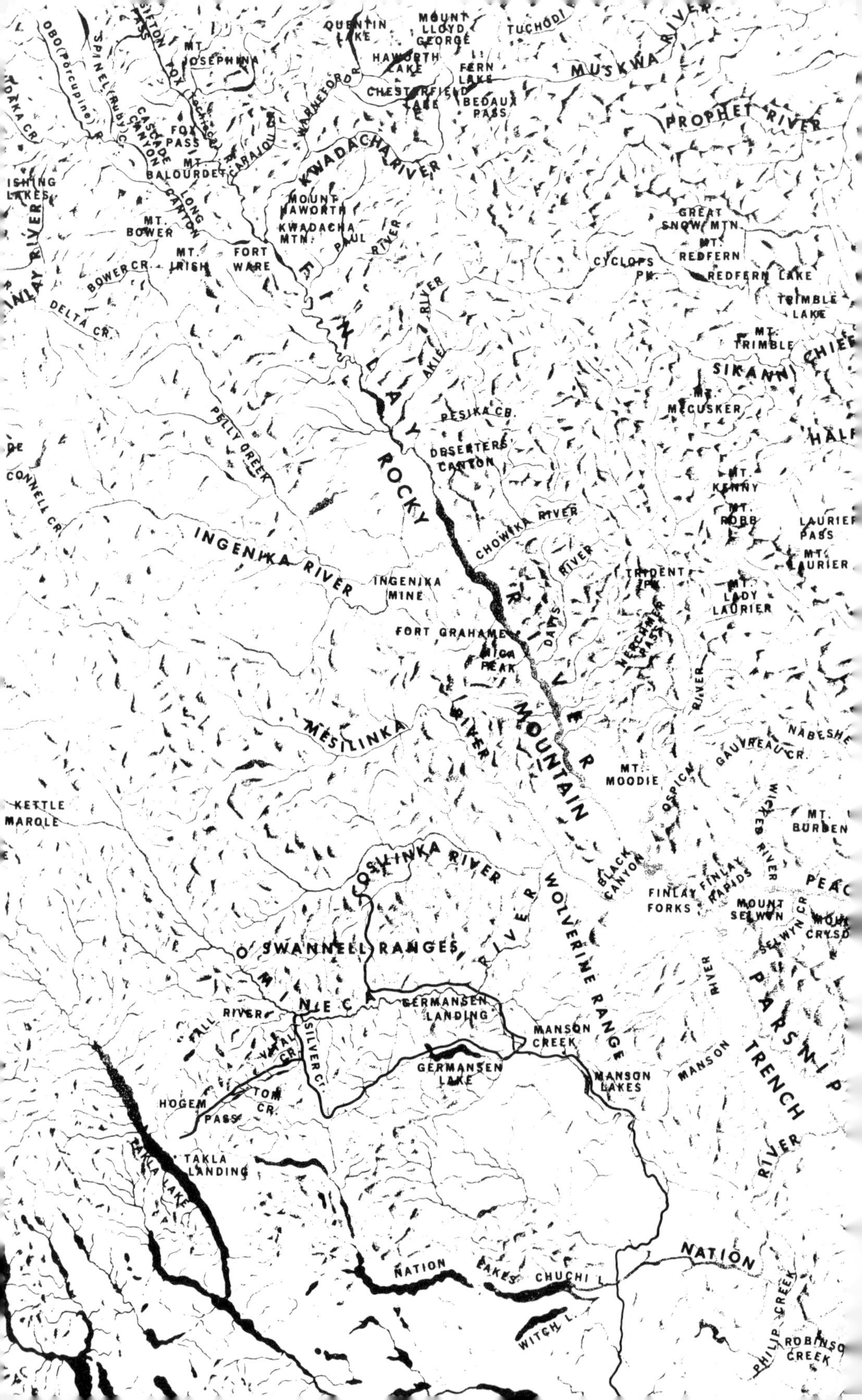

QUENTIN LAKE
MOUNT LLOYD GEORGE
TUCHODI
MUSKWA RIVER
OBO (Porcupine) R.
SPINEL (Ruby) C.
MT. JOSEPHINE
HAWORTH LAKE
FERN LAKE
CHESTERFIELD LAKE
BEDAUX PASS
WARNEFORD R.
CASCADE CANYON
FOX PASS
MT. BALOURDET
CARAJOU CR.
KWADACHA RIVER
PROPHET RIVER
ISHING LAKES
LONG CANYON
MOUNT HAWORTH
KWADACHA MTN.
PAUL RIVER
MT. BOWER
MT. IRISH
FORT WARE
GREAT SNOW MTN.
MT. REDFERN
REDFERN LAKE
CYCLOPS PK.
TRIMBLE LAKE
MT. TRIMBLE
BOWER CR.
DELTA CR.
FINLAY RIVER
AKIE RIVER
SIKANNI CHIEF
MT. MCCUSKER
PESIKA CR.
PELLY CREEK
DESERTERS' CANYON
ROCKY MOUNTAIN
CONNELL CR.
MT. KENNY
MT. ROBB
LAURIER PASS
MT. LAURIER
CHOWIKA RIVER
INGENIKA RIVER
INGENIKA MINE
TRIDENT PK.
MT. LADY LAURIER
FORT GRAHAME
MICA PEAK
DAVIS RIVER
NEWCHMIE PASS
MESILINKA RIVER
NABESHE
GAUVREAU CR.
MT. MOODIE
OSPICA RIVER
KETTLE
MAROLE
WICKED RIVER
MT. BURDEN
BLACK CANYON
OSILINKA RIVER
FINLAY FORKS
FINLAY RAPIDS
MOUNT SELWYN
SELWYN CR.
SWANNELL RANGES
OMINECA
WOLVERINE RANGE
OMINECA RIVER
PARSNIP RIVER
TRENCH
FALL RIVER
GERMANSEN LANDING
MANSON CREEK
VITAL CR.
SILVER CR.
GERMANSEN LAKE
MANSON LAKES
MANSON RIVER
HOGEM PASS
TOM CR.
TAKLA LANDING
TAKLA LAKE
NATION
NATION LAKES
CHUCHI L.
WITCH L.
PHILIP CREEK
ROBINSO CREEK